The Break-up of Yugoslavia and International Law

Various secessionist movements seeking international recognition of statehood brought about the demise of the former Yugoslavia. Peter Radan's book provides a critical analysis of this break-up from an international law perspective.

Although international recognition was granted to the former Yugoslav republics of Slovenia, Croatia, Bosnia-Hercegovina and Macedonia, the claims of secessionist movements that sought a revision of existing internal federal borders were rejected. The basis upon which the post-secession international borders were accepted in international law involved novel applications of certain principles: primarily, self-determination of peoples and *uti possidetis*. Against the background of the historical development of Yugoslavia's internal borders, this book traces the developments of these principles and their application to Yugoslavia by the Arbitration Commission established by the European Community.

In addition, it charts the course of the various claims to secession within former Yugoslavia, and concludes that none of these provide a principled legal basis for holding that Yugoslavia's internal administrative borders should have become post-secession international borders.

Encapsulated within the central argument, the book covers several key issues in detail:

- The meaning of 'people'
- The *uti possidetis* principle
- Yugoslavia's constitutional and legal history
- Yugoslavia's secessions
- The Arbitration Commission Opinions

Students and scholars working in the fields of international law and political science will find this thorough and persuasive work both interesting and valuable.

Peter Radan is a senior lecturer in law at Macquarie University, New South Wales, Australia.

Routledge Studies in International Law

1 **International Law in the Post-Cold War World**
Essays in memory of Li Haopei
Edited by Sienho Yee and Wang Tieya

2 **The Break-up of Yugoslavia and International Law**
Peter Radan

The Break-up of Yugoslavia and International Law

Peter Radan

London and New York

First published 2002
by Routledge
2 Park Square, Milton Park, Abingdon, Oxon OX14 4RN

Simultaneously published in the USA and Canada
by Routledge
270 Madison Ave, New York, NY 10016

Routledge is an imprint of the Taylor & Francis Group

Transferred to Digital Printing 2005

Typeset in Baskerville by
M Rules

British Library Cataloguing in Publication Data
A catalogue record for this book is available from the British Library

Library of Congress Cataloging in Publication Data

Radan, Peter
The break-up of Yugoslavia and international law/Peter Radan.
p. cm.
Includes bibliographical references and index.
1. Secession–Yugoslavia. 2. Self-determination, National–Yugoslavia.
3. Yugoslavia–International status. 4. Self-determination,
National–Former Yugoslav republics. 5. Former Yugoslav
republics–International status. I. Title.
KZ4255.R33 2002
341.26–dc21 2001019668

ISBN 0-415-25352-7

Contents

Maps

Acknowledgements

The research and writing of this book would not have been possible without the support and encouragement of my family and a number of my friends and colleagues. All in their own way made the completion of this work possible.

First and foremost, I wish to acknowledge the love, support, encouragement and understanding given to me by my wife Sybil and our children, Rade, Andrija and Aleksandra, over the six years that this book has been a part of our lives. Without them this book would never have been written. It is to them that it is dedicated.

The support of two friends and colleagues needs to be acknowledged in particular. This book has its origins in my doctoral dissertation completed under the supervision of Professor Ivan Shearer at the University of Sydney. In addition to a keen critical and expert eye, he provided the kind of guidance, advice and encouragement that made it a privilege to have him as my supervisor. To my colleague at Macquarie University, Associate-Professor Aleksanadar Pavković, I owe an enormous debt given the countless hours he spent discussing my work with me and providing valuable comments on the various drafts through which this book passed before it was completed.

I also wish to thank the following friends and colleagues who made their own contributions to the final completion of this book: Dr Mile Bjelajac, Susan Fitzpatrick, Paul Joffe, Dr Margaret Kelly, Dr Thomas Musgrave, Libby O'Reilly, Petar Samardžija, Zoran Veljić and Ilija Vickovich.

At Routledge I wish to thank James Whiting and his editorial team of Annabel Watson and Yeliz Ali for their support in publishing this work. Their professionalism and efficiency have made it a pleasure for me to work with them.

Parts of Chapters 6 and 8 of this book were previously published. I am obliged to the Editors of *Melbourne University Law Review* and *East European Quarterly* for permission to reproduce the following articles: 'Post-Secession International Borders: A Critical Analysis of the Opinions of the Badinter Arbitration Commission', *Melbourne University Law Review*, 2000, vol. 24, pp. 50–76; and 'Yugoslavia's Internal Borders: A Question of Appropriateness', *East European Quarterly*, 1999, vol. 33, pp. 137–55.

Peter Radan
4 January 2001

Introduction

On 9 November 1989 the Berlin Wall came down. This event, more than any other of that tumultuous year, symbolised the end of the Cold War. The Cold War itself had been the defining aspect of the bi-polar international order that had emerged in the wake of World War II. With the passing of the Cold War a new international order emerged. An important feature of this new international order is that 'peace is less often threatened by conflicts between states than by friction, power contests, and the breakdown of order within states'.[1] States today are more concerned with internal rather than external threats to their security and territorial integrity. Most of these internal threats come from nationalist groups seeking to secede, by force if necessary, and establish their own independent states.[2] In what Allen Buchanan suggests is 'the age of secession',[3] the right to self-determination of peoples as developed principally by the United Nations (UN), is almost universally relied upon as the legal basis for secession.

The reasons for the upsurge of nationalist secessionist claims are much debated. Some see nationalism as a response to the forces of globalisation. Others argue that nationalism has its own autonomous history and is not a response to globalisation.[4]

1 G. A. Craig and A. L. George, *Force and Statecraft: Diplomatic Problems of Our Time*, 3rd edition, New York, Oxford University Press, 1995, p. 146. See also H. Hannum, 'The Specter of Secession, Responding to Claims for Ethnic Self-Determination', *Foreign Affairs*, 1998, vol. 77, no. 2, p. 13.

2 A partial list of these conflicts, as of mid-1992, is found in M. H. Halperin and D. J. Scheffer with P. L. Small, *Self-Determination in the New World Order*, Washington, DC, Carnegie Endowment for International Peace, 1992, pp. 123–60.

3 A. Buchanan, 'Self-Determination, Secession, and the Rule of Law', in R. McKim and J. McMahan (eds), *The Morality of Nationalism*, New York, Oxford University Press, 1997, p. 301. See also T. M. Franck, 'Postmodern Tribalism and the Right to Secession', in C. Brölmann, R. Lefeber and M. Zieck (eds), *Peoples and Minorities in International Law*, Dordrecht, Martinus Nijhoff Publishers, 1993, pp. 3–4.

4 For a summary of the debate on this issue see I. Clark, *Globalization and Fragmentation, International Relations in the Twentieth Century*, Oxford, Oxford University Press, 1997, pp. 28–31. For more detailed statements of the competing views see J. L. Comaroff, 'Ethnicity, Nationalism, and the Politics of Difference in an Age of Revolution', in E. N. Wilmsen and P. McAllister (eds), *The Politics of Difference: Ethnic Premises in a World of Power*, Chicago, University of Chicago Press, 1996, pp. 162–83; A. D. Smith, *Nations and Nationalism in a Global Era*, Cambridge, Polity Press, 1995.

Whatever the truth of this matter may be, there is general agreement that the spectre of fragmentation of states as the result of nationalism and the quest for self-determination represent a major challenge to international order and security.[5] The challenges posed by claims to self-determination stem from the fact that 'the international order is based on a states system rather than a system of nation-states'.[6] As Shehadi has observed:

> The wave of ethnic claims to self-determination challenges the very foundations of the international order and the security of the international system. . . . The existing international order based on state sovereignty, territorial integrity, the inviolability of international borders and non-intervention in the internal affairs of another state is giving way to international disorder.[7]

The international community's response to the problem of nationalist self-determination has been discussed and debated in a variety of international organisations, particularly the UN and the European Union (EU). Active UN engagement in some of the most significant secessionist conflicts has been a feature of the post-Cold War period. During the Cold War era with its bi-polar international order, the UN was rendered powerless because of vetoes cast in the Security Council.[8] With the passing of bi-polarity, the 1990s have witnessed a near total absence of the use of the veto, thereby facilitating action by the UN in response to the major cases involving secessionist self-determination claims.

The response of the UN towards secessionist conflicts was set out by its then Secretary-General Boutros Boutros-Ghali in *An Agenda for Peace*, where he asserted that its 'foundation stone' was respect for the fundamental sovereignty and integrity of the State. The Secretary-General recognised the threat that nationalism posed to such a statist view of the world's order. He went on to say that, 'if every ethnic, religious or linguistic group claimed statehood, there would be no limit to fragmentation, and peace, security and economic well-being for all would

5 K. von Hippel, 'The Resurgence of Nationalism and its International Implications', *The Washington Quarterly*, 1995, vol. 17, no. 4, p. 185; A. I. Singh, 'Democracy and Ethnic Diversity: A New International Priority?', *The World Today*, 1996, vol. 52, no. 1, p. 20. This does not mean that all multi-national states are susceptible to fragmentation. Some, even in circumstances of tension and hostility between national groups, have not been threatened with fragmentation. Nationalism alone is not always sufficient to ignite and sustain secessionist demands: J. Mayall and M. Simpson, 'Ethnicity is Not Enough: Reflections on Protracted Secessionism in the Third World', *International Journal of Comparative Sociology*, 1992, vol. 33, pp. 5–25; A. I. Singh, 'On the Absence of War', *The World Today*, 1998, vol. 54, no. 8–9, pp. 236–9.

6 S. M. Makinda, 'Sovereignty and International Security: Challenges for the United Nations', *Global Governance*, 1996, vol. 2, p. 159.

7 K. S. Shehadi, *Ethnic Self-Determination and the Break-up of States*, London, Adelphi Paper 283, International Institute for Strategic Studies, 1993, p. 8.

8 B. Boutros-Ghali, *An Agenda for Peace: Preventive Diplomacy, Peacemaking and Peace-keeping*, New York, United Nations, 1992, p. 7.

become ever more difficult to achieve'.[9] While the Secretary-General recognised the importance of the principle of self-determination of peoples, he was nevertheless committed to the sovereignty and territorial integrity of established states within the present international system. In his view, claims to statehood based upon self-determination must, in general, be subordinated to the interests of existing states. Unrestrained fragmentation of states would seriously hamper efforts towards securing 'peace, security and economic well-being for all'.[10]

In the practical implementation of this policy the UN has consistently insisted that secessionist conflicts be resolved by peaceful negotiation and without the use of force. Active engagement of UN personnel has focused on deployment of UN forces for peacekeeping and humanitarian purposes. However, this approach has failed to suppress the use of force by the protagonists in most secessionist conflicts. On this basis alone the UN response to such conflicts must be seen as a failure.

The generally accepted perspective of international law on secession has been, according to Crawford, that 'secession is neither legal nor illegal in international law, but a legally neutral act the consequences of which are, or may be, regulated internationally'.[11] The principal legal regulations to which he refers relate to the recognition of belligerency and the laws of war in the context of secessionist conflicts.[12] Implicit in this approach is the notion that the success of any secessionist demand will be determined by the use of force, notwithstanding the prohibition against the use of force contained in Article 2(4) of the UN Charter.[13] The consequence of this traditional perspective is international recognition of statehood for a secessionist group that prevails on the battlefield.[14]

Almost invariably, the justification for secessionist demands is based on the right of self-determination of peoples. One of the means by which self-determination is realised is 'the establishment of a sovereign and independent state'.[15] The critical

9 Ibid., p. 9. The Secretary-General's views echoed those of Hector Gros Espiell, Special Rapporteur to a sub-commission of the Commission on Human Rights, who noted that 'the proliferation of very small States might have the effect of destroying or seriously undermining the very foundations of the existing community of nations': quoted in J. Duursma, *Fragmentation and the International Relations of Micro-States, Self-determination and Statehood*, Cambridge, Cambridge University Press, 1996, p. 40.

10 Boutros-Ghali, note 8, pp. 9–10.

11 J. Crawford, *The Creation of States in International Law*, Oxford, Clarendon Press, 1979, p. 268. See also C. Haverland, 'Secession', in R. Bernhardt (ed.), *Encyclopedia of Public International Law*, vol. 10, Amsterdam, North-Holland, 1987, p. 385.

12 Crawford, note 11, pp. 268–70.

13 Ibid., p. 266. Article 2(4) stipulates: 'All Members shall refrain in their international relations from the threat or use of force against the territorial integrity or political independence of any State, or in any other manner inconsistent with the Purposes of the United Nations.' An exception to Article 2(4) is the use of force by a state in self-defence: Article 51.

14 Duursma, see note 9, pp. 101–2. '[I]nternational law declares the lack of either a blanket right to, or prohibition against, secession and seemingly relegates its achievement to a pure power calculus': S. R. Ratner, 'Drawing a Better Line: *Uti Possidetis* and the Borders of New States', *American Journal of International Law*, 1996, vol. 90, p. 590.

15 Declaration on Principles of International Law Concerning Friendly Relations and Co-operation

question for self-determination relates to the meaning of 'peoples'. Only a 'people' has the right to the establishment of a sovereign and independent state. The dominant interpretation of 'people' since World War II has been a territorial one. A 'people' was defined as the population of a territorial entity, be it an internationally recognised state or a colonial entity. This interpretation precludes a part of a state's population from being a 'people'.[16] The main application of self-determination has been in the context of decolonisation. Independent statehood was granted to the populations of colonial entities on the basis of their right to self-determination as peoples. If this territorial interpretation of self-determination is correct, the right to self-determination will be devoid of any relevance once the populations of the few remaining colonial entities exercise their right to self-determination. This territorial interpretation of a 'people' effectively denies a legal right of secession based upon the right of peoples to self-determination. Indeed, on the basis of such an interpretation, the UN Security Council in 1961 declared Katanga's secession from the Congo illegal,[17] and in 1983 and 1984 declared the secession of the Turkish Republic of Northern Cyprus from Cyprus illegal.[18] In effect, the territorial definition of a 'people' renders secession illegal and flies in the face of the generally accepted view in international law that secession is neither legal nor illegal.

In the post-Cold War era the territorial definition of a 'people' has been extended to include the population of a federal unit of an internationally recognised and independent state, with the break-up of Yugoslavia in the 1990s the most vivid illustration. Secessionist demands from within four of Yugoslavia's republics have been accepted by the international community on the basis that the claims to statehood were expressions, through referenda, of the right to self-determination of the populations of those republics. The consequence of this development to the right of peoples to self-determination is that it enables a national group that is dominant within a federal unit to proceed to independent statehood within the territorial limits of that federal unit.

If a 'people' does not mean the population of specified types of political units, but is defined so as to include certain groups within a state, then it can be argued that the right of peoples to self-determination supports a legal right to secession, at least in some circumstances, irrespective of whether such groups live within or

Among States in Accordance with the Charter of the United Nations, General Assembly Resolution 2625 (XXV), 24 October 1970.

16 R. Higgins, *Problems and Process: International Law and How We Use It*, Oxford, Clarendon Press, 1994, p. 124; H. A. Wilson, *International Law and the Use of Force by National Liberation Movements*, Oxford, Clarendon Press, 1988, p. 80.

17 Security Council Resolution 169 (1961), 24 November 1961.

18 Security Council Resolution 541 (1983), 18 November 1983; Security Council Resolution 550 (1984), 11 May 1984. 'When the international community in 1983 refused to recognize the [Turkish Republic of Northern Cyprus] as a new State under international law . . . it by the same token implicitly rejected the claim of the [Turkish Republic of Northern Cyprus] to self-determination in the form of secession': *Loizidou -v- Turkey (Merits)* (1996) 108 ILR 445, at 471, per Judge Wildhaber.

across political border lines. This is of importance given that most secessionist demands are made by nationalist groups justifying their aspirations to statehood on the basis of a right to self-determination. On this interpretation of a 'people', such nationalist groups have, at least in some circumstances, a right to establish their own sovereign and independent states, provided they can satisfy the international law criteria for recognition of statehood.

If the right of peoples to self-determination supports such an international law right to secession, a critical aspect of any secessionist conflict will be the borders of any new emerging state. In the post-Cold War period the international community has relied on the principle of *uti possidetis* in an attempt to resolve this question. Historically the principle of *uti possidetis* in international law was used in the context of decolonisation, especially in Latin America and later in Africa. When applied, the principle mandated that former colonial borders became international borders upon independence. The principle of *uti possidetis* has two variants. *Uti possidetis juris* relates to borders based upon the new state's right of territorial possession as determined by the legal documents of the former colonial power. *Uti possidetis de facto* relates to borders based upon territory actually possessed and controlled by the colonial entity at the time of independence, irrespective of legal rights of possession. In the secessionist conflicts of the 1990s the international community asserted that where a federal unit of an internationally recognised state sought to secede, the borders of a future state would, on the principle of *uti possidetis juris*, correspond to the pre-existing borders of the federal unit. In the absence of agreement to the contrary between relevant federal units, these borders would be regarded as sacrosanct. Such an adaptation of the principle of *uti possidetis juris* complements the already noted adaptation of the territorial definition of a 'people' with respect to the right of peoples to self-determination.

The sum total of the developments in the post-Cold War period in relation to the application of the territorial definition of a 'people' and *uti possidetis* has been a recognition in international law of a right of a federal unit to secede from a federal state. That there are shortcomings with the development of such a right has been conceded, even by proponents of such a right. One such shortcoming is that the rule admits of no right of secession in the context of a unitary state.[19] More significantly, this new right has not facilitated the resolution of secessionist conflicts by negotiation and mediation rather than the use of force. In particular, the interpretation given to the principle of *uti possidetis juris* has removed from negotiations arguably the most significant matter, namely, that of borders.

The case of the secessionist wars of the 1990s in Yugoslavia provides the most important illustration of the application of the territorial definition of a 'people' and the use of the principle of *uti possidetis juris* to determine the international borders of the seceding republics that gained international recognition as states. Although the initial reaction of the international community to secessionist

19 T. M. Franck, *Fairness in International Law and Institutions*, Oxford, Clarendon Press, 1995, p. 160.

demands from within Yugoslavia was overwhelmingly opposed to secession, within six months of the secessions of Slovenia and Croatia from Yugoslavia in June 1991, the international community had effectively decreed that all secessionist claims in Yugoslavia had to be determined in accordance with the territorial definition of a 'people' and the principle of *uti possidetis juris* as developed in the post-Cold War period. It was believed that this approach would avert the use of force and facilitate the partition of Yugoslavia by means of mediation and negotiation. However, this hope was not realised. The bloody conflicts within the former Yugoslavia that have been waged during the 1990s have resulted in Slovenia, Croatia, Bosnia-Hercegovina and Macedonia successfully gaining independence and international recognition. Whether this situation represents the end of the redrawing of maps remains uncertain. Slovenia, and possibly Croatia, appear to be excluded from the possibility of further conflict and violence. In all other parts of the former Yugoslavia the threat of war remains.

The fundamental purpose of this book is to examine, from the perspective of international law, the territorial interpretation of 'a people'. In the context of the break-up of Yugoslavia, this examination will explore the legality and wisdom of the international community's response to the break-up of that state as to the question of the borders and territorial extent of the new states that emerged as the result of secession.

Initially this book questions the generally accepted view that secession is neither legal nor illegal. It will be argued that an analysis of international documents, especially those of the UN, as well as international practice do not support the territorial definition of a 'people' and that they support a definition that includes within its ambit national groups within a state. It will be argued that the right of self-determination of peoples is a legal right in international law, and that on its proper interpretation makes secession legal in international law in certain situations.

This book also questions recent international practice in applying the principle of *uti possidetis juris* to cases of establishing the borders of new states following secession. It will be argued that there is no principled basis upon which *uti possidetis juris* should be adapted or extended to apply to cases of secession. It will also be argued that, even if *uti possidetis juris* could be so adapted or extended, it would be inappropriate to do so. Although not a central theme of this book, some suggestions will be offered as to appropriate means by which borders of seceding states could be determined.

The questions under discussion in this book will start with an analysis of the meaning of nationalism and the theories of self-determination in Chapter 1. This analysis serves as a necessary preliminary to the closer analysis of the meaning of a 'people' for the purposes of the right to self-determination in Chapter 2. Chapters 3 and 4 will trace and analyse the meaning and application of the principle of *uti possidetis*, first, in Latin America since the early nineteenth century and then in Asia and Africa during the post-World War II era. All three of these chapters will essentially confine their analyses up to the period just prior to the secessions that took place in Yugoslavia from 1991 onwards. Chapter 5 will examine the political and constitutional background to the Yugoslav secessionist conflicts. A particular emphasis in this chapter is an analysis of the establishment of, and rationales behind, the four systems of internal administrative borders Yugoslavia experimented with during its history to 1991 in an attempt to establish a viable political and constitutional structure. Chapter 6 gives an account of the various secessions in Yugoslavia during the 1990s as well as the international response to them. Chapter 7 will critically evaluate the Opinions of the Arbitration Commission established by the European Community as part of its institutional framework for dealing with the Yugoslav crisis. These Opinions pronounced important and novel interpretations on the dissolution of states, the right of peoples to self-determination and the principle of *uti possidetis* which provided a legal basis for the recognition of four republics that successfully seceded from Yugoslavia. Chapter 8 will draw together conclusions based upon the preceding seven chapters. It will also offer some alternative approaches for the peaceful resolution of secessionist conflicts suggested by these conclusions.

1 Nationalism and self-determination

The origins of the modern right of self-determination of peoples are to be found in the Enlightenment ideas pertaining to popular sovereignty. The principle of popular sovereignty had as its fundamental goal the transfer of sovereignty from the ruler to the ruled. Sovereignty, and therefore political legitimacy, were to be transferred from the absolutist monarch to the people. An individual's loyalty was to pass from the monarch to the state. The American Revolution, and more significantly the French Revolution, were defining moments in the emergence of the modern right of peoples to self-determination.[1]

From these historical events two theoretical versions of self-determination emerged. The point of departure between them is over how to define the holders of the right to self-determination, that is, 'the people'. The 'classical' theory has it that a people is defined in essentially territorial terms. According to this theory, a people is constituted by the population of a particular territorial entity, namely the state. The 'romantic' theory of self-determination proclaims a people to be a group of persons forming a cultural group based upon a common history and language.[2] In both theories it is common to refer to the people as the 'nation'. Indeed, it was under the label of nationalism that claims to self-determination were usually sought until early in the twentieth century. The term self-determination was first used in this context in 1848.[3]

On 8 January 1918 President Woodrow Wilson outlined to the American Congress his celebrated Fourteen Points as the basis of the post-World War I political settlement for Europe. At the heart of his outline was the principle of self-determination which Wilson saw as 'an imperative principle of action, which statesmen will henceforth ignore at their peril'.[4] The significance of

1 B. J. Wells, 'United Nations Decisions on Self-Determination', unpublished doctoral dissertation, New York University, 1963, pp. 1–14.

2 The 'classical' and 'romantic' labelling of self-determination theories is adopted from M. Koskenniemi, 'National Self-Determination Today: Problems of Legal Theory and Practice', *International and Comparative Law Quarterly*, 1994, vol. 43, pp. 249–50.

3 S. Wambaugh, *Plebiscites Since the World War*, vol. I, Washington, DC, Carnegie Endowment for International Peace, 1933, p. 3.

4 A. S. Link (ed.), *The Papers of Woodrow Wilson*, vol. 46, Princeton, NJ, Princeton University Press,

Wilson's championing of self-determination was that the post-World War I political settlement was the first time that the great powers used the principle as the basis for re-drawing the political map of Europe. Since then self-determination has arguably evolved to the status of one of the few peremptory and non-derogable norms of international law (*jus cogens*).[5] In 1995 the International Court of Justice ruled that the right of peoples to self-determination was an essential principle of contemporary international law and an *erga omnes* obligation.[6]

The meaning of 'peoples'

The legal basis of claims to self-determination stems from brief references to the 'principle of equal rights and self-determination of peoples' in Articles 1(2) and 55 of the United Nations Charter. These provisions were subsequently developed by a series of resolutions and declarations of the General Assembly of the United Nations (UN), to the point where self-determination has been described as 'the imperative right of peoples'.[7] Critical to the legal justification of any claims to self-determination is whether the claimants can be seen as a people within the terms of the principle of self-determination of peoples. As Crawford has observed, 'from the perspective of international law, the key feature of the phrase "rights of peoples" is not the term "rights", but the term "peoples"'.[8] According to Schoenberg:

1984, p. 321. Wilson's enthusiasm for self-determination was matched by the deep concern of his Secretary of State Robert Lansing: D. P. Moynihan, *Pandemonium: Ethnicity in International Politics*, Oxford, Oxford University Press, 1993, p. 83.

5 The Special Rapporteur of the Sub-Committee on Prevention of Discrimination and Protection of Minorities, stated in his study that 'no one can challenge the fact that, in the light of contemporary international relations, the principle of self-determination necessarily possesses the character of *jus cogens*': E/CN.4/Sub.2/405/Rev. 1, p. 12. See also *Barcelona Traction, Light, & Power Co (Belgium -v- Spain)* [1970] ICJ Rep. 3, at 304; *Legal Consequences for States of the Continued Presence of South Africa in Namibia (South West Africa) Notwithstanding Security Council Resolution 276* [1971] ICJ Rep. 16, at 89–90; I. Brownlie, *Principles of Public International Law*, 5th edition, Oxford, Oxford University Press, 1998, p. 515; A. Cassese, *Self-Determination of Peoples: A Legal Reappraisal*, Cambridge, Cambridge University Press, 1995, pp. 133–40; E. A. Laing, 'The Norm of Self-Determination', *California Western International Law Journal*, 1991–1992, vol. 22, pp. 248–50, 307–8. For a contrary view see L. Gross, 'The Right of Self-Determination in International Law', in M. Kilson (ed.), *New States in the Modern World*, Cambridge, MA, Harvard University Press, 1975, pp. 136–57.

6 *Case Concerning East Timor (Portugal v Australia)* (1995) 105 ILR 227, at 243. *Erga omnes* obligations have been defined as 'obligations of a State towards the international community as a whole. . . . In view of the importance of the rights involved, all States can be held to have a legal interest in their protection': *Barcelona Traction, Light, & Power Co (Belgium -v- Spain)* [1970] ICJ Rep. 3, at 32.

7 *Legal Consequences for States of the Continued Presence of South Africa in Namibia (South West Africa) Notwithstanding Security Council Resolution 276* [1971] ICJ Rep. 16, at 75, per Judge Ammoun.

8 J. Crawford, 'The Rights of Peoples: "Peoples" or "Governments"?', in J. Crawford (ed.), *The Rights of Peoples*, Oxford, Clarendon Press, 1988, p. 55.

> The central and most challenging problem of self-determination is the identification of the units, the 'peoples', entitled to its exercise, particularly at a time when men and women are becoming more acutely aware of the groups to which they belong and more forcibly expressive about the needs and demands of their groups.[9]

It is widely accepted that a people is defined according to territorial criteria. A people is seen as the population or inhabitants of a defined territorial unit, irrespective of other identities and affiliations. This is consistent with the classical theory of self-determination. Higgins, in seeking a definition of people, has written:

> There are really two possibilities – that 'peoples' means the entire people of a state, or that 'people' means all the persons comprising distinctive groupings on the basis of race, ethnicity, and perhaps religion. The emphasis in all the relevant instruments, and in the state practice . . . on the importance of territorial integrity, means that 'peoples' is to be understood in the sense of *all* the peoples of a given territory. . . . [M]inorities *as such* do not have a right to self-determination.[10]

A consequence of this view is that self-determination 'cannot be utilized as a legal tool for the dismantling of sovereign states. . . . Self-determination does not provide groups . . . with the legal right to secede from existing independent States and create a new State'.[11] On the other hand, this statist view has been criticised by lawyers,[12] political scientists and philosophers.[13] These criticisms point out that

9 H. O. Schoenberg, 'Limits of Self-Determination', *Israel Yearbook on Human Rights*, 1976, vol. 6, p. 91.

10 R. Higgins, *Problems and Process, International Law and How We Use It*, Oxford, Clarendon Press, 1994, p. 124. See also Cassese, note 5, pp. 327, 339; J. Crawford, *The Creation of States in International Law*, Oxford, Clarendon Press, 1979, pp. 91–102; G. Welhengama, *Minorities' Claims: From Autonomy to Secession, International Law and State Practice*, Aldershot, Ashgate, 2000, pp. 255–81. Shaw is of the view that 'peoples' is confined to 'a colonial people within the framework of the existing territorial unit as established by the colonial power': M. Shaw, *Title to Territory in Africa: International Legal Issues*, Oxford, Clarendon Press, 1986, p. 140.

11 M. N. Shaw, 'The Heritage of States: The Principle of *Uti Possidetis Juris* Today', *British Year Book of International Law*, 1996, vol. 67, p. 123.

12 The views of Professor Higgins on self-determination as expressed in *Problems and Process* have been criticised, and, it is claimed, the dismemberment of Yugoslavia and the Soviet Union clearly establish that 'the right of self-determination today embraces the right of secession': L-C. Chen, 'Problems and Process: International Law and How We Use It', *New York Law School Journal of International and Comparative Law*, 1996, vol. 16, p. 157. See also E. Suzuki, 'Self-Determination and World Public Order: Community Response to Territorial Separation', *Virginia Journal of International Law*, 1976, vol. 16, pp. 779–862; D. Z. Cass, 'Re-Thinking Self-Determination: A Critical Analysis of Current International Theories', *Syracuse Journal of International Law and Commerce*, 1992, vol. 18, pp. 21–40; D. Murswiek, 'The Issue of a Right of Secession – Reconsidered', in C. Tomuschat (ed.), *Modern Law of Self-Determination*, Dordrecht, Martinus Nijhoff Publishers, 1993, pp. 21–39, at 37; D. Wippman, 'Treaty-Based Intervention: Who Can Say No?', *University of Chicago Law Review*,

such a view is outdated and unjust. Although these critics are not in agreement on all issues, they agree that, in some circumstances, national groups or minorities should be granted the right of self-determination, including the right of secession. The approaches inherent in these criticisms are in varying degrees consistent with the romantic theory of self-determination. In the words of McCorquodale:

> [A] restriction on the definition of 'peoples' to include only all the inhabitants in a State would tend to legitimate an oppressive government operating within unjust State boundaries and create disruption and conflict in the international community. This approach also upholds the perpetual power of a State at the expense of the rights of the inhabitants, which is contrary to the clear development of the right of self-determination and international law generally.[14]

In the literature on this issue the word 'nation' is commonly used as a synonym for people. Depending on the writer, the nation can mean the population of a certain territorial unit (classical theory of self-determination), or a cultural group based upon a common history and language (romantic theory of self-determination). This has led to what Connor labels 'terminological chaos',[15] and it warrants a deeper analysis of the meaning of nation in the context of self-determination.

1995, vol. 62, pp. 628–30, 663–5; J. Duursma, *Fragmentation and the International Relations of Micro-States, Self-Determination and Statehood,* Cambridge, Cambridge University Press, 1996, pp. 7–109, esp. at p. 81. Michalska rejects the statist interpretation of 'peoples' on another basis. She writes: 'I cannot accept the concept that a State is vested with the "right of peoples to self-determination". A number of international norms can be quoted in which principles of sovereignty and independence in international relations is expressly voiced, therefore since the right of states to independence is proved there is no need here to recall "the right of peoples to self-determination". Besides, identifying "state" with "peoples" brings the danger of relaxing the international protection of rights of peoples': A. Michalska, 'Rights of Peoples to Self-determination in International Law', in W. Twining (ed.), *Issues of Self-Determination*, Aberdeen, Aberdeen University Press, 1991, p. 74.

13 H. Beran, 'A Liberal Theory of Political Self-Determination for a New World Order', in P. B. Lehning (ed.), *Theories of Secession*, London, Routledge, 1998, pp. 32–59; D. Miller, *Citizenship and National Identity*, Cambridge, Polity Press, 2000, pp. 110–24; A. Buchanan, *Secession, The Morality of Political Divorce from Fort Sumter to Lithuania and Quebec*, Boulder, CO, Westview Press, 1991. Support for a wide right of secession is also found in a volume of articles in D. Gordon (ed.), *Secession, State & Law*, Transaction Publishers, New Brunswick, 1998.

14 R. McCorquodale, 'Self-Determination: A Human Rights Approach', *International and Comparative Law Quarterly*, 1994, vol. 43, p. 868. Oko writes: '[A] policy that emphasizes national sovereignty over self-determination will simply embolden despotic regimes and majority groups to engage in acts of oppression and human rights violations. Nations should be encouraged to redraw boundary lines whenever the current government fails to meet the aspiration of its people. To continue to ignore minority rights violates basic standards of decency and makes a mockery of human rights championed by the United Nations and the "super powers"': O. Oko, 'Partition or Perish: Restoring Social Equilibrium in Nigeria Through Reconfiguration', *Indiana International and Comparative Law Review*, 1998, vol. 8, pp. 370–1.

15 W. Connor, *Ethnonationalism: The Quest for Understanding*, Princeton, NJ, Princeton University Press, 1994, pp. 90–117.

The meaning of 'nation'

In the romantic theory of self-determination the nation is briefly defined as a group linked by a common history and culture and bound to a national ideal that the nation should be autonomous, united and distinct in its recognised homeland. As Smith has written:

> Each nation defines the identity of its members, because its specific culture moulds the individual. The key to that culture is history, the sense of special patterns of events peculiar to successive generations of a particular group. An historical culture is one that binds present and future generations, like links in a chain, to all those who preceded them, and one that therefore has shaped the character and habits of the nation at all times. A man identifies himself, according to the national ideal, through his relationship to his ancestors and forebears, and to events that shaped their character. The national ideal therefore embodies both a vision of a world divided into parallel and distinctive nations, and also a culture of the role of the unique event that shapes the national character.[16]

On the basis of this definition, nationalism can be viewed as the identification of a significant number of people with a particular nation. A state based upon a nationalist ideology is thus a nation-state. Such a state will, in most cases, also contain a segment of the population who are not members of the nation in question. In a 1971 survey of 132 states only 12 (9.1 per cent) could be described as true nation-states. A further 25 (18.9 per cent) contained a national group that accounted for more than 90 per cent of the population, but also contained a significant minority. In 39 states (29.5 per cent) no nation accounted for 50 per cent of the population.[17]

Of particular significance in the development of romantic nationalism were German thinkers, especially Johann Gottfried Herder (1744–1803) and Johann Gottlieb Fichte (1762–1814). In Herder's view, each nation was a distinct organic entity different from all other nations and thus entitled to be master of its own destiny. The individual member of any nation could only be fulfilled by being true to the national whole of which that individual was a part. In this romantic theory of nationalism, the will of the individual was secondary to the national will. Service to the nation was the highest endeavour of any individual. As Wilson has observed:

> In contradistinction to liberal nationalism, romantic nationalism emphasized passion and instinct instead of reason, national differences instead of common

16 A. D. Smith, *Nationalism In The Twentieth Century*, Canberra, Australian National University Press, 1979, pp. 2–3.

17 Connor, note 15, p. 96.

aspirations, and above all, the building of the traditions and myths of the past – that is, on folklore – instead of on the political realities of the present.[18]

The most significant building block of romantic nationalism is that of culture, especially language, literature and religion. As Gellner has observed, it is cultures that define and make nations.[19] As to language and literature, Herder and Fichte were of the view that they were integrally involved in moulding national consciousness.[20] Herder observed that language is the basis by which a group's identity is established. Without its own language the idea of a nation is an absurdity and a contradiction in terms.[21] For Fichte the existence of a separate language meant the existence of a separate nation, which had the right to take independent charge of its affairs. Consequentially, 'where a people has ceased to govern itself, it is equally bound to give up its language and to coalesce with conquerors'.[22] Thus, literary elites were often in the vanguard of nationalist movements as they strove to develop national languages based upon the languages used by the masses. Nowhere was this more evident than in the Balkans during the nineteenth century.[23] Once the goal of a nation-state had been achieved, the entrenchment of the national language was often a major item on the state's political agenda.[24]

Religion, especially Christianity, also plays a significant role in moulding national consciousness. This aspect of nationalism is usually neglected by 'modernist' scholars of nationalism who see the emergence of nationalism in the 'secularism' of the Enlightenment, French Revolution and Napoleonic Wars.[25] However, as Hastings has shown, religion had a significant role in shaping and canonising the origins of various nationalisms. It has been instrumental in commemorating great threats to national identity, defining the role of the clergy, and in producing vernacular literatures. It has provided biblical models for the nation,

18 W. A. Wilson, 'Herder, Folklore and Romantic Nationalism', *Journal of Popular Culture*, 1973, vol. 6, p. 820.

19 E. Gellner, *Nationalism*, London, Weidenfeld & Nicolson, 1997, p. 69.

20 Herder wrote: 'Has a nation . . . anything more precious than the language of its fathers? In it dwells its entire world of tradition, history, religion, principles of existence; its whole heart and soul': quoted in I. Berlin, *The Proper Study of Mankind: An Anthology of Essays*, London, Chatto & Windus, 1997, pp. 380–1. Fichte wrote: 'Men are formed by language far more than language is formed by men': quoted in D. Heater, *The Theory of Nationhood: A Platonic Symposium*, London, Macmillan Press, Ltd, 1998, p. 69.

21 N. Berman, 'Nationalism Legal and Linguistic: The Teachings of European Jurisprudence', *New York Journal of International Law and Politics*, 1992, vol. 24, p. 1520.

22 Quoted in Heater, note 20, p. 69.

23 R. L. Lencek, 'The Enlightenment's Interest in Languages and the National Revival of the South Slavs', *Canadian Revue of Studies in Nationalism*, 1983, vol. 10, pp. 111–34.

24 On Croatia's language policy after its declaration of independence in 1991 see K. Langston, 'Linguistic Cleansing: Language Purism in Croatia After the Yugoslav Break-Up', *International Politics*, 1999, vol. 36, pp. 179–201.

25 Typical of the 'modernist' school are B. Anderson, *Imagined Communities: Reflections on the Origin and Spread of Nationalism*, revised edition, London, Verso, 1991, and E. J. Hobsbawm, *Nations and Nationalism Since 1780: Programme, Myth, Reality*, Cambridge, Cambridge University Press, 1990.

established the presence of autocephalous national churches, and 'discovered' unique national destinies.[26] The impact of religion on the development of nationalism necessarily dates the historical origins of nationalism to periods before the latter part of the eighteenth century. This is contrary to what is argued by the 'modernists'. The religious roots of English and Serbian nationalisms serve as examples.[27] In contemporary times religion is inextricably tied to many nationalist movements.[28]

The above definitions of 'nation' and 'nation-state' do not accord with the common usage of these terms in the post-World War II era. This is because the prevailing ideology of the state during the past half-century rejected romantic nationalist ideology. The so-called nation-state of this period was not the nation-state as defined above. Rather, it could more aptly be described as the 'citizen-state'. In the citizen-state the focal point of an individual's loyalty and identification is to the state itself. In a nation-state the individual's loyalty and identification are focused on the nation, rather than the state as such.

The citizen-state ideology is not romantic–nationalist in orientation. With its focus on the state, it would be more appropriate to label it as 'patriotic' in orientation. The romantic notion of national identity is of no consequence in the citizen-state. Rather, it is citizenship that entitles the individual to participation in state affairs. If romantic–nationalist identity is of no consequence in the citizen-state, then state creation based upon a romantic–nationalist ideology cannot be supported. Romantic–nationalist identity is seen as a negative concept which is destined to diminish and ultimately disappear with the progressive achievement of modernity. Thus, the citizen-state ideology applied state integration theory to the aim of building patriotic loyalty towards the integration and consolidation of existing states.[29] Karl Deutsch was perhaps the most influential political theorist of such state integration theory, in which patriotism was to be built 'from above' by

26 A. Hastings, *The Construction of Nationhood, Ethnicity, Religion and Nationalism*, Cambridge, Cambridge University Press, pp. 187–96. See also A. D. Smith, 'Social and Religious Origins of Nations', in D. M. Clarke and C. Jones (eds), *The Rights of Nations: Nations and Nationalism in a Changing World*, New York, St Martin's Press, 1999, pp. 35–40.

27 Hastings, note 26, pp. 14–18, 35–65. Greenfeld, although essentially a 'modernist', recognises the religious roots of English nationalism in a chapter appropriately entitled 'God's Firstborn: England': L. Greenfeld, *Nationalism: Five Roads to Modernity*, Cambridge, MA, Harvard University Press, 1992, pp. 29–87. On Serbian nationalism, see M. B. Petrovich, 'Religion and Ethnicity in Eastern Europe', in P. F. Sugar (ed.), *Ethnic Diversity and Conflict in Eastern Europe*, Santa Barbara, ABC-Clio, 1980, pp. 383–91, 399–401.

28 M. E. Marty and R. S. Appleby (eds), *Religion, Ethnicity, and Self-Identity: Nations in Turmoil*, Hanover, University Press of New England, 1997.

29 In most cases of decolonisation the one-party state was seen as the most effective way of promoting patriotic loyalty to the new state. Opposition parties were eliminated because they were often supported by individual nations within the state. The authoritarian nature of most of the newly independent states was further enhanced by their refusal to adopt genuine federalist constitutional structures and enact minority rights provisions, fearing that the same would lead to secessionist claims: D. Welsh, 'Ethnicity in Sub-Saharan Africa', *International Affairs*, 1996, vol. 72, pp. 484–5.

the utilisation of the tools of mobilisation and assimilation.[30] The citizen-state ideology is thus consistent with the meaning of nation in the classical theory of self-determination.

However, the citizen-state ideology appropriated romantic–nationalist terminology for itself. Thus, what is here referred to as the citizen-state is referred to elsewhere as the 'nation-state'. State integration was referred to as 'nation-building', whereas it would have been more accurately described as 'nation-destroying'.[31] International legal documents are replete with instances of this (mis)appropriated terminology. The clearest example is in the very name of the United Nations Organisation. The appropriation of romantic–nationalist terminology by the citizen-state ideology has led to the result that 'slipshod use of the key terms, nations and nationalism, is more the rule than the exception, even in works purportedly dealing with nationalism'.[32] What is defined by Smith as nationalism has, to avoid confusion with its meaning in the citizen-state ideology, been referred to as ethnonationalism, ethnofidelity, primordialism, tribalism, communalism, parochialism, and the like.[33]

In this book, unless the context clearly indicates otherwise, the meaning of the words 'nation', 'nationalism' and 'nation-state' is that as understood within the romantic theory of self-determination. There are a number of reasons for adopting this approach. First, the romantic meaning of nation was the dominant understanding of the word for nearly all of the nineteenth century and the first half of the twentieth century. Although the American and French Revolutions saw the nation defined in a manner consistent with the classical theory of self-determination, this was not its generally accepted meaning until after World War II. As Schoenberg has established, the meaning of the nation in the nineteenth century was essentially consistent with its romantic variant.[34] This is illustrated by the examples of the German and Italian unifications, as well as the recognition of statehood for Greece, Serbia, Romania and Bulgaria in the nineteenth century. It is also relevant to the emergence of independent Sweden, Norway and Albania in the early years of the twentieth century, and to the fact that the stability of the Austro-Hungarian empire was threatened by the nationalist aspirations of many of its non-German and non-Hungarian nations. Second, most of the recent and current claims to self-determination are based on the romantic theory of self-determination, including those relating to the former Yugoslavia.

30 A. Heraclides, *The Self-Determination of Minorities in International Politics*, London, Frank Cass & Co Ltd, 1991, p. 3. For a critique of Deutsch's views, see Connor, note 15, pp. 30–5.

31 Connor, note 15, p. 42.

32 Ibid., p. xi.

33 Ibid., pp. 90–117.

34 H. O. Schoenberg, 'The Concept of "People" in the Principle of Self-Determination', unpublished doctoral dissertation, Columbia University, 1972, pp. 38–60.

Implications of the meaning of nation for theories of self-determination

In broad terms, the romantic theory of self-determination found its most fertile ground in central and eastern Europe. The classical theory of self-determination was more widely adopted in western Europe. The neighbouring European states of Germany and France provide apt illustrations of the romantic and classical theories of self-determination respectively. The German and French models of statehood have been described as 'distinctive, even antagonistic models of nationhood and national self-understanding'.[35] The establishment of the modern German and French states clearly illustrates the applications of the two theories of self-determination.

In France, the Revolution of 1789 occurred within an established state. The Revolution saw the end of royal absolutism. Victory went to the people or, more specifically, to the political representatives of the people. It was therefore logical to assert that the people were the population of the territorial state known as France. The French case is thus one where the state preceded, in point of time, the demand for self-determination.

With Germany the historical circumstances were different. The culmination of the self-determination of the German people was the creation of a unified German state in 1871. Unlike France, there was no pre-existing German state. The German demand for self-determination was a demand for the creation of a German state. However, before a German state could be created, one had to determine who the German people were. In this process the German people were defined on the basis of culture and language.[36]

The differing historical experiences of France and Germany therefore resulted in different understandings of nationhood.[37] German national consciousness has always centred on the concept of the *Volk*. As Brubaker has written:

> This prepolitical German nation, this nation in search of a state, was conceived not as the bearer of universal political values, but as an organic cultural, linguistic, or racial community. . . . On this understanding, nationhood is an ethnocultural, not a political, fact.[38]

On the other hand, the French tradition of nationhood has been irrevocably tied to the institutional and territorial framework of the state. French national identity is tied to membership, via citizenship, of the territorial state. Nationhood in France is a political fact dependent on citizenship. It is not an ethnocultural concept. This

35 R. Brubaker, *Citizenship and Nationhood in France and Germany*, Cambridge, MA, Harvard University Press, 1992, p. 1.

36 Schoenberg, note 34, pp. 26–7, 43–4.

37 These differing conceptions of nationhood profoundly influenced and continue to influence French and German conceptions and laws on citizenship: Brubaker, note 35.

38 Ibid., p. 1.

understanding stems from the fact that French national consciousness was developed in the context of a pre-existing political state. However, what is crucial in the case of France is that the process of self-determination required the creation of a French nation in the sense of a cultural and linguistic community. As Brubaker observes: '[W]hile French nationhood is constituted by political unity, it is centrally expressed in the striving for cultural unity. Political inclusion has entailed assimilation, for regional minorities and immigrants alike.'[39] This was recognised by the leaders of the French Revolution from the outset. If they had accepted the romantic theory of self-determination it would have probably led to the break-up of the French state. The French monarchy had been tolerant towards the languages and customs of minority groups such as the Bretons and Basques. French nationalism required the assimilation of such groups.[40] This has been a major task for France ever since the Revolution of 1789. As late as the end of the nineteenth century most of France was characterised by an absence of French national consciousness despite significant efforts to culturally assimilate all areas of the state.[41]

The distinctive German and French conceptions of nationhood offered competing models to other European nations. In the case of the nations that ultimately comprised the state of Yugoslavia, it was the German model that emerged as dominant.[42] This was hardly surprising. Like the German nation, the Yugoslav nations were nations in search of a state.

The implications of the two theories of self-determination for state creation are significant. In the classical theory, because an individual's identity is tied to the state or territorial unit, self-determination takes place within the confines of an existing state or territorial unit. Self-determination takes place when the population of that state or territorial unit elects a representative government of its choice.[43] It is consistent with the principles of territorial integrity and the inviolability of state borders. In the romantic theory, an individual's loyalty is to the nation rather than to the state in which that individual is found. Self-determination thus takes place

39 Ibid. It can also be noted that the populations of French colonies were, and continue to be, subject to the same processes, given that France's colonial policy has consistently maintained that its colonies were in fact integral parts of the French state. Such a policy has generally failed, in that most French colonies have sought and obtained independence from France. Occasionally, however, French colonies sought to maintain their status as parts of France, as is evidenced by the island of Mayotte which declined to become part of the archipelago Republic of Comoros in 1975. On French colonial theory see W. F. S. Miles, *Elections and Ethnicity in French Martinique: A Paradox in Paradise*, New York, Praeger, 1986, pp. 12–31.

40 Schoenberg, note 34, pp. 22-3. In a report to the Committee of Public Safety in January 1794 it was said: 'Federalism and superstition speak low Breton; emigration and hatred of the [French] Republic speak German; the counterrevolution speaks Italian, and fanaticism speaks Basque': quoted in Brubaker, note 35, p. 7.

41 E. Weber, *Peasants into Frenchmen: The Modernization of Rural France, 1870-1914*, London, Chatto & Windus, 1979.

42 Schoenberg, note 34, pp. 48–50.

43 T. D. Musgrave, *Self-Determination and National Minorities*, Oxford, Clarendon Press, 1997, pp. 96–101.

when that nation obtains its own state.[44] It thus permits the alteration of existing state borders and clearly contemplates secession as well as irredentism.

In practice, the application of either of the two theories was determined by the prevailing 'configurations of power and interest between dominant and oppressed groups and between competing states'.[45] In the twentieth century the most significant event affecting such a configuration was World War II, and in particular, the policies of Nazi Germany. Adolf Hitler's racist and genocidal policies committed in the name of the German *Volk* meant that the romantic theory of self-determination fell out of favour in the aftermath of World War II.[46] For most of the post-World War II era, secession from internationally recognised states has not been, at least until recently, widely accepted by the international community of states. Indeed, as Heraclides has written, 'the main legal bulwark against secession is the principle of self-determination which developed during the late 1950s and 1960s'.[47] In other words, secession was not acceptable because of the widespread acceptance of the classical theory of self-determination.

The dominance of the classical theory of self-determination in the first few decades after World War II was most dramatically illustrated in the process of the decolonisation of Africa and Asia on the basis of the right to self-determination of colonial peoples. Decolonisation saw the emergence of a significant number of new states. The self-determination of colonial peoples was in most, but not all, cases achieved within the territorial framework of former colonial units. The retention of existing borders, even though they cut across cultural and linguistic boundaries, was justified on the grounds that alteration of such borders would result in fratricidal strife after the departure of the imperial powers, thereby endangering the process of decolonisation itself. The preservation of former colonial borders was given legal sanction by the adaptation of the principle of *uti possidetis juris* which had been applied to a number of cases in Latin America in the early nineteenth century and by which existing colonial administrative borders were transformed into state borders following decolonisation.

However, even during the intensive decolonisation of the post-World War II period, claims to romantic self-determination did not disappear. The establishment in 1947 of the state of Israel for Hitler's primary victims, the Jews, represented a significant exception to the prevailing practice.[48] Even though the case of Israel

44 Ibid., pp. 102–8.
45 Schoenberg, note 34, p. 2.
46 Ibid., p. 178.
47 Heraclides, note 30, p. 21.
48 Schoenberg, note 34, p. 2. The Israeli independence declaration referred to 'the right of the Jewish people to establish their State' and declared 'the establishment of a Jewish state in Eretz-Israel, to be known as the State of Israel': Declaration of the Establishment of the State of Israel, 14 May 1948, in F. Gervasi, *The Case for Israel*, New York, The Viking Press, 1967, pp. 204–8. The Jewish demand for statehood was justified by its first Foreign Minister, and later Prime Minister, on the UN Charter's provisions on self-determination: G. Sheffer, *Moshe Sharett: Biography of a Political Moderate*, Oxford, Clarendon Press, 1996, p. 256.

could be seen as unique because of the extent of Jewish suffering during World War II, it proved that oppression and victimisation of a nation could lead to the establishment of a state based upon the romantic theory of self-determination. The successful secession of Bangladesh from Pakistan in 1971 served as another example of the same process.

The case of Bangladesh is significant, for it served as a precursor to events that would occur, and are likely to continue to occur, as the shadow cast by Nazi Germany in World War II continues to recede with the passage of time. The state of Pakistan emerged in the wave of decolonisation after World War II. The secession of Bangladesh was ignited by the sense of oppression and victimisation felt by the Bengali Muslims of East Pakistan at the hands of the Muslims of West Pakistan. The former spoke a Sanskrit-based Bengali language while the latter were Urdu-speaking non-Bengalis.[49] What the case of Bangladesh illustrates is that Pakistan was unable to achieve what France did in relation to the moulding of cultural unity. The Bengali population resisted the assimilationist policies of the Pakistani government dominated by politicians from West Pakistan. The Pakistan scenario is one found across the globe today. The cases of the failed Katanga and Biafra secessions, the successful secession of Eritrea, the on-going secession in Southern Sudan, the anarchical strife in Somalia, and the mass slaughters in Rwanda and Burundi are only the most prominent illustrations in Africa. The Tamil rebellion in Sri Lanka, the Bougainville rebellion in Papua-New Guinea and the claims to political domination of Fiji by its indigenous people are prominent illustrations in the Asia-Pacific region. The collapse of the Soviet Union, Yugoslavia and Czechoslovakia serve as prominent illustrations in eastern and central Europe. Nor is the West immune, as is illustrated by Quebec's attempt to secede from Canada. All of these claims have been or are essentially based upon allegations of oppression and victimisation of nations. All these claims to self-determination invoke the meaning of nation as understood within the romantic theory of self-determination.[50]

The dominance of the classical theory of self-determination in international practice in the post-World War II era has largely been the result of self-determination being seen as a political, rather than a legal principle. However, it is doubtful whether this essentially political approach to self-determination can be maintained. The character of self-determination as a *jus cogens* norm with its *erga omnes* attributes makes it imperative to view self-determination in legal terms.

49 V. P. Nanda, 'Self-Determination Outside the Colonial Context: The Birth of Bangladesh in Retrospect', in Y. Alexander and R. A. Friedlander (eds), *Self-Determination: National, Regional, and Global Dimensions*, Boulder, CO, Westview Press, 1980, pp. 205–6.

50 Brubaker observes that 'for the foreseeable future . . . the nation-state and national citizenship will remain very much – perhaps too much – with us. It is not only that, as Western Europe moves fitfully *beyond* the nation-state, multinational Yugoslavia and the Soviet Union have disintegrated *into* nation-sates. It is not only that a powerful German nation-state has been recreated in the heart of Europe. It is also that throughout Western Europe nationhood has been revived as a political theme, and nativism as a political program, in response to the unprecedented immigration of the last thirty years': Brubaker, note 35, p. 187.

Since the adoption of the United Nations Charter in 1945, self-determination has been defined in terms of a right of 'peoples'. In any legal interpretation of the right of peoples to self-determination, two fundamental questions need to be answered. The first relates to what the right to self-determination entails, in the sense of what consequences are acceptable upon the exercise of the right. The second relates to the meaning of 'peoples', for it is only peoples that are entitled to exercise the right to self-determination.

As to what the right to self-determination entails, this is clearly set out in the Declaration on Principles of International Law Concerning Friendly Relations and Co-operation Among States in Accordance With the Charter of the United Nations (Declaration on Friendly Relations) passed by the General Assembly of the UN in October 1970.[51] In the principle dealing with self-determination the Declaration stipulates:

> The establishment of a sovereign and independent State, the free association or integration with an independent State or the emergence into any other political status freely determined by a people constitute modes of implementing the right of self-determination by that people.[52]

As to the meaning of a people, the rival theories of self-determination differ. The classical theory holds that a people is defined as the population or inhabitants of a defined territorial unit. The romantic theory holds that a people means, or at least includes, a nation. This difference has profound significance in relation to the existence of a right of secession from an internationally recognised state.

The right to self-determination includes, as noted above, the right to 'the establishment of a sovereign and independent State'. According to the classical theory of self-determination, secession from an internationally recognised state would be a logical impossibility. This is because a people, defined as the population of a state, already have a 'sovereign and independent State'. However, this does not mean that this method of implementing the right of self-determination is rendered meaningless

51 General Assembly Resolution 2625 (XXV), 24 October 1970. This Resolution echoed the provisions of an earlier resolution on self-determination in the context of decolonisation, where the General Assembly declared that self-determination for colonial entities could be achieved by '(a) Emergence as a sovereign independent State; (b) Free association with an independent State; or (c) Integration with an independent State': General Assembly Resolution 1541 (XV), Annex, Principle VI, 15 December 1960. The great majority of states emerging as the result of decolonisation achieved joint or separate independence: Crawford, note 10, p. 369.

52 Some commentators seek to downplay the independent statehood option in relation to self-determination. Thus, Brownlie stresses that 'in practice the claim to self-determination does not necessarily involve a claim to statehood or secession': I. Brownlie, 'The Rights of People', in J. Crawford (ed.), note 8, p. 6. However, as Tomuschat observes: 'It is the attraction, but also the tragedy of self-determination that according to . . . prevailing doctrine it necessarily includes a right to independent statehood. . . . [A people] cannot be prevented from choosing independent statehood': C. Tomuschat, 'Self-Determination in a Post-Colonial World', in C. Tomuschat (ed.), note 12, p. 12.

if one accepts the classical meaning of people. Establishing 'a sovereign and independent State' is available to peoples under colonial rule or administration, given that such peoples do not live in a 'sovereign and independent State'.

If the meaning of 'people' according to the romantic theory of self-determination is correct, the right of a people to self-determination would permit secession of a nation from an internationally recognised state. It could be argued that a nation within a multi-national state could not secede on the basis that it already has 'a sovereign and independent State', namely the multi-national state of which it is part, and thus secession becomes a logical impossibility. For example, nations A and B agree, by implementing their rights of self-determination, to form a multinational state, thereby establishing 'a sovereign and independent State'. Thus, both nations have formed one 'sovereign and independent State', with the consequence that neither can secede from it. However, this argument must be rejected for the following reason. It is now generally accepted that the right to self-determination is a continuing right.[53] Thus, the fact that nations A and B may have opted for a multi-national state as the mode of exercising their rights to self-determination does not mean that they have forever exhausted the exercise of their rights to self-determination. It is open to both to assert their rights again at a later time. Therefore, nation A could, at a later time, exercise its right to self-determination by seceding from the multi-national state to form another 'sovereign and independent State'.

It must be noted that the right to secede from a state on the romantic theory of self-determination is only a *prima facie* right. Sovereignty and independent statehood can only be achieved if the seceding entity fulfils the criteria for statehood.[54] The classical criteria for statehood are reflected in the often cited Montevideo Convention of 1933 which, in Article 1, stipulates that a state should possess a permanent population, a defined territory, a government and a capacity to enter into relations with other States.[55] Even though recognition of statehood by member states of the international community is usually as much a political question as it is a legal one, non-compliance with the provisions of Article 1 will generally result

53 Self-determination was the basis of decolonisation in Africa and Asia in the wake of World War II. Many of the new African leaders asserted that with independence the right to self-determination had expired. However, as McCorquodale has shown, 'the right to self-determination did not cease once colonies ceased': R. McCorquodale, 'Self-Determination Beyond the Colonial Context and its Potential Impact in Africa', *African Journal of International and Comparative Law*, 1992, vol. 4, pp. 601–8. In the Final Act of Helsinki of 1 August 1975, in Principle VIII of the part on Questions Relating to the Security of Europe, the right of self-determination is expressed to be exercisable by peoples 'always' and 'when and as they wish', making it clearly an ongoing right: (1975) 24 ILM 1292–325. See also Cassese, note 5, p. 285; P. Thornberry, 'The Principle of Self-Determination', in V. Love and C. Warbrick (eds), *The United Nations and Principles of International Law, Essays in Honour of Michael Akehurst*, London, Routledge, 1994, pp. 185–6.

54 McCorquodale, note 53, p. 595; G. Nettheim, '"Peoples" and "Populations" – Indigenous Peoples and the Right of Peoples', in J. Crawford (ed.), note 8, p. 120.

55 Convention on Rights and Duties of States Adopted by the Seventh International Conference of American States, 26 December 1933, (1936) 165 LTNS 21–31.

in non-recognition, thereby effectively precluding the exercise of the right to self-determination by the means of establishing 'a sovereign and independent State'. It is thus almost universally the case that the major initial preoccupation of any secessionist movement is gaining international recognition, especially that of major powers in the international system.

Historically, international recognition of statehood has been the major foreign policy goal of any secessionist movement.[56] Although recognition is not necessary to achieve statehood, in the context of secession 'the viability of a would-be state in the international community depends, as a practical matter, upon recognition by other states'.[57] Without such recognition the seceding entity cannot be regarded as a member of the international community, and the secession will most likely end in failure. The importance of recognition in secessionist conflicts can be illustrated by a number of examples. The recognition of the independence of the Spanish American states by the United States of America (USA) in 1822 has been described as 'the greatest assistance rendered by any foreign power to the independence of Latin America'.[58] The recognition by India, a significant regional power, of Bangladesh in 1971 was a key to the success of the Bangladesh secession from Pakistan.[59]

On the other hand, the failure to gain international recognition has been a major contributing factor to the failure of various secessions. In the case of the secessions of southern states from the USA in 1861 and their formation of the Confederate States of America, the major foreign policy goal of the USA was to prevent international recognition of the southern Confederacy. President Abraham Lincoln was prepared to risk war with Great Britain over this issue. For the Confederacy international recognition was the single most important diplomatic goal.[60] Lincoln's strategy succeeded.[61] However, had Great Britain and the rest of Europe recognised the Confederacy, it is arguable that the latter's secession from the USA would have succeeded. Widespread international condemnation of the secessions of Katanga from the Congo in 1960 and Biafra from Nigeria in 1967 doomed them to eventual failure. The fact that only Turkey has recognised the 1983 secession of the Turkish Republic of Northern

56 Crawford, note 10, p. 248.

57 *Reference re: Secession of Quebec* (1998) 161 DLR (4th) 385, at 443.

58 Samuel Flagg Bemis, quoted in P. Gleijeses, 'The Limits of Sympathy: The United States and the Independence of Spanish America', *Journal of Latin American Studies*, 1992, vol. 24, p. 487.

59 Crawford, note 10, p. 115.

60 J. M. Taylor, *William Henry Seward, Lincoln's Right Hand*, New York, HarperCollins Publishers, 1991, pp. 177-9; H. Jones, *Union in Peril: The Crisis Over British Intervention in the Civil War*, Lincoln, University of Nebraska Press, 1992. On British policy towards recognition of the Confederacy see W. K. Pattison, 'The International Law of Recognition in Contemporary British Foreign Policy', unpublished doctoral dissertation, University of Virginia, 1981, pp. 38–40.

61 H. Jones, 'History and Mythology: The Crisis Over British Intervention in the Civil War', in R. E. May, *The Union, the Confederacy, and the Atlantic Rim*, West Lafayette, Purdue University Press, 1995, p. 52.

Cyprus means that the latter's secession has not, at least to date, been successful.[62]

In light of the above, the meaning of 'people' is the critical issue in any legal interpretation of the right of peoples to self-determination. In this respect it is imperative to analyse the various UN and other international documents that concern themselves with self-determination. The results of such an analysis will enable an assessment of whether post-World War II practice has been in accord with international law. The meaning of 'people' is the subject of a detailed analysis in the next chapter.

62 *Loizidou -v- Turkey (Merits)* (1996) 108 ILR 445 at 471; R. Jennings and A. Watts, *Oppenheim's International Law*, Volume I, *Peace*, 9th edition, London, Longman, 1992, p. 130.

2 The 'nation' as a 'people'

Any analysis of whether a nation is a people for the purposes of the right to self-determination in international law must begin with World War I and the Peace Conference of 1919 that finally concluded it. It was in the events of the war and the peace settlement that self-determination started its transformation from political principle to its present normative status in international law.

During the early years of World War I both sides to the conflict adopted policies of national self-determination as tactics to weaken each other. Each side sought to incite rebellion in each other's empires amongst dissatisfied national groups as a means of gaining military advantage. Thus, the Allies proclaimed that they were fighting for the liberation of the Italians, the South Slavs, and the Czechs and Slovaks from foreign domination. On the other hand, the Germans made similar claims in relation to the Irish, Finns and various national groups within the Russian Empire.[1] One of the first statements for the use of self-determination as the basis of a territorial settlement after the war was a British Foreign Office memorandum in the autumn of 1916. It declared that an essential condition of peace required that 'the principle of nationality should therefore be one of the governing factors in the consideration of territorial arrangements after the war'.[2] However, neither side in the early years of the war was totally committed to the principle of self-determination, for they saw in it an inherent danger to the continuance and stability of their own empires.[3]

The two events that most significantly led to the adoption of national self-determination as a basis of any post-war peace settlement were the outbreak of the Russian Revolution and the almost simultaneous entry of the United States of America into the war on the side of the Allies.[4] These two events triggered the emergence of the Leninist and Wilsonian conceptions of self-determination which are fundamental to an understanding of self-determination in the post-World War I era.

1 H. O. Schoenberg, 'The Concept of "People" in the Principle of Self-Determination' unpublished doctoral dissertation, Columbia University, 1972, pp. 62–72.
2 R. A. Friedlander, 'Self-Determination: A Legal-Political Inquiry', *Detroit College of Law Review*, 1975, Issue 1, p. 72.
3 T. D. Musgrave, *Self-Determination and National Minorities*, Oxford, Clarendon Press, 1997, p. 17.
4 Schoenberg, note 1, p. 72.

The word 'people' was not generally used in the discourse on self-determination at that time. Its use in this context came with the adoption of the United Nations Charter in 1945. However, an understanding of the Leninist and Wilsonian conceptions of self-determination serves as a useful introduction to the meaning of 'people' as used in the primary sources on the right of peoples to self-determination after 1945.

Leninist self-determination

On 8 November 1917, the day after assuming power in Russia, the Bolshevik government affirmed its support for national self-determination, including the right of secession from Russia.[5] The Bolshevik policy on self-determination was principally developed by Vladimir Ilyich Lenin.

Lenin never defined what he meant by 'nation'. However, he relied on the 1913 formulation by his colleague Joseph Stalin which read:

> A nation is a historically produced stable community of people originating on the basis of a community of language, of territory, of economic life, and a psychological form of existence which reveals itself in the community of culture. Only the existence of all these features together constitutes a nation.[6]

Stalin's definition of a nation is consistent with the romantic theory of self-determination. For Lenin the right to national self-determination meant the right of an oppressed national minority to political independence. In accordance with socialist theory, Russian national minorities had the right of self-determination because Russia was at that time in the first stage of capitalist development which required the formation of nation-states. However, Lenin believed that if national minorities were given the right to self-determination, including the right of secession, they would choose to unite with Russia into a unitary state. For Lenin, the recognition of the right of secession was proof that national inequality had been eliminated. This would end the nationalism of Russians as oppressors, and that of Russia's national minorities as the oppressed. Lenin believed that none of the oppressed nations would exercise the right of secession because once that right was recognised it lost its meaning.[7]

Once in power the oppressed nations did in fact exercise the right to secession. Initially the Bolshevik government had no option but to permit this process since the promise of self-determination was an instrumental part of Bolshevik political

5 W. Connor, *The National Question in Marxist-Leninist Theory and Strategy*, Princeton, NJ, Princeton University Press, 1984, pp. 45–6.

6 Quoted in H. E. Asenbauer, *On the Right of Self-Determination of the Armenian People of Nagorno-Karabakh*, New York, The Armenian Prelacy, 1996, p. 121.

7 R. Pipes, *The Formation of the Soviet Union, Communism and Nationalism 1917–1923*, revised edition, Cambridge, MA, Harvard University Press, 1997, pp. 44–5; B. J. Wells, 'United Nations Decisions on Self-Determination', unpublished doctoral dissertation, New York University, 1963, pp. 22–6.

strategy. To successfully gain control of Russia and its empire the Bolsheviks realised that they had to appeal to the oppressed nations. As a result, at least thirteen new states came into being within what was formerly the Russian Empire, many of which were recognised by the new Bolshevik government.[8] In fact, Leninist theory failed the test of reality in its underestimation of the forces of nationalism. To achieve the Bolshevik goal of control over all of the former Russian Empire there was a need to redefine Lenin's original policy. The key figure in that process was Stalin.

Stalin's key contribution to the Bolshevik approach to self-determination was to limit the exercise of the right to self-determination to the proletariat of any given oppressed nation. Only the proletariat, or its spokesperson, the party, had the right to declare secession. No true working class would seek independence. This meant, by definition, that all secessionist movements were led by bourgeois or counter-revolutionary elements and had to be suppressed. Despite differences with Stalin over this reformulation of the right to national self-determination, Lenin was forced to concede that Stalin was correct.[9] This led Lenin to another concession, namely, acceptance of a federal form of government. Lenin recognised that some form of federalism, even if devoid of substance, was necessary to reintegrate the Russian Empire in the form of the Union of Soviet Socialist Republics (USSR), as it was renamed in 1922. This process of reintegration required war, but success in that war would not have come without formal adherence to the right of national self-determination, including the right of secession.[10]

The federalism of the USSR was one of form and no real substance. The republics were designed as the homelands of the various nations that constituted the USSR. Although all Soviet constitutions explicitly recognised the right of federal republics to secede,[11] this right was interpreted as purely theoretical. Lenin's concession to federalism was more apparent than real because of the continued adherence to his injunction to maintain a single centralised Communist Party. As long as the Communist Party retained real political power, federalism was little more than a symbolic concession to national feelings. The significance of the Leninist formulation of self-determination was that the right belonged to the nation.

Wilsonian self-determination

Woodrow Wilson's concept of self-determination was one of granting statehood to nations. This was the fundamental ideal in his plans for the 1919 Peace

8 Connor, note 5, pp. 46–7.
9 Pipes, note 7, pp. 109–11.
10 Connor, note 5, p. 47.
11 See the 1924 constitution, Chapter 3, Article 4; the 1936 constitution, Article 17; and the 1977 constitution, Article 72.

Conference. For Wilson language was the fundamental basis of any nation. This linguistic basis of defining the nation was developed by Wilson during his days as an academic at Princeton University.[12]

These views were later reinforced by a team of experts that provided Wilson with the necessary geographic, historical, economic and legal data he required in preparation for the Peace Conference of 1919.[13] The Wilsonian conception of national self-determination was not universally applied at the Peace Conference, being confined to a part of Europe only and not applied against the victorious powers in World War I.[14] The dominant motives of the Peace Conference were the gratification of faithful allies, punishment of the defeated enemies, and the establishment of a new political order in Europe.[15] As a result, the application of self-determination principles was essentially confined to the dismantling of the empires of the defeated Germans, Austro-Hungarians and Ottomans.

The new states of Czechoslovakia, Yugoslavia and Poland which emerged out of the Peace Conference were all justified on the principle of self-determination.[16] However, territorial delimitation did not always conform with the principle of national self-determination. In many cases political, economic and strategic considerations prevailed over national self-determination.[17] In a few cases exchanges of populations acted as a substitute for self-determination. Thus, population exchanges took place between Greece and Turkey and Greece and Bulgaria.[18] In other cases the peace makers approved the holding of plebiscites as a means of resolving disputed border regions. This idea was not strongly supported because the victors did not want to endanger the spoils of war with

12 D. Heater, *National Self-Determination, Woodrow Wilson and His Legacy*, New York, St Martin's Press, 1994, p. 26.

13 Ibid., pp. 38, 56.

14 Wilson claimed that pressure from the other Allies forced him to confine self-determination to the territories of the defeated powers. This is not altogether correct as Wilson refused to consider many requests for self-determination from nations that were with the Allied powers. After the Peace Conference he admitted that he was not aware at the time of outlining the Fourteen Points of the existence of a number of nations. Thus, the Irish were given short shrift when their delegation petitioned him for independence: A. Cobban, *National Self-Determination*, Oxford, Oxford University Press, 1945, pp. 21-2. On the other hand, the partition of Ireland in 1921 was justified by the British by the principle of self-determination: T. M. Franck, 'Legitimacy in the International System', *American Journal of International Law*, 1988, vol. 82, p. 744.

15 P. M. Brown, 'Self-Determination in Central Europe', *American Journal of International Law*, 1920, vol. 14, p. 237.

16 The new states that emerged as a result of the Peace Conference could all be regarded as being based upon the principle of national self-determination. However, those that were on the winning side of the war often found themselves with substantial numbers of persons who would otherwise have been within the borders of states that were on the losing side of the war: Brown, note 15, pp. 237–8. The rights of these and other minorities were to be protected by a network of minorities treaties.

17 Heater, note 12, pp. 70–7; Schoenberg, note 1, pp. 80–6.

18 C. Meindersma, 'Population Exchanges: International Law and State Practice – Part I', *International Journal of Refugee Law*, 1997, vol. 9, pp. 338–51.

possibly hostile plebiscites. Wilson himself was reticent on the holding of plebiscites, preferring to be guided by the evidence of his experts rather than the expressed will of the population at the ballot box.[19] Rather than being seen as a panacea of universal application, the holding of plebiscites was approved for only a handful of contested regions. Not all the approved plebiscites were actually held.

The Aaland Islands dispute

In the inter-war era national self-determination was a political ideal. It was not a rule of international law, at least insofar as definitively constituted sovereign states were concerned. This was confirmed by the resolution of the dispute between Finland and Sweden over the Aaland Islands in the years following World War I.

In the Aaland Islands dispute the Swedish population of the islands sought unification with Sweden after the collapse of the Russian Provisional government in October 1917, on the basis of an overwhelming referendum vote to that effect on 31 December 1917. Prior to that date the islands had been part of the Grand Duchy of Finland within Tsarist Russia. With the collapse of the Russian Provisional government, Finland declared its independence, claiming the Aaland Islands as part of its territory. Finland was recognised by the new Bolshevik government in Russia on 4 January 1918, by France on 5 January 1918, by Denmark and Norway on 10 January 1918 and by Switzerland on 22 February 1918. Sweden recognised Finland on 4 January 1918 without making any reservation as to Finland's claim over the islands or its territorial boundaries.[20] Nevertheless, Sweden supported the islanders' claims for incorporation into Sweden, and the matter was eventually referred to the Council of the League of Nations in July 1920.

An International Commission of Jurists, appointed by the Council to investigate the matter, said:

> Although the principle of self-determination of peoples plays an important part in modern political thought, especially since the Great War, it must be pointed out that there is no mention of it in the Covenant of the League of Nations. The recognition of this principle in a certain number of international treaties cannot be considered as sufficient to put it upon the same footing as a positive rule of the Law of Nations.[21]

19 Heater, note 12, pp. 78–9.

20 S. N. Lalonde, 'Uti Possidetis and Internal Administrative Borders', unpublished doctoral dissertation, University of Cambridge, 1997, pp. 65–6.

21 *Report of the International Commission of Jurists* (1920) LNOJ Spec. Supp. 3, p. 5. A similar view was taken by the Commission of Rapporteurs in their report on the Aaland Islands dispute: *The Aaland Islands Question: Report Submitted to the Council of the League of Nations by the Commission of Rapporteurs* (1921) League Doc. B7.21/68/106, pp. 27–8.

However, this statement was qualified by the Commission of Jurists who went on to say that the statement that the principle of self-determination was not a rule of international law:

> only applies to a nation which is definitively constituted as a sovereign State, and an independent member of the international community, and so long as it continues to possess these characteristics. From the point of view of both domestic and international law, the formation, transformation and dismemberment of States as a result of revolutions and wars create situations of fact which, to a large extent, cannot be met by the application of normal rules of positive law. . . . Under such circumstances, the principle of self-determination of peoples may be called into play.[22]

The consequence of this qualification was that, in the transitional period between the dissolution of Tsarist Russia and the definitive constitution of new states, the normal rules of international law did not apply. A different kind of international law rule, one which included the principle of national self-determination, applied. The Commission of Jurists said of this transitional period:

> New aspirations of certain sectors of the nation, which are sometimes based on old traditions or on a common language and civilization, may come to the surface and produce effects which must be taken into account in the interests of the internal and external peace of nations. The principle recognising the rights of peoples to determine their political fate may be applied in various ways: the most important of these are, on the one hand the formation of an independent State, and on the other hand the right of choice between two existing States.[23]

The Commission of Jurists was careful to note that in such transitional periods:

> the principle that nations must have the right to self-determination is not the only one to be taken into account. Even though it be regarded as the most important of the principles governing the formation of States, geographical, economic and other similar considerations may put obstacles in the way of its complete recognition.[24]

The Commission of Jurists formed the view that, at the time, Finland was not a definitively established state, but rather a revolutionary entity. Thus, self-determination could have a role to play regarding the fate of the Aaland Islands. However, a subsequent Commission of Rapporteurs disagreed with the Commission of

22 *Report of the International Commission of Jurists* (1920) LNOJ Spec. Supp. 3, pp. 5–6.
23 Ibid., p. 6.
24 Ibid.

Jurists on this point and found that Finland was a definitively constituted state, with the consequence that self-determination had no role to play and that the Aaland Islands were part of Finland. This was all the more so given that Swedish recognition of Finland made no reservation as to the latter's claim to sovereignty over the islands.[25] Even so, the Commission of Rapporteurs noted that if Finland did not guarantee the Aaland Islanders cultural autonomy within Finland, the principle of national self-determination would justify 'the separation of the islands from Finland, based upon the wishes of the inhabitants which would be freely expressed by means of a plebiscite'.[26]

The importance of the Aaland Islands dispute lies in the report of the Commission of Jurists. Although the dispute has been cited as authority for the view that there is no normative concept of self-determination in international law,[27] the Jurists' report clearly indicates otherwise. The report clearly states that in revolutionary situations, such as the dissolution of a state, the principle of national self-determination is the most important, although not the only, principle affecting the creation of new states.

The United Nations Charter

With the coming into force of the United Nations Charter in 1945, the word 'peoples' was associated with self-determination for the first time in any international legal instrument. In the Charter it appears in a number of places. The Preamble commences with the words 'WE, THE PEOPLES OF THE UNITED NATIONS' and goes on to list the organisation's general aims and objectives, including 'the promotion of the economic and social advancement of all peoples'.

Articles 73 and 76, dealing with non-self-governing and trust territories respectively, both speak of the populations of such territories as 'peoples' and 'inhabitants'. In Article 80, the placing of territories under the trusteeship system would not, except as stipulated in individual trusteeship agreements, alter in any respect existing rights, *inter alia*, of 'any peoples'.

The 'self-determination of peoples' is specifically referred to in Articles 1(2) and 55. In Article 1(2) it is stated that a purpose of the United Nations is:

> To develop friendly relations among nations based on respect for the principle of equal rights and self-determination of peoples, and to take other appropriate measures to strengthen universal peace.

By Article 55 the goal of 'peaceful and friendly relations among nations based upon respect for the principle of equal rights and self-determination of peoples' is

25 *The Aaland Islands Question: Report Submitted to the Council of the League of Nations by the Commission of Rapporteurs* (1921) League Doc. B7.21/68/106, p. 27.

26 Ibid., p. 34.

27 H. A. Wilson, *International Law and the Use of Force by National Liberation Movements*, Oxford, Clarendon Press, 1988, p. 57.

to be achieved by the UN promoting various policies relating to economic and social conditions and respect for human rights.

Given that the Charter contains no definition of peoples, the meaning of the word has to be ascertained by giving it its 'ordinary meaning . . . in . . . the context and in the light of [the Charter's] object and purpose'.[28] Subsequent state practice in the application of the Charter is also relevant in determining the meaning of peoples.[29] The *travaux préparatoires* may be taken into account to establish the meaning of peoples if interpretation based upon the ordinary meaning of the word in the light of the Charter's object and purpose 'leaves the meaning ambiguous or obscure'.[30] In applying these canons of construction no clear definition of peoples emerges. However, it can be concluded, at the very least, that a nation is not excluded from being a people.

The introductory part of Article 73 speaks of the populations of non-self-governing territories as 'peoples' and 'inhabitants'. In paragraphs (a) and (b) reference is made only to 'peoples'. 'Inhabitants' clearly means the total population of any such territory and it is reasonable to assume that 'peoples' means the same as 'inhabitants' in this article. However, nothing in Article 73 precludes a nation from being a people. This follows from the article using the plural 'peoples' and not the singular 'people'. Article 73 does not equate 'inhabitants' with a single people, but rather with peoples. Thus, the population of any given non-self-governing territory is made up of its 'inhabitants' or a number of peoples. This is specifically stated in paragraph (b) with its reference to developing self-government in non-self-governing territories 'according to the particular circumstances of each territory and its peoples'. Thus, a number of peoples can occupy a single territory. Given the multi-national composition of most of these territories it is thus reasonable to equate peoples with nations, and conclude that a people means a nation. If a people were to mean the total population of a territorial unit irrespective of national identity, paragraph (b) would have referred to 'people' and not 'peoples'.

Support for this conclusion can also be drawn from paragraph (a) with its reference to 'due respect for the culture of the peoples concerned' in relation to their political, economic, social and educational advancement, just treatment and protection against abuses. The reference to 'culture' echoes some aspects of the definition of a nation, thus pointing to the meaning of a people as being a nation.

A similar comment could be made in relation to Article 76. Here the basic objectives of the trusteeship system include, in paragraph (b), the promotion of various interests of 'the inhabitants of trust territories' and progression towards self-government or independence 'as may be appropriate to the particular circumstances of each territory and its peoples and the freely expressed wishes of the

28 Vienna Convention on the Law of Treaties, UN Doc A/Conf 39/27 (1969), Article 31(1).
29 Ibid., Article 31(3)(b).
30 Ibid., Article 32(a).

people concerned'. Here too there is reference to a number of peoples occupying a single territory.[31]

Reference to 'peoples' in Articles 1(2) and 55 is made specifically in the context of the purpose of developing 'friendly relations among nations based upon respect for the principle of equal rights and self-determination of peoples'.[32] The inclusion of 'the principle of equal rights and self-determination of peoples' in the Charter was at the insistence of the delegation from the USSR whose Foreign Minister called upon the UN to expedite 'the realization of the principle of self-determination of nations'.[33]

The Charter *travaux préparatoires* indicate that the word 'nation' as used in the Charter included colonies, mandates, protectorates, quasi-states and states, or, in other words, all types of political entities.[34] In the light of this definition of 'nation', the UN Secretariat, after analysing the Charter as a whole, indicated that the meaning of 'peoples' in Articles 1(2) and 55 meant 'groups of human beings who may, or may not, comprise states or nations'.[35] The Charter *travaux* reveal no conclusive interpretation of the term 'people'. However, nor do the Charter *travaux* rule out a meaning of people that is consistent with a nation.[36] Reference by the UN Secretariat to 'groups of human beings' clearly could include a nation. On the basis of the UN Secretariat's definition, there is nothing to exclude a nation from the definition of a people. The view of the Belgian delegate at San Francisco that peoples meant 'national groups which do not identify with the population of a state'[37] would support such a conclusion. It is also the view of Ofuatey-Kodjoe, who observes that 'peoples' as used in Article 1(2) refers to all 'distinct groups' such as 'nations'.[38] In a similar vein, Franck opines that the term peoples 'recognize[d] the importance of the ethnic dimension in determining who is entitled to invoke self-determination'.[39] The consequences of such a definition of 'peoples' as used in the Charter led to

31 This interpretation of the meaning of 'peoples' as used in Articles 73 and 76 was supported by *ad hoc* Judge van Wyck in *South West Africa Cases (Ethiopia -v- South Africa; Liberia -v- South Africa) Second Phase* [1966] ICJ Rep 4, at 166, and by Turkey in UN debates over the claim of Turkish Cypriots to the right of self-determination: Musgrave, note 3, p. 228.

32 Article 14 of the Charter also speaks of the General Assembly having a role in the preservation of 'friendly relations among nations'.

33 R. B. Russell, *A History of the United Nations Charter: The Role of the United States 1940–1945*, Washington, DC, The Brookings Institution, 1958, p. 811; Wells, note 7, pp. 59, 62–3.

34 *United Nations Documents of the Conference on International Organisation*, 18 vols, San Francisco, 1945–1952, vol. XVIII, p. 657.

35 Ibid., p. 658.

36 Musgrave, note 3, p. 156.

37 *UNCIO*, note 34, vol. VI, p. 300.

38 W. Ofuatey-Kodjoe, 'Self-Determination', in O. Schachter and C. C. Joyner (eds), *United Nations Legal Order*, Volume 1, Cambridge, Cambridge University Press, 1995, p. 354.

39 Franck, note 14, p. 745.

French[40] and Colombian[41] concerns that Article 1(2) introduced the right of secession.[42]

The right to secession on the basis of self-determination of peoples was apparently conceded by the Chairman, Rapporteur and Secretary of the Technical Committee I/1, who, when asked by the Coordination Committee whether self-determination meant the capacity of peoples to govern themselves and whether it included a right of secession on the part of peoples within a state, replied that 'the right of self-determination meant that a people may establish any regime which they favour'.[43] This reply does not exclude the right of a people to establish its own state.[44]

On the other hand, it must be observed that the Charter does refer to the principle of territorial integrity of states. Article 2(4) precludes member states from 'the threat or use of force against the territorial integrity or political independence of any State'. The preservation of the territorial integrity of states can be enhanced by confining the meaning of people to the population of a state as a whole without differentiation according to the national identification of various segments of that population. By thus confining the definition of people, a nation within a state could not be a people. A nation cannot be the claimant to a right to self-determination resulting in secession from a state, thereby preserving the territorial integrity of that state. Only if the Charter sanctified territorial integrity over and above any other principle could such a confined interpretation of the meaning of peoples be justified. However, the ordinary meaning of Article 2(4) does not lead to the conclusion that all other Charter principles are subordinated to the overriding demands of territorial integrity. If that was the intention of its framers, one would have expected a clear statement to that effect to appear in the Charter. Article 2(4) is not such a statement.

Before analysing the text of Article 2(4), the usually proffered justifications for the primacy of territorial integrity over other Charter principles need to be examined. It is often argued that if secession from independent states is legitimated on the basis of the principle of self-determination of peoples, the results would be the proliferation of a large number of economically non-viable small states, and the fragmentation of the present international system.[45] However, these two claims do not withstand the slightest of scrutiny.

40 *UNCIO*, note 34, vol. VI, p. 298.

41 A. Cassese, *Self-Determination of Peoples: A Legal Reappraisal*, Cambridge, Cambridge University Press, 1995, pp. 39–40.

42 Other delegates argued that Article 1(2) did not grant a right of secession: *UNCIO*, note 34, vol. VI, at 296. Buchheit accurately states that no right of secession can be 'supported or discredited by reference to the *travaux préparatoires* of the San Francisco Conference': L. C. Buchheit, *Secession: The Legitimacy of Self-Determination*, New Haven, CT, Yale University Press, 1978, p. 73.

43 *UNCIO*, note 34, vol. XVII, p. 143.

44 J. Duursma, *Fragmentation and the International Relations of Micro-States: Self-Determination and Statehood*, Cambridge, Cambridge University Press, 1996, pp. 14–15.

45 C. O. Quaye, *Liberation Struggles in International Law*, Philadelphia, Temple University Press, 1991, p. 220; R. Khan, *Kashmir and the United Nations*, Delhi, Vikas Publications, 1969, pp. 101–3, arguing that, because of such reasons, self-determination is confined to the process of decolonisation.

First, there is no demonstrated connection between the political and economic viability of a state and its size.[46] As to political viability, if anything, one could more plausibly argue that the size of a state is inversely proportionate to its viability, rather than the opposite. Thus, the USSR, at the time the largest state in the world, proved to be non-viable by 1991, with its demise into fifteen new states corresponding to its former republics. The viability of Russia, now the largest state in the world and one of the new states emerging from the former USSR, is by no means guaranteed given the conflicts in some of its federal units, most notably in Chechnya. The continued viability of Canada, the second largest state in the world, is in question notwithstanding, and largely because of, the very slender vote against secession in late 1995 in the province of Quebec. In India, the seventh largest state in the world, the viability of that state has been in constant focus since its creation in 1947, due to the threat of Sikh and Kashmiri separatism. In these and many other examples[47] the viability of large states has been threatened by nations that have not been satisfied with their position within the frameworks of a multi-national state. The states that have emerged from successful secessions or have been claimed in the case of unsuccessful secessions, have not generally been as small in size as many of the new states admitted to the UN after independence from colonisation.

As to economic viability, some of the largest states are amongst the world's poorest, while some of the smallest are amongst the most economically prosperous.[48] Smallness does not correlate with poverty. The Editor of *The Round Table*, after referring to the economic success of the small Commonwealth states of Brunei and Mauritius, made the following observation in relation to small states:

> In general, their security and prosperity depend on the quality, including the probity and provenance, of each state's government and administration. Beyond these simple but fundamental verities, it is unwise to deal unduly in generalities. The problems, and opportunities, of small states are specific not generic; and it is in specific terms that they must mostly be seen and handled.[49]

On the other hand, rather than discouraging the emergence of new states, the UN has generally acted in quite the opposite manner. Thus, in 1970 the UN General

46 Dahl and Tufte have shown that no significant relationship exists between the size of states and either their Gross National Product *per capita* or their ability to survive as politically independent entities: R. A. Dahl and E. R. Tufte, *Size and Democracy*, Stanford, CA, Stanford University Press, 1973.

47 Some of the more prominent examples would include the failed attempts at secession in the Congo (Katanga) and Nigeria (Biafra), the successful secessions from Pakistan (Bangladesh), Ethiopia (Eritrea), and Yugoslavia (Croatia, Slovenia, Bosnia-Hercegovina, Macedonia), the partition of Czechoslovakia (Czech Republic, Slovakia), and the as yet unresolved secession in Sudan (Southern Sudan). None of the states affected by the events could be described as small states.

48 M. R. Islam, 'Secession Crisis in Papua New Guinea: The Proclaimed Republic of Bougainville in International Law', *University of Hawaii Law Review*, 1991, vol. 13, p. 470.

49 Editorial 2, 'Small States Reconsidered', *The Round Table*, October, 1996, no. 340, p. 403.

Assembly, by a vote of 120 for, 1 against and 1 abstention, passed Resolution 2734, which, in paragraph 1:

> solemnly reaffirms the universal and unconditional validity of the purposes and principles of the Charter of the United Nations as the basis of relations among States *irrespective of their size, geographical location, level of development or political, economic and social systems* and declares that breach of these principles cannot be justified in any circumstances whatsoever.
>
> (emphasis added)[50]

As observed by Hector Gros Espiell, Special Rapporteur to a sub-commission of the Commission on Human Rights, there is 'no legal basis for denying the right to self-determination on the ground that the population of which a people is composed, or the territory which it inhabits, is small'.[51]

Given that since 1960 the General Assembly has annually passed resolutions calling for the speedy end to colonisation in accordance with the principle of self-determination of peoples, and that in paragraph 2 of Resolution 2734 the General Assembly called upon all states to comply with their obligations as to self-determination of peoples, it is clear that the UN is prepared to end colonisation by granting independence to non-self-governing and trust territories irrespective of their size and viability.[52] This is amply evidenced by the many small and micro-states that have been admitted to the UN over the last few decades. What this establishes is that the size and economic viability of states are of no major concern to the UN, and further, that small and potentially non-viable states overwhelmingly emerge from the process of decolonisation rather than from secession from existing independent states. In these circumstances it is hard, if not impossible, to maintain that matters of size and economic viability of states justify the paramountcy of territorial integrity over other principles found in the UN Charter.

Second, it is argued that the multiplication of states leads to the breakdown and fragmentation of the international system. This claim is also demonstrably false. Empirical evidence supports the view that fragmentation of the international system is unrelated to the number of states in that system, despite claims to the contrary by the then UN Secretary-General Boutros Boutros-Ghali in *An Agenda for Peace*. The evidence is found in Boutros-Ghali's other comments in the very same document, where he observes:

50 Declaration on the Strengthening of International Security, General Assembly Resolution 2734 (XXV), 16 December 1970. A similar approach is seen in the context of decolonisation where the General Assembly in the Declaration on the Granting of Independence to Colonial Countries and Peoples in 1960 declared in paragraph 3 that '[i]nadequacy of political, economic, social or educational preparedness should never serve as a pretext for delaying independence': General Assembly Resolution 1514(XV), 14 December 1960.

51 Quoted in Duursma, note 44, p. 39.

52 J. Rapaport, E. Muteba and J. J. Therattil, *Small States and Territories: Status and Problems*, New York, Arno Press, 1971, pp. 21–7.

> Since the creation of the United Nations in 1945, over 100 major conflicts around the world have left some 20 million dead. The United Nations was rendered powerless to deal with many of these crises because of the vetoes – 279 of them – cast in the Security Council, which were a vivid expression of the divisions of that period.[53]

It is clear that since the end of the Cold War the UN, unhampered by the use of the veto within the Security Council, has been far more active in attempting to resolve conflicts around the world, as is evidenced by UN involvement in the Gulf War, Cambodia, Somalia, and the former Yugoslavia. But this increased activity, at a time of decreased divisions in the international system, also came at a time when there was a significant increase of 27 in the number of new states admitted to the UN in the years 1990–93 inclusive. The 'divisions' that Boutros-Ghali referred to were divisions of a time when the world had fewer states than at present.

Furthermore, the UN practice of encouraging non-self-governing and trust territories to seek independence upon decolonisation is hard to reconcile with a concern that a multiplicity of states leads to fragmentation and division in the international system. If such a concern did exist, then the UN Committee on Decolonisation would presumably have looked upon other means of achieving decolonisation, such as free association or integration with an existing state or some other political status, short of independent statehood, determined by the peoples of the relevant territory. These alternatives were explicitly recognised as options to independent statehood.[54] However, the UN Committee on Decolonisation has consistently favoured and emphasised independence as the preferred option of achieving decolonisation, and has with reluctance accepted decisions of the peoples of relevant territories either to retain their existing dependent status, or choose some form of association with an independent state.[55] Thus, the generally proffered arguments justifying the sanctity of the territorial integrity of states do not withstand scrutiny. Nor does the actual interpretation of Article 2(4) in the UN Charter justify the subordination of other Charter principles, such as that of self-determination of peoples, to that of territorial integrity of states. Article 2(4) does not, directly or indirectly, proclaim the paramountcy of territorial integrity over other principles in the Charter. In other words, it does not sanction the territorial integrity of states absolutely. The prohibition is only and specifically directed against the activities of members of the UN. Nothing in Article 2(4) or elsewhere in the Charter precludes a challenge to a state's territorial integrity from within the state itself.[56] Indeed, Article 2(7), in precluding the UN from intervening 'in matters

53 B. Boutros-Ghali, *An Agenda for Peace*, New York, United Nations, 1992, para. 14.

54 Declaration on Friendly Relations, Principle of Equal Rights and Self-Determination of Peoples, Principle 5, Paragraph 4.

55 R. Emerson, 'Self-Determination', *American Journal of International Law*, 1971, vol. 65, p. 470, where the author notes that the decision in 1965 of the Cook Islands to continue ties with New Zealand was accepted by the Committee 'with surprised dismay'.

56 J. Crawford, *The Creation of States in International Law*, Oxford, Clarendon Press, 1979, p. 266.

which are essentially within the domestic jurisdiction of any State', indicates that, if the territorial integrity of a state is challenged from within, for example, by secession, the obligation of the UN, and by implication its members, is not to interfere, even if the territorial integrity of the state in question is at stake. Of course, the provisions of Article 2(7) are subject to UN intervention, including the use of force, pursuant to Chapter VII of the Charter. Article 39 permits such intervention in the internal affairs of a state if there is 'any threat to peace, breach of peace, or act of aggression', with the purpose of such intervention being 'to maintain or restore international peace and security'. In cases of secession threatening the territorial integrity of a state, nothing in Article 39 implies that the intervention pursuant to Chapter VII must be directed towards the preservation of the territorial integrity of the state. UN intervention in these cases must be with the aim of maintaining or restoring international peace and security. The fact that in cases such as Congo[57] and Cyprus[58] the UN supported the territorial integrity of those states against secessionist forces does not change the meaning of Article 39. In both cases the call for maintaining the territorial integrity of those states was seen as the means by which international peace and security could be restored. It is open to the UN to support, or at least not oppose, a secession from a state if it is of the view that that is the most effective way of carrying out its duty under Article 39 of maintaining and restoring international peace and security. This was implicitly the case with former Yugoslavia, where the Security Council, before any secessionist republic had been internationally recognised, sought a negotiated settlement between the disputant parties as the means of restoring peace and security to that country.[59] The end of Yugoslavia's territorial integrity was clearly a possible outcome of negotiations, and, for the Security Council, was an acceptable solution of the crisis.

These observations clearly demonstrate that Article 2(4) does not, of itself, guarantee the territorial integrity of states absolutely. Therefore, it cannot justify a meaning of people as being confined to the entire population of a state. In effect, Article 2(4) sheds no further light on the meaning of peoples as used in the Charter.

Whatever one may claim to be the meaning of peoples in the Charter, the practice of the UN in the few years immediately following its ratification indicated acceptance of the idea that a people meant, or at least included, a nation. The partition of the Indian sub-continent into the Muslim state of Pakistan and the predominantly Hindu state of India was to some extent an application of the principle of self-determination in which the peoples invoking self-determination were defined essentially by nationalist criteria.[60] Furthermore, the UN General Assembly, in 1950 and 1965 respectively, referred to both the Ewe tribe in West Africa[61] and the Tibetans[62] as groups that were nations.

57 General Assembly Resolution 1600 (XV), 15 April 1961.

58 General Assembly Resolution 3212 (XXXIX), 1 November 1974.

59 Security Council Resolution 713 (1991), para. 5, 21 September 1991.

60 Schoenberg, note 1, p. 199.

61 General Assembly Resolution 441(V), 2 December 1950.

62 General Assembly Resolution 2079 (XX), 18 December 1965.

Decolonisation

Given that the UN Charter in Articles 1(2) and 55 refers to 'self-determination of peoples' it is not surprising that the meaning of 'self-determination' has impacted on the meaning of 'peoples'. Self-determination means the right to self-government. This notion of self-determination stemmed from the Atlantic Charter of 1941 which endorsed an Anglo-American commitment to 'respect the right of all peoples to choose the form of government under which they will live'.[63] The British saw this commitment aimed primarily at the 'restoration of the sovereignty, self-government, and national life of the States and nations of Europe now under the Nazi yoke, and the principles governing any alterations in their territorial boundaries which may have to be made'.[64] However, the universality of the commitment meant that it could also apply to the colonies of both the Allied and Axis powers. By the time of the proclamation of the Charter the application of self-determination to colonial territories was clearly indicated with the provisions of Chapters XI and XII. These provisions committed the UN to seek self-government of what were defined as non-self-governing and trust territories respectively. The earlier commitment to other parts of the world, especially Eastern Europe, was ignored in practice, despite the generality of the expression of self-determination of peoples as used in Articles 1(2) and 55 of the Charter. The rapidly evolving international climate into a Cold War, and the West's inaction in Eastern Europe, meant that the demand for self-determination in Eastern Europe descended to the level of political propaganda in the West, but with no desire or commitment to go any further.[65] The West was unwilling to risk a major war with the Communist East which it believed would almost certainly eventuate if it actively supported claims to self-determination in Eastern Europe.

However, the pressure for self-government for colonial territories continued after the Charter's proclamation, and ultimately resulted in the 1960 General Assembly Resolution on the Granting of Independence to Colonial Countries and Peoples (Declaration on Colonialism).[66] The wording of the Declaration in its references to 'peoples' and 'self-determination of peoples' makes it difficult to glean exactly what is meant by the word 'peoples'.

The Declaration, either directly or indirectly, consistently speaks in terms of 'all peoples' subject to colonial rule as being entitled to independence. Nothing in the Declaration states or implies that a people is by definition the whole population of a given colonial territory. Nothing in the Declaration is inconsistent

63 The Atlantic Charter is reproduced in *United Nations Documents, 1941–1945*, London, Royal Institute of International Affairs, 1946, pp. 9–10.

64 R. E. Sherwood (ed.), *The White House Papers of Harry L Hopkins*, Volume I, London, Eyre & Spottiswoode, 1948, pp. 363–4.

65 On Western policy towards the 'liberation' of Eastern Europe see B. Kovrig, *The Myth of Liberation: East-Central Europe in US Diplomacy and Politics Since 1941*, Baltimore, Johns Hopkins University Press, 1973.

66 General Assembly Resolution 1514 (XV), 14 December 1960.

with the proposition that a given colonial territory consists of a number of peoples. The strong emphasis in the Declaration on the preservation of the territorial integrity of former colonial territories[67] upon independence does not alter that conclusion. It is often asserted that, because of the Declaration's insistence on the maintenance of a colonial territory's territorial integrity at the time of independence, a people must mean the population of that territory as a whole.[68] There is, however, no logical reason for such an assertion. The fundamental concern of the Declaration, made abundantly clear by its provisions, is the independence from foreign rule of all peoples in non-self-governing and trust territories. Sovereignty and political power were to be vested in the colonial peoples to the exclusion of the UN members administering such territories pursuant to Chapters XI and XII of the Charter. The Declaration's provisions on continued territorial integrity simply meant that former multi-national colonial territories became multi-national states. In fact, the Declaration's insistence on the continued territorial integrity of colonial territories was recognition of the fact that these territories were usually populated by a number of different peoples or nations. Mindful of the bloodshed and dislocation that had occurred in the decolonisation of British India, the UN members, in drafting the Declaration, found it necessary to insist on the continued territorial integrity of former colonial entities.[69] Without such provisions in the Declaration there was the expectation of demands by individual peoples for nation-states based upon the principle of self-determination of peoples where national boundaries did not correspond to colonial boundaries. This promised the probable result of war and suffering of a type that had characterised the decolonisation of British India.[70]

Thus, one must conclude that the effect of the Declaration on the meaning of peoples was negligible. Its major significance was in the fact that independence from colonial rule did not allow for the alteration of colonial borders upon gaining independence. Whatever the definition of a people had been prior to the Declaration remained unaltered by its adoption.[71]

67 Curiously the Declaration's references to territorial integrity are referenced variously to the nation, a country and a people. In the Preamble it states that 'all peoples have an inalienable right to complete freedom, the exercise of their sovereignty and the integrity of their national territory'. Article 4 speaks of 'the integrity of . . . national territory'. Article 6 speaks of 'territorial integrity of a country'. Article 7 speaks of 'territorial integrity' of 'peoples'.

68 Cassese, note 41, pp. 72–3; Ofuatey-Kodjoe, note 38, p. 358.

69 T. M. Franck, 'Postmodern Tribalism and the Right to Secession', in C. Brölmann, R. Lefeber and M. Zieck (eds), *Peoples and Minorities in International Law*, Dordrecht, Martinus Nijhoff Publishers, 1993, pp. 8, 10.

70 Such concerns were uppermost in the minds of member states of the Organisation for African Unity in 1964 when it resolved to respect the borders of colonial territories upon these territories achieving independence. The full text of the Cairo Resolution is reprinted in I. Brownlie, *African Boundaries: A Legal and Diplomatic Encyclopaedia*, London, C Hurst & Co, 1979, p. 11.

71 Even if one were to assert that a people meant the whole population of a colonial territory as a result of the Declaration, such a definition would be of no relevance in non-colonial contexts. As

It must also be noted that the General Assembly passed Resolution 1541(XV) on the day after the Declaration on Colonialism. Resolution 1541(XV) dealt with principles guiding UN members on their obligations, required by Article 73(e) of the Charter, to transmit information concerning the economic, social and educational conditions within their non-self-governing territories.[72] References in Resolution 1541(XV) to 'peoples' are consistently in the form of one territory and its 'peoples', implying that a number of peoples occupy any given territory.[73] Thus, Resolution 1541(XV) is quite explicit in denying that a people is the same as the whole population of a colonial territory, and is consistent, or at least not inconsistent, with a definition of people that means, or at least includes, a nation. Given that Resolution 1541(XV) was adopted at essentially the same time as the Declaration on Colonialism, and further that the latter declaration does not indicate anything as to the meaning of peoples, it would be reasonable to suggest that the meaning of peoples in both declarations is the same, and that the meaning is as indicated by Resolution 1541(XV).

In the practice of implementing the provisions of the Declaration on Colonialism, the UN did not always abide by the Declaration's requirement as to territorial integrity of former colonial boundaries. On a number of occasions the UN subordinated the principle of territorial integrity to the demands of nationalism, thereby recognising that the population of a colonial territory did include a number of peoples rather than only one people.

For example, in 1962 the former trust territory of Ruanda-Urundi acceded to independence as two separate states, namely Rwanda and Burundi. In both states the population was overwhelmingly Hutu with a small Tutsi minority, but at the time of independence Rwanda was politically dominated by the Hutus and Burundi by the Tutsis. Although in early 1962 the UN General Assembly supported decolonisation of Ruanda-Urundi as a single state,[74] it shortly thereafter

Crawford has observed, the meaning of people is 'context-dependent' in that 'what constitutes a people may be different for the purposes of different rights': J. Crawford, 'The Rights of Peoples: Some Conclusions', in J. Crawford (ed.), *The Rights of Peoples*, Oxford, Clarendon Press, 1988, pp. 169–70.

72 General Assembly Resolution 1541(XV), 15 December 1960. Whereas the Declaration on Colonialism, especially in Articles 3 and 5, spoke of the need for immediate steps to be taken towards independence as the desired means to end colonialism, Resolution 1541(XV) spoke of evolution and progress towards reaching a full measure of self-government by one of three means, namely independence, free association with an independent state and integration with an independent state. Pomerance has expressed the view that these two resolutions were 'in many ways mutually contradictory' and aptly labelled the Declaration on Colonialism revolutionary and Resolution 1541(XV) evolutionary: M. Pomerance, *Self-Determination in Law and Practice*, The Hague, Martinus Nijhoff Publishers, 1982, pp. 10–11.

73 Thus, in Principle VII reference is made to 'the peoples of the territory concerned', 'the territory and its peoples' and 'the peoples of the territory'. In Principle VIII there is reference to 'the peoples of the erstwhile Non-Self-Governing Territory'. In Principle IX there is reference to 'the integrating territory . . . [and] . . . its peoples' and 'the territory's peoples'.

74 General Assembly Resolution 1743 (XVI), 23 February 1962.

acceded to the formation of two separate states as desired by the two parts of the former Belgian colony.[75] In the British Cameroons, the UN General Assembly eventually agreed to dividing the trust territory into two parts for the purpose of a plebiscite to determine its future.[76] The Northern Cameroons voted to join Nigeria, while the Southern Cameroons opted to federate with the Republic of Cameroon as the Federal Republic of Cameroon.[77] The Republic of Cameroon, independent only since January 1960, had previously been the trust territory of French Cameroun. Had the plebiscite been taken in British Cameroons as a whole the result would have been in favour of joining the Republic of Cameroon.[78] In the single colony of the Gilbert and Ellice Islands the UN permitted a split along national lines, with the mainly Polynesian Ellice Islands voting to separate from the mainly Micronesian Gilbert Islands.[79] The Gilbert Islands became independent in 1977, and in 1979 assumed the name of Kiribati. The Ellice Islands achieved independence as Tuvalu in 1978.

Violations of the principle of territorial integrity occurred in other ways, notably in allowing former colonial units, after independence, to absorb areas that had never been within their pre-independence borders.[80] Such a situation had occurred before the Declaration on Colonialism with the emergence of an independent India from parts of the former British colony on the sub-continent. The new

75 General Assembly Resolution 1746 (XVI), 27 June 1962. See Wells, note 7, pp. 183–201.

76 General Assembly Resolution 1350 (XIII), 13 March 1959. A proposal for the British Togoland plebiscite to be held in four parts of that colony, determined along essentially national and linguistic criteria, was put to the UN General Assembly by its own special mission to the colony. However, the proposal was not accepted by the Assembly and a plebiscite in the colony as a whole was ordered: General Assembly Resolution 944(X), 15 December 1955. The plebiscite resulted in a majority vote for the unification of British Togoland with Gold Coast to form the new state of Ghana: Wells, note 7, pp. 124–51.

77 Proceedings by the Federal Republic of Cameroon to contest the validity of the plebiscite in the International Court of Justice were dismissed: *Case Concerning the Northern Cameroons Case (Cameroon -v- United Kingdom)* [1963] ICJ Rep. 15.

78 Wells, note 7, pp. 159–83.

79 General Assembly Resolution 3426 (XXX), 8 December 1975.

80 It should also be noted that some colonial powers absorbed their colonial territories in circumstances where the populations of these territories were not consulted or the process of consultation has been alleged to have been dubious. Thus, the non-self-governing territory of Greenland was unilaterally integrated by Denmark into the Danish Kingdom in 1953, and removed from the list of non-self-governing territories by the General Assembly in 1954: H. Hannum, *Autonomy, Sovereignty, and Self-Determination: The Accommodation of Conflicting Rights*, revised edition, Philadelphia, University of Pennsylvania Press, 1996, p. 342. In 1954 the non-self-governing territories of the Netherlands Antilles and Suriname were absorbed into the Kingdom of the Netherlands and the General Assembly removed them from the list of non-self-governing territories in 1955. Suriname achieved independence in 1975: Hannum, see above, p. 347. Finally, in 1959, Hawaii voted to become a state of the USA, and was removed by the General Assembly from the list of non-self-governing territories. However, various factors taint the conduct of the plebiscite as illegitimate, and its validity is keenly contested to this day by Native Hawaiians: S. J. Anaya, 'The Native Hawaiian People and International Human Rights Law: Toward a Remedy for Past and Continuing Wrongs', *Georgia Law Review*, 1994, vol. 28, pp. 333–5.

Indian state absorbed the princely states of Hyderabad, Junagadh and Kashmir, even though they had never been part of British India. They had operated as princely states with a measure of autonomy, as distinct from British India which was the object of direct British rule, and their right to retain their independence had been guaranteed by the Indian Independence Act 1947.[81] Kashmir, given that it was predominately populated by Muslims, and that it was contiguous to both India and Pakistan, has remained a source of conflict between the two states, particularly since the political insurgency that swamped it in 1989. In December 1961, just over a year after the adoption of the Declaration on Colonialism, India forcibly seized Goa, a Portuguese colony, ignoring the opinion of the population of Goa which would probably have decided against incorporation with India.[82] Indonesia's incorporation of Irian Jaya serves as another example. The Indonesian claim that West New Guinea and the Dutch East Indies formed one colony was denied by the former colonial power itself as well as by many Third World states.[83] The yet unresolved situation in Western Sahara, where Morocco and Mauritania partitioned and occupied the former colony after Spain's departure in January 1976, is another illustration. Another instance is the Indonesian annexation of Portuguese East Timor in July 1976. Notwithstanding that the annexation was condemned by the UN Security Council[84] and by slim majorities of the UN General Assembly[85] and despite the fact that East Timor's right to self-determination was

81 The precise legal status of the princely states is a matter of controversy. The Indian Independence Act 1947, in s. 2(4) stated that nothing in the Act could be construed 'as preventing the accession of Indian States to either of the new Dominions'. Section 7(1)(b) stipulated the end of British paramountcy over these princely states. What that meant had been made clear in a British Government Memorandum of 12 May 1946 which declared 'all the rights surrendered by the States to the paramount power will return to the States': Memorandum on States' Treaties and Paramountcy, 12 May 1946, reprinted in H. S. G. Rao, *Legal Aspects of the Kashmir Problem*, Bombay, Asia Publishing House, 1967, p. 177. On this basis the preferable conclusion is that the princely states became independent states for the purposes of international law after the passage of the Indian Independence Act 1947. For an alternative perspective see Rao, *Legal Aspects of the Kashmir Problem*, pp. 16–24. Not all princely states were absorbed by India or Pakistan. Thus, Bhutan became an independent state.

82 Q. Wright, 'The Goa Incident', *American Journal of International Law*, 1962, vol. 56, p. 627. According to Crawford, the Goa annexation is an exception to the principle of self-determination which only applies 'to minute territories which approximate, in the geographical sense, to "enclaves" of the claimant State, which are ethnically and economically parasitic upon or derivative of that State, and which cannot be said in any legitimate sense to constitute separate territorial units': Crawford, note 56, p. 384. Other retrocessions of small colonial enclaves, such as Ifni to Morocco and Walvis Bay to Namibia, have been achieved by the process of negotiation and treaty: Duursma, note 44, pp. 86–7.

83 Pomerance, note 72, p. 87. Cassese views the Goa and Irian Jaya cases as ones of 'gross disregard for the principle [of self-determination]': Cassese, note 41, pp. 79–86.

84 Security Council Resolutions 384 (1975), 22 December 1975, and 389 (1976), 22 April 1976.

85 The General Assembly Resolutions 3485 (XXX), 12 December 1975; 31/53, 1 December 1976; 32/34, 28 November 1977; 33/39, 13 December 1978; 34/40, 21 November 1979; 35/27, 11 November 1980; 36/50, 24 November 1981; 37/30, 23 November 1982. These resolutions were passed with decreasing majorities, with negative votes and abstentions outweighing positive votes after 1976.

confirmed by the International Court of Justice,[86] the UN only became engaged in East Timor after Indonesia granted the population the right to vote on whether they wanted independence from, rather than autonomy within, Indonesia.[87] Following a strong vote in favour of independence in August 1999 the UN authorised a multinational force to enter into East Timor to facilitate East Timor's transition to independence.[88]

In the light of the above, it is not surprising that, in his separate opinion in *Case Concerning the Frontier Dispute (Burkina Faso and Mali)*,[89] Judge *ad hoc* Luchaire said:

> [T]he exercise of the right of self-determination may evidently lead certain plainly individualized parts of the former colony to a different option from that followed by the other parts. . . . [T]he frontiers of an independent State emerging from colonization may differ from the frontiers of the colony which it replaces, and this may actually result from the exercise of the right of self-determination.[90]

Implicit in the judge's comments is the fact that the population of a colony could contain a number of peoples rather than only one people.

International covenants on human rights

In December 1966 the UN General Assembly adopted two human rights covenants, namely the International Covenant on Economic, Social, and Cultural Rights (Economic Rights Covenant)[91] and the International Covenant on Civil and Political Rights (Civil Rights Covenant).[92] These two covenants, based upon the general principle of respect for human rights in the UN Charter, enumerate a long list of human rights belonging to individuals, and stem from the desire of UN member states to incorporate into treaty form more detailed provisions protecting human rights. The UN Universal Declaration of Human Rights of 1948[93] was the first step in the process that ultimately led to the two international covenants of 1966.

Article 1 of both covenants, containing three paragraphs, is identical. Article 1(1) states:

86 *East Timor (Portugal -v- Australia)* (1995) 105 ILR 227, at 243.

87 Security Council Resolutions 1236 (1999), 7 May 1999 1246 (1999), 11 June 1999, and 1257 (1999), 3 August 1999.

88 Security Council Resolution 1264 (1999), 15 September 1999.

89 [1986] ICJ Rep. 554.

90 *Case Concerning the Frontier Dispute (Burkina Faso and Mali)* [1986] ICJ Rep. 554, at 653.

91 General Assembly Resolution 2200 (XXI), 16 December 1966. The Economic Rights Covenant entered into force on 3 January 1976.

92 General Assembly Resolution 2200 (XXI), 16 December 1966. The Civil Rights Covenant entered into force on 23 March 1976.

93 General Assembly Resolution 217, 10 December 1948.

> All peoples have the right of self-determination. By virtue of that right they freely determine their political status and freely pursue their economic, social and cultural development.

Article 1(2) states that 'all peoples' have the right to freely dispose of their natural wealth and resources. The paragraph goes on to say that in no case can a people be deprived of its own means of subsistence. By Article 1(3) all states which are parties to the two international covenants must promote the 'realization of the right of self-determination'.

In another identical provision, Article 25 of the Economic Rights Covenant and Article 47 of the Civil Rights Covenant (Article 25/47), it is stated that nothing in the covenants shall be interpreted as impairing the right of 'all peoples' to utilise and enjoy their natural wealth and resources.

In the Civil Rights Covenant two further provisions should be noted. Article 2(1) provides that state parties to the covenant are obliged to respect the various rights recognised in the covenant and to ensure that those rights are guaranteed to 'all individuals within its territory' without discrimination or distinction based upon race, sex, colour, language, religion, political views, national or social origin, property, birth or other status. Article 27 stipulates that in states with 'ethnic, religious or linguistic minorities', 'persons belonging to such minorities' have the 'right, in community with other members of their group', to cultural, religious and linguistic freedoms.[94]

In construing the two international covenants it must be noted that all the stipulated rights, with the exceptions of common Article 1 and the common Article 25/47, are rights of individuals. The subjects of these rights are described variously as 'every human being', 'everyone', 'anyone', 'all persons', and the like, clearly indicating the individual, rather than the collective, nature of the rights. In particular it must be stressed that this applies to Article 27 of the Civil Rights Covenant. Article 27 does not confer rights on a minority as a collective, but rather on 'persons belonging to such minorities'. An individual member of a minority has rights 'in community with other members'. The 'community' requirement necessitates the existence of a minority as a collective group before an individual member of a minority can assert the rights conferred by Article 27. This, however, does not make the minority as a collective group the subject of the rights in Article 27.

On the other hand, the common Article 1 and Article 25/47 clearly do not

94 The provisions of paragraphs 1 and 2 of Article 1 of the two international covenants are essentially identical to Article 1A of the Arab Charter on Human Rights, 15 September 1994, which stipulates: 'All peoples have the right to self-determination and to have control over their wealth and natural resources. By virtue of that right, they have the right to freely determine their political status and to freely pursue their economic, social, and cultural development.' Article 2 of the Arab Charter is almost identical to Article 2(1) of the Civil Rights Covenant. Article 37 of the Arab Charter is very similar to Article 27 of the Civil Rights Covenant. The Arab Charter is reproduced in *The Review, International Commission of Jurists*, 1996, no. 56, pp. 58–64.

grant rights to individuals, but rather to peoples as groups.[95] In the debate leading to the formulation of the two international covenants there was considerable opposition to including the collective right of self-determination of peoples in documents fundamentally dealing with the legal rights of individuals.[96] Opposition to the inclusion of Article 1 was also based upon the uncertainties surrounding the scope and meaning of self-determination.[97] The inclusion of Article 1 has been attributed to the still strong anti-colonial sentiment of the time and the desire to reaffirm the right to independence of existing colonial territories based upon the right of all peoples to self-determination.[98]

In one respect, the inclusion of Article 1 in the two international covenants made a significant contribution to the development of the right to self-determination. Article 1 established that the right of peoples to self-determination is universal and not confined to colonial peoples.[99] The language of Article 1 is unambiguous on this point and clearly removes any lingering doubts as to whether the provisions on self-determination in the UN Charter were confined to colonial situations. The Human Rights Committee has confirmed this view in its General Comment 12 dealing with Article 1. In paragraph 6 of General Comment 12 the Committee, after reciting Article 1(3), states:

> [T]he obligations [under Article 1] exist irrespective of whether a people entitled to self-determination depends on a State party to the Covenant or not. It follows that all State parties to the Covenant should take positive action to

95 This point is confirmed by the decision of the Human Rights Committee in *Kitok -v- Sweden*, UN Doc A/45/40, vol. II, App A (1990). This case involved a claim by an individual concerning alleged violations of Article 1. Because the Committee only had jurisdiction to hear cases concerning alleged infringements of individual rights, it ruled that it could not adjudicate on allegations pertaining to Article 1. The Committee noted, at para. 6.3, that the applicant 'as an individual, could not claim to be the victim of the right to self-determination . . . *Whereas the Optional Protocol provides a recourse procedure for individuals claiming that their rights have been violated, Article 1 ... deals with the rights conferred upon peoples as such.*' (Emphasis added.) Similar rulings were made in *Committee in Bernard Omivayak Chief of the Lubicon Lake Band -v- Canada*, UN Doc A/45/40, vol. II (1990), at para. 13.3, and *Whispering Pines Indian Band -v- Canada*, UN Doc A/46/40 (1991), at para. 6.2.

96 Cassese, note 41, pp. 48–52; Buchheit, note 42, pp. 76–84.

97 M. J. Bossuyt, *Guide to the 'Travaux Préparatoires' of the International Covenant on Civil and Political Rights*, Dordrecht, Martinus Nijhoff Publishers, 1987, p. 20.

98 Buchheit, note 42, p. 84. It has been suggested that the inclusion of Article 1 was merely a reflection of the perception that, in its external form, it was confined to the colonial context: M. C. R. Craven, *The International Covenant on Economic, Social, and Cultural Rights: A Perspective on its Development*, Oxford, Clarendon Press, 1995, p. 24.

99 Cassese, note 41, pp. 48–52; J. Crawford, 'Outside the Colonial Context', in W. J. A. Macartney (ed.), *Self-Determination in the Commonwealth*, Aberdeen, Aberdeen University Press, 1988, pp. 5–6. The universality of the right to self-determination has been affirmed by the General Assembly by resolution to that effect in every year since 1980: Duursma, note 44, p. 26. The Supreme Court of Canada recognised the right of self-determination as a general principle of international law and that it extends, in certain cases, to secession outside the colonial context: *Reference re: Secession of Quebec* (1998) 161 DLR (4th) 385, at 434–40.

> facilitate realization of and request for the right of peoples to self-determination.[100]

A significant example confirming the universality of the right to self-determination was the absorption of the former German Democratic Republic by the Federal Republic of Germany, neither of which was a colonial entity. The Preamble to the Treaty on the Final Settlement With Respect to Germany of 1990, signed by four of the five Permanent Members of the UN Security Council, declared that the 'German people, freely exercising their right to self-determination, have expressed their will to bring about the unity of Germany as a State'.[101] However, the Treaty itself makes no contribution to the clarification of the pivotal issue of who qualifies as a people for the purpose of the exercise of the right to self-determination.

As to the meaning of 'all peoples' as used in the two international covenants, Cassese interprets the expression to mean the entire population of either an independent state, a colonial territory or a population living under foreign military occupation.[102] Implicit in this interpretation is that a nation is not a people.[103] This interpretation is based upon the 'general spirit and context of Article 1, combined with the preparatory work'[104] leading to its inclusion in the two international covenants.[105] It is not based upon the text alone. Insofar as the text of the covenants is concerned, there is little to which one can point that clarifies the meaning of 'all peoples'.

One could argue that the obligation of states in Article 2(1) of the Civil Rights Covenant to ensure the granting of its rights 'to all individuals within its territory' sheds light on the meaning of a people. There are two possible ways of looking at Article 2(1) and its connection with the meaning of 'all peoples' in Article 1. First, the reference in Article 2(1) to 'all individuals' could indicate that a people, on the one hand, and 'all individuals' of one state or colonial territory, on the other hand, are not the same thing. Hence the use of different expressions. If, as Cassese

100 General Comment 12, paragraph 6, the Human Rights Committee, adopted by the Committee at its 516th meeting on 12 April 1984, and reprinted in M. Nowak, *UN Covenant on Civil and Political Rights: CCPR Commentary*, Kehl am Rhein, N P Engel, 1993, pp. 856–7.

101 (1990) 29 ILM 1186-93, at p. 1188. West Germany's Foreign Minister Hans-Dietrich Genscher saw reunification as an act of self-determination: H.-D. Genscher, *Rebuilding a House Divided: A Memoir by the Architect of Germany's Reunification*, New York, Broadway Books, 1998, p. 370.

102 Cassese, note 41, p. 59.

103 In earlier writings Cassese stated a different view, claiming that a national or ethnic group constitutionally recognised as a component part of a multinational state is a people entitled to self-determination under Article 1: A. Cassese, 'The Self-Determination of Peoples', in L. Henkin (ed.), *The International Bill of Rights: The Covenant on Civil and Political Rights*, New York, Columbia University Press, 1981, pp. 94–6.

104 Cassese, note 41, p. 59.

105 McCorquodale takes the view that the preparatory work makes 'it clear that "peoples" was not intended to be limited to all the inhabitants of a state as a single group': R. McCorquodale, 'The Right of Self-Determination', in D. Harris and S. Joseph (eds), *The International Covenant on Civil and Political Rights and United Kingdom Law*, Oxford, Clarendon Press, 1995, p. 97.

argues, a people is in fact the entire population ('all individuals') of a state or colonial territory, then Article 2(1) should logically have referred to 'its people' rather than to 'all individuals within its territory'. Whatever one makes of the strengths of this argument, it does not support the territorial concept of a people advocated by Cassese.

Second, it could be argued that the reference to 'all individuals within its territory' in Article 2(1) implies that a people is the entire population ('all individuals') of a state or colonial territory for the purposes of determining who are the holders of the right to self-determination conferred by Article 1. However, this argument cannot be sustained. The obligation upon states contained in Article 2(1) must be confined to the rights conferred by the Civil Rights Covenant that are enumerated in the articles appearing after Article 2(1). These rights are all individual rights and it is entirely appropriate that a state's obligation to ensure these rights be expressed as being owed to 'all individuals within its territory'. That the obligation imposed upon states contained in Article 2(1) does not relate to the collective or group right to self-determination in Article 1 is clear from paragraph 3 of Article 1. This paragraph explicitly imposes upon states the obligation to 'promote the realization of the right of self-determination'. Given the collective nature of the right to self-determination, this obligation is, quite properly, not expressed in terms of being owed to individuals. That the provisions of Article 2(1) are unrelated in any way to the provisions of Article 1 is further reinforced by the fact that they appear in separate Parts of the Civil Rights Covenant. It would in any event be inappropriate to relate Article 2(1) to Article 1 because one would be left with a curious proposition. It would mean that a state would be required by Article 2(1) to ensure an individual's right of self-determination where such a right does not belong to individuals as such, but to a group of individuals as a collective. Such an interpretation of Article 2(1) would also render the obligation upon states in Article 1(3) superfluous. Thus, one can properly conclude that Article 2(1) is of no relevance in shedding light on the meaning of 'all peoples' as used in Article 1.

Cassese's interpretation is, however, based on the context and spirit in which Article 1 was introduced. He states that, in the context of independent and sovereign states, Article 1 is concerned with the 'right to be free from an authoritarian regime'.[106] This conclusion is unobjectionable, but why it should mean that a people means the entire population of a state is not made clear. Cassese is in fact confusing the content of self-determination with its subject. What Cassese is in effect saying is that the expression 'All peoples have the right of self-determination' as used in Article 1 means 'All peoples have the right to be free from an authoritarian regime.' Whilst this is a legitimate interpretation of the content of the right enunciated in Article 1, it does not clarify the meaning of the Article's subject, namely, 'all peoples'.

In the considerable debate preceding the adoption of the two international

106 Cassese, note 41, pp. 59–60.

covenants many states expressed concerns as to the secessionist implications of Article 1. The fear was that Article 1 did not mean simply the entire population of an independent and sovereign state. The fear was expressed that disaffected groups within states, especially national groups claiming to be peoples, would make secessionist claims based on Article 1.[107] The very existence of the debate on this issue indicates a belief held by many states that a people is not simply a state's entire population and could well mean a national group within that state.[108] Cassese's interpretation of 'all peoples' in Article 1 is based simply upon what amounted to little more than wishful thinking at the time the two international covenants were adopted that such secessionist claims would not be permitted. Such a belief was unfounded at the time and it has subsequently been demonstrated that Cassese's interpretation is mistaken. Article 1 has been used as the basis for a successful secession from an independent and sovereign state. The secession of the Yugoslav republic of Slovenia in 1991 is a case in point.

That a people is not the entire population of a state is also confirmed by the practice of the Human Rights Committee, established pursuant to Part IV of the Civil Rights Covenant, and some states. In its General Comment on Article 1, the Committee requests states to 'describe the constitutional and political processes which in practice allow the exercise of [the] right [of self-determination]'.[109] As McCorquodale observes, this implies 'that as a state's internal constitutional and political processes are relevant to the protection of the right, the right can be exercised by peoples within a state'.[110] Furthermore, state practice by the United Kingdom in reporting to the Committee with respect to the Scottish, Welsh and Irish as peoples within the United Kingdom confirms that a people is not the entire population of a state.[111] The fact that some state constitutions speak in terms of the state being constituted by a number of different peoples further enforces this view.[112]

107 S. Morphet, 'Article 1 of the Human Rights Covenants: Its Development and Current Significance', in D. M. Hill (ed.), *Human Rights and Foreign Policy: Principles and Practice*, Houndmills, Macmillan Press, 1989, pp. 77–8.

108 Seven states (Denmark, Lebanon, New Zealand, Philippines, USSR, the United Kingdom and the USA) thought secession was inherent in the right to self-determination. Eight states (Australia, Colombia, Egypt, Greece, Iraq, Saudi Arabia, Syria and Venezuela) took the opposite view: Duursma, note 44, p. 31.

109 General Comment 12, paragraph 4, reprinted in Nowak, note 100, pp. 856–7.

110 McCorquodale, note 105, p. 98.

111 R. McCorquodale, 'Negotiating Sovereignty: The Practice of the United Kingdom in Regard to the Right of Self-Determination', *British Year Book of International Law*, 1995, vol. 66, pp. 294–8.

112 For example, the Constitution of the Socialist Federative Republic of Yugoslavia (1974) in paragraph I of Basic Principles stated: 'The peoples of Yugoslavia, accepting the right of all peoples to self-determination, including the right of secession, . . . have united in a federal republic of free and equal peoples and nationalities'. Article 3 stipulated that the state is, in part, 'based upon the sovereignty of the peoples'.

Cassese also supports his interpretation of 'a people' by reference to Article 27 of the Civil Rights Covenant.[113] He argues that because Article 27 only grants rights to individual members of a minority and does not contemplate its political, economic or social autonomy, a minority cannot be seen as a people for the purposes of Article 1. It thus follows that, if a minority within a state's population is not a people, only a state's entire population can be a people.[114] Whilst his stated limitations on the subject of the rights conferred by Article 27 is correct, it is difficult to see why a minority is thus disqualified from being a people. Cassese is asserting that a minority has no rights because Article 27 does not explicitly confer any rights upon it. However, Article 27 has nothing to do with the rights of minority groups. It is concerned with the rights of individuals who are members of minority groups. It is invalid reasoning to assert that because Article 27 does not positively confer rights on minority groups, such groups have no rights and therefore are not a peoples for the purposes of Article 1. One cannot validly infer, simply because a provision of the Civil Rights Covenant does not confer certain rights on a particular group, that the group has no such rights. Of course, this does not mean that Article 27 suggests that a minority group is a people – nor does any other article in either of the two international covenants. Article 27 is silent on this issue.[115]

However, there is considerable scholarly support[116] for the view that minorities can be considered holders of the right of self-determination, a point recently confirmed by the Supreme Court of Canada which asserted that it was clear that a

113 Franck also relies on Article 27 to support the view that a people is the entire population of a state and that a minority within a state cannot be a people. His argument is even less convincing than that of Cassese. Franck selectively quotes Article 27 as follows: 'ethnic, religious or linguistic minorities . . . shall not be denied the right, in community with the other members of their group, to enjoy their own culture, to profess and practice their own religion, or to use their own language'. He then goes on to say: 'Evidently, they are not given the right to *secede*'. Later in his article, after referring to Article 27, he says: 'This permits minorities not to secede but the right to enjoy their own culture, to profess and practice their own religion, or to use their own language': Franck, note 69, pp. 11, 17. The objection to Franck's analysis is his selective quoting of Article 27, leaving out words that clearly establish that its benefits accrue to individual ('persons belonging to such minorities') and not to minorities as groups. By falsely asserting that Article 27 deals with minorities as groups he is able to deduce that because only limited rights are granted to minorities, they have no right to self-determination. See also J. Castellino, *International Law and Self-Determination: The Interplay of the Politics of Territorial Possession with Formulations of Post-Colonial 'National' Identity*, The Hague, Martinus Nijhoff Publishers, 2000, pp. 64–8.

114 Cassese, note 41, pp. 61–2.

115 The Declaration on the Rights of Persons Belonging to National or Ethnic, Religious and Linguistic Minorities, General Assembly Resolution 47/135, 18 December 1992, which extensively details the rights of persons belonging to minority groups is similar to Article 27 in that it consistently speaks of rights belonging to individuals and not to groups. Thus, just as Article 27 sheds no light on whether minority groups are 'peoples', nor does this declaration.

116 R. N. Kiwanuka 'The Meaning of "People" in the African Charter on Human and Peoples' Rights', *American Journal of International Law*, 1988, vol. 82, at 92–4; D. Murswiek, 'The Issue of a Right of Secession – Reconsidered' in C. Tomuschat (ed.), *Modern Law of Self-Determination*, Dordrecht, Martinus Nijhoff Publishers, 1993, p. 37; Nowak, note 100, pp. 19–22; I. Brownlie, 'International Law at the Fiftieth Anniversary of the United Nations, General Course on Public

people may include only a portion of the population of an existing state.[117] The Court then suggested that the French-speaking population of Quebec shared many of the characteristics, such as a common language and culture, that would be considered in determining whether a specific group was a people.[118]

It can also be noted that if the logic of Cassese's argument on Article 27 is correct, and if the same logic is applied to Article 2 of the Civil Rights Covenant, his view that a people means the entire population of a state or colonial territory is wrong. As noted, Article 2 obliges states to ensure that the various rights contained in the Civil Rights Covenant are respected and recognised for 'all individuals within its territory', regardless of an individual's race, colour, sex, language, religion, political or other opinion, national or social origin, property, birth or other status. Essentially, Article 2 means that the covenant's rights cannot be denied to an individual on any of the grounds stated therein. Thus, Article 2 confers a 'negative' right upon 'all individuals within [a state's] territory', that is, upon the entire population of a state. If Article 27, by conferring rights upon individual members of a minority, means that a minority as a group has no rights, then it must logically follow that Article 2, by conferring a right upon individuals forming the entire population of a state, means that the entire population of a state as a group has no rights. It follows that if a minority is not a people, then neither is the entire population of a state. Given that neither a minority nor the entire population of a state is a people, neither are the subject of the right to self-determination contained in Article 1. Cassese's argument that Article 27 supports his definition of a people, when applied in the context of Article 2, leads, in fact, to the opposite conclusion.

Thus, the view that the two international covenants indicate that a people is the entire population of a state or territory is not sustainable. In effect, the text of the covenants' provisions do little to advance the search for the meaning of people as used by the UN in its Charter and subsequent declarations. However, the views of the Human Rights Committee and state practice tend to suggest that a people is not the entire population of a state or colonial territory.

Declaration on friendly relations

In October 1970 the UN General Assembly passed the Declaration on Principles of International Law Concerning Friendly Relations and Co-operation Among States in Accordance With the Charter of the United Nations (Declaration on

International Law', *Recueil De Cour*, 1995, vol. 255, p. 62; J. Wright, 'Minority Groups, Autonomy, and Self-Determination', *Oxford Journal of Legal Studies*, 1999, vol. 19, pp. 625–8. Capotorti has a more restrictive view on the collective rights of minorities. He asserts that a minority can only be a people with the right to self-determination if it has a 'historical right to be called a "people"': F. Capotorti, 'Are Minorities Entitled to Collective International Rights?', *Israel Yearbook on Human Rights*, 1990, vol. 20, pp. 355–6.

117 *Reference re: Secession of Quebec*, (1998) 161 DLR (4th) 385, at 437.

118 Ibid., at 437.

Friendly Relations).[119] As its title indicates, the Declaration on Friendly Relations expounds a number of principles relating to friendly relations and co-operation among states. One such principle is 'the principle of equal rights and self-determination of peoples' (Principle 5) enshrined in the UN Charter. Principle 5 and its elaboration reads as follows:

The principle of equal rights and self-determination of peoples

> [1] By virtue of the principle of equal rights and self-determination of peoples enshrined in the Charter of the United Nations, all peoples have the right freely to determine, without external interference, their political status and to pursue their economic, social and cultural development, and every State has the duty to respect this right in accordance with the provisions of the Charter.
> [2] Every State has the duty to promote, through joint and separate action, realization of the principle of equal rights and self-determination of peoples, in accordance with the provisions of the Charter, and to render assistance to the United Nations in carrying out the responsibilities entrusted to it by the Charter regarding the implementation of the principle, in order:
> (a) to promote friendly relations and co-operation among states; and
> (b) to bring a speedy end to colonialism, having due regard to the freely expressed will of the peoples concerned;
>
> and bearing in mind that subjection of peoples to alien subjugation, domination and exploitation constitutes a violation of the principle, as well as a denial of fundamental human rights, and is contrary to the Charter.
> [3] Every State has a duty to promote through joint and several action universal respect for and observance of human rights and fundamental freedoms in accordance with the Charter.
> [4] The establishment of a sovereign and independent State, the free association or integration with an independent State or the emergence into any other political status freely determined by a people constitute modes of implementing the right of self-determination by that people.
> [5] Every State has a duty to refrain from any forcible action which deprives peoples referred to above in the elaboration of the present principle of their right to self-determination and freedom and independence. In actions against, and resistance to, such forcible action in pursuit of the exercise of their right to self-determination, such peoples are entitled to seek and receive support in accordance with the purposes and principles of the Charter.
> [6] The territory of a colony or other non-self-governing territory has, under the Charter, a status separate and distinct from the territory of the State administering it; and such separate and distinct status under the Charter shall exist until the people of the colony or non-self-governing territory have

119 General Assembly Resolution 2625 (XXV), 24 October 1970.

> exercised their right of self-determination in accordance with the Charter, and particularly its purposes and principles.
> [7] Nothing in the foregoing paragraphs shall be construed as authorizing or encouraging any action which would dismember or impair, totally or in part, the territorial integrity or political unity of sovereign and independent States conducting themselves in compliance with the principle of equal rights and self-determination of peoples as described above and thus possessed of a government representing the whole people belonging to the territory without distinction as to race, creed or colour.
> [8] Every State shall refrain from any action aimed at the partial or total disruption of the national unity and territorial integrity of any other State or country.[120]

The Declaration on Friendly Relations contains a number of references to peoples apart from those in Principle 5. However, these references do not in any way clarify the meaning of a people. The most significant parts of the Declaration that have been used to assign a meaning to a people are the references to maintaining the continued territorial integrity of existing states. The Declaration's first principle is that states should not use force or the threat of force 'against the territorial integrity and political independence of any State'. Furthermore, paragraphs 7 and 8 of Principle 5 deal with the territorial integrity and political independence of states.

Paragraph 7 of Principle 5 is significant in extrapolating the meaning of a people. Its emphasis on territorial integrity, together with the references in the Declaration on Colonialism which insist on the territorial integrity of colonial territories being maintained upon the grant of independence, is used to argue that a people means the entire population of a state. The rejection of such an argument in the context of the Declaration on Colonialism has already been discussed. The argument is also rejected in the context of the Declaration on Friendly Relations.

The very essence of paragraph 7 is that a state's territorial integrity is assured only under certain conditions. These conditions require a state to conduct itself in such a way that certain groups within the state are not subjected to particular discrimination. If groups are subjected to discrimination they are entitled to secede. The propositions that emerge from an analysis of paragraph 7 are, first, that a people is not defined as the entire population of a state,[121] and, second, that in the definition of a people is included a group defined as a nation. These propositions

120 The numbering of the paragraphs in Principle 5 does not appear in the original text and is inserted here for convenience in relation to the discussion of Principle 5.

121 In the 1966 Special Committee deliberations dealing with the then proposed Friendly Relations Declaration, the USA effectively took this view. Its delegation argued that self-determination would *prima facie* apply where sovereignty is exercised by a state 'over a territory geographically distinct and ethnically or culturally diverse from the remainder of that State's territory': quoted in G. W. Haight, 'Principles of International Law Concerning Friendly Relations and Co-operation Among States', *International Lawyer*, 1966, vol. 1, p. 124.

flow from the combined effect of interpreting the wording of the obligation as expressed in paragraph 7, and the fact that a state's territorial integrity is not absolutely assured by paragraph 7.

In interpreting the wording of the obligation in paragraph 7, it is clear that paragraph 7 protects the territorial integrity of a state that conducts itself 'in compliance with the principle of equal rights and self-determination of peoples'. In paragraph 1 of Principle 5 it is stated that by virtue of the principle of equal rights and self-determination of peoples 'all peoples have the right freely to determine, without external interference, their political status and to pursue their economic, social and cultural development, and *every State* has the duty to respect this right'. (Emphasis added.) Thus, a state's conduct is bound by a principle that requires it to allow 'all peoples' the right to freely determine their political status and pursue their economic, social and cultural development. For convenience we can refer to this right as the right to 'representative government'.[122] In other words, in requiring a state to conduct itself in accordance with the principle of equal rights and self-determination of peoples, paragraph 7 obliges it to guarantee 'all peoples' the right to representative government. If a state does not so conduct itself, its territorial integrity is not protected by paragraph 7.[123]

If, pursuant to paragraph 7, a state's obligation to conduct itself in accordance with the principle of equal rights and self-determination of peoples means, pursuant to paragraph 1, the obligation to guarantee the right of representative government to 'all peoples', this raises the question of what is meant by 'all peoples'. In the context of paragraph 7 this obligation upon a state must mean an obligation to 'all peoples' of that state. It would be an absurdity if, for the purposes of paragraph 7, the obligation extended to peoples in other states. If this were so, then state A's territorial integrity would not be assured if it did not respect the right to representative government of peoples in State B. State A would perhaps be in breach of paragraph 2 of Principle 5, but it could hardly mean that its territorial integrity would be in jeopardy. There have been many instances in which states could be said to have committed such breaches of paragraph 2, but in no such case has it ever been suggested that the territorial integrity of such states is threatened. Thus, a state's obligation to 'all peoples' does not extend to 'all peoples' in other states, but is confined to 'all peoples' of that state.

If, in the context of paragraph 7, a state's obligation is confined to 'all peoples' of that particular state, then any given state's population could be constituted by one people or a number of peoples.[124] If that is so, then the entire population of a

122 What is here referred to as 'representative government' is defined by Cassese as 'equal access to government': Cassese, note 41, p. 114.

123 V. P. Nanda, 'Self-Determination Outside the Colonial Context: The Birth of Bangladesh in Retrospect', in Y. Alexander and R. A. Friedlander (eds), *Self-Determination: National, Regional, and Global Dimensions*, Boulder, CO, Westview Press, 1980, p. 201; P. H. Kooijmans, 'Tolerance, Sovereignty and Self-Determination', *Netherlands International Law Review*, 1996, vol. 43, p. 212.

124 This is also the opinion of Rosenstock who, in the context of discussing paragraph 7, observes that paragraph 7 creates 'difficulties for states possessing different and distinct peoples':

state cannot be the definition of a people. This analysis of paragraph 7 does not significantly clarify the meaning of 'a people'. It does not shed any light on what 'a people' is or means. Rather, it simply confirms that the entire population of a state is not 'a people'. Significantly, nothing in this analysis precludes a nation from being 'a people'.

The argument that a people is not the entire population of a state is further reinforced by the fact that paragraph 7 does not absolutely guarantee a state's territorial integrity. By not absolutely assuring a state's territorial integrity, paragraph 7 implicitly envisages the emergence of a new state or states from an existing state. In other words, paragraph 7 sanctions secession in certain circumstances.[125]

Paragraph 7 clearly implies a right to secede. It makes it clear that the territorial integrity of a state is conditional upon it conducting itself 'in compliance with the principle of equal rights and self-determination of peoples'. A state that does not so conduct itself is not assured of its territorial integrity. This aspect of paragraph 7 echoes comments made by the Commission of Jurists and the Commission of Rapporteurs in the Aaland Islands dispute. The Commission of Jurists ruled that '[p]ositive International Law does not recognize the right of any national groups, as such, to separate themselves from the State of which they form a part'.[126] However, this finding was qualified with a statement that the Commission

> does not give an opinion concerning the question as to whether a manifest and continued abuse of sovereign power, to the detriment of a section of the population of a State, would . . . give to [an] international dispute arising therefrom, such a character . . . which is not confined to the domestic jurisdiction of the State concerned.[127]

The implication of this qualification is that, in circumstances of oppression against a section of a state's population, secession could be justified. The Commission of Rapporteurs noted that if cultural autonomy was not granted to the people of the Aaland Islands, they would have the right to secede from Finland. Thus, the Commission's decision on this point assumes the existence of the right of secession to a minority that has suffered oppression.

The scope for secession within paragraph 7, while noted by some commentators,

R. Rosenstock, 'Declaration of International Law Concerning Friendly Relations', *American Journal of International Law*, 1971, vol. 65, p. 732. The US delegation at the 1966 Special Committee meeting effectively argued that a state could be composed of more than one 'people' when it pressed for the inclusion of wording in the proposed Declaration which spoke of states 'possessing a representative Government, effectively functioning as such to *all distinct peoples within its territory*' (emphasis added): quoted in Haight, note 121, p. 124.

125 Although secession is permitted in certain situations, there are no generally accepted rules regulating such a process. For a summary of state practice on opposed secessions, see Duursma, note 44, pp. 92–102.

126 *Report of the International Commission of Jurists* (1920) LNOJ Spec. Supp. 3, p. 5.

127 Ibid.

has more often than not been overlooked[128] or downplayed[129] and occasionally denied.[130] However, Cassese and others do recognise the significance of the undoubted scope for secession in paragraph 7.[131] What is critical is that, given that paragraph 7 envisages the right to secede, a people cannot be defined as the entire population of a state. If secession is, as will be argued, the exercise of the right of 'a people' to self-determination, a people cannot at the same time be the entire population of a state as well as a group that secedes from that state. The only logical conclusion is that, because paragraph 7 sanctions secession, and because secession is by a people that necessarily forms only part of the population of a state,

128 In their analyses of self-determination within the context of the Declaration on Friendly Relations neither Arangio-Ruiz nor Šuković make any reference at all to the secessionist implications of paragraph 7: G. Arangio-Ruiz, *The United Nations Declaration on Friendly Relations and the System of the Sources of International Law*, Alphen aan den Rijn, Sijthoff & Noordhoff, 1979, pp. 131–42; O. Šuković, 'The Principle of Equal Rights and Self-Determination of Peoples', in M. Šuković (ed.), *Principles of International Law Concerning Friendly Relations and Cooperation*, Belgrade, Institute of International Politics and Economics, 1972, pp. 323–73. Higgins, although mentioning paragraph 7 does not cite the end qualification and concludes that the requirement of territorial integrity precludes secession: R. Higgins, *Problems and Process: International Law and How We Use It*, Oxford, Clarendon Press, 1994, p. 121.

129 Ofuatey-Kodjoe states that the qualification to paragraph 7 'may represent a minute breach in the United Nations' prohibition against secession': Ofuatey-Kodjoe, note 38, pp. 362–3. Shaw opines that the paragraph cannot justify secession in the light of explicit references to territorial integrity of states and that it operates merely 'as a relevant factor in determining the views taken by the international community generally, and states particularly, as to recognition': M. N. Shaw, 'Peoples, Territorialism and Boundaries', *European Journal of International Law*, 1997, vol. 8, p. 483. See also C. Antonopoulos, 'The Principle of *Uti Possidetis Iuris* in Contemporary International Law', 1996, *Revue Hellénique de Droit International*, vol. 49, no. 1, pp. 75–6.

130 After citing paragraph 7 in full Gravelle claims that 'according to this text, the principle of self-determination cannot be regarded as authorizing dismemberment or amputation of sovereign States exercising their sovereignty by virtue of the principle of self-determination of peoples': J. F. Gravelle, 'The Falkland (Malvinas) Islands: An International Law Analysis of the Dispute Between Argentina and Great Britain', *Military Law Review*, 1985, vol. 107, p. 42.

131 Buchheit, note 42, pp. 92–7. Kirgus also recognises the secessionist impact of paragraph 7 and argues that secession is permitted if a government is 'quite unrepresentative' even if serious destabilisation may result: F. L. Kirgus, Jr, 'The Degrees of Self-Determination in the United Nations Era', *American Journal of International Law*, 1994, vol. 88, pp. 304–10. Kooijmans notes that 'the right of secession is not a normal emanation of the right to self-determination, but an *ultimum remedium*, to be resorted to only if all efforts to find a solution within the State structure have been to no avail and if local and international remedies have turned out to be fruitless': Kooijmans, note 123, p. 216. See also R. C. A. White, 'Self-Determination: Time for a Re-assessment?', *Netherlands International Law Review*, 1981, vol. 28, pp. 159–61; R. McCorquodale, 'Self-Determination Beyond the Colonial Context and Its Potential Impact on Africa', *African Journal of International and Comparative Law*, 1992, vol. 4, pp. 603–4; C. Tomuschat, 'Self-Determination in a Post-Colonial World', in C. Tomuschat (ed.), note 116, pp. 9–10; J. Klabbers and R. Lefeber, 'Africa: Lost Between Self-Determination and *Uti Possidetis*', in C. Brölmann, R. Lefeber and M. Zieck (eds), note 69, pp. 47–9; Duursma, note 44, p. 25; V. P. Nanda, 'The New Dynamics of Self-Determination: Revisiting Self-Determination as an International Law Concept: A Major Challenge in the Post-Cold War Era', *ILSA Journal of International and Comparative Law*, 1997, vol. 3, p. 449.

it is impossible for the entire population of a state to be a people. This argument is dependent upon a finding that the group that secedes is in fact a people.

It can readily be established that a group which secedes pursuant to paragraph 7 is a people. As has already been shown, paragraph 7 asserts that a state's territorial integrity is conditional upon it guaranteeing representative government to all of its peoples. If a state's territorial integrity is not protected by paragraph 7, due to its failure to comply with the obligation of providing representative government, then its territorial integrity is justifiably violated by the act of secession of a group within that state. If a state denies representative government to a group within the state, it denies that group the right described in paragraph 1 as the right 'to pursue their economic, social and cultural development'. Such a right, as is made clear by paragraph 1, is the right to self-determination. Thus, a state that denies representative government to a group, denies that group the right to self-determination. Simply to deny a group the right to self-determination does not mean that the group possesses the right to self-determination. However, because that group has the right to secede pursuant to paragraph 7, the group must be a people. This is because secession is the process of establishing a sovereign and independent state, separate and distinct from the former state to which the group belonged. Paragraph 4 stipulates that the establishment of a sovereign and independent state is one of the 'modes of implementing the right of self-determination' by a people. Thus, in seceding from a state pursuant to paragraph 7, a group is doing something which, by paragraph 4, a people is entitled to do in the exercise of its right of self-determination. The conclusion that is inescapable is that a group that secedes pursuant to paragraph 7, being a group that is denied the right to self-determination, and which acts in a way that is consistent with implementing the right of self-determination, must be a group possessed of the right to self-determination. As only peoples have the right to self-determination, a group that secedes pursuant to paragraph 7 must therefore be a people.[132]

It must be noted that the right to secede implied by paragraph 7 is unaffected by paragraph 8. Paragraph 8 protects a state's territorial integrity from the actions of other *states*. As Robin White has observed, there is no prohibition in paragraph 8 against a people seeking self-determination either by secession or by replacement of an unrepresentative government.[133]

132 Cassese effectively, but not explicitly, comes to the same conclusion. In his discussion of paragraph 7 he observes that when a group is denied representative government it is 'entitled to claim the right to self-determination': Cassese, note 41, p. 112. Cassese does not then conclude that such a group is a people but it is hard to see how he could deny such a conclusion, given that only peoples have the right to self-determination. This conclusion reveals a significant inconsistency in Cassese's work. This is because elsewhere Cassese argues that a people means the entire population of a state: Cassese, note 41, pp. 327, 339. However, in the context of the right to secede pursuant to paragraph 7, the necessary conclusion of what Cassese states means that a group that forms part of the population of a state is also a people, or at least becomes a people due to the actions of the state in question denying that group the right to representative government.

133 White, note 131, p. 159.

On the preceding analysis, the right to secede pursuant to paragraph 7 rests with a people. However, after stipulating that nothing can affect the territorial integrity of a state which conducts itself in accordance with the principle of equal rights and self-determination of peoples, paragraph 7 further stipulates that a state which does so conduct itself is 'possessed of a government representing the whole population belonging to the territory *without distinction as to race, creed or colour*' (emphasis added). The only inference that can be drawn from the 'without distinction' provision is that the right to secede is open only to groups defined in terms of 'race, creed or colour'. As has already been established any group seceding pursuant to paragraph 7 must be 'a people'. Given that only groups defined in terms of 'race, creed or colour' can secede pursuant to paragraph 7, it logically follows that 'a people' is a group defined in terms of 'race, creed or colour'. If that is so, then it is critical to determine the meaning of 'race, creed or colour' in order to establish if a nation comes within the expression 'race, creed or colour' and thus within the definition of a people.

Cassese gives a very narrow definition of the words 'race, creed or colour'. He claims that 'race' and 'colour' are identical expressions of the concept of race.[134] He also confines 'creed' to 'religious beliefs', and gives a narrow interpretation to 'religious beliefs'. The effect of such a narrow interpretation is that Cassese excludes from the range of groups that are entitled to secede pursuant to paragraph 7, groups that he refers to as '*linguistic* or *national* groups'.[135] In effect, Cassese confines groups defined in terms of 'race, creed and colour' to racial and religious groups, and significantly for present purposes, excludes national groups. However, the narrowness of Cassese's definition, and thus the narrowness of the scope for secession, are open to dispute.

There is some merit in Cassese's interpretation of 'creed'. However, given the centrality of religious identification to many national groups,[136] discrimination on grounds of religious beliefs is, in many cases, tantamount to discrimination on grounds of nationality. Furthermore, his reasoning justifying the interpretation

134 Cassese, note 41, p. 112.

135 Ibid., pp. 113–14.

136 'Religion attaches itself to nationalism, in the first instance, because of its capacity for providing political legitimacy. There is something close to sacred about the way many peoples or ethnic groups come to regard their language and cultural tradition. They readily think of themselves as being, in Weber's words, a "chosen people" with "a providential mission" that is undergirded by a belief in "the superiority, or at least the irreplacability, of the [group's peculiar] cultural values". Under modern conditions, an appealing way of protecting a group's peculiarity, and of advancing its holy mission, is to form a self-determining nation-state': D. Little, 'Religion and Self-Determination', in D. Clark and R. Williamson (eds), *Self-Determination: International Perspectives*, London, Macmillan, 1996, p. 142. 'In many parts of the world, however, religious and ethnic identities are intertwined. The nationalist aspirations of Muslims in China and Central Asia have been rightly described as "ethnoreligious" . . . [I]n these locales the crucial symbols and ideas of the regions' cultural heritage are most often the religious ones': M. Juergensmeyer, *The New Cold War?: Religious Nationalism Confronts the Secular State*, Berkeley, CA, University of California Press, 1993, p. 4.

that 'race' and 'colour' are identical in meaning, is not convincing. He claims the two words are a pleonasm and reflect 'redundant language' rooted in Article 2(1) of the Universal Declaration on Human Rights of 1948. However, the words 'race' and 'colour' were also used together in both the Economic Rights Covenant[137] and the Civil Rights Covenant,[138] and although Cassese may feel they amount to a pleonasm, one must question whether the UN General Assembly at the time was of the same view. If it were, one would have expected the General Assembly not to have used both words. At the time the two international covenants were passed by the General Assembly, just four years before the Declaration on Friendly Relations, it was common to refer to different national groups as belonging to different races, but not necessarily as being of different colour. Thus, the references to 'race' and 'colour' in paragraph 7 were not seen as being expressions of an identical concept, but rather meant different things.

Perhaps the most significant of the three words used in paragraph 7 is that of 'race'. This is so because there are grounds to suggest that 'race' was, in the decades leading up to the adoption of the Declaration on Friendly Relations, often seen as meaning much the same as nation. Hobsbawm, in his study of modern nationalism, has written:

> [W]hat brought 'race' and 'nation' even closer was the practice of using both as virtual synonyms, generalizing equally wildly about 'racial'/'national' character, as was then the fashion. Thus before the Anglo-French Entente Cordiale of 1904, a French writer observed, agreement between the two countries had been dismissed as impossible because of the 'hereditary enmity' between the two races.[139]

The interchangeable use of 'race' and 'nation' was also evident at the Paris Peace Conference after World War I when, in the context of the post-World War I minorities treaties, both President Woodrow Wilson and his legal adviser David Hunter Miller used the words 'race' or 'racial' in the sense of 'nation' or 'national'.[140] This habit was also current at the time of the San Francisco Conference which finalised the terms of the UN Charter. The *travaux préparatoires* to the UN Charter contain a number of references which clearly indicate that the word race was synonymous with people. Although these references stipulate the

137 Article 2(2).

138 Articles 2(1), 4(1), 24(1), 26(1).

139 E. J. Hobsbawm, *Nations and Nationalism Since 1780: Programme, Myth, Reality*, Cambridge, Cambridge University Press, 1990, pp. 108–9. See also W. Connor, *Ethnonationalism: The Quest for Understanding*, Princeton, NJ, Princeton University Press, 1994, p. 94; K. R. Minogue, *Nationalism*, London, B T Batsford Ltd, 1967, pp. 8–9, T. K. Oommen, *Citizenship, Nationality and Ethnicity*, Cambridge, Polity Press, 1997, p. 67.

140 See quoted comments of Wilson and Miller in J. Robinson, O. Karbach, M. M. Laserson, N. Robinson and M. Vichniak, *Were the Minorities Treaties a Failure?*, New York, Institute of Jewish Affairs, 1943, p. 8. International lawyers also used 'race' interchangeably with 'people' and 'nation' as is illustrated in Brown, note 15.

synonym of race as being people rather than nation, it must be recalled that many at San Francisco saw the words nation and people as themselves synonymous. Thus, in the Summary Report of the Sixth Meeting of Committee II/4 of 17 May 1945, there appears the following sentence:

> Nothing in the Charter should contravene the principle of the equality of all races; and their right to self-determination, whether it resulted in independence or not, should be recognized.[141]

Given that this sentence clearly states that a race has the right to self-determination, it must be understood that a race equates to a people. Similarly, the Philippines delegate explained that the principle of self-determination was deeply rooted in the concept of 'equality of races'.[142] This clearly equates a race with a people. Furthermore, the International Convention on the Elimination of All Forms of Racial Discrimination, in its definition of 'racial discrimination', includes, *inter alia*, discrimination on grounds of 'national or ethnic origin'.[143] Finally, the Oxford Dictionary defines 'race', *inter alia*, as 'a tribe, nation, or people, regarded as of common stock'.[144] The conclusion that one can draw from this is that the word race was often understood as meaning nation. Thus, a group defined in terms of 'race' in paragraph 7 could mean a group defined as a nation. On this basis it is difficult to justify Cassese's narrow interpretation of the last words of paragraph 7. Consequently, his interpretation of the limited scope of permissible secession pursuant to paragraph 7 is also not justified.

Thus, on the above analysis of paragraph 7, two basic conclusions are forthcoming. The first is that the entire population of a state cannot be the meaning of 'a people'. The second is that, in implying that 'a people' is a group defined in terms of 'race, creed or colour', there are good reasons for holding that such a group does include a nation, with the consequence that the definition of a people includes a nation.

However, the above conclusions, in particular the first, must be tested against the fact that paragraph 7 includes the phrase 'whole people belonging to the territory'. Paragraph 7 stipulates that a state that fulfils its obligations pursuant to paragraph 7 is one 'possessed of a government representing the *whole people* belonging to the territory' of that state 'without distinction as to race creed or colour' (emphasis added). The reference to 'the whole people belonging to the territory' of a state suggests a view that 'a people' must mean the entire population of a state. The question that arises is to what extent, if any, does this suggestion displace the conclusions reached above on the analysis of the remainder of paragraph 7?

141 *UNCIO*, note 34, vol. X, p. 453.

142 Ibid., vol. VI, p. 704.

143 General Assembly Resolution 2106 (XX), Article 1(1), 20 November 1963.

144 *The Compact edition of the Oxford English Dictionary*, Volume II, Oxford, Oxford University Press, 1971, p. 2400.

If one accepts the view that a people is not by definition the entire population of a state and that a number of peoples can constitute the population of a state, then the words 'all peoples' would logically have been included in paragraph 7 in place of 'the whole people'. On the other hand, if it is accepted that a people means the entire population of a state, then the word 'whole' is superfluous in the context of paragraph 7 and logically should not have been included. More importantly, if one accepts that a people is the entire population of a state, one must also take into account the 'without distinction' provision when construing 'the whole people' expression. Paragraph 7 stipulates that a state which fulfils its obligation pursuant to paragraph 7, is one 'possessed of a government representing the whole people of the territory without distinction as to race, creed or colour'. This 'without distinction' provision implies the existence of different groups as parts of a state's entire population. If there was no recognition that such groups could exist within a state, the 'without distinction' provision would be superfluous.[145] Given that it has been established that any such group is a people, and given that logically such a group is only part of the entire population of any particular state, then the 'without distinction' provision implies that a people does not mean the entire population of a state, and thus contradicts the argument that the expression 'the whole people' implies that a people means the entire population of a state.[146]

What is clear is that the drafting of paragraph 7 is far from satisfactory and not without its difficulties. It is submitted that in construing it to shed light on the meaning of a people, one should reject any conclusion that 'the whole people' reference implies that the meaning of a people is the entire population of a state. Two reasons can be submitted in support of this submission. First, reference to 'the whole people' appears only once in Principle 5. If the supposed implication drawn from the use of 'the whole people' was what the framers of the document intended, then it would have been used in other paragraphs of Principle 5 and indeed in other parts of the Declaration on Friendly Relations. Second, its single appearance in paragraph 7 should not be permitted to counter implications drawn from other parts of paragraph 7 and Principle 5 to the effect that a people does not mean the entire population of a state. On this basis the previously established conclusions as to the effect of paragraph 7 remain intact. Thus, an analysis of paragraph 7 does not establish that a people is the entire population of a state, but rather that a people is a group within a state which forms part only of that state's population. Further, it strongly indicates that a nation is included within the meaning of a people.

145 P. Thornberry, 'The Principle of Self-Determination', in V. Love and C. Warbrick (eds), *The United Nations and Principles of International Law: Essays in Honour of Michael Akehurst*, London, Routledge, 1994, pp. 181–2.

146 Duursma supports this interpretation when she writes that '"[t]he whole people" of paragraph 7 of the Declaration means either that one State can have but one people, or within a State more than one people can co-exist. The latter meaning seems correct if we read it in combination with the prohibition of discrimination on grounds of race, creed or colour': Duursma, note 44, p. 25.

The potential impact of paragraph 7 was confirmed soon after its adoption with the secession of Bangladesh from Pakistan in 1971. An International Commission of Jurists observed, in its 1972 study entitled *The Events in East Pakistan, 1971*, that the right to self-determination and the principle of territorial integrity were conflicting principles, and that paragraph 7 gave primacy to the principle of territorial integrity. However, the Commission also noted:

> It is submitted, however, that this principle is subject to the requirement that the government does comply with the principle of equal rights and does represent the whole people without distinction. *If one of the constituent peoples of a state* is denied equal rights and is discriminated against, it is submitted that their full right of self-determination will revive.[147] (Emphasis added.)

Thus, according to the Commission, if the circumstances are present, as indeed they were with the Bangladesh situation, secession as the exercise of a people's right to self-determination is permissible.[148]

The final reference to the Declaration on Friendly Relations that is relevant to the meaning of 'a people' is paragraph 6 of Principle 5 which deals with colonial and non-self-governing territories. In paragraph 6 reference is made to 'the people', as opposed to 'the peoples', of individual colonial territories. This wording raises the implication that in the colonial context the right to self-determination is vested in the entire population of the relevant colony. Whilst the wording in the Declaration on Friendly Relations is in terms of 'a people' as the entire population of any given colonial territory, the Declaration on Colonialism implies that a number of peoples can constitute the entire population of a colonial territory. Thus, paragraph 6 and the Declaration on Colonialism are inconsistent on the question of what is 'a people'. However, it is submitted for several reasons that the interpretation based upon the Declaration on Colonialism should be preferred.

First, the Declaration on Friendly Relations is not primarily concerned with colonial territories, but rather with friendly relations and co-operation among states. The Declaration on Colonialism is concerned precisely with colonial territories and should be accepted as the primary authority on the issue of whether or not a people is the entire population of a colonial territory. The implications of the numerous references to peoples in the Declaration on Colonialism, none of which is consistent with a people as the entire population of a colonial territory, should be preferred to the alternative definition based, as it is, on only one reference to that issue found in the Declaration on Friendly Relations.

Second, if one accepts the interpretation of the Declaration on Friendly Relations in paragraph 6, and that, in the context of independent states referred to

147 International Commission of Jurists, 'East Pakistan Staff Study', *The Review*, 1972, no. 8, p. 46.

148 It can be noted that the secession of Bangladesh was justified on the basis of the right of self-determination of the people of Bangladesh. See Bangladesh Proclamation of Independence, 10 April 1971, (1972) 11 ILM 119.

in paragraph 7, a people is not necessarily the entire population of a state but rather that a number of peoples can constitute the entire population of a state, one is left with the curious result that, prior to independence, a people means one thing, but after independence it means something else. This could hardly have been the intention of the General Assembly. For the purposes of self-determination, the definition of a people should be the same, be it in the context of colonial territories or independent states. On the basis of the discussion of the Charter and the various General Assembly resolutions, the only relatively clear assertion that a people means the entire population of a territorial unit is within paragraph 6 of the Declaration on Friendly Relations. All other references point to the opposite conclusion, namely, that a people is not co-extensive to the population of a colonial territory or independent state, and that a number of peoples can populate such colonial territories or independent states. Accordingly, the single reference in paragraph 6 should not displace the consistent meaning of a people flowing from the Charter and other General Assembly resolutions.

Fiftieth anniversary declaration of the United Nations

In October 1995 the General Assembly adopted the Declaration on the Occasion of the Fiftieth Anniversary of the United Nations (Fiftieth Anniversary Declaration).[149] By Article 1, the UN declared that it would, *inter alia*:

> Continue to reaffirm the right of self-determination of all peoples, taking into account the particular situation of peoples under colonial or other forms of alien domination or foreign occupation, and recognize the right of peoples to take legitimate action in accordance with the Charter of the United Nations to realize their inalienable right of self-determination. This shall not be construed as authorizing or encouraging any action that would dismember or impair, totally or in part, the territorial integrity or political unity of sovereign and independent States conducting themselves in compliance with the principle of equal rights and self-determination of peoples and thus possessed of a Government representing the whole people belonging to the territory without distinction of any kind.[150]

As can be seen from its wording, Article 1 has similarities to Principle 5, and in particular paragraph 7, of the Declaration on Friendly Relations. The standard of

149 General Assembly Resolution 50/6, 24 October 1995.

150 At the second World Conference on Human Rights organised by the UN and held in Vienna in June 1993, the more than 180 states adopted, on 25 June 1993, by consensus, the Vienna Declaration and Programme of Action. The declaration, in Article 2, paragraph 1, reaffirmed the right of all peoples to self-determination in terms identical to Article 1 of the two international covenants of 1966, and in Article 2, paragraph 3 stated in identical terms the last sentence of Article 1 of the Fiftieth Anniversary Declaration: The Vienna Declaration and Programme of Action, United Nations Department of Public Information, (1993) 32 ILM 1661–87.

conduct of states required by Article 1 is expressed in identical terms to that found in paragraph 7. Article 1 refers, as does paragraph 7, to 'the whole people'. Thus, the comments on these two aspects of Article 1 are the same as for paragraph 7.

The critical difference between Article 1 and paragraph 7 is the qualification at the end of both provisions. Paragraph 7 speaks in terms of representative government 'without distinction as to race, creed or colour', whereas Article 1 is unlimited in scope, speaking of representative government 'without distinction of any kind'. Whatever doubts may have existed on the extent of the right to secession contained in the limiting words of paragraph 7 by writers such as Cassese, they are removed by Article 1. Any group within an unrepresentative or discriminatory state has the right to secede.[151] Discrimination by a state along national lines is clearly envisaged by Article 1. If a particular state's government is not representative of its national groups, it is not conducting itself 'in compliance with the principle of equal rights and self-determination of peoples', and thus, its territorial integrity is not absolutely protected by Article 1. Secession by such a national group would be possible. Such a secession would be by a people and its justification would be the exercise of that people's right to self-determination. The reasoning that justifies the conclusion that a nation or national group is a people is the same reasoning outlined above concerning a group's entitlement to secede pursuant to paragraph 7 as a people possessed of the right to self-determination.

Decisions of the International Court of Justice

The right of peoples to self-determination has been discussed in decisions of the International Court of Justice concerning the three non-self-governing territories of South West Africa (later Namibia),[152] Western Sahara[153] and East Timor.[154] All three cases confirmed the applicability of self-determination to the decolonisation of non-self-governing territories.[155] In none of these cases was the meaning of peoples in issue, nor was it discussed in any of the judgments. However, in the case dealing with Western Sahara, the Court more often than not used the word 'population' rather than 'people' when referring to the exercise of the right of self-determination in Western Sahara.[156] The Court decision ended with reference to 'the decolonization of Western Sahara and, in particular, of the principle of self-

151 S. P. Sharma, *Territorial Acquisition, Disputes and International Law*, The Hague, Martinus Nijhoff Publishers, 1997, p. 226.

152 *Legal Consequences for States of the Continued Presence of South Africa in Namibia (South West Africa) Notwithstanding Security Council Resolution 276* [1971] ICJ Rep. 16.

153 *Advisory Opinion of the International Court of Justice on the Western Sahara* [1975] ICJ Rep. 12.

154 *Case Concerning East Timor (Portugal -v- Australia)* (1995) 105 ILR 227.

155 *Legal Consequences for States of the Continued Presence of South Africa in Namibia (South West Africa) Notwithstanding Security Council Resolution 276* [1971] ICJ Rep. 16, at 31–3; *Western Sahara, Advisory Opinion* [1975] ICJ Rep. 12, at 31–3 (paras. 54–9); *Case Concerning East Timor (Portugal -v- Australia)* (1995) 105 ILR 227, at 243.

156 'Population' is used four times: *Western Sahara, Advisory Opinion* [1975] ICJ Rep. 12, at 34, 36 (twice), 84. 'People' is used three times: ibid., at 34, 35 (twice).

determination through the free and genuine expression of the will of *the peoples of the Territory*' (emphasis added).[157] Although not too much can be read into these references, they do give some support to the view that the population of a territorial unit is not a people, and that such a territorial unit may be constituted by a number of peoples.

Other international instruments

Apart from the UN, a number of other international organisations have adopted various instruments relating to the right of self-determination of peoples. These include the Conference on Security and Cooperation in Europe (CSCE),[158] and the Organisation of African Unity (OAU).

The major document of the CSCE is the Final Act of Helsinki of 1 August 1975.[159] Self-determination is dealt with in Principle VIII of the part of the document which deals with Questions Relating to Security in Europe. Principle VIII confirms that 'all peoples' have the right to self-determination. Nothing in the Helsinki Final Act explicitly defines what is meant by peoples. Cassese argues that because of the expressed concerns of many of the member states with national minorities, a people for the purposes of Principle VIII is the total population of a member state and cannot include a national minority. Cassese argues that this conclusion is further reinforced by the provisions of Principle VII which guarantee the human and other rights of individuals within the national minorities of member states. Cassese does concede that national minorities could be covered by both Principles VII and VIII, but because individual members of national minorities are granted rights, he concludes that such minorities are not granted the right of self-determination.[160] His argument here is in effect similar to the argument he pursues in relation to the effect of Article 27 upon Article 1 of the Civil Rights Covenant. However, just as the argument in relation to the Civil Rights Covenant cannot be sustained, neither can it be sustained in relation to the Helsinki Final Act.

A second basis upon which Cassese supports his conclusion is the provisions in

157 Ibid., at 68.

158 The CSCE changed its name to the Organisation on Security and Cooperation in Europe (OSCE) in January 1995.

159 (1975) 14 ILM 1292–325. The relevant provisions were subsequently reaffirmed by the CSCE in the Concluding Document of the Vienna Meeting of the CSCE of 19 January 1989: reprinted in A. Bloed (ed.), *From Helsinki to Vienna: Basic Documents of the Helsinki Process*, Dordrecht, Martinus Nijhoff Publishers, 1990, p. 184, and the Charter of Paris for a New Europe of 21 November 1990: (1991) 30 ILM 190–228. Cassese claims that these two documents restricted the scope and meaning of self-determination as stipulated in the Helsinki Final Act: Cassese, note 41, pp. 292–3. However, this contention is not supported by a reading of the relevant texts. Both of the later documents are almost identical in wording to the Helsinki document in relation to provisions on self-determination and territorial integrity of states, and explicitly reaffirm the full commitment of member states to the continuing validity of all principles contained in the Helsinki document.

160 Cassese, note 41, pp. 283, 289.

the Helsinki Final Act relating to the territorial integrity of states, especially the reference in Principle VIII.[161] Principle VIII stipulates that the right to self-determination is to be respected by member states 'acting at all times in conformity with the purposes and principles of the Charter of the United Nations and with relevant norms of international law, including those relating to territorial integrity of States'. As already noted, neither the Charter provisions on territorial integrity of states nor paragraph 7 of Principle 5 of the Declaration on Friendly Relations shed clear light on the meaning of peoples. However, paragraph 7, by clearly permitting secession, clearly implies that a people is not defined as the entire population of a state.

Furthermore, Principle VIII places the obligation to respect the right to self-determination upon states. As Cassese correctly notes, this does not qualify the rights of peoples. Cassese then concludes:

> It would follow that, under the Helsinki Declaration, a 'people' can claim a right to secede if they consider secession the only means available to implement their right to self-determination (but that which was stressed above must be recalled: 'peoples' is not synonymous with 'minorities'; the latter are not entitled to self-determination and certainly not to secession).[162]

This is a curious sentence. The first part is correct, and on its own clearly supports the view that a people is not defined as the whole population of a state. However, the portion of the sentence in brackets renders the first part an absurdity. If one accepts Cassese's definition of a people, and if there is a right of secession, then secession in these circumstances involves an entire state seceding from itself.

The only sensible conclusion that can be drawn from the territorial integrity provision in Principle VIII is, as Cassese concludes, that it does not qualify the right of a people to self-determination and that it permits secession as the only means of implementing the right of a people to self-determination. This conclusion implies that a people is not defined as the whole population of a state.

A final aspect of the CSCE documents on self-determination which sheds light on the meaning of peoples relates to the unification of Germany in 1990. On Cassese's definition of a people, the two states of West and East Germany constituted two peoples. This is expressly confirmed by Cassese.[163] However, the CSCE, in the Charter of Paris for a New Europe of 21 November 1990,[164] referred to and welcomed, 'the fact that *the German people* have united to become one State in accordance with the principles of [the Helsinki Final Act]' (emphasis added). The literal interpretation of this provision is that the two former German states constituted a single people. Factually, this provision is also correct.

161 Ibid., pp. 288–9.
162 Ibid., p. 289.
163 Ibid., p. 288.
164 (1991) 30 ILM 190–228.

The two former German states, and consequently the unified state after 1990, were true nation-states, that is, states of the German nation. Reunification was in accordance with the historic German adherence to the romantic theory of self-determination. The provision in the Charter of Paris is a validation of that theory.

Article 20 of the African Charter on Human and Peoples' Rights of 27 June 1981[165] stipulates that 'all peoples . . . have the unquestionable and inalienable right to self-determination'. Nothing in this Charter defines or indicates the meaning of peoples. Debate about the meaning of people has drawn upon conclusions about the meaning of people in other contexts, especially the UN Charter and subsequent UN documents on self-determination. In commentaries on Article 20 some authors, wedded to the interpretation of writers such as Cassese, have accepted that such an interpretation also applies to this Charter.[166] Others take a wider view and leave open the possibility that Article 20 may contemplate secession from African states.[167]

Conclusion

This chapter's analysis of the meaning of peoples in the context of self-determination reveals that international documents from the date of the UN Charter onwards do not readily lend themselves to easy interpretation. Prior to the UN Charter there were no similar documents for interpretive analysis. Self-determination during the nineteenth and early twentieth centuries was primarily a political principle. However, it was understood throughout that time as being applicable for the benefit of nations and was generally referred to as national self-determination, and included the right of secession. The Leninist and Wilsonian interpretations accord with this appellation.

In relation to the meaning of people in the context of self-determination after the adoption of the UN Charter there has been a strong body of opinion that has argued that a people is defined as the total population of a political unit, such as a colonial entity or an independent state. Whether an analysis of UN and other international documents supports such an interpretation has been the subject of the greater part of this chapter. The view taken in this chapter is that it does not and that a nation is within the meaning of a people. The principal argument for the territorial definition of a people rests on references in most of the relevant documents to the continued territorial integrity of colonial entities and independent

165 (1982) 21 ILM 58–68.

166 R. Gittleman, "The African Charter on Human and Peoples' Rights: A Legal Analysis', *Virginia Journal of International Law*, 1982, vol. 22, pp. 678–80; G. J. Naldi, *The Organization of African Unity: An Analysis of its Role*, London, Mansell, 1989, pp. 125–6.

167 M. K. Addo, 'Political Self-Determination Within the Context of the African Charter on Human and Peoples' Rights', *Journal of African Law*, 1988, vol. 32, pp. 185–90; S. K. N. Blay, 'Changing African Perspectives on the Right of Self-Determination in the Wake of the Banjul Charter on Human and Peoples' Rights', *Journal of African Law*, 1985, vol. 29, pp. 157–9.

states. However, it has been argued that the provisions on territorial integrity do not mean that such colonial entities and states cannot be populated by a number of peoples. This is recognised in the Declaration on Friendly Relations and Fiftieth Anniversary Declaration by the inclusion of provisions that permit secession. Furthermore, if a people meant the population of a colonial entity or independent state, the stipulations on territorial integrity of the relevant territorial unit would have been unnecessary because the exercise of the right of self-determination by a people so defined, by definition could never threaten such a unit's territorial integrity.

International practice, while often insisting that self-determination occurred within the confines of a territorial unit, especially in the context of decolonisation, could be said to support the territorial interpretation of a people. However, as argued in relation to the Declaration on Colonialism, this does not automatically imply that such colonial units were populated by only one people. Indeed, the insistence on maintaining the territorial integrity of the colonial units upon independence was indicative of the recognition that most of these colonial units were populated by more than one people. It was felt that if each of these peoples were to enjoy the right to self-determination, there would be the need to re-draw former colonial borders. This would have had two possible consequences. First, the process of decolonisation would have slowed down considerably. Second, the possibility of war breaking out over future borders was seen as very likely. The international community was determined to prevent both these consequences. It did so by generally requiring that decolonisation take place within existing colonial borders irrespective of the numbers of peoples who lived within them.

Furthermore, the insistence on territorial integrity upon decolonisation was not always adhered to. A number of cases of decolonisation involved partition of the relevant colonial unit. In each case this was in recognition of the fact that different peoples within the units desired partition. The peoples in such cases were universally distinguished as belonging to different nations, thereby reinforcing the argument that a nation is within the meaning of a people.

To the extent that the *travaux préparatoires* of many of the relevant international documents dealing with self-determination assist in extrapolating the meaning of a people, it can be said that they, on balance, support the view that a nation is within the meaning of a people. This is based on the often expressed concern of diplomats in these discussions that the right of self-determination would permit the right of secession. Given that many of these diplomats came from multi-national states, their concerns clearly revealed a belief that a people is coterminous with a nation and not with the total population of a state. If a people meant the population of a colonial entity or an independent state one would not have expected these concerns to surface at all.

If, as is argued in this chapter, a people does include a nation within its scope, secession from an internationally recognised state pursuant to the right of self-determination of peoples is clearly possible. The right to secede is tempered by the condition that it can only occur when a state discriminates against, and thereby denies self-determination to, a group within that state.[168] In the realisation of independent statehood through secession the precise territorial parameters of the seceding state will be a major issue. In the 1990s it was argued that, in the context of secession from a federal state, secession must be within the confines of internal federal borders. The legal justification for this approach was the adaptation of the principle of *uti possidetis* to such situations. The principle of *uti possidetis*, insofar as it relates to international borders, dates back to the independence of Latin America from Spanish and Portuguese colonial rule. In order to properly assess the relevance, if any, of the principle's application to instances of secession from internationally recognised states, an analysis of the origins of the principle of *uti possidetis* and its application to cases of independence from colonial rule needs to be undertaken. This is the focus of the next two chapters.

168 This conclusion is confirmed by the Canadian Supreme Court where the Court said that the right to secede, apart from the context of decolonisation, existed 'where a definable group is denied meaningful access to government to pursue their political, economic, social and cultural development': *Reference re: Secession of Quebec* (1988) 161 DLR (4th) 385, at 442. Whilst this conclusion is acceptable, it has been suggested that such groups are not, at least initially, peoples. This rather peculiar line of reasoning suggests they only become peoples once extreme discrimination has been inflicted upon them: G. Lauwers and S. Smis, 'New Dimensions of the Right to Self-Determination: A Study of the International Response to the Kosovo Crisis', *Nationalism and Ethnic Politics*, 2000, vol. 6, no. 2, p. 57.

3 The principle of *uti possidetis* in Latin America

This chapter sets out the historical development of the principle of *uti possidetis* from its origins in Roman law to its transformation as a principle of international law. Its use in international law was initially related to territorial rights following war. It was only with the liberation of Latin America from Spanish and Portuguese colonial rule at the beginning of the nineteenth century that *uti possidetis* began to be used as a principle in the resolution of border disputes following decolonisation.

The next chapter details the further development of *uti possidetis* in resolving post-decolonisation border disputes following the decolonisation of Africa and Asia in the wake of World War II. A conclusion to the two chapters on *uti possidetis* appears at the end of the next chapter.

Uti possidetis in Roman law

The term *uti possidetis* has its origins in Roman law where it designated an interdict of the Praetor which precluded the disturbance of the existing state of possession of immovable property. In a dispute over possession between two individuals, in the absence of any established title to land, the possessor, by virtue of his possession, was awarded the right to be free from disturbance by his adversary.[1] The formula adopted by the Praetor was: *Uti eas aedes, quibus de agitur, nec vi nec clam nec precario alter ab altero possidetis, quominus ita possidetis, vim fieri veto.*[2] The essence of the decree was embraced in the words *uti possidetis, ita possidetis* (as you possess, so you may possess). In short, the interdict is referred to as *uti possidetis.*[3]

Although the interdict confirmed the right of the current possessor of immovable property, the victor's right to remain in possession was only provisional. His

1 H. J. Roby, *Roman Private Law in the Times of Cicero and of the Antonines*, vol. I, Cambridge, Cambridge University Press, 1902, p. 460.

2 'As you possess the house in question, the one not having obtained it by force, clandestinely, or by permission from the other, I forbid force to be used to the end that you may not continue so to possess it': translation in J. B. Moore, 'Memorandum on *Uti Possidetis*: Costa Rica–Panama Arbitration, 1911', in *The Collected Papers of John Bassett Moore in Seven Volumes*, vol. III, New Haven, CT, Yale University Press, 1944, p. 329.

3 Ibid., p. 330.

possession would always give way to the rights of any person who could establish ownership of the property. Thus, the *uti possidetis* interdict did not confer permanent rights to the victor.

With the emergence of the modern state in the wake of the Renaissance and Reformation there arose a need for a system of law to regulate relations between states. In the development of international law, scholarly jurists were significantly influenced by Roman law principles. Roman law had always been a powerful influence on the development of law in Western Europe, and it was the scholarly jurists of Western Europe who took the lead in the initial development of international law.[4] Thus, the Spanish jurist Francisco de Vitoria conceived a theory of relations between states, which, borrowing from Roman law, he called *jus gentium*. Whereas *jus gentium* was a part of the private law of Rome, it was transformed by Vitoria to mean a branch of public law regulating the relations between one people and another.[5] The eminent Dutch jurist Hugo de Groot, or Grotius as he is better known, was also heavily influenced by Roman law. In his treatise *De Jure Belli ac Pacis* (On the Rights of War and Peace), published in 1625, Grotius relied almost entirely on writings from the classical period as textual authority for his own work.[6]

In these formative years of international law, given that jurists viewed sovereignty of states as similar to ownership of private property, it was not surprising that Roman law concepts pertaining to the acquisition of private property were utilised and adapted to international law rules and principles dealing with the modes of acquisition of territory in international law.[7] In this way these jurists effected the transformation of the Roman law principle of *uti possidetis* and its incorporation into the corpus of international law.[8]

Uti possidetis and the termination of war

The transformation of *uti possidetis* from its Roman law origins into a principle of international law began with its use by international lawyers 'to connote a method of determining the territorial changes that had occurred as a result of armed conflict'.[9]

Prior to the nineteenth century, wars often ended by the simple cessation of

4 H. Wheaton, *History of the Law of Nations in Europe and America: From the Earliest Times to the Treaty of Washington, 1842*, New York, Gould, Banks & Co, 1845, pp. 29–34.

5 J. H. Parry, *The Age of Reconnaissance*, London, Weidenfeld & Nicolson, 1963, p. 305.

6 D. J. Bederman, 'Reception of the Classical Tradition in International Law: Grotius' *De Jure Belli ac Pacis*', *Emory International Law Review*, 1996, vol. 10, p. 3.

7 J. Dugard, *International Law: A South African Perspective*, Kenwyn, Juta & Co Ltd, 1994, p. 96.

8 Pursuant to Article 38(1)(d) of the Statute of the International Court of Justice such juristic works are a recognised source of international law: I. A. Shearer, *Starke's International Law*, 11th edition, London, Butterworths, 1994, pp. 44–5.

9 *Case Concerning the Territorial Dispute (Libyan Arab Jamahiriya/Chad)* [1994] ICJ Rep. 6, at 84, per Judge Ajibola.

hostilities. No formal peace treaty was concluded. In such cases the question of entitlement to territory which had changed hands during the war was determined by the principle whereby each party gained legal title to the territory actually possessed at the time hostilities ceased.[10] This was subject to the provision that the party in possession intended, and proceeded, to annex territory gained from its adversary during the war.[11] In the words of Schwarzenberger, '[i]n this primordial stage, effective control of a territory and power to defend it was the title deed'.[12] This principle can be dated back to the mid-sixteenth century and is stated in the works of Pierino Belli (1563), Alberico Gentili (1612), Emer de Vattel (1758) and Christian Wolff (1764).[13] The first use of the Roman expression *uti possidetis* to label this principle appears to be in the 1737 work of Cornelius Van Bynkershoek.[14] With the increased use of treaties to terminate wars after the Peace Treaties of Westphalia of 1648, *uti possidetis* was the principle applied to govern legal rights to property in the absence of specific provisions to the contrary.[15] In the words of Wheaton, in a paragraph headed 'Uti Possidetis the basis of every treaty of peace, unless the contrary be expressed':

> The treaty of peace leaves everything in the state in which it found it – according to the principle of *uti possidetis* – unless there be some express stipulation to the contrary. The existing state of possession is maintained, except so far as altered by the terms of the treaty. If nothing be said about the conquered country or places, they remain with the conqueror, and his title cannot afterwards be called in question. During the continuance of the war, the conqueror in possession has only a usufructuary right, and the latent title of the former sovereign continues, until the treaty of peace, by its silent operation or express provisions, extinguishes his title forever.[16]

In this sense, unlike its Roman law predecessor, the *uti possidetis* principle validated

10 C. G. Fenwick, *International Law*, 3rd edition, New York, Appleton-Century-Crofts Inc, 1948, p. 661; C. Phillipson, *Termination of War and Treaties of Peace*, London, Sweet & Maxwell Ltd, 1916, p. 221.

11 G. Fitzmaurice, 'The Juridical Clauses of the Peace Treaties' (1948), an extract of which is quoted in M. M. Whiteman, *Digest of International Law*, vol. 2, Washington, DC, Department of State Publication 7553, 1963, p. 1088. The means of completing the annexation of conquered territory were compulsory cession in a peace treaty, proclamation of annexation, and performance of state functions on the conquered territory: S. Korman, *The Right of Conquest: The Acquisition of Territory by Force in International Law and Practice*, Oxford, Clarendon Press, 1996, pp. 123–31.

12 G. Schwarzenberger, 'Title to Territory: Response to a Challenge', *American Journal of International Law*, 1957, vol. 51, p. 310.

13 S. N. Lalonde, '*Uti Possidetis* and Internal Administrative Borders', unpublished doctoral dissertation, University of Cambridge, 1997, pp. 15–16.

14 Ibid., p. 18.

15 C. C. Hyde, *International Law Chiefly as Interpreted and Applied by the United States*, (3 vols), 2nd revised edition, Boston, Little, Brown & Company, 1947, in vol. 3, pp. 2416–17; Shearer, note 8, p. 517.

16 A. B. Keith, *Wheaton's International Law*, vol. 2 – *War*, 7th English edition, London, Stevens & Sons Ltd, 1944, pp. 622–3.

the use of force.[17] However, the application of *uti possidetis* in these situations was based upon a presumption

> that the previous territorial sovereign, having voluntarily ceased hostilities, had given up hope of regaining the conquered territory, and that the status which existed between the parties at the time when they ceased hostilities . . . had been silently recognized and could be upheld as the basis of the future relations of the parties.[18]

Moore is correct when he observes that the principle of *uti possidetis* 'was a rule of peace; since it furnished a date from which rights were to be reckoned, without recurring to prior controversies and hazarding the consequences of their renewal'.[19]

In cases where peace treaties specifically dealt with territorial settlements, the principle of *uti possidetis* was often the explicit basis of such settlements. Many peace treaties expressly provided that each state was entitled to keep the territories actually possessed at the time of cessation of hostilities.[20] In such situations, the treaty, based upon *uti possidetis*, was regarded as an express abandonment of title by the former sovereign.[21]

By the early twentieth century, the application of *uti possidetis* as a principle relating to peace treaties had, according to Coleman Phillipson, become obsolete. Phillipson asserted that by that time, unless a peace treaty stipulated otherwise, all invaded territory was to be restored to the state which had legal ownership before hostilities commenced.[22] With the adoption of the Charter of the United Nations (UN) in 1945, the use of *uti possidetis* as the basis for justifying title to territory obtained by conquest is no longer justified,[23] largely because of Article 2(4) of the Charter which stipulates that:

> All Members shall refrain in their international relations from the threat or use of force against the territorial integrity or political independence of any State, or in any manner inconsistent with the Purposes of the United Nations.

The essence of Article 2(4) is reaffirmed in the 1970 Declaration on Friendly Relations,[24] and resolutions of the UN General Assembly[25] and the UN Security

17 Lalonde, note 13, pp. 19–20.
18 Korman, note 11, p. 112.
19 Moore, note 2, p. 330.
20 Phillipson, note 10, pp. 221–2.
21 Korman, note 11, pp. 112–13.
22 Phillipson, note 10, p. 222.
23 Korman, note 11, pp. 135-307; F. Wooldridge, '*Uti Possidetis* Doctrine', in R. Bernhardt (ed.), *Encyclopedia of Public International Law*, vol. 12, Amsterdam, North-Holland, 1990, p. 519.
24 General Assembly Resolution 2625 (XXV), 24 October 1970, which stipulates, that '[t]he territory of a State shall not be the object of acquisition by another State resulting from the threat or use of force' and further that '[n]o territorial acquisition resulting from the threat or use of force shall be recognized as legal'.
25 General Assembly Resolution 2949, 8 December 1972, which reaffirms 'that the territory of a

Council.[26] Furthermore, Article 52 of the Vienna Convention on the Law of Treaties, which entered into force on 27 January 1980, stipulates that a treaty will be void if it is imposed by unlawful force in violation of the principles of international law embodied in the UN Charter.

The resolution of boundary disputes in Latin America

The principle of *uti possidetis* achieved its most significant application in international law in the early decades of the nineteenth century with the resolution of boundary disputes in Central and South America upon the achievement of independence of these regions from the Spanish and Portuguese empires. Prior to that time *uti possidetis* had been applied to resolve international boundary disputes between European colonial powers following the discovery, exploration and settlement of the New World. In many cases of conflicting claims the contestants were obliged, as a basis of dispute resolution, 'to accept as the only possible solution the principle of actual possession – the *uti possidetis*'.[27] Thus, Spain and Portugal, by treaties in 1750 and 1777, resolved their conflicting claims in South America, relying, in part, on the actual possession of territory by each colonial power.[28]

However, it was with the independence of the former Spanish colonies in Latin America in the early decades of the nineteenth century that *uti possidetis* achieved its most significant application in international law. The leaders of the independence movement in Spanish America quickly adopted *uti possidetis* as the basis for the territorial delimitation of the new states that emerged after liberation from Spanish rule. The principle was also adopted by Brazil following the eventual departure of the Portuguese, and was applied in the boundary disputes involving the British, Dutch and French Guyana colonies. The United States of America also supported the principle of *uti possidetis* for all cases of independence of colonial entities in America.[29]

State shall not be the object of occupation or acquisition by another State resulting from the threat or use of force'.

26 Security Council Resolution 242 (1970), 24 October 1970, dealing with the situation in the Middle East, and which *inter alia* emphasised 'the inadmissibility of the acquisition of territory by war'.

27 Moore, note 2, p. 332.

28 Ibid., p. 335.

29 In his instruction to George M. Dallas, Minister to Great Britain, on 26 July 1856, Secretary of State William L. Marcy wrote: 'The United States regard it as an established principle of public law and international right that when a European Colony in America becomes independent, it succeeds to the territorial limits of the colony as it stood in the hands of the parent country': quoted in Hyde, note 15, vol. 1, p. 508. Ireland cites this instruction as evidence that the USA supported the principle of *uti possidetis* for all of America: G. Ireland, *Boundaries, Possessions, and Conflicts in South America*, New York, Octagon Books, 1971, p. 328. On the other hand, Hyde doubts Ireland's conclusion, claiming that the instruction was focused on denying the right of other European states to the territory of former colonial entities in America when they declared their independence from the relevant colonial power, and that as such the instruction did not prevent alterations to colonial boundaries by any other rules as may be agreed by the relevant states: Hyde, note 15, vol. 1, p. 508.

In its application *uti possidetis* stipulated that the borders of newly independent states would be the same as those of the former colonial administrative units.[30] A logical corollary of this principle was the right of each colonial administrative unit to attach itself to the state of its choice.[31] That such administrative boundaries would ever emerge as international borders could never have been in the contemplation of the colonial powers. As the Chamber of the International Court of Justice observed in *Land, Island and Maritime Frontier Dispute* (*El Salvador/Honduras*) (*El Salvador/Honduras*), the principle of *uti possidetis* was 'a retrospective principle, investing as international boundaries administrative limits intended originally for quite other purposes'.[32] The principle of *uti possidetis* had particular relevance to the mainland colonial possessions of the European powers in Central and South America. At the time of independence the Spanish colonial possessions in mainland Central and South America were divided into four viceroyalties – Mexico (New Spain), New Granada, Peru and Rio De La Plata, and four Captaincies-General – Yucatan, Guatemala, Venezuela and Chile.[33] Portugal's empire consisted of Brazil, and the British, Dutch and French had separate colonies in Guyana.

It has been observed that the application of the Roman law principle of *uti possidetis* to the independence of Latin America involved two significant alterations. First, there was a change in the scope of its application from private land claims to that of a state's territorial sovereignty. Second, there was the transformation of a provisional status into a permanent one.[34] As observed by Ratner, the Latin American transformation of *uti possidetis* meant that colonial administrative control 'became ten-tenths of the law'.[35]

30 S. W. Boggs, *International Boundaries: A Study of Boundary Functions and Problems*, New York, Columbia University Press, 1940, p. 79.

31 G. Maier, 'The Boundary Dispute Between Ecuador and Peru', *American Journal of International Law*, 1969, vol. 63, p. 36, referring to the decisions of the provinces of Jaen and Guayaquil within the Audiencia of Quito to join Peru and Colombia respectively.

32 [1992] ICJ Rep. 383, at 388.

33 Originally Spain's American possessions were divided into two viceroyalties – Mexico (eventually the independent states of Mexico, Honduras, Guatemala, El Salvador, Nicaragua and Costa Rica) and Peru. In 1717, the viceroyalty of Peru which covered South America was broken up by the formation of the new viceroyalty of New Granada (eventually the independent states of Colombia, Venezuela, Ecuador and Panama). In 1776 the viceroyalty of Rio De La Plata was created (eventually the independent states of Argentina, Uruguay, Paraguay and part of Bolivia). In the truncated viceroyalty of Peru (eventually the independent states of Peru, Chile and part of Bolivia) the captaincy-general of Chile was all but independent of the viceroyalty of Peru. It was only in military matters that the viceroy had authority: see W. J. Dennis, *Tacna and Arica: An Account of the Chile–Peru Boundary Dispute and of the Arbitrations by the United States*, New Haven, CT, Yale University Press, 1931, pp. 3–5.

34 Moore, note 2, p. 330; S. R. Ratner, 'Drawing a Better Line: *Uti Possidetis* and the Borders of New States', *American Journal of International Law*, 1996, vol. 90, p. 593; E. J. de Aréchaga, 'Boundary Disputes in Latin America: *Uti Possidetis* Doctrine', in R. Bernhardt (ed.), *Encyclopedia of Public International Law*, vol. 1, Amsterdam, North-Holland, 1992, p. 450.

35 Ratner, note 34, p. 593. Ratner incorrectly refers to 'possession' rather than administrative control.

However, a third difference can be noted. In its Roman law context, *uti possidetis* was based upon the concept of possession of property. In Latin America the application of *uti possidetis* was dependent upon the concept of a colony's administrative control of territory, given that the newly independent states did not, in the colonial period, have any rights of possession or ownership of territory. Such possession or ownership vested in full in the Crown of the former colonial states. On this basis, Bernárdez may well be correct in asserting that the principle of *uti possidetis* in Spanish America did not derive from its Roman law namesake, but rather from Spanish domestic law on succession. Under Spanish succession law the beneficiaries of deceased persons were entitled to judicial protection of their heritage, without prejudice to third parties with better rights.[36] If Bernárdez is correct, the first two distinctions between *uti possidetis* as applied in Latin America and in Roman law would also exist if it had derived from Spanish succession law. However, the third distinction would not arise.

Just as the application of the principle of *uti possidetis* in Latin America differed from its Roman law original, so too did it differ from its application as a principle in international law to sanction title to territory gained by conquest. As detailed below, the Latin American use of the principle, in insisting on the sanctity of former colonial borders as new international borders, effectively rejected the validity of *uti possidetis* as a principle justifying title to territory gained by conquest.

The independence movement in Central and South America began in the Spanish American colonies and was triggered by the Napoleonic seizure of the Spanish throne in 1808. The Spanish colonial elites responded by governing themselves ostensibly in the name of the deposed Spanish king.[37] However, with the restoration of the king to the throne in 1814 many of the creoles,[38] who dominated the colonial bureaucracies to which they owed their primary allegiances,[39] were not prepared to return to the days of royal absolutism, and began to seek formal independence. By 1825 the Spanish colonies on mainland Central and South America successfully fought for their liberation from Spanish imperial rule. The independence of Brazil from Portugal was also a by-product of Napoleon's European ambitions. In 1808 Napoleon's armies forced the Portuguese king to flee and set up his court in exile in Brazil. In 1821 the king was able to return to Portugal. The

36 S. T. Bernárdez, 'The "Uti Possidetis Juris Principle" in Historical Perspective', in K. Ginther, G. Hafner, W. L. H. Neuhold and L. Sucharipa-Behrmann (eds), *Völkerrecht zwischen normativem Anspruch und politischer Realität: Festschrift für Karl Zemanek zum 65. Geburtstag*, Berlin, Duncker & Humbolt, 1994, pp. 426–7.

37 The regional juntas formed in various parts of Hispanic America were often called 'Supreme Councils for the Conservation of the Rights of Ferdinand VII'. In 1810 the Supreme Junta of Venezuela was proclaimed 'in order to safeguard the rights of Ferdinand VII': J. A. Crow, *The Epic of Latin America*, 4th edition, Berkeley, CA, University of California Press, 1992, pp. 424–31.

38 A creole (*criollo*) was defined as a person of pure European descent born in the Americas, and was contrasted with the *peninsulares* who were born in Spain but served in the imperial administration where they dominated the highest political and church offices.

39 B. Anderson, *Imagined Communities: Reflections on the Origin and Spread of Nationalism*, revised edition, London, Verso, 1991, pp. 56–9.

king's son, who remained in Brazil, declared himself emperor of an independent Brazil in 1822. The movement towards independence of the British, Dutch and French colonies in Guyana followed much later. British Guyana became independent in 1966 as Guyana, and Dutch Guyana became independent in 1975 as Suriname. French Guyana became a department of France in 1946 and a region in 1974, a status it still has to the present day. In the still not finalised process of border determination, of the eight independent states in Central America[40] and twelve independent states in South America which emerged from the colonial administrations of the European imperial powers, the principle of *uti possidetis* played, and continues to play, a key role.[41]

Reasons for the development of *uti possidetis* as a principle in boundary disputes

Denial of the doctrine of terra nullius

The transformation of the Roman law principle of *uti possidetis* into a principle of international law applicable to the Americas was the product of a number of inter-related factors. Primarily, the leaders of the independence movement in Spanish America were determined to free themselves from colonial rule and to prevent a return of European control over any part of Spanish America. The fear of

40 Not all of Spain's colonial territory in Central America ended up as new independent states. The northern part of the former Viceroyalty of New Spain, which declared its independence as Mexico in 1821, lost territory north of the Rio Grande to the USA. On 2 March 1836 the Mexican province of Texas seceded and sought annexation by the USA. The latter recognised Texan independence on 3 March 1837, and Texas was ultimately annexed by the USA on 29 December 1845: R. H. Brock, '"The Republic of Texas is No More": An Answer to the Claims that Texas was Unconstitutionally Annexed by the United States', *Texas Tech Law Review*, 1997, vol. 28, pp. 683–93. Following the 1846–1848 war between Mexico and the USA and its conclusion pursuant to the Treaty of Guadalupe Hidalgo of 2 February 1848, Mexico recognised the Texas annexation and ceded to the USA the provinces of Upper California and New Mexico. On 30 December 1853, with the Gadsden Purchase, the USA negotiated the purchase from Mexico of a thin strip of land, which now forms the southern part of the state of Arizona. Notwithstanding the provisions of the Treaty of Guadalupe Hidalgo and the Gadsden Purchase, the USA–Mexican border was the subject of continued dispute. It was only when the two states concluded a Boundary Treaty of 1970 that border issues were finally resolved.

41 Moore, note 2, pp. 336–7. As recently as 1995, the Foreign Minister of Colombia invoked the continued relevance of *uti possidetis* in the context of a dispute between Colombia and Nicaragua over title to the Caribbean island of San Andres. Although Colombia was awarded the island by a treaty between the two states in 1928, the Foreign Minister, in maintaining Colombia's right to the island, in addition to referring to the treaty, observed that the island 'used to belong to the Viceroyalty of Santa Fé. That is clearly established in a document dated 1803 in which the king specifies that the jurisdiction of these territories is transferred to the Viceroyalty of Santa Fé. That was the situation in 1810 when the process of independence of the Americas began. Therefore that was the boundary that was established between the two countries': Colombian Foreign Minister interviewed on talks with Nicaragua, *BBC Summary of World Broadcasts*, EE/D2403/L, 8 September 1995.

European attempts to re-colonise South and Central America was real, as independence from Spain came in the wake of Spain's acceptance that it no longer had a monopoly over settlement and trade in the Americas.[42] Other European maritime powers increasingly had the force to compel a Spanish retreat in this respect. The Americas were thus open to Spain's imperial rivals. It was by no means certain that Spain's rivals, especially France, would not seek to fill the vacuum created by her withdrawal from South and Central America. *Uti possidetis* was thus at first much less legal than political in its implications.[43] According to Alejandro Alvarez, the independence leaders in Spanish America:

> would not admit the possibility of a future return to the condition of their former dependence on the mother country; nor would they agree to the extension on the new continent of that policy of the balance of power and of intervention which was at that time the foundation of the international politics of the Old World; nor would they tolerate the idea that the States of Europe might acquire any part of the American continent, however unexplored it might be, that is to say, regions 'nullius' according to the then dominant doctrines of law.[44]

The development of the principle of *uti possidetis* as the basis of preventing further European colonisation of Latin America meant the exclusion of any further application of the doctrine of *terra nullius* to the Americas.[45] Under this doctrine land that was not appropriated was susceptible to occupation. Because former colonial boundaries served as new state boundaries, the new Latin American states claimed to be legally entitled to all the territory within these boundaries irrespective of whether they had been explored or inhabited by the former colonial power.[46] Indeed, much of Central and South America was unexplored or uninhabited by the colonial powers and remained inhabited only by the native Indian peoples.

42 Throughout the eighteenth century the British wanted Spanish America opened to British merchants and generally favoured emancipating the Spanish colonies from Spanish imperial rule: J. Lynch, *Spanish Colonial Administration, 1782–1810: The Intendant System in the Viceroyalty of Rio de la Plata*, Westport, CT, Greenwood Press, 1969, p. 20. As early as 1778, by the Ordinance of Free Commerce, Spain had felt it necessary to permit indirect commerce between the Spanish colonies and powers other than Spain: A. P. Whitaker, *The United States and the Independence of Latin America, 1800–1830*, New York, W. W. Norton & Co, 1964, pp. 3–9.

43 'This doctrine [of *uti possidetis*] – possibly, at least at first, a political tenet rather than a true rule of law – is peculiar to the field of the Spanish-American states whose territories were formerly under the rule of the Spanish Crown': *The Beagle Channel Arbitration* (1977) 52 ILR 93, at 125–6.

44 A. Alvarez, 'Latin America and International Law', *American Journal of International Law*, 1909, vol. 3, p. 275.

45 The doctrine of *terra nullius* was never used by Spanish lawyers to justify their colonial empire. However, it was the justification adopted by the English and French for their empires: A. Pagden, *Lords of all the World: Ideologies of Empire in Spain, Britain and France c.1500–c.1800*, New Haven, CT, Yale University Press, 1995, pp. 76–9, 91–2.

46 L. M. D. Nelson, 'The Arbitration of Boundary Disputes in Latin America', *Netherlands International Law Review*, 1973, vol. 20, p. 271.

Native Indian occupation of land did not preclude the operation of the *terra nullius* doctrine.[47] Nor did, initially, the territorial limitations, established by Spanish colonial authorities, of native Indian communities affect territorial delimitation in accordance with the principle of *uti possidetis*.[48] This was so because these grants '[were] not Spanish colonial law documents concerning the definition of the administrative boundaries of the colonial provinces or intendancies'.[49] However, in 1992 the International Court of Justice did rule that 'grants to Indian communities . . . might indicate where the boundaries were thought to be or ought to be'.[50]

In effect, the principle of *uti possidetis* declared that no territory in former Spanish America was without an owner and thus was not open to further European colonisation on the basis of territory being *terra nullius*. Agreements between Latin American states occasionally expressly stipulated that no Latin American territory could be considered *terra nullius*.[51] In the *Colombia–Venezuela Arbitral Award*[52] the Federal Council of Switzerland observed that the principle of *uti possidetis* meant that although territories were not occupied in fact, they were deemed to be occupied in law by the new states at the very moment of independence. By this legal fiction of constructive possession, in the words of the Federal Council, 'no territory of old Spanish America was without an owner' and the principle of *uti possidetis* served to 'put an end to the designs of the colonizing states of Europe against lands which otherwise they could have sought to proclaim as *res nullius*'.[53] As was stated in the *Beagle Channel Arbitration*, title to the entire territorial scope of Latin America belonged to the newly independent states, and in each case was based on the denial of any further application of the *terra nullius* doctrine to Latin America.[54] The views of the Federal Council were cited with approval in *El Salvador/Honduras* where the Chamber of the International Court of Justice observed that 'a key aspect of the principle [of *uti possidetis*] is the denial of the possibility of *terra nullius*'.[55]

47 The rights of indigenous populations were, in accordance with the times, not legally recognised and they became part of the populations of the relevant states. However, such a view of the rights of indigenous peoples is no longer accepted: *Advisory Opinion of the International Court of Justice on the Western Sahara* [1975] ICJ Rep. 12, at 39.

48 *Case Concerning the Land, Island and Maritime Frontier Dispute* (*El Salvador/Honduras*) [1992] ICJ Rep. 383, at 636, 644–9, per sep. op. Judge Torres Bernárdez.

49 Ibid., at 648, per sep. op. Judge Torres Bernárdez.

50 Ibid., at 394.

51 See Protocol between Argentina and Chile, 6–7 December 1878: A. Marchant, *Boundaries of the Latin American Republics: An Annotated List of Documents 1493–1943*, Washington, DC, United States Government Printing Office, 1944, p. 226.

52 *Colombia–Venezuela Arbitral Award* (1922) 1 RIAA 223.

53 Ibid., at 228. See also *Case Concerning the Arbitral Award Made by the King of Spain on 23 December 1906* (*Honduras -v- Nicaragua*) [1960] ICJ Rep. 192, at 226–7, per diss. op. Judge Urrutia Holguin.

54 *The Beagle Channel Arbitration* (1977) 52 ILR 93, at 645.

55 [1992] ICJ Rep. 383, at 387. See also *The Beagle Channel Arbitration* (1977) 52 ILR 93, at 124–5. The suggestion in *Case Concerning the Frontier Dispute* (*Burkina Faso and Mali*) [1986] ICJ Rep. 554, at 565, that the primary purpose of *uti possidetis* in Latin America was to prevent fratricidal conflict between newly independent states cannot be sustained. The Chamber's comments in that case were applicable to the adoption of the principle in Africa.

A somewhat different interpretation involving the denial of the operation of the doctrine of *terra nullius* is offered by Bernárdez. According to Bernárdez, the denial of *terra nullius* was a corollary of the primary purpose of *uti possidetis* as a principle of succession by the former Spanish colonies to the international law title of the Spanish Crown. On this interpretation, the title of the Spanish Crown denied the possibility of the existence of *terra nullius* within Spanish America from the time of Spanish colonisation of the region. The Spanish colonies, by virtue of the principle of *uti possidetis*, succeeded to the territorial rights derived from the title of the Spanish Crown.[56] A consequence of this view is that the principle of *uti possidetis* was not an assertion that, as from independence, the doctrine of *terra nullius* would cease to apply to Hispanic America, but rather, that it would continue, as always, not to apply.

The title to territory claimed by the new states was not in any sense a transfer of any 'historic title' belonging to the colonial powers. The colonial powers ultimately derived their titles from the 1493 Bull of the Spanish Pope Alexander VI which purported to deal with all rights of property in the lands discovered by Christopher Columbus in 1492.[57] The Bull's terms, which 'donate, concede and assign', and in some passages 'invest' in the Spanish and Portuguese monarchs, 'full, free and all-embracing authority and jurisdiction' over the islands and mainland discovered by Columbus, provided the legal legitimation to the empires in the New World.[58] Such 'historic title' as was held by the colonial powers lapsed with the recognition by Spain of the new Hispanic republics.[59] Title during the colonial era, rooted in the Papal Bull of 1493, was vested exclusively in the Spanish Crown. This legal legitimation continued to be applied until the decolonisation of Latin America, notwithstanding that the concept of Papal donation as the basis of title to territory had been eclipsed

56 Bernárdez, note 36, pp. 423–5.

57 The Papal Bull *Inter caetera* of 4 May 1493 granted to Spain all the islands and mainlands found and to be found beyond a line drawn from pole to pole at a distance of 100 leagues west of the islands of the Azores and Cape Verde, unless any such island or land was in the actual possession, as at 25 December 1492, of some other Christian king or prince. Portugal was entitled to territory east of this line. This line was moved further west by 270 leagues as the result of the Treaty of Tordesillas of 7 June 1494 between Spain and Portugal. The Treaty of Tordesillas was formally confirmed by the Papal Bull *Ea quae* of 24 June 1506: Marchant, note 51, pp. 332–3; G. Francalanci and T. Scovazzi (eds), *Lines in the Sea*, Dordrecht, Martinus Nijhoff Publishers, 1994, pp. 2–4; W. G. Grewe, *The Epochs of International Law*, Berlin, Walter de Gruyter, 2000, pp. 233–4. The effect was to leave a sizeable part of the eastern part of South America open for Portuguese occupation after its discovery in 1500 and thereby grant Portugal a substantial area of South America. On the theoretical writings of Francisco de Vitoria, Bartolomé de las Casa and Juan Ginés de Sepúlveda aimed at establishing justifications for Spanish colonialism in Latin America based on principles of conquest pursuant to a just war rather than the declining theory based upon the Papal Bull, see Pagden, note 45, pp. 46–62, 91–102; Parry, note 5, pp. 303–19; Grewe, above, pp. 240–4.

58 M. Gongora, *Studies in the Colonial History of Spanish America*, Cambridge, Cambridge University Press, 1975, pp. 34–5.

59 *Case Concerning the Land, Island and Maritime Frontier Dispute* (*El Salvador/Honduras*) [1992] ICJ Rep. 383, at 565 and 671–2, per sep. op. Judge Torres Bernárdez.

elsewhere in the sphere of international relations by the late seventeenth century.[60] The Crown had absolute ownership and was deemed to be in possession, in fact and in law, at all times. This was made clear in the arbitral award of 1933 in *Honduras Borders* (*Guatemala/Honduras*) (*Honduras Borders*) in which the arbitrator observed:

> Prior to independence, each colonial entity being simply a unit of administration in all respects subject to the Spanish King, there was no possession in fact or law, in a political sense, independent of his possession. The only possession of [any] colonial entity before independence was such as could be ascribed to it by virtue of the administrative authority it enjoyed. The concept of '*uti possidetis* of 1821' thus necessarily refers to an administrative control which rested on the will of the Spanish Crown.[61]

The 'administrative control' which colonial entities possessed was subject entirely to the 'will of the Spanish King' who 'was at liberty at all times to change [the Crown's] royal commands or interpret them by allowing what it did not forbid'. Proof of such 'administrative control' was to be found in 'any manifestations of that will – royal *cédulas*, or rescripts, to royal orders, laws and decrees, and in the absence of precise laws or rescripts, to conduct indicating royal acquiescence in colonial assertions of administrative authority'.[62] It followed that only imperial documents were relevant in determining former colonial boundaries. It was on this basis that evidence of grants to individuals or Indian communities was excluded as evidence of the *uti possidetis juris* of 1821 in the boundary dispute in *El Salvador/Honduras*.[63]

The new states' title to territory was thus established, not from a transfer of the colonial powers' historic title, but rather 'either by *uti possidetis juris* or by any other norms of international law governing succession of States which might be applicable'.[64] As was observed by the Chamber in *El Salvador/Honduras*, *uti possidetis* was concerned as much with title to territory as it was with the location of boundaries.[65]

In this sense, the principle of *uti possidetis* complemented the policy of the USA, largely triggered by the independence movement in Spanish America, encapsulated in the Monroe Doctrine of 1823.[66] In his annual message to Congress on 2

60 Gongora, note 58, p. 34.

61 (1933) 2 RIAA 1307, at 1324. See also *Case Concerning the Land, Island and Maritime Frontier Dispute* (*El Salvador/Honduras*) [1992] ICJ Rep. 383, at 672, per sep. op. Judge Torres Bernárdez.

62 *Honduras Borders* (*Guatemala/Honduras*) (1933) 2 RIAA 1307, at 1324.

63 *Case Concerning the Land, Island and Maritime Frontier Dispute* (*El Salvador/Honduras*) [1992] ICJ Rep. 383, at 392–3.

64 Ibid., at 672, per sep. op. Judge Torres Bernárdez.

65 Ibid., at 387.

66 D. Perkins, *The Monroe Doctrine 1823–1826*, Gloucester, Peter Smith, 1965, pp. 3, 40–69; C. Tower, 'The Origin, Meaning and International Force of the Monroe Doctrine', *American Journal of International Law*, 1920, vol. 14, pp. 4–5; C. E. Hughes, 'Observations on the Monroe Doctrine', *American Journal of International Law*, 1923, vol. 17, pp. 613–14; Whitaker, note 42, pp. 467–8, 471.

December 1823, President Monroe declared that 'the American continents, by the free and independent condition which they have assumed and maintain, are henceforth not to be considered as subjects for future colonization by any European powers'.[67] The Monroe Doctrine declared that, in relation to 'the existing colonies or dependencies of any European power' the USA '[had] not interfered and shall not interfere',[68] but warned against any European interference in the political affairs of the American states. The USA saw considerable potential for its traders moving into South American markets at the expense of the European powers.[69] In effect, the USA declared itself as protector of the independence of the new states in Latin America.[70]

Not surprisingly, the Monroe Doctrine was generally endorsed by the Latin American states which had gathered for the Congress of Panama in 1826. Subsequent gatherings of Latin American states during the nineteenth century did the same.[71] In effect, the Hispanic American adherence to the principle of *uti possidetis*, when combined with the Monroe Doctrine, amounted to a rejection of the use of *uti possidetis* as a principle to sanction the right to territory by conquest. The principle of *uti possidetis* implied that the Hispanic American states would respect each other's territorial integrity, thereby prohibiting acquisition of territory by conquest. If any Hispanic American state violated this principle, the other Hispanic American states agreed not to recognise such territorial gains.[72] The

67 Quoted in Whitaker, note 42, p. 465. See also instruction to George M. Dallas, Minister to Great Britain on 26 July 1856, from Secretary of State William L. Marcy in which the latter wrote: 'When a colony is in revolt, and before its independence has been acknowledged by the parent Country, the colonial territory belongs, in the sense of revolutionary right, to the former, and in that of legitimacy, to the latter. It would be monstrous to contend that in such a contingency, the colonial territory is to be treated as derelict, and subject to voluntary acquisition by any third nation. That notion is abhorrent to all the notions of right, which constitute the international code of Europe and America': quoted in Hyde, note 15, vol. 1, p. 508.

68 Quoted in Whitaker, note 42, p. 465.

69 J. Clarke, *British Diplomacy and Foreign Policy 1782–1865: The National Interest*, London, Unwin Hyman, 1989, p. 166. Clarke notes, at 167–9, that Britain, without the means or will to take over any former Spanish colonies, also supported recognition of the new Hispanic states as a means of gaining the commercial and diplomatic advantage in the region over other powers, especially the USA. This policy was successful. By 1826 British trade and influence dominated South America.

70 Whitaker, note 42, p. 520. Others see in the Monroe Doctrine the assertion of imperialist intentions by the USA with respect to Latin America. By insisting that the European powers were excluded from the region, the USA was asserting that the two American continents were within its sphere of influence: P. Gleijeses, 'The Limits of Sympathy: The United States and the Independence of Spanish America', *Journal of Latin American Studies*, 1992, vol. 24, pp. 488–9.

71 Alvarez, note 44, p. 312.

72 J. Dugard, *Recognition and the United Nations*, Cambridge, Grotius Publications, 1987, pp. 25–6; J. B. Moore, 'Fifty Years of International Law', *Harvard Law Review*, 1936, vol. 50, pp. 434–6. See also M. M. McMahon, *Conquest and Modern International Law: The Legal Limitations on the Acquisition of Territory by Conquest*, Washington, DC, Catholic University of America Press, 1940, pp. 122–4, 174–7, where the writer notes that the non-recognition principle although proclaimed by most of the Americas, was ultimately ineffective to prevent title by conquest in the War of the Pacific (1879–1883) and the Chaco War (1932–1935).

effect of the Monroe Doctrine was to preclude European conquest of territory in the Americas. The principle of *uti possidetis* in Latin American decolonisation was a repudiation of *uti possidetis* as a principle 'concerning acquisition of . . . titles *jure belli*'.[73]

Prevention of boundary disputes and international conflict

Apart from confronting the possibility of further European colonisation of Latin America, the principle of *uti possidetis* was aimed at preventing, or at least peacefully resolving, boundary disputes between the new states.[74] The emergence of a number of new independent states in Spanish America was always going to be the reality, notwithstanding the dreams of men such as Simon Bolívar that the former colonies would form a federation, or at least confederate. Notwithstanding the influence of Enlightenment principles in the independence movement in Spanish America, they were not of such strength to overcome regional differences and the nascent sense of national identity. Even before the independence movement, 'the various constituent parts of the Spanish empire had already gone far towards developing a proto-national consciousness, based upon a sense of not only their difference from the mother country but from each other'.[75] Difficulties in communication, combined with the variety of soils and climates, tended to give the various administrative centres a self-contained character which was exacerbated by Spanish policy which was aimed at thwarting colonial interdependence or patterns of regional integration, and turning the various centres into separate economic zones that were forbidden to trade with each other.[76] The different experiences of these centres contributed to the adoption of the principle of *uti possidetis* after independence.[77]

To achieve the aim of preventing boundary disputes, it was deemed necessary to accept the principle that the borders of future independent states corresponded to Spanish colonial boundaries. This meant the boundaries, at the date of independence from Spain, of the viceroyalties, captaincies-general, Court districts, *intendencias*, *mayores*, *alcaldias* and *corregimientos* or 'provinces'.[78] In the case of Spanish South America the date of independence from Spain was taken as being 1810 (the

73 *Case Concerning the Land, Island and Maritime Frontier Dispute* (*El Salvador/Honduras*) [1992] ICJ Rep. 383, at 635, per sep. op. Judge Torres Bernárdez. Korman argues that the Latin American principle of *uti possidetis* and the Monroe Doctrine amount to the first attempt to eliminate the right to territory by conquest in international law: Korman, note 11, pp. 234–6.

74 *Colombia–Venezuela Arbitral Award* (1922) 1 RIAA 223, at 228; Nelson, note 46, p. 269.

75 D. Bushnell, 'The Independence of Spanish South America', in L. Bethell (ed.), *The Independence of Latin America*, Cambridge, Cambridge University Press, 1987, p. 146.

76 A. Hennessy, *The Frontier in Latin American History*, Albuquerque, University of New Mexico Press, 1978, pp. 106, 128–9; J. V. Fifer, *Bolivia: Land, Location and Politics Since 1825*, Cambridge, Cambridge University Press, 1972, p. 3.

77 Anderson, note 39, pp. 52–3.

78 *Case Concerning the Land, Island and Maritime Frontier Dispute (El Salvador/Honduras)* [1992] ICJ Rep. 383, at 387.

uti possidetis of 1810), and in the case of Spanish Central America it was taken as being 1821 (the *uti possidetis* of 1821).[79]

Boundary disputes were not an immediate problem after independence. This was, in part, due to the need for unity and co-operation amongst the new states in the face of possible European attempts to lay claim to the former Spanish empire. Furthermore, the pattern of colonial settlement based upon strategically located towns meant that great tracts of unoccupied territory separated them. These vacant and usually non-vital border regions militated against boundary disputes. On the other hand, it was also recognised by many that the principle of *uti possidetis* was not without its problems. Bolívar accepted that former colonial boundaries served as a starting point for the new states. He also recognised that they were unsatisfactory, because of the inexact basis upon which they were drawn, and that modifications would have to be made to provide natural and stable borders.[80] On the other hand, Bolívar's dreams of a Latin American federation or confederation implied that border issues would not be of major significance. However, with the gradual expansion of settlement, exploration and economic exploitation[81] of the previously unexplored regions of South America, the decreased threat of European conquest, and the failure of Bolívar's dreams of union, border disputes became increasingly important. Disputes over boundaries came to dominate the relationships between the Latin American states.[82] This situation was accompanied by an increased reliance on *uti possidetis* as the guiding principle in the resolution of such disputes.

For Bolívar, who was against the formation of smaller states, the *uti possidetis* of 1810 meant that only the larger Hispanic administrative units, the viceroyalties, captaincies-general and presidencies, could form the basis of new states. This was reflected in his 1825 statement rejecting Peruvian claims to Upper Peru when he wrote of 'what has come to be recognized as a principle of international law in America, namely: that the republican governments are founded within the boundaries of the former viceroyalties, captaincies general, or presidencies'.[83] However, this limitation was not maintained in practice.[84] Two examples are illustrative. First, the province of Chiapas, within the Captaincy-General of Guatemala, joined Mexico following independence, despite it being claimed as part of the Federal Republic of Central America, and then by Guatemala after the dissolution of the federation. Plebiscites in the province in 1824 and 1825 revealed a strong majority in favour of incorporation into Mexico.[85] Guatemala nevertheless maintained

79 Nelson, note 46, p. 268.

80 Ireland, note 29, pp. 324–8.

81 The discovery of nitrates in the Desert of Atacama in the 1850s ignited a boundary dispute between Bolivia and Chile: R. D. Talbott, *A History of the Chilean Boundaries*, Ames, Iowa State University Press, 1974, p. 33.

82 Alvarez, note 44, p. 291; Talbott, note 81, p. ix.

83 Bolívar letter to General Antonio Jose de Sucre, 21 February 1825, in H. A. Bierck Jr (ed.), *Selected Writings of Bolivar*, Volume Two, *1823–1830*, New York, Colonial Press Inc, 1951, p. 470.

84 Moore, note 2, p. 337.

85 G. Ireland, note 29, p. 98; Lalonde, note 13, p. 39.

its claims until 1882, when by treaty with Mexico, it renounced its claims to Chiapas.[86] Second, the provinces of Upper Peru declared their independence in 1825, claiming the Audiencia of Charcas as the territorial basis of the new state of Bolivia.[87]

Furthermore, just as Enlightenment ideas permeated Spanish America, so too did those of Romanticism. The Romantics were preoccupied with the concept of group identity rather than with the Enlightenment's focus on the individual. The ideas of Jean Jacques Rousseau, who saw the necessity of establishing the collective personality of the nation as the centre and justification of society and the social order, were well known in Spanish America. Although Rousseau was influenced by the ideas of John Locke, he never placed as much emphasis on the individual as did Locke. The influence of Romanticism in Spanish America was apparent from the fact that individuals saw themselves more as Mexicans, Venezuelans, Peruvians and Chileans than as Americans. Their states were 'the homes of societies, each of them unique, . . . [and] all with different interests'.[88]

In these circumstances boundary problems were of major significance with the new states that emerged in the wake of independence from Spain, and later with the break-up of some of these new states into smaller states.[89] At the time of independence not one boundary line had actually been agreed upon and defined.[90] A significant factor contributing to the intensity of some boundary disputes was the legacy of the redrawing of colonial boundaries by the Bourbon rulers of Spain after they had replaced the Habsburgs in the early eighteenth century.[91] Bourbon reforms of the imperial system in the mid-eighteenth century led to a redrawing of the Habsburg boundaries of the sixteenth century. This had the effect of 'creating conflicts of allegiance between newer centres and older focuses of authority' with the result that it was precisely the areas most affected by Bourbon reforms which provided the most bitter boundary disputes after independence.[92] In addition, disputes arose in the wake of these administrative reforms with two states claiming to

86 Treaty Between Mexico and Guatemala for Fixing the Boundaries Between the Respective States, Article 1, 27 September 1882, 73 BFSP 273–6.

87 Fifer, note 76, pp. 6–16.

88 J. Lynch, 'The Origins of Spanish American Independence', in Bethell (ed.), note 75, p. 39. On the development of creole nationalisms, see Anderson, note 39, pp. 47–65.

89 The Viceroyalty of New Granada and the Captaincy-General of Venezuela united on independence to became the Republic of Gran Colombia, but in 1830 split into the states of Colombia, Venezuela and Ecuador. In 1903 Panama, encouraged by the USA, seceded from Colombia and became independent. The Viceroyalty of Rio De La Plata in 1810 became known as the United Provinces of Rio De La Plata (later Argentina) but later saw the emergence of Paraguay (1811), and Bolivia (1825) and Uruguay (1828). The Captaincy-General of Guatemala became the Federal Republic of Central America in 1821 but in 1838 split into the states of Guatemala, Honduras, El Salvador, Nicaragua and Costa Rica.

90 Moore, note 2, p. 338.

91 Bourbon reforms were partially motivated by the need to improve the defence capabilities of the colonies from possible attack by Spain's imperial competitors: Lynch, note 42, pp. 20–2.

92 E. Williamson, *The Penguin History of Latin America*, London, Penguin Books, 1992, p. 240.

have succeeded the same colonial administrative division.[93] The competing and still unresolved claims of Peru and Ecuador to the Oriente province is one such example. In this dispute Ecuador claims that, at the time of independence, the province was administered by the Viceroyalty of New Granada, whereas Peru claims it was administered by the Viceroyalty of Peru.[94]

Another factor of significance, particularly after the break-up of the initial larger states into smaller ones, related to the economic viability of these smaller states, in particular their continuing ability to participate in overseas trade. Bolivia serves as a good illustration. After its independence from the United Provinces of Rio De La Plata, its once recognised and protected lines of movement to ports and shipping lines became precarious. Whilst it could function as part of the United Provinces, Bolivia's economic future as an isolated and landlocked state was uncertain because the principal routes to the coast lay outside its jurisdiction, that of the former colonial Audiencia of Charcas. The *uti possidetis* of 1810 forced Bolivia to accept an inappropriate distribution of territory, and led to a number of protracted border disputes with its various neighbouring states all aimed at securing internationally recognised, free and permanent access to the sea.[95]

Not all these problems were strictly boundary disputes. Boundary disputes are concerned with the lines drawn between the areas of sovereignty of adjacent states. On the other hand, territorial disputes are concerned with attempts by one state to dislodge another from an area of the latter's sovereignty on the ground of better title.[96] In Latin America some of the disputes, although covering significant areas of territory, were in essence boundary disputes. Thus, the dispute between Brazil and Argentina over the territory of the Missions, which involved over 30,000 square kilometres of land, was one in which there were differing interpretations over which two pairs of rivers, 160 kilometres apart from each other, formed the boundary pursuant to an express boundary agreement. The neutral arbitration of the President of the USA, basing his decision on earlier reports, surveys and maps, awarded the territory to Brazil in 1895.[97] The same could also be said of Ecuador's dispute with Peru, notwithstanding that it is over an area of approximately 325,000

93 *Case Concerning the Land, Island and Maritime Frontier Dispute* (*El Salvador/Honduras*) [1992] ICJ Rep. 383, at 387.

94 Ireland, note 29, pp. 219–30; Marchant, note 51, pp. 306–9; R. B. St John, 'The Ecuador-Peru Dispute: A Reconsideration', in P. O. Girot (ed.), *The Americas, World Boundaries,* Volume 4, London, Routledge, 1994, pp. 113–32; D. S. Palmer, 'Peru-Ecuador Border Conflict: Missed Opportunities, Misplaced Nationalism, and Multilateral Peacekeeping', *Journal of Interamerican Studies and World Affairs*, 1997, vol. 39, no. 3, pp. 109–48.

95 Fifer, note 76, pp. 3–5.

96 M. Shaw, *Title to Territory in Africa: International Legal Issues*, Oxford, Clarendon Press, 1986, p. 225. For a more detailed discussion of the boundary–territorial dispute distinction, see S. P. Sharma, *Territorial Acquisition, Disputes and International Law*, The Hague, Martinus Nijhoff Publishers, 1997, pp. 21–30.

97 Ireland, note 29, pp. 10–17; J. B. Moore, *History and Digest of the International Arbitrations to Which the United States Has Been a Party*, 6 Vols, Washington, Government Printing Office, Washington, 1898, in vol. II, pp. 1969-2026.

square kilometres of territory within the Amazon Basin. By way of contrast, the dispute between Chile and Argentina over Los Andes and Patagonia, which affected 94,000 square kilometres, was a true territorial dispute. The Patagonia region had been part of the Viceroyalty of Rio De La Plata. However, the region had not been inhabited by any Spaniards by the time of independence. Chile, in its constitutions of 1823, 1828 and 1833, claimed that part of Patagonia, south of the former Captaincy-General of Chile, west of the Andes to the Pacific Ocean and south to Cape Horn. This claim was disputed by Argentina. War threatened between the two states over the dispute. It was finally resolved by acceptance of the arbitrations in 1902[98] and 1966,[99] by which Argentina received approximately 40,000 square kilometres and Chile received approximately 54,000 square kilometres of the disputed territory.[100]

Whether the disputes are characterised as boundary disputes or territorial disputes is not, however, of any great practical significance. In either event the result of any arbitral adjudication is to establish a dividing line separating the disputant states.[101]

Finally, there was the fear that the establishment of independent states would lead to bloody wars and conflict of the type that characterised Europe at that time.[102] Latin American independence leaders, much like their counterparts in the independence struggle in North America against Great Britain, were determined to avoid this possibility.[103] It was hoped that the adoption of the principle of *uti possidetis* would contribute to minimising the possibility of war between the newly independent states.

Adoption of *uti possidetis* in Latin America

Political declarations and organisation

The principle of *uti possidetis* was voiced in various ways. Independence leaders such as Bolívar were steeped in the thinking of the European Enlightenment of the mid-eighteenth century.[104] They were also inspired by the example of the USA and its

98 *The Cordillera of the Andes Boundary Case (Argentina/Chile)* (1902) 9 RIAA 29.

99 *Argentine-Chile Frontier Case* (1966) 16 RIAA 109.

100 Boggs, note 30, pp. 85–92; Ireland, note 29, pp. 17–27; Talbott, note 81, pp. 90–115.

101 *Case Concerning the Frontier Dispute (Burkina Faso and Mali)* [1986] ICJ Rep. 554, at 563. See also H. Thirlway, 'The Law and Procedure of the International Court of Justice 1960–1989, Part Seven', *British Year Book of International Law*, 1995, vol. 66, pp. 27–31.

102 Declaration of the Rights of the People of Chile, 1810, quoted in Alvarez, note 44, p. 276; Antonio Muñoz Tebar to Bolívar, 31 December 1813, in H. A. Bierck (ed.), *Selected Writings of Bolivar*, Volume I, *1810–1822*, 2nd edition, New York, Colonial Press, Inc., 1951, p. 56; Bolívar to Francesco De Paula, 6–7 January 1825, in Bierck, note 83, pp. 461–2. See also *Case Concerning the Frontier Dispute (Burkina Faso and Mali)* [1986] ICJ Rep. 554, at 566 and 661–2, per sep. op. of Judge ad hoc Abi-Saab.

103 D. J. Hauptly, *'A Convention of Delegates': The Creation of the Constitution*, New York, Atheneum, 1987, pp. 96–7.

104 On the influence of European thinkers on Bolívar, see G. Masur, *Simon Bolivar*, Albuquerque,

struggle for independence.[105] The political and economic writings of Enlightenment thinkers such as John Locke and Adam Smith resulted in a liberalism which had inspired many constitutions of the new states of former Spanish America.[106] Enlightenment ideas focused on the rights of the individual over those of the group. The impact of Enlightenment thought was that, although the colonial order was destroyed, the new states that emerged did so within the former imperial territorial framework. White has explained this process in another context as follows:

> Enlightenment ideas created the need to re-evaluate the social organization of space. Since tradition was rejected, dynastic order lost its legitimacy and with it the basis for dividing the world up into dynastic territories. A new spatial order could arise, yet its structure was not obvious. Enlightenment philosophers placed the rights of the individual over those of any group identity (i.e. the nation). Consequently, there was no pressing need to redraw boundaries according to the spatial distribution of groups. Individuals could consent to pool their individual wills into a general will and thereby exchange their natural but chaotic freedom for civil liberty. The rights of individuals could be achieved through a change in institutional structures within the existing territorial framework. Therefore, state boundaries did not need to be redrawn at all. The old dynastic territories could be, and were, used for the new states.[107]

Thus, the first governments of the new states generally accepted former colonial boundaries as new international borders. This reflected the earlier policies of the leaders of the independence armies who, in their proclamations and manifestos issued at times of incursion into neighbouring provinces, consistently declared that they had come in aid of the independence struggle of a future separate state.[108]

An early public manifestation of the *uti possidetis* principle was at the Congress of Angostura in 1819, convened by Bolívar, at which it was declared that the Captaincy-General of Venezuela and the Viceroyalty of New Granada constituted the independent state of Colombia. This approach was accepted by the emerging Hispanic republics in 1821 as a common policy of territorial division with the critical date in South America being 1810 – the *uti possidetis* of 1810.[109]

University of New Mexico Press, 1969, pp. 35–6. On the influence of the Enlightenment on the independence movement in Spanish America, see J. Kinsbruner, *Independence in Spanish America: Civil Wars, Revolutions, and Underdevelopment*, Albuquerque, University of New Mexico Press, 1994, pp. 9–14.

105 Essay on Public Education, in Bierck, note 83, p. 555.

106 Kinsbruner, note 104, p. 12.

107 G. W. White, 'The Territorial Component of Nationalism in Southeastern Europe: The Cases of the Hungarians, Romanians, and Serbs', unpublished doctoral dissertation, University of Oregon, 1994, pp. 37–8.

108 Ireland, note 29, p. 327.

109 E. J. Sahurie, *The International Law of Antarctica*, Dordrecht, Martinus Nijhoff Publishers, 1992, p. 225; Wooldridge, note 23, p. 215.

The principle of *uti possidetis* was also reflected in the various, but unsuccessful, attempts to establish Central and South American federations or confederations after independence from Spanish rule.[110] In Central America the Federation of Central America, formed in 1821, collapsed in 1838, whereupon its five constituent states all claimed as their boundaries, lines based upon former Spanish colonial provinces.[111] Subsequent confederation treaties involving the Central American states in 1842, 1849, 1895 and 1921 all failed to be implemented.[112] None of the efforts to form a South American confederation were successful.[113] The idea of federation or confederation was seen as a way of establishing a strong and united force against any possible European attempts to re-colonise Latin America. It was also thought that the likelihood of war within Latin America would be reduced if a fewer, rather than a greater, number of independent states emerged after liberation from European colonial domination.[114]

At the congresses aimed at establishing a confederation the various states agreed that the principle of *uti possidetis* was the basis for ascertaining mutual boundaries. These attempts at confederation were important in consolidating the acceptance of the principle of *uti possidetis*. By the time of the 1848 Congress of Lima *uti possidetis* was firmly entrenched in American international law.[115] This was reflected in Article 7 of the Treaty of Confederation, between New Granada, Chile, Peru and Bolivia, signed at the Congress of Lima on 8 February 1848 which stated:

> The confederated Republics declare that they have a perfect right to the conservation of their territories as they existed at the time of independence from Spain, those of the respective Viceroyalties, captaincies-general or presidencies into which Spanish America was divided.[116]

110 Some of the new states did adopt federalism as a basis of internal constitutional law, but they were generally failures and most states became centralist states in due course. The federal units in these states usually corresponded to former administrative units established during the period of Spanish rule. On federalism in Spanish America after independence, see Kinsbruner, note 104, pp. 116–24, 141–7.

111 *Case Concerning the Land, Island and Maritime Frontier Dispute* (*El Salvador/Honduras*) [1992] ICJ Rep. 383, at 631, per sep. op. Judge Torres Bernárdez.

112 D. G. Munro, *The Five Republics of Central America*, New York, Oxford University Press, 1918, pp. 164–71. The closest the Central American states came to again federating was in 1921: S. Evans, 'At Union's Brink: Ideals and Problems in Restoring the United Provinces of Central America, 1920–1922', *Latin American Research Review*, 1997, vol. 32, no. 1, pp. 69–87.

113 Alvarez, note 44, pp. 276–87.

114 In *The Federalist*, No. 5 of *The Federalist Papers*, John Jay put forth almost identical reasons in favour of one state, and not four states, emerging in the wake of the American War of Independence: Hauptly, note 103, pp. 96–7.

115 Marchant, note 51, pp. 247–8.

116 Quoted in Hyde, note 15, vol. 1, p. 500; Alvarez, note 44, p. 281. This treaty was never ratified, but the reasons for such failure had nothing to do with the provisions of Article 7.

Domestic constitutional provisions

The principle of *uti possidetis* was also incorporated into the constitutional law of various Latin American states. This was particularly so in the two major federations established at the time of independence, namely, Gran Colombia and the Federal Republic of Central America.[117] Military expediency was the major factor in establishing these federations. However, once independence was gained and the threat of re-colonisation by any of the European imperial powers receded, these federations disintegrated.[118] The principle of *uti possidetis* was to be found in the constitutions of the federations and in the successor states, although the only cases in which the expression '*uti possidetis*' was used are those of Colombia and Costa Rica.

In Gran Colombia, Article 6 of the constitution of 30 August 1821 stipulated:

> The territory of Colombia is the same which was formerly comprehended in the ancient Vice-royalty of New Granada and the Captain-Generalship of Venezuela.[119]

In 1822 Ecuador entered into a confederal arrangement with Gran Colombia. The boundary line between Ecuador and Gran Colombia was declared to be that which 'separated the provinces of the ancient Department of the Cauca from that of Equator'.[120] Article VI of Gran Colombia's constitution of 11 September 1830 defined Ecuador as the 'three Departments of the Equator, within the ancient Kingdom of Quito'.[121]

In 1830 the federation of Gran Colombia came to an end, resulting in the new states of Colombia, Venezuela and Ecuador. The principle of *uti possidetis* was reflected in the constitutions of the new states. Article VII of Colombia's constitution of 20 April 1843 referred to the 'Vice-Royalty of New Granada' as the territorial scope of the state.[122] A similar expression was used in Article 3 of the constitution of 5 August 1886, but the stipulation went on to say that Colombia's

117 Another illustration was the Peruvian constitution of 12 November 1823, which in Article VI referred to the state's territory as being 'Upper and Lower Peru': 10 BFSP 701–22. This was a reference to *uti possidetis* as is made clear in the Address of the Commission on Presenting the Project of Constitution to the Constituent Congress on 14 June 1823, where it was stated that '[t]he Peruvian Nation . . . is, from circumstances of a local nature, composed of distinct divisions which the former Government denominated Provinces, and subjected to the authority of the Viceroy': 10 BFSP 668.

118 W. H. Riker, *Federalism, Origin, Operation, Significance*, Boston, Little, Brown & Co, 1964, pp. 41–3.

119 9 BFSP 698–723. Virtually identical provisions were stipulated in two earlier constitutions of 17 December 1819 (Article II): 9 BFSP 407–9, and 12 July 1821 (Article V): 9 BFSP 696–8, as well as subsequent constitutions of 29 April 1830 (Article IV): 17 BFSP 1198–220, and 29 February 1832 (Article II): 19 BFSP 911–41.

120 20 BFSP 1206–11 (Article II).

121 18 BFSP 1065–76.

122 32 BFSP 1160–86. Subsequent Venezuelan constitutions stipulated virtually identical provisions: 22 May 1858 (Article II): 48 BFSP 1250–67; 8 May 1863 (Article III): 53 BFSP 286–306.

boundaries could be amended by treaty with neighbouring states 'without reference to the principle of *uti possidetis* recognized in 1810'.[123] Article 5 of the Venezuelan constitution of 1830 declared that the territory of Venezuela consisted of 'all that which, previously to the political changes of 1810, was denominated the Captain-Generalship of Venezuela'.[124] Article II of Ecuador's constitution of 9 June 1869 referred to Ecuador's territory as being the 'Ancient Presidency of Quito'.[125]

In the Federal Republic of Central America, the Declaration of Independence of 1 July 1823 referred to the territory of the new state as being constituted by 'the Provinces of the ancient Kingdom of Guatemala'.[126] In its constitution of 22 November 1824, Article V declared that the federation's territory was 'that which formerly composed the Ancient Kingdom of Guatemala, with the exception, for the present, of the Province of Chiapas'.[127] Following the collapse of the federation in 1838, the principle of *uti possidetis* was reflected in the constitutions of some of the five successor states. In its constitutions of 22 November 1848,[128] 26 December 1859,[129] 15 April 1869[130] and 7 December 1871,[131] Costa Rica defined its boundary with Colombia as that 'of the *uti possidetis* of 1826'. Honduras, in its constitutions of 11 January 1839,[132] 8 February 1848[133] and 28 September 1865,[134] claimed that the former colonial province of Honduras constituted the territory of the independent state of Honduras. El Salvador in its constitution of 18 February 1841 defined its boundaries as being 'composed of the ancient provinces of San Salvador, Tonsonate, San Vincente, and San Miguel'.[135]

Treaties

The principle of *uti possidetis* was also embodied in a number of the early treaties between the new states that emerged after the wars of independence.[136] In an 1811

123 77 BFSP 836–71.

124 18 BFSP 1119–52. Subsequent Venezuelan constitutions stipulated virtually identical provisions: 24 December 1858 (Article III): 50 BFSP 1341–62; 28 March 1864 (Article III): 57 BFSP 471–89; 27 May 1874 (Article 3): 69 BFSP 1148–68; 27 April 1881 (Article 3): 72 BFSP 977–1000; 21 June 1893: 85 BFSP 1203-31. All of Venezuela's constitutions to date have contained similar stipulations: O. V. Masot, *The Gulf of Venezuela: A Case Study of Historic Waters*, Carácas, Editorial Arte, 1991, pp. 72–4.

125 59 BFSP 1229–46. A similar provision was stipulated in the constitution of 14 February 1884 (Article 2): 77 BFSP 1295–317.

126 11 BFSP 874–5.

127 13 BFSP 725–47.

128 37 BFSP 777–93 (Article VII).

129 50 BFSP 1092–111 (Article IV).

130 59 BFSP 216–35 (Article III).

131 63 BFSP 294–313 (Article III).

132 30 BFSP 1192–207 (Article IV).

133 36 BFSP 1086–104 (Article IV).

134 58 BFSP 287–305 (Article V).

135 29 BFSP 206–22 (Article I).

136 Hyde, note 15, vol. 1, p. 499. Ireland's contention that the principle of *uti possidetis* was not embodied in any of the early treaties between the new Latin American states is mistaken: Ireland, note 29, p. 327.

treaty between Venezuela and New Granada, the parties agreed that the boundaries would be those of the former Captaincy-General of Venezuela and Viceroyalty of New Granada.[137] In the Treaty of Alliance between Peru and Chile of 26 April 1823, Article IX stated:

> For greater security of payment, the Government of Peru pledges in favor of the State of Chile, first the sums received from the cited loans contract of London in favor of Peru, and subsidiarily all the fiscal income of the Peruvian Republic, including all the extent of its territory as it was under the Spanish dominion, comprised in the ancient Viceroyalty of Peru in January 1810.[138]

Similar provisions were found in treaties between Colombia and Mexico in 1823,[139] Colombia and the Republic of Central America in 1825,[140] and Gran Colombia and Peru in 1829.[141] The latter treaty was reaffirmed in the Treaty of Peace, Friendship and Alliance of 25 January 1860 between Peru and Ecuador, which in Article VI provided for a boundary commission to fix a boundary line, and went on to stipulate:

> In the meantime they accept for such boundaries those which arise from the *uti possidetis*, acknowledged in Article V of the Treaty of September 22, 1829, between Columbia and Peru, and which were those of the ancient Vice-Royalties of Peru and Santa Fé, according to the Royal Decree of July 15, 1802.[142]

Problems in applying *uti possidetis*

In *El Salvador/Honduras* the Chamber observed that, even though the principle of *uti possidetis* was important in providing many certain and stable boundaries in Latin America, in cases of unsettled boundaries its application in resolving boundary disputes was itself 'the subject of dispute'.[143] Such boundary disputes were often difficult to resolve. Two particular problems were immediately apparent. The first was in the actual determination of colonial boundaries as they existed at the time of independence. The second problem arose because of the two different meanings which *uti possidetis* acquired.

137 Lalonde, note 13, p. 28.
138 Quoted in Hyde, note 15, vol. 1, p. 499.
139 73 CTS 493–6, Article VII, 31 December 1823.
140 75 CTS 149–59, Article V, 15 March 1825.
141 80 CTS 97–109, Article V, 22 September 1929.
142 50 BFSP 1086–92.
143 *Case Concerning the Land, Island and Maritime Frontier Dispute* (*El Salvador/Honduras*) [1992] ICJ Rep. 383, at 386.

Inadequate or non-existent documentary evidence of boundaries

The problem of precisely establishing boundaries at the time of independence was due to the fact that much of the territory of Latin America was unexplored and unmapped. Hence, the imperial decrees, proclamations and other declarations purporting to establish the limits of any territorial unit were only abstract lines delimiting the various colonial entities in Hispanic America. This stemmed from the fact that Spanish sovereigns usually named natural features such as mountains and deserts as boundaries.[144] In the words of Talbott, 'frontier areas rather than definite boundary lines were established in the colonial period'.[145] As such, they often failed to indicate even approximately accurate boundaries.[146] This factor severely impeded the utility of *uti possidetis*. As McEwen has aptly observed:

> [A] doctrine which attempts to crystallize, or maintain the status quo of, boundaries is little more than an abstract proposition unless there is factual and tangible identification of the boundaries themselves. At the time of independence in Latin America, this was seldom the case.[147]

The fact that much of Spanish America was unoccupied and unexplored was clearly recognised by the new states themselves. In the *Boundary Case Between Bolivia and Peru*[148] it was observed that:

> [I]n reality the disputed zone was, in 1810 and up to a recent period, perfectly unexplored, as appears from the numerous maps of the colonial period and of periods subsequent to the latter, which were submitted by both parties, and this the latter themselves recognize, which explains that the demarcations of the said administrative entities, subject to one and the same Sovereign, had not been fully determined.[149]

Thus, in areas where there were no maps in existence, or where no colonial

144 By necessity this practice was initially adopted by the new Latin American states. Thus, in the first Chilean constitution the northern boundary or limits of the state was defined simply as 'the Desert of Atacama': Dennis, note 33, p. 11–12.

145 Talbott, note 81, p. vii.

146 *Honduras Borders (Guatemala/Honduras)* (1933) 2 RIAA 1307, at 1325; *The Beagle Channel Arbitration* (1977) 52 ILR 93, at 645. Chile's boundaries as at 1810 were defined in terms of boundary areas rather than boundary lines. After independence Chile's constitutions of 1811, 1812, 1818, 1822, 1823, 1828 and 1833 all defined Chilean boundaries in terms of geographical areas rather than demarcated lines: Talbott, note 81, pp. 3–15, 21–9.

147 A. C. McEwen, *International Boundaries of East Africa*, Oxford, Clarendon Press, 1971, p. 28.

148 *Boundary Case Between Bolivia and Peru* (1902) 11 RIAA 133.

149 Ibid., at 143. See also *Honduras Borders (Guatemala/Honduras)* (1933) 2 RIAA 1307, at 1325; *Case Concerning the Land, Island and Maritime Frontier Dispute (El Salvador/Honduras)* [1992] ICJ Rep. 383, at 380.

occupation had occurred, the application of *uti possidetis* was not possible and other means of resolving disputes had to be utilised.[150] Such areas included the Patagonia region which was subject to competing Argentinian and Chilean claims,[151] the Tacna-Arica provinces which were the subject of a dispute between Chile and Peru,[152] and the El Chaco region which was subject to competing Argentinian and Paraguayan claims.[153] In areas where documents and maps existed but were either contradictory or unclear the application of *uti possidetis* became problematical. As the Chamber in *El Salvador/Honduras* observed:

> It is rather as if the disputed boundaries must be construed like a jig-saw puzzle from certain already cut pieces so that the extent and location of the resulting boundary depend upon the size and shape of the fitting piece.[154]

Even where administrative boundaries did exist, they were often of different degrees and kinds. As the Chamber observed in *El Salvador/Honduras*:

> To apply [the principle of *uti possidetis*] is not easy when, as in Spanish Central America, there were administrative boundaries of different kinds or degrees; for example, besides 'provinces' (a term of which the meaning was different at different periods), there were *Alcadias Mayores* and *Corregimientos* and later on, in the 18th century, *Intendencias*, as well as the territorial jurisdictions of a higher court (*Audiencias*), Captaincies-General and Vice-Royalties. . . . Furthermore, the jurisdictions of general administrative bodies such as those referred to did not necessarily coincide in territorial scope with those of [sic] bodies possessing particular or special jurisdictions, e.g., military commands. Besides, in addition to the various civil territorial jurisdictions, general or special, there were ecclesiastical jurisdictions, which were supposed to be

150 S. B. Jones, *Boundary-Making: A Handbook for Statesmen, Treaty Editors and Boundary Commissioners*, Washington, DC, Carnegie Endowment for International Peace, 1945, pp. 52–3; D. P. O'Connell, *International Law*, Volume 1, London, Stevens & Sons Ltd, 1965, p. 491.

151 C. Escude, 'Argentine Territorial Nationalism', *Journal of Latin American Studies*, 1988, vol. 20, pp. 145–50.

152 The arbitrator in the Tacna-Arica dispute said: 'It is quite apparent that the representatives of the Parties who negotiated the treaty had little exact knowledge of the geography of the region to the east and wrote into the treaty an inaccurate description. It should also be said that there has not been furnished to the Arbitrator satisfactory evidence as to the exact line of the old Peruvian provincial boundaries. The record is strikingly deficient in appropriate maps and geographical information bearing upon these questions': *Tacna-Arica Question* (1925) 2 RIAA 921, at 954.

153 Moore, note 97, vol. II, p. 1924. In the case of the boundary dispute between Chile and Bolivia, '[b]oth governments gave proof of ownership dating back to the colonial period and invoked the principle of *uti possidetis* of 1810. The appeal to colonial documents was no help because the disputed area was one of those unimportant border areas which was not definitely assigned to any administrative sub-division of South America': Talbott, note 81, p. 3.

154 *Case Concerning the Land, Island and Maritime Frontier Dispute* (*El Salvador/Honduras*) [1992] ICJ Rep. 383, at 388.

> followed in principle, pursuant to general legislation, by the territorial jurisdiction of the main civil administrative units in Spanish America.[155]

Applying the principle of *uti possidetis* was very difficult when states claimed territory on the basis of overlapping and conflicting colonial administrative boundaries.

Competing meanings of uti possidetis

A further difficulty with the application of *uti possidetis* concerned the two different meanings ascribed to it. On one interpretation, *uti possidetis* referred to territory to which a state had legal rights of possession based upon former Spanish instruments. This interpretation was known as *uti possidetis juris*. The alternative meaning granted legal title based upon territory actually possessed and administered by the colonial unit at the time of independence. This interpretation was known as *uti possidetis de facto*. The assumption involved in the original use of *uti possidetis* in Hispanic America was that it was possible to accurately determine the borders of colonial administrative units. As previously noted, this was often not the case. In many cases, at the time of cessation of Spanish rule, colonial administrative authorities in fact exercised control beyond an apparent border.[156] In the boundary disputes that followed independence, states in the former Spanish American colonies chose the interpretation that was most helpful in any given claim.[157] The same state would in different disputes argue for differing interpretations of *uti possidetis*.[158]

In most cases in Hispanic America the states adopted *uti possidetis juris* as the basis of resolving boundary disputes. In a separate opinion in *El Salvador/Honduras*, Judge Torres Bernárdez noted:

> By virtue of the Spanish-American Republics' *uti possidetis juris* principle the colonial administrative boundaries of Spanish *virreinatos*, *capitanias*, *intendencias* or *provincias* became international boundaries between neighbouring Spanish-American States as from the very date of independence. This also means that 'possession' was *not* defined in terms of effective possession or occupation but by reference to the former Spanish legislation as ascertainable through the relevant *Reales Cédulas*, *Providencias*, *Ordenanzas*, etc., or indirectly from Spanish colonial documents recording '*colonial effectivités*', namely the exercise of territorial jurisdiction by Spanish authorities. It therefore confers preference on '*el derecho*' (the Spanish legislation) over '*el hecho*' (effective possession or occupation). Thus the concept of 'possession' embodied in the *uti possidetis juris* principle of the Spanish-American Republics is the concept of the right to

155 Ibid., at 387.

156 A. O. Cukwurah, *The Settlement of Boundary Disputes in International Law*, Manchester, Manchester University Press, 1967, pp. 114–15; Nelson, note 46, p. 270.

157 *Honduras Borders* (*Guatemala/Honduras*) (1933) 2 RIAA 1307, at 1322–3; Ireland, note 85, p. 359.

158 Sharma, note 96, p. 120, citing the example of Venezuela.

> possess according to Spanish legislation ('title') and not a reflection of factual situations of usurpations by former Spanish colonial authorities, such as might have existed, or of the fact of occupation or control by this or that Spanish-American Republic following independence (the *de facto* situations).[159]

However, even though *uti possidetis juris* was the general rule applied in Hispanic America, it would be a mistake to presume that, in its application, considerations based upon *uti possidetis de facto* were totally excluded. As Moore has observed:

> To say that the word 'juris' excludes altogether the consideration of possession *de facto*, is to make the word destructive. The judgment of '*uti possidetis*' cannot be predicated of a situation from which the thought of continued physical possession is wholly excluded. Such a use of the terms would be wholly fanciful.[160]

Moore further observed that if *uti possidetis juris* were to be the only basis upon which boundary issues could be resolved in Hispanic America, the effect would be 'to leave countries of Spanish-America for the most part without any basis for the fixing of their limits'.[161]

Moore's first observation is confirmed by the arbitral award of the King of Spain of 1891[162] in the dispute between Venezuela and Colombia which was, according to a treaty of 14 September 1881,[163] to be determined on the basis of the *uti possidetis* of 1810. By an additional protocol of 15 February 1886, it was stipulated that the arbiter could 'fix the line in the way which he thinks the closest to the existing documents when, in one or another part of the line, those documents are not sufficiently clear'.[164] In relation to two sections of the disputed boundary both parties relied on the same imperial Royal Warrant of 1768 to advance their conflicting claims. The arbitrator ruled that the Royal Warrant's terms were not clear and precise, and he invoked the provision in the 1886 additional protocol ruling that Venezuela was 'in *bona fide* possession' of the relevant territories 'which form the boundaries . . . assigned in the . . . Royal Warrant of 1768'. Furthermore, Venezuelan interest in the relevant territories was 'encouraged by the confident belief that they were established in the dominions of the United States of Venezuela'. Finally, the relevant territories were bounded by certain rivers, and the arbiter expressed the view that the rivers traced 'a clear, definite and natural

159 *Case Concerning the Land, Island and Maritime Frontier Dispute* (*El Salvador/Honduras*) [1992] ICJ Rep. 383, at 635, per sep. op. Judge Torres Bernárdez.

160 Moore, note 2, p. 350.

161 Ibid.

162 *Arbitral Award About the Limits Between Venezuela and Colombia*, 16 March 1891, 83 BFSP 387; Ireland, note 29, p. 210–11; Moore, note 2, pp. 351–2.

163 73 BFSP 1107–8; Masot, note 124, pp. 169–70; Ireland, note 29, p. 209.

164 Ad Referendum Act of Paris of 15 February 1886, between Venezuela and Colombia; 77 BFSP 1012–13; Moore, note 2, p. 351.

frontier'.[165] Thus, the boundary allocation, although to be decided upon the *uti possidetis juris* of 1810, did in fact include elements of *uti possidetis de facto*.[166]

The boundary dispute between El Salvador and Honduras is also a case in which, although the parties agreed that the dispute was to be resolved by virtue of *uti possidetis juris*, the principles of *uti possidetis de facto* were applied in determining the *uti possidetis juris*. In that case the parties and arbitral chamber referred to '*effectivités*', rather than *uti possidetis de facto*, but it is clear that the two expressions are synonymous. This is evident in the separate opinion of Judge Torres Bernárdez, who, after describing the meaning of *uti possidetis juris* as based on possession according to 'Spanish Legislation', and distinguishing it from *effectivités* or possession according to 'factual situations', declared that 'this distinguishes the *uti possidetis juris* from the Brazilian *uti possidetis* or from the so-called *uti possidetis de facto*'.[167]

In *El Salvador/Honduras*, although the parties agreed that the *uti possidetis juris* was the basis of the delimitation of the disputed boundary, in some areas the sovereign acts of the Spanish crown did not determine the boundary line. In such a situation the Chamber observed:

> What the Chamber has to do in respect of the land frontier is to arrive at a conclusion as to the position of the 1821 *uti possidetis juris* boundary; to this end it cannot but take into account . . . the colonial *effectivités* as reflected in the documentary evidence of the colonial period submitted by the Parties. The Chamber may have regard also, in certain circumstances, to documentary evidence of post-independence *effectivités* when it considers that they afford indications in respect of the 1821 *uti possidetis juris* boundary, providing a relationship exists between the *effectivités* concerned and the determination of the boundary.[168]

The Chamber, in dealing with title to a number of islands in the Gulf of Fonseca, relied exclusively on post-independence *effectivités*. In relation to the islands the Chamber ruled:

> Possession backed by the exercise of sovereignty may be taken as evidence confirming the *uti possidetis juris* title . . . [I]n the case of the islands, where historical material of colonial times is confused and contradictory, and the accession to independence was not immediately followed by unambiguous acts

165 *Arbitral Award About the Limits Between Venezuela and Colombia*, 16 March 1891, in Moore, note 97, vol. V, p. 4860.

166 The 1891 award was not accepted by Venezuela. It continued to be the subject of further negotiations between the two states and was the subject of further award in 1922. For details of the post-award negotiations, see Ireland, note 29, pp. 211–19; Masot, note 124, pp. 75–93.

167 *Case Concerning the Land, Island and Maritime Frontier Dispute* (*El Salvador/Honduras*) [1992] ICJ Rep. 383, at 635, per sep. op. Judge Torres Bernárdez.

168 Ibid., at 399.

of sovereignty, that is practically the only way in which the *uti possidetis juris* could find formal expression so as to be judicially recognized and determined.[169]

Thus, *El Salvador/Honduras* confirms Moore's observation that the determination of the *uti possidetis juris* could not entirely be divorced from considerations of *uti possidetis de facto*, or *effectivités*, to use the terminology of the arbitral chamber.

Moore's second observation is confirmed by the resolution of the dispute between Argentina and Paraguay over a portion of the El Chaco region. At the time of independence from Spain the El Chaco region was unmapped and not clearly assigned to a particular colonial entity. It was not populated by Spanish colonists, except for some Spanish fugitives. After independence Paraguay occupied the region and, in part, based its claim to it on the fact of occupation, that is, *uti possidetis de facto*.[170] Argentina invoked the principle of *uti possidetis juris* and claimed that it was legally entitled to it based on royal Spanish decrees.[171] Most of the Argentinian–Paraguayan boundary dispute was resolved by the Treaty of Limits of 3 February 1876.[172] However, one part of the disputed El Chaco region was to be resolved by arbitration. The treaty did not mention the rules or principles by which the arbitrator was to decide the dispute. No mention was made of *uti possidetis* in either form. The award of President Rutherford B. Hayes of 13 November 1878[173] declared that the area in dispute 'legally and justly' belonged to Paraguay. No reasons were given in the short arbitral award, but given the result, it would suggest that the arbitrator applied the principle of *uti possidetis de facto*, thereby confirming Paraguay's long period of occupation of the territory. In light of the undefined nature of Argentina's claim, based upon the principle of *uti possidetis juris*, it is clear that whatever the reasoning behind the arbitrator's award, it was not based upon application of *uti possidetis juris*. Given that the application of *uti possidetis juris* was not possible, another principle, arguably that of *uti possidetis de facto*, was applied.

In the case of Brazil's boundary disputes with its Hispanic neighbours, the former consistently based its territorial claims on *uti possidetis de facto*.[174] In so doing Brazil followed the approach taken by Portugal during the colonial era. The Spanish–Portuguese division of South America was initially formalised by the Papal Bull of 1493 and subsequently revised by the Treaty of Tordesillas in 1494. Precise demarcation of the boundary line was impossible, until the early eighteenth century, because of inadequate cartographic techniques.[175] Aggressive penetration

169 Ibid., at 566.
170 Moore, note 97, vol. II, pp. 1932–3.
171 Ibid., pp. 1936–9.
172 68 BFSP 97–100, Moore, note 97, vol. V, pp. 4783–5.
173 Reprinted in Moore, note 97, vol. II, pp. 1943–4.
174 Cukwurah, note 156, p. 115; Nelson, note 46, p. 270; *Case Concerning the Territorial Dispute (Libyan Arab Jamahiriya/Chad)* [1994] ICJ Rep. 6, at 86, per sep. op. Judge Ajibola.
175 D. M. Davidson, 'How the Brazilian West Was Won: Freelance & State on the Mato Grosso Frontier, 1737–1752', in D. Alden (ed.), *Colonial Roots of Modern Brazil*, Berkeley, CA, University of California Press, 1973, p. 67.

by Portuguese traders and Jesuit missionaries across the Tordesillas line into Spanish America, especially during the Spanish–Portuguese Union between 1580 and 1640, eventually led to an attempt to establish a new boundary by the terms of the Treaty of Madrid in 1750.[176] Dissatisfaction with this treaty led to its annulment in 1761.[177] However, a new boundary line was established by the Treaty of San Ildefonso in 1777. This treaty reflected the expansionist programme of the Portuguese commercial and missionary interests, and was seen by Spain as a means by which further Portuguese penetration into Spanish America would end. The San Ildefonso boundary gave Portugal legal title, based upon occupation, to territory more than twice the size of territory conferred by the Treaty of Tordesillas.[178] However, the agreed boundary lines were never subjected to survey and demarcation as stipulated by the treaty.[179]

All the various boundary treaties between Spain and Portugal reflected the principle of *uti possidetis de facto*. Portuguese expansionism rendered each treaty in turn unrealistic as a *de facto* division of territory. This expansion soon rendered the San Ildefonso line inappropriate. With the passing of the colonial era Brazil pursued its former colonial master's expansionist activities at the expense of the successor states to Spanish America. Brazil insisted on the principle of *uti possidetis de facto* as the basis of territorial delimitation between herself and the new Hispanic states. The latter consistently argued *uti possidetis juris*, based on the Treaty of San Ildefonso, as the appropriate basis of resolving boundary disputes. Brazil argued that the Treaty was no longer in force, claiming it had been revoked in 1801. With the void thus created, Brazil argued that the relevant *uti possidetis* principle was that based upon actual possession.[180] Brazil's acceptance of the principle of *uti possidetis* occurred only upon the signing of treaties with its Hispanic neighbours.[181] These treaty provisions invariably referred to *uti possidetis*, without clearly indicating whether they meant *de jure* or *de facto*. However, Brazil consistently pressed an interpretation of these treaties consistent with *uti possidetis de facto*. For instance, following its 1857 treaty with Argentina, Brazil asserted that its acceptance of *uti possidetis* was on the basis that 'there was no intention of prejudging by that clause the *facts of possession* on the part of each nation'[182] (emphasis added).

176 Ibid., pp. 101–2.

177 Fifer, note 76, pp. 94–5; Moore, note 2, p. 335. On Portuguese expansionism, see Crow, note 37, pp. 368–71.

178 Fifer, note 76, p. 95.

179 Moore, note 2, p. 335; Ireland, note 29, p. 12.

180 Bernárdez, note 36, pp. 429–30; J. Castellino, *International Law and Self-Determination*, The Hague, Martinus Nijhoff Publishers, 2000, pp. 112–13.

181 Brazil entered into border treaties which incorporated the principle of *uti possidetis*, with Argentina (14 December 1857): 49 BFSP 1316–19 (Article IV); Bolivia (27 March 1867): 59 BFSP 1161–9 (Article II); Colombia (24 April 1907): 100 BFSP 810–12; Paraguay (6 April 1856): 46 BFSP 1299–304; Peru (23 October 1851): 42 BFSP 1308–12 (Article VII); Uruguay (12 October 1851): 40 BFSP 1151–4 (Article II) and supplementary treaty (15 May 1852) 40 BFSP 1145–50 (Article I); and Venezuela (25 November 1852): 49 BFSP 1213–15 (Article II).

182 Quoted in Moore, note 2, p. 336.

Brazil's disputes with its Hispanic neighbours were finally determined in its favour, reflecting the principle of *uti possidetis de facto*. In this way Brazil gained legal confirmation, based upon occupation, of its territorial expansion during the nineteenth century.[183] This effectively negated the boundary line established by the Treaty of San Ildefonso, which, if the principle of *uti possidetis juris* had been applied, would have been the boundary between Brazil and her Hispanic neighbours.[184] The principle of *uti possidetis juris* applied only, and then not always, in cases of boundary disputes involving states that emerged from Spain's colonial empire in the Americas.

In Brazil's boundary dispute with Great Britain over whether the Pirara region belonged to British Guyana or Brazil, the principle of *uti possidetis de facto* was applied. Article 4 of an arbitration treaty of 6 November 1901[185] stipulated that the arbitrator was to determine the dispute according to 'such principles of international law as he shall determine to be applicable to the case'. In his award of 6 June 1904,[186] King Victor Emmanuel III ruled that sovereignty over the disputed territory must be determined by effective, uninterrupted and permanent possession. This amounted to an application of *uti possidetis de facto* in relation to those areas where either party had established effective and permanent possession. In relation to the remaining areas, territory was divided according to principles of equity. This approach was inevitable given that claims based on historical and legal rights did not fix with any precision the limits of either party's sovereignty. The award resulted in just over 40 per cent of the disputed territory being awarded to Brazil.[187]

The problem of the competing interpretations of *uti possidetis* were summed up by Ireland who wrote:

> [I]t may be pointed out here that merely to invoke the *uti possidetis* at a given time does not of itself determine the solution of conflicting claims, since the boundaries as set down on paper of an administrative, judicial, or even ecclesiastical division often differ materially from the lines to which permanent occupation or occasional jurisdictional authority has actually been carried. Hence properly to settle a controversy by this doctrine it is commonly necessary first to know to which greater weight is to be given, possession *de jure* or possession *de facto*.[188]

183 These disputes included ones with Argentina, Bolivia, Colombia, Paraguay, Peru, Uruguay and Venezuela and are discussed in detail in Ireland, note 29, pp. 10–17, 40–53, 109–15, 117–23, 123–30, 130–8 and 138–44 respectively.

184 *The Minquiers and Ecrehos Case* (*France/United Kingdom*) [1953] ICJ Rep. 4, at 104–5, per sep. op. Judge M. Levi Carneiro.

185 94 BFSP 23–9.

186 *The Guiana Boundary Case* (1904) 11 RIAA 10.

187 Brazil's disputes with France and the Netherlands were effectively resolved by negotiated treaties. These resulted, especially in the case of the dispute with France, in substantial parts of the territories in dispute being awarded to Brazil. On these disputes, see Ireland, note 29, pp. 144–51, 158–60.

188 Ibid., p. 329.

The importance of boundary treaties

In the resolution of boundary disputes in Latin America prior to 1986, the legally binding nature of *uti possidetis* depended upon its being specifically fixed by treaty as the basis for resolving a dispute. If the relevant states did not stipulate that the principle of *uti possidetis* applied as the basis of establishing boundaries or of resolving boundary disputes, it was not relevant.[189] Thus, Articles 1 and 2 of the arbitration convention of 10 April 1897[190] between Brazil and France, stipulated that the arbitrator had simply to decide which of two versions of the boundary line between Brazil and French Guyana was applicable. In the treaty of 5 May 1906[191] between Brazil and the Netherlands the frontier between Brazil and Surinam was actually determined by the treaty itself. In both of these cases the principle of *uti possidetis* was effectively excluded as a basis of resolving the boundary dispute in question.

If a treaty referred to boundaries being based upon former colonial boundaries, then the principle of *uti possidetis* was given legal force. Any arbitrator appointed by such a treaty was bound to apply *uti possidetis* on the basis of the principle in arbitration that the state parties to a dispute can determine the rules of law upon which the arbitrator is to determine the award.[192] In the words of Bloomfield, the principle of *uti possidetis* was one by which:

> the American Republics have decided to adjust their boundary differences. But in no case has the International Community recognized, as an institution of international law, the principle of *uti possidetis*. It remains . . .

189 'It should be observed that the term *uti possidetis* was in reality a description of a practice that was being roughly followed. The Latin American States of Spanish origin did not at the time regard the phrase ... as expressive of a legal principle to which they owed deference or were endeavouring to conform in the establishment of new frontiers. . . . [T]he American Republics of Spanish origin felt no obligation to agree to respect and were not in fact disposed to respect, a boundary line laid down by the Monarch even in the last monarchical hour if for any reason it did not correspond with what revolutionary or post-revolutionary acts served to place within the control of neighbouring States': Hyde, note 15, vol. 1, pp. 501, 507. 'It must be emphasized that the principle [of *uti possidetis*] is by no means mandatory and the states concerned are free to adopt other principles as the basis of settlement': I. Brownlie, *Principles of Public International Law*, 5th edition, Oxford, Oxford University Press, 1998, p. 133. Bello also states that the principle of *uti possidetis* was not mandatory, but he overstates his case with the assertion that it was 'broadly ignored' and 'hardly entertained in any treaty contemplating arbitration': E. G. Bello, 'The Effects of the Application of the Uti Possidetis Principle in Africa', *Proceedings of the Second Amsterdam International Law Conference on the Rights of Peoples and Minorities in International Law*, Amsterdam, 18–20 June 1992, pp. 2, 3, 28.

190 90 BFSP 952–3.

191 99 BFSP 932–3.

192 H-J. Schlochauer, 'Arbitration', in R. Bernhardt (ed.), *Encyclopedia of Public International Law*, vol. 1, Amsterdam, North-Holland, 1992, p. 224; Shearer, note 8, p. 444. It was on the basis of this principle that any decision on the basis of principles of equity was ruled out in *Case Concerning the Land, Island and Maritime Frontier Dispute* (*El Salvador/Honduras*) [1992] ICJ Rep. 383, at 390–1.

> derogatory to general international law, which insists on occupation as a basis for sovereignty. A rule derogating to generally accepted customary international law is *binding only on those persons which have, by a convention, expressly agreed to it.*[193] (Emphasis added)

If a treaty's stipulations as to the principles upon which a boundary dispute was to be resolved were not adhered to by the arbitral body, this was sufficient ground for the resulting arbitral award being declared void and of no effect.[194]

Since 1986, following the Chamber's decision in *Case Concerning the Frontier Dispute (Burkina Faso -v- Mali)*[195] (the *Frontier Dispute Case*), a treaty need not explicitly stipulate that the principle of *uti possidetis juris* governs a boundary dispute for that principle to apply. In the *Frontier Dispute Case* the Chamber ruled that the principle of *uti possidetis juris* was 'a firmly established principle of international law where decolonization is concerned'.[196] This meant that if, as occurred in *El Salvador/Honduras*,[197] a treaty stipulated that a dispute was to be determined by principles of international law, then the principle of *uti possidetis juris* was to apply if the disputants were former colonies. Prior to 1986 such a treaty provision would not necessarily have invoked the application of the principle of *uti possidetis*. On the other hand, the *Frontier Dispute Case* ruling does not apply if 'parties to the dispute . . . specifically agree to the contrary that the principle of *uti possidetis* should not apply'.[198]

When a treaty stipulated the application of the principle of *uti possidetis* it became the 'first duty'[199] of any appointed tribunal to establish the boundary line according to that principle. If the treaty stipulated other principles as the basis of an arbitral tribunal's basis for determining a boundary dispute, then those principles applied and, by implication, the principle of *uti possidetis* was irrelevant. Thus, the

193 L. M. Bloomfield, *The British Honduras–Guatemala Dispute*, Toronto, The Carswell Company Ltd, 1953, p. 94; L. M. Bloomfield, *Egypt, Israel and the Gulf of Aqaba in International Law*, Toronto, The Carswell Company Ltd, 1957, pp. 107–8; Y. Z. Blum, *Historic Titles in International Law*, The Hague, Martinus Nijhoff, p. 342. Shaw has asserted that '[i]t is beyond question that the principle of *uti possidetis* became established as a binding norm of international law with regard to Latin America': M. N. Shaw, 'Peoples, Territorialism and Boundaries', *European Journal of International Law*, 1997, vol. 8, p. 493. This assertion, on the basis of the following discussion, must be rejected.

194 In *Case Concerning the Arbitral Award Made by the King of Spain on 23 December 1906* (*Honduras -v- Nicaragua*) [1960] ICJ Rep. 192 an application to have an arbiter's award declared void failed because it was not established that the arbiter had failed to adhere to the application of principles stipulated in the relevant treaty.

195 [1986] ICJ Rep. 554.

196 Ibid., at 565.

197 *Case Concerning the Land, Island and Maritime Frontier Dispute* (*El Salvador/Honduras*) [1992] ICJ Rep. 383.

198 *Case Concerning the Territorial Dispute* (*Libyan Arab Jamahiriya/Chad*) [1994] ICJ Rep. 6, at 89, per sep. op. Judge Ajibola; *Dubai-Sharjah Border Arbitration* (1981) 91 ILR 543, at 578; Bernárdez, note 36, pp. 420–1.

199 *Honduras Borders* (*Guatemala/Honduras*) (1933) 2 RIAA 1307, at 1322.

Treaty of Peace, Friendship and Boundaries of 21 July 1938[200] between Bolivia and Paraguay stipulated that principles of equity, subject to certain geographical limits, were to be the basis of the arbitrators' decision in the wake of the Chaco War between the two countries. Accordingly, the principle of *uti possidetis* was of no relevance.[201] Similarly, following Great Britain's forcible appropriation of Venezuelan frontier territory and diplomatic intervention by the USA, an Arbitration Treaty of 2 February 1897[202] between Venezuela and Great Britain was entered into to resolve the boundary dispute between Venezuela and British Guyana. Article IV(a) of the treaty stipulated that the arbitrators had to determine good title to territory on the basis of whether either of the claimants had 'adverse holding or prescription during a period of fifty years'. Further, Article IV(b) stipulated that the arbitrators could recognise claims according to other grounds valid in international law, but only if the rule in Article IV(a) was inapplicable. Following the arbitral award of 3 October 1899[203] which gave the bulk of the contested territory to British Guyana, Venezuela contested the award and claimed it was invalid. One of Venezuela's grounds of complaint against the validity of the award was that Article IV(b) permitted the application of *uti possidetis juris* as the guiding principle. According to Venezuela, if the principle of *uti possidetis juris* applied, the arbitral award was wrong and most of the territory in dispute should have been awarded to Venezuela. However, the problem with the Venezuelan argument was that Article IV(b), and thus the principle of *uti possidetis juris*, was inapplicable if the rule in Article IV(a) was able to determine the dispute. Given that the Guyanan case was governed by the rule in Article IV(a), any argument that *uti possidetis juris* applied was clearly ruled out by the terms of Article IV(b).[204]

If a treaty did not stipulate the principles upon which a boundary dispute was to be resolved, it was up to the arbitral tribunal to determine the relevant principles. In such a case the principle of *uti possidetis* could be a basis upon which an arbitral tribunal made its decision.[205] Such a situation was not common in Central and South America. In the arbitration treaty of 6 November 1901[206] between Brazil and Great Britain over whether the Pirara region belonged to Brazil or British Guyana, Article IV left it to the arbitrator to determine what principles of international law were to be applied. The arbitrator effectively applied the principle of *uti possidetis de facto* to those areas where territory was effectively occupied by either of the parties,

200 Quoted in Hyde, note 15, vol. 1, p. 376–7. An earlier Protocol of 3 August 1894 between Bolivia and Paraguay provided for an equitable agreement to define territorial rights without any discussion or examination of titles, but failing that based upon a discussion and examination of titles: Marchant, note 51, p. 249.

201 Marchant, note 51, pp. 250–1.

202 89 BFSP 57–65; J. A. Braveboy-Wagner, *The Venezuela-Guyana Border Dispute: Britain's Colonial Legacy in Latin America*, Boulder, CO, Westview Press, 1984, pp. 315–19.

203 Braveboy-Wagner, note 202, pp. 319–21.

204 Ibid., pp. 121–3.

205 Masot's assertion that *uti possidetis* is binding only if a treaty stipulates so is thus too broad a statement: Masot, note 124, pp. 51–2.

206 94 BFSP 23–9.

and principles of equity for the rest of the area in dispute. Similarly, in the dispute between Argentina and Paraguay over part of the El Chaco region, the Treaty of Limits of 3 February 1876[207] was completely silent on which principles of international law were to be applied by the arbitrator. The arbitral award of 12 November 1878[208] determined the dispute in favour of Paraguay, but without stating his reasons, although arguably the principle of *uti possidetis de facto* was applied.

In other cases, although the principle of *uti possidetis* may have been a governing principle to a certain date, a boundary treaty could render it irrelevant thereafter. Thus, in the boundary dispute between Argentina and Chile, the Boundary Treaty of 23 July 1881[209] provided a regime for the delimitation of the disputed boundary. In *The Beagle Channel Arbitration* of 18 February 1977, the Tribunal noted that, given that the Boundary Treaty 'was intended to provide, and must be taken as constituting, a complete, definitive and final settlement of all territorial disputes still outstanding at that time', the consequence was that 'the regime created by the 1881 Treaty, whatever it was, superseded and replaced all previous territorial arrangements or understandings between the Parties, together with any former principles governing territorial allocation in Spanish-America'.[210]

It was thus, as the Tribunal further noted, 'no part of its task to pronounce on what would have been the rights of the Parties on the basis of the *uti possidetis* of 1810 because . . . these rights . . . are supposed to have been overtaken and transcended by the regime deriving from the 1881 Treaty'.[211] However, the Tribunal indicated that the principle of *uti possidetis* and the historical record before 1881 could be of relevance in the interpretation of the treaty.[212]

However, the above examples were more the exception than the rule. Because of the considerable acceptance of the idea that former colonial boundaries should form the basis of international boundaries, the principle of *uti possidetis* was often incorporated into boundary treaties. These treaties were common from the latter half of the nineteenth century when boundary disputes became more prominent in Latin America. Incorporation was usually by reference to the disputant parties agreeing that their territories extended to the boundaries of some former imperial unit of administration. Incorporation by the use of the expression '*uti possidetis*' was much rarer.[213] After 1986 incorporation of *uti possidetis* resulted from a reference in the treaty to principles of international law.

207 68 BFSP 97–100.

208 Reprinted in Moore, note 97, vol. II, pp. 1943–4.

209 72 BFSP 1103–5.

210 *The Beagle Channel Arbitration* (1977) 52 ILR 93, at 123–4.

211 Ibid., at 125. Earlier at 125–6 the Tribunal had noted that prior to 1881 territorial issues were *prima facie* governed by the *uti possidetis* of 1810.

212 Ibid., at 125–6.

213 Explicit use of the words '*uti possidetis*' is found in treaties between Peru and Ecuador, 25 January 1860, 50 BFSP 1086–92 (Article VI); Columbia and Venezuela, 14 September 1881, Preamble, 73 BFSP 1107–8; Bolivia and Peru, Article 8, 21 November 1901, *American Journal of International Law (Supplement)*, 1909, vol. 3, pp. 378–81; Guatemala and Honduras, 16 July 1930, Article V, 132 BFSP 823–5.

However, in some of these cases the express or implied references to the principle of *uti possidetis* were irrelevant. This was so, even though the treaty may have referred to *uti possidetis juris* as the guiding principle, because the relevant boundary areas in dispute were either not occupied by the relevant colonial power and/or they were not the subject of imperial acts or maps. The examples of the Bolivia–Peru boundary, the Argentina–Chile boundary and the El Salvador–Honduras boundary are illustrative.

In the Bolivia–Peru boundary dispute, following a number of treaties[214] aimed at resolving the boundary issues, a final Treaty of Arbitration was signed on 30 December 1902.[215] Article I of the treaty referred the boundary dispute to arbitration and invoked the principle of *uti possidetis juris* of 1810 by referring to the boundaries of the two states as being the territories within the 'jurisdiction or district' of either the Audiencia of Charcas or the Viceroyalty of Peru 'in virtue of the enactments of the former Sovereign'. Article V invoked *uti possidetis juris* by stipulating that 'the rights over territory exercised by one of the High Contracting Parties shall not be a bar to or prevail against titles or royal dispositions establishing the contrary'. By Article II, the entire Bolivia–Peru boundary was subject to arbitration pursuant to the treaty, with the exception of the boundary immediately north and south of, and including, the Lake Titicaca region. In *The Boundary Case Between Bolivia and Peru*[216] in 1909, it was noted that 'the Royal Acts and dispositions, which were in force in 1810, did not define in a clear manner the ownership of the disputed territory'.[217] This conclusion flowed from a finding that the evidence presented by both sides showed that, in 1810, the disputed areas were 'perfectly unexplored', with the consequence that the 'demarcation of the said administrative entities, subject to one and the same Sovereign, had not been fully determined'.[218] The arbitrator was left to determine the boundary on other grounds. The arbitral award was so unsatisfactory to both states that it was subsequently adjusted by voluntary agreements.[219] As for the Lake Titicaca region, a treaty between Bolivia and Peru of 23 September 1902[220] provided that if the parties could not resolve the dispute by means of a mixed demarcation commission, it was to be referred to arbitration. In 1932 the Commissioners did reach a demarcation agreement that divided the area, especially the Copacabana peninsula, by using the criterion of the nationality of the resident population.[221]

In the Argentina–Chile boundary dispute, Article XXXIX of the Treaty of Friendship, Commerce and Navigation of 30 August 1855[222] referred to the

214 Treaties were entered into in 1826 (not ratified), 1831, 1839, 1847, 1848, 1863, and 1886: Ireland, note 29, pp. 95–102.

215 100 BFSP 803–4.

216 (1909) 11 RIAA 133.

217 Ibid., at 144.

218 Ibid., at 143.

219 Ireland, note 29, p. 109.

220 Ibid., pp. 102–3.

221 Fifer, note 76, pp. 78–81.

222 49 BFSP 1200–13.

boundary between the two states as being those the two states possessed as such at the time of separating from Spanish dominion in 1810. This reference to the *uti possidetis* of 1810 'offered no solution of the problem, for throughout the dependency period the territory had not been inhabited by any Spaniards, and neither the viceroys of Buenos Aires nor the captains-general of Chile had concerned themselves about it'.[223] A further Boundary Treaty of 23 July 1881,[224] after specifically referring to Article XXXIX of the 1855 Treaty, went on to stipulate the boundary between the two states. An Additional and Explanatory Protocol of the 1881 Treaty of 1 May 1893[225] provided for the precise demarcation of the lines provided for by the 1881 Treaty. By the terms of an agreement of 17 April 1896 provision was made for arbitration of disputes relating to the demarcation.[226] Four regions in dispute were referred to arbitration in *The Cordillera of the Andes Boundary Case* of 1902.[227] The areas in dispute were those in which the orographical and hydrographical lines did not coincide. Argentina argued that the 1881 treaty referred to the orographical line as the boundary. Chile argued that the hydrographical line was the true boundary. The arbitrator ruled that the 1881 treaty was ambiguous. The arbitrator did not determine the issue by simply choosing one of the competing interpretations of the 1881 treaty. Rather, the determination was expressed to be one 'which would best interpret the intention of the diplomatic instruments submitted [for] consideration'.[228] The principle of *uti possidetis* was of no relevance in either the arbitral award or any of the three treaties and agreements that preceded it. The arbitral award was based upon considerations relating to the value of the disputed territory, the nationality of the occupants and the advantages of having a good strategic boundary.[229]

Following the 1902 arbitral award, further arbitration was necessary because of a geographical mistake in the award. The *Argentine–Chile Frontier Case*[230] resolved the competing claims over an area of 478 square kilometres in the Palena region immediately to the north of Lake General Paz. Almost the entire disputed zone which was populated and farmed by Chileans was awarded to Chile.[231]

223 Ireland, note 29, p. 22.
224 72 BFSP 1103–5.
225 178 CTS 423–8.
226 88 BFSP 553–4.
227 (1902) 9 RIAA 29.
228 Ibid., at 40.
229 A. L. W. Munkman, 'Adjudication and Adjustment – International Judicial Decision and the Settlement of Territorial and Boundary Disputes', *British Year Book of International Law*, 1972–1973, vol. 45, pp. 28–33. Claims to border regions based upon nationalist affiliations of the local population were not uncommon, both in Latin America and later in Africa. Part of Mali's claim to the region disputed with Burkina Faso was based upon the fact that the inhabitants were Malian by nationality: J. B. Allcock *et al.* (eds), *Border and Territorial Disputes*, 3rd edition, Harlow, Longman Group (UK) Limited, 1992, p. 222.
230 (1966) 16 RIAA 109.
231 R. Y. Jennings, 'The Argentine–Chile Boundary Dispute – A Case Study', in *International Disputes: The Legal Aspects*, London, Europa Publications, 1972, p. 324. See also Munkman, note 229, pp. 33–41.

In the resolution of both the disputes over the Lake Titicaca region and over the Argentina–Chile border the result was effectively determined by an analysis of the nationality of the populations occupying the regions. In relying so heavily on actual occupation of territory a principle somewhat analogous to *uti possidetis de facto* was in effect applied. Indeed, Fifer has described the Lake Titicaca result as one in which the Commissioners 'applied the principle of *uti possidetis de facto*'.[232] Professor Jennings, who appeared as one of the counsel on behalf of Argentina in the 1966 arbitration between Argentina and Chile, noted that the nature of the distribution of territory in that case was 'perhaps the most important result of the Award' and surmised that the fact that Chileans lived in the area awarded to Chile 'was not without its effect on the mind of the Court'.[233] The nature of Jennings' comments appear to infer that a principle akin to *uti possidetis de facto* was applied in the resolution of the dispute over the Palena region.[234]

In the El Salvador–Honduras boundary dispute the provisions of Article 5 of the Special Agreement of 24 May 1986 between the two states stated that 'the rules of international law' were to be used to determine the disputed boundary areas. This meant, as the parties agreed, the application of the principle of *uti possidetis juris*. However, as there were areas where Spanish imperial decrees could not identify the boundary, the principle of *uti possidetis juris* could not be strictly applied. As the Chamber in *El Salvador/Honduras* observed:

> [T]he suitability of topographical features to provide a readily identifiable and convenient boundary is a material aspect where no conclusion unambiguously pointing to another boundary emerges from the documentary material.[235]

The Chamber stated that the use of topographical features was not used as a concept of 'natural frontiers'. Rather, the topographical features were used on the assumption that 'those who made the provincial boundaries previous to 1821' also used the same topographical features to establish colonial boundaries.[236] In effect, the Chamber was using topographical features to establish what it presumed were the legal colonial administrative borders at the time of independence from Spain. This enabled the Chamber to claim that the *uti possidetis juris* principle applied even in these situations.[237] However, the Chamber's claim rests on a legal fiction, namely,

232 Fifer, note 76, at 81.

233 Jennings, note 231, pp. 324–5. See also Munkman, note 229, p. 41.

234 It has been suggested that the *Argentine–Chile Frontier Case* in dividing the disputed territory according to the nationality of its residents in fact applied equity principles: M. Miyoshi, *Considerations of Equity in the Settlement of Territorial and Boundary Disputes*, Dordrecht, Martinus Nijhoff Publishers, 1993, pp. 159–62.

235 *Case Concerning the Land, Island and Maritime Frontier Dispute (El Salvador/Honduras)* [1992] ICJ Rep. 383, at 422.

236 Ibid., at 390.

237 The Chamber applied the same reasoning when referring to grants to Indian communities and

that colonial administrative boundaries existed in places where, almost certainly, no such boundaries had ever existed. Whereas in earlier boundary disputes, such as the Bolivia–Peru and Argentina–Chile disputes, an arbitral tribunal faced with such a problem would simply have used other principles to determine the boundary and would not have claimed to have established a boundary line in accordance with the principle of *uti possidetis juris*, the Chamber was compelled to use such a fiction because, following the 1986 decision in the *Frontier Dispute Case*, which ruled that *uti possidetis juris* was the principle of international law to be used in determining the boundaries between former colonial entities, a boundary could only be determined by the use of *uti possidetis juris*, unless otherwise specifically stipulated. Without the use of such a fiction, the Chamber could not have determined the boundary dispute, because without the use of such a fiction it could not establish a boundary line according to the principle of *uti possidetis juris*. However, the use of the fiction does not avoid the reality that topographical considerations, and not the principle of *uti possidetis juris* were used in *El Salvador/Honduras* to determine some of the disputed boundary lines.

In other cases in which the principle of *uti possidetis* was referred to in a treaty as a guiding principle for resolution of boundary disputes, the meaning of *uti possidetis* and its scope of application in resolving a dispute were in each case governed by the terms of the relevant treaty.

As to the meaning of *uti possidetis* in any given treaty, a distinction must be made between treaties that determined boundaries following a war, and treaties that provided for the resolution of such disputes without, and often with the aim of preventing, war. Although Latin American leaders saw one of the aims of the principle of *uti possidetis* as being the prevention of wars over boundaries, this aim was not always realised. In the plethora of boundary disputes between the states that emerged in post-independence Latin America, the principle of *uti possidetis* was an important means by which they were resolved. However, on occasion, states resorted to war to resolve these disputes. The most significant such war of the nineteenth century was the War of the Pacific (1879–1883) in which the provinces of Antofagasta, Tarapaca, Tacna and Arica were the subject of rival and inter-related claims by Chile, Bolivia and Peru. By the Treaty of Ancon of 20 October 1883,[238] Peru ceded Tarapaca to Chile, with Tacna and Arica to remain in Chilean possession pending the holding of a plebiscite after ten years to determine whether they should remain part of Chile or be returned to Peru. Negotiations for the holding of a plebiscite failed, and, despite an arbitral ruling in 1925 that the plebiscite go ahead,[239] it was never held. The Tacna-Arica dispute was eventually resolved by the second Treaty of Ancon of 3 June 1929,[240] which stipulated that Tacna would

so-called 'republican titles' as other factors that could be used to establish the *uti possidetis juris* position in 1821: *Case Concerning the Land, Island and Maritime Frontier Dispute* (*El Salvador/Honduras*) [1992] ICJ Rep. 383, at 394–5.

238 74 BFSP 349–53.

239 *Tacna–Arica Question* (1925) 2 RIAA 921, at 927–44.

240 130 BFSP 605–10.

be returned to Peru and that Arica would remain part of Chile, eventually to be incorporated into the Chilean province of Tarapaca.[241]

By the Treaty of Peace, Friendship and Commerce of 20 October 1904,[242] Chile and Bolivia, in confirming the terms of a truce of April 1884, agreed that Bolivia would cede Antofagasta to Chile.[243] The effect of the War of the Pacific was to deprive Bolivia of an outlet to the Pacific Ocean. Bolivia's perennial, but unsuccessful, attempt to secure an outlet to the sea also provided the most significant territorial war of the twentieth century in Latin America, with the Chaco War (1932–1935) between Bolivia and Paraguay over the Chaco Boreal.[244] The war resulted in a victory for Paraguay and was confirmed by the Treaty of Peace, Friendship and Boundaries concluded on 21 July 1938.[245] The treaty did not determine the boundary dispute by reference to the principle of *uti possidetis*. Rather, the arbitrators had to exercise their functions as arbitrators in equity, who, acting *ex aequo et bono*, were to give their award in accordance with the treaty provisions. These provisions laid down certain geographical limits on the arbitrators' freedom.[246] The arbitral award of 10 October 1938 was one in which:

> The six Presidents were by no means free to apply historical judgment and legal doctrine; for Paraguay had won, and they were required by the peace treaty to give precision to the boundaries of that conquest, although within those limits they were authorized to decide as 'arbitrators in equity,' *ex aequo et bono*.[247]

Thus, the peace treaty and the arbitration confirmed the results of the border

241 Dennis, note 33, at 211–89; S. Wambaugh, *A Monograph on Plebiscites*, New York, Oxford University Press, 1920, pp. 156–65; S. Wambaugh, *Plebiscites Since the World War*, vol. I, Washington, DC, Carnegie Endowment for International Peace, 1933, pp. 331–410.

242 98 BFSP 763–9.

243 Fifer, note 76, pp. 64–6.

244 Bolivia has since the Chaco War consistently claimed an entitlement to a sea outlet to the Pacific Ocean. Bolivia's proposal, in 1987, for a strip of land from Chile along the Chile–Peru border with a sea coast on the Pacific Ocean of between 40 and 50 kilometres, was rejected by Chile: Allcock, note 229, pp. 576–7. In its declaration upon signing the United Nations Convention on the Law of the Sea of 1982, Bolivia stated that it 'wishes to place on record that it is a country that has no maritime sovereignty as a result of war and not as a result of its natural geographic position and that it will assert all rights of coastal States under the Convention once it recovers the legal status in question as a consequence of negotiations on the restoration to Bolivia of its own sovereign outlet to the Pacific Ocean': *United Nations, Multilateral Treaties Deposited with the Secretary General: Status as at 31 December 1992*, New York, United Nations, p. 764. Some success was achieved by Bolivia with a 1992 agreement with Peru in which the latter ceded 327 hectares of land in southern Peru to Bolivia for development as a free zone in the port of Ilo. Bolivia would thus attain a free port for its international trade: *The World Guide 1887/98: A View from the South*, Oxford, New Internationalist Publications, Ltd, 1997, p. 141.

245 Fifer, note 76, p. 218.

246 Quoted in Hyde, note 15, vol. 1, pp. 376–7.

247 Ibid., p. 377, quoting P. C. Jessup and B. Wood, 'The Chaco Award' (1938).

dispute as determined on the battlefield. The treaty that followed the Chaco War was actually an application of *uti possidetis* as used in international law to indicate territorial change that occurs as the result of war.[248] As Fifer correctly notes in the context of the ceasefire following the Chaco War, '[t]he truce line . . . represented the *uti possidetis de facto* demarcation'.[249] The subsequent arbitration simply endorsed that demarcation.

In the peaceful resolution of boundary disputes where treaties provided for the application of the principle of *uti possidetis*, disputes often centred on whether the relevant treaty referred to *uti possidetis juris* or *uti possidetis de facto*. Not all treaties were clear on the issue. Some quite clearly stipulated one or the other. Thus, in the Juris Arbitral Limits Treaty of 14 September 1881[250] between Colombia and Venezuela, it was explicitly stated that *uti possidetis juris* was to be the principle that the arbitrator was to apply in resolving the boundary dispute. The treaty, in its preamble, noted the parties' unsuccessful attempts to date 'to come to an agreement as to their respective rights or *uti possidetis juris* of 1810', and then in Article 1 it submitted the dispute to arbitration for determination of the boundary. Article 3 of an additional protocol between the two states of 15 February 1886[251] stipulated that '[t]he arbiter will decide according to the acts and documents from the Government of Spain and its authorities and agents in America until 1810',[252] implying the application of the principle of *uti possidetis juris*. However, the additional protocol stipulated that if a line could not be fixed upon the basis of *uti possidetis juris* because the documentation was unclear, the arbitrator was empowered to 'fix the line in the way which he thinks closest to the existing documents'.[253] As previously noted, when the arbitrator acted upon this power in the additional protocol, elements of *uti possidetis de facto* were used to set the boundary line.

On other occasions a treaty would simply refer to the application of *uti possidetis* without it being clear whether it was meant to be *uti possidetis juris* or *uti possidetis de facto*. Thus, Article V of the Treaty of Arbitration of 16 July 1930 between Guatemala and Honduras stipulated that '[t]he High Contracting Parties are in agreement that the only juridical line which can be established between their respective countries is that of the *Uti Possidetis* of 1821. Consequently they are in

248 Woolsey observed that the Bolivia/Paraguay dispute 'was largely determined by the military victory of doughty Paraguay': L. H. Woolsey, 'The Settlement of the Chaco Dispute', *American Journal of International Law*, 1939, vol. 33, p. 128. Much the same could be said about the outcome of the earlier War of the Pacific: Korman, note 11, p. 236. Although in both of these disputes the principle of non-recognition of territory acquired by force was voiced in the Americas, it was not sufficient to preclude ultimate recognition of title to territory by conquest: McMahon, note 72, pp. 122–4, 174–7.

249 Fifer, note 76, pp. 217–18.

250 159 CTS 87–91.

251 Ad Referendum Act of Paris of 15 February 1886, between Venezuela and Colombia, 77 BFSP 1012–13.

252 Masot, note 124, p. 173.

253 Ibid., p. 172.

accord that the Tribunal shall determine this line.'[254] Guatemala argued that Article V referred to *uti possidetis de facto*. Honduras argued that it meant *uti possidetis juris*.[255] In treaties of this kind the arbitrator is left with the difficulty of establishing the meaning of '*uti possidetis*'.

In the boundary dispute between Haiti and the Dominican Republic, differing interpretations of *uti possidetis* were presented by the two states in response to their peace treaty of 9 November 1874.[256] Article 4 stipulated that the boundary would be based on the signatories' 'actual possessions'. The Dominican Republic, on the basis of *uti possidetis juris*, claimed territory to which it was legally entitled by virtue of the Preliminary Convention of Peace between the two states dated 26 July 1867.[257] By Article 7 of the 1867 convention the states were entitled to maintain 'their present possessions'. Thus, according to the Dominican Republic, the *uti possidetis de facto* of 1867 became, by virtue of the 1867 convention, the *uti possidetis juris* of 1867. Haiti, who had not ratified the 1867 convention, argued that on the basis of the principle of *uti possidetis de facto*, it was entitled to such territory as it occupied in 1874. This claim was surprising given that Haiti's occupation of territory in 1874 was beyond the line established by the 1867 convention.[258] It was not until a treaty of 21 January 1929,[259] when both sides abandoned their conflicting claims based upon differing interpretations of *uti possidetis*, that a boundary treaty was agreed upon. The 1929 treaty laid out a detailed boundary line to be demarcated by a boundary commission. The results of the demarcation were incorporated into a protocol of revision of the 1929 treaty on 9 March 1936.[260]

Principles of equity, *uti possidetis* and boundary treaties

Although the principle of *uti possidetis* was found in many treaties, it was usually not the only one. Most commonly, treaties stipulated that if the boundary could be ascertained by application of *uti possidetis*, that would be the determinative criterion. However, as already established, in many cases *uti possidetis* could not be applied. In such circumstances treaties often provided for boundary delimitation on other grounds.[261] One of the major alternative grounds was what can be described as the application of principles of equity.

The three functions of equity in international arbitral and judicial decisions have been described by Miyoshi as follows:

254 132 BFSP 823–8.
255 *Honduras Borders* (*Guatemala/Honduras*) (1933) 2 RIAA 1307, at 1322–3.
256 65 BFSP 235.
257 135 CTS 293–6.
258 Ireland, note 85, pp. 59–60.
259 130 BFSP 572.
260 Ireland, note 85, p. 67.
261 In the Treaty between Great Britain and Venezuela of 2 February 1897 the principle of adverse holding or prescription was the guiding principle to be used: 89 BFSP 57–64. For the Arbitral Award of 3 October 1899 pursuant to this Treaty see 92 BFSP 160–2.

> (1) the modification of law to apply it to particular facts; (2) the supplementing of law by filling in 'gaps' in the positive law; and (3) the correction of law, or its supplanting as a distinct basis of decision. These correspond to equity *infra legem*, equity *praeter legem* and equity *contra legem*.[262]

Although principles of equity were often applied, they could be excluded by the terms of the arbitration treaty or agreement between the relevant states. This was the situation in *El Salvador/Honduras*.[263]

In Latin America, equity was a principle that was used first in ascertaining boundaries by the principle of *uti possidetis*, and second, to occasionally permit changes in the boundary lines established by the principle of *uti possidetis*. An example of the first situation was in the Bonilla-Gamez Treaty of 7 October 1894[264] between Honduras and Nicaragua, which in Article II(7) stipulated:

> In studying the plans, maps and other similar documents which the two Governments may submit, the Mixed Commission shall prefer those which it *deems more rational and just*. (Emphasis added)

This provision was directed to establishing the boundary in accordance with the principle of *uti possidetis juris*, but the 'more rational and just' reference is to equity having a role to play in the assessment of relevant evidence going to establishing the *uti possidetis juris* line. In the arbitration of 1906 based upon the Bonilla-Gamez Treaty, equity principles were invoked to assist in ascertaining the Honduras–Nicaragua border.[265] The International Court of Justice rejected Nicaragua's later claim that the arbitral award was void because of the tribunal's application of equity principles.[266]

An example of equity being used to alter the boundary line established by the principle of *uti possidetis* was Article V of the Treaty of Arbitration of 16 July 1930[267] between Guatemala and Honduras. Following a reference to 'the *Uti Possidetis* of 1821' it stipulated:

> If the Tribunal finds that one or both parties, in their subsequent development, have established, beyond that line, interests which should be taken into account in establishing the permanent boundary, the Tribunal shall modify as it may see fit the line of the *Uti Possidetis* of 1821, and shall fix the territorial or other compensation which it may deem just that either party should pay to the other.

262 Miyoshi, note 234, p. 12.

263 *Case Concerning the Land, Island and Maritime Frontier Dispute* (*El Salvador/Honduras*) [1992] ICJ Rep. 383, at 390–1, 633–4, per sep. op. Judge Torres Bernárdez.

264 180 CTS 347–51.

265 *The Boundary Case Between Honduras and Nicaragua* (1906) 11 RIAA 101.

266 *Case Concerning the Arbitral Award Made by the King of Spain on 23 December 1906* (*Honduras -v- Nicaragua*) [1960] ICJ Rep. 192, at 214–15.

267 132 BFSP 823.

As the Tribunal in *Honduras Borders* observed, this provision was 'expressly authorized in the interests of justice . . . to depart from the line of the *uti possidetis* of 1821, even where the line was found to exist'.[268]

However, the greatest significance of equity was as an alternative to the principle of *uti possidetis*. The Bonilla-Gamez Treaty of 7 October 1894[269] in Article II(5) provided a typical example. It stipulated:

> In case of lack of proof of ownership the maps of both Republics and public or private documents, geographical or of any other nature, which may shed light upon the matter, shall be consulted; and the boundary line between the two Republics shall be that which the Mixed Commission shall equitably determine as a result of such study.

Apart from stipulating the use of equity, this clause clearly indicated the parameters within which that principle was to be applied. In other cases a variety of expressions were used to invoke the use of equity principles in resolving boundary disputes. One of the more often used expressions to indicate equity was a direction that a case be determined 'according to the circumstances peculiar to a given case'.[270]

An illustrative case in which a boundary dispute was resolved partly on the basis of the principle of *uti possidetis* and partly on the basis of equity principles was *Honduras Borders*.[271] In that case Guatemala argued that the *uti possidetis* of 1821 referred to *uti possidetis de facto*, while Honduras argued that it meant *uti possidetis juris*. The Tribunal ruled that reference to *uti possidetis* referred to 'administrative control' and proceeded to examine whether such control was exercised by either state in 1821 in order to establish a boundary based on the principle of *uti possidetis*. However, because much of the disputed area was unexplored, colonial predecessors of the two states had not by 1821 made any 'effort to assert any semblance of administrative control'.[272] Thus, only part of the boundary could be delineated by reference to the *uti possidetis* of 1821.[273] The remaining parts of the border were determined by reference to principles of equity. The Tribunal had no specific authorisation to use equitable principles in relation to areas where no line could be fixed in reliance on the principle of *uti possidetis*, but it construed the relevant treaty as giving it such jurisdiction indirectly. In doing so it rejected the argument that, because a definite line could not be established by reference to the *uti possidetis* of 1821, the Tribunal was 'relieve[d] . . . of the duty to determine the definitive boundary to its full extent'.[274]

268 (1933) 2 RIAA 1307, at 1352.
269 108 CTS 347–51.
270 Miyoshi, note 234, pp. 16–17, 93–173.
271 *Honduras Borders* (*Guatemala/Honduras*) (1933) 2 RIAA 1307.
272 Ibid., at 1325.
273 Ibid., at 1351.
274 Ibid., at 1352.

The Tribunal noted that Article XIV of the Treaty of Arbitration of 16 July 1930[275] stipulated that the arbitral award 'shall decide the boundary controversy finally' and further, in Article XII, that the Tribunal had 'the necessary authority to settle by itself any difference which may arise with regard to the interpretation or carrying out of this Treaty and the decisions of the said Tribunal'. Although Article V stated that 'the only line that can be established de jure between their respective countries is that of the *Uti Possidetis* of 1821', that article also stated that equity principles could be used to depart from the line established by the principle of *uti possidetis*. After observing that the treaty did not require the Tribunal to establish a boundary line on the basis of the *uti possidetis* of 1821 where there was insufficient evidence, the Tribunal ruled that:

> [A]s the Tribunal is expressly authorized in the interests of justice, as disclosed by subsequent developments, to depart from the line of *uti possidetis* of 1821, even where that line is found, the Treaty must be construed as empowering the Tribunal to determine the definitive boundary as justice may require throughout the entire area in controversy, to the end that the question of territorial boundaries may be finally and amicably settled.[276]

In exercising its authority to determine the boundary line according to equity principles, the Tribunal rejected the view that it was not able to construe the treaty 'according to an idealistic conception, without regard to the settlement of the territory and existing equities created by the enterprise of the respective Parties'.[277] Reference merely to geographical features could be considered only insofar as they were consistent with these equities. The Tribunal ruled that, in establishing the boundary line, it had to have regard:

> (1) to the facts of actual possession; (2) to the question whether possession by the one Party has been acquired in good faith, and without invading the right of the other Party; and (3) to the relation of territory actually occupied to that which is as yet unoccupied.[278]

In applying these principles the Tribunal refused, in one area, to adopt 'the continental divide of the Merendon range, however acceptable as a natural boundary' and ruled that 'it is necessary to approach the region . . . with appropriate regard to the actual occupation established by the Parties in good faith, and without a preconception that the mountain range, as such, must be deemed to constitute the dividing line'.[279] In another region the Tribunal noted that, given that it had long been uninhabited and unknown, the 'advances in good

275 132 BFSP 823.
276 *Honduras Borders* (*Guatemala/Honduras*) (1933) 2 RIAA 1307, at 1351–2.
277 Ibid., at 1352.
278 Ibid.
279 Ibid., at 1357–8.

faith, followed by occupation and development' by the respective states 'unquestionably created equities'.[280] The Tribunal then noted:

> When it appears that the two Parties, seeking to extend their area of possession, have come into conflict, the question of priority of occupation necessarily arises. Priority in settlement in good faith would appropriately establish priority of right.[281]

The critical date and *uti possidetis*

In establishing the boundary line according to the principle of *uti possidetis* reference had to be made to the 'critical date'. In international law, according to Fitzmaurice, the doctrine of the critical date refers to a point of time at which material facts in a dispute have occurred, after which the parties by their actions can no longer affect the issue.[282] The principle of the critical date, although sometimes invoked, has not been of major significance in resolving international boundary disputes.[283] This has been because it arises for determination when the question posed relates to who was entitled to sovereignty over territory at a specified date, and not to who is presently entitled to sovereignty over disputed territory.[284]

In Spanish South America the critical date was 1810. In Spanish Central America it was 1821. These two dates were the deemed years of independence from colonial rule. These dates did not change in circumstances involving the fragmentation of the states that emerged immediately upon independence from Spain. Thus, even after Gran Colombia disintegrated in 1830, to eventually result in the new states of Colombia, Venezuela, Ecuador and Panama, the critical date remained 1810.

However, the years of 1810 and 1821 were not always the critical dates in Latin American boundary cases.[285] The Chamber in *El Salvador/Honduras*, said:

> A later critical date clearly may arise, for example, either from adjudication or from a boundary treaty. Thus, in the previous Latin American boundary

280 Ibid., at 1359.

281 Ibid.

282 G. Fitzmaurice, 'The Law and Procedure of the International Court of Justice, 1951–4: Points of Substantive Law, Part II', *British Year Book of International Law*, 1955–1956, vol. 32, p. 20; L. F. Goldie, 'The Critical Date', *International and Comparative Law Quarterly*, 1963, vol. 12, p. 1254; *Argentine–Chile Frontier Case* (1966) 16 RIAA 109, at 166. Fitzmaurice's views have been criticised as being artificial: Thirlway, note 101, p. 31.

283 *Dubai–Sharjah Border Arbitration* (1981) 91 ILR 543, at 594.

284 D. W. Bowett, 'The Dubai/Sharjah Boundary Arbitration of 1981', *British Year Book of International Law*, 1994, vol. 65, pp. 111–14; Thirlway, note 101, p. 33.

285 M. N. Shaw, 'The Heritage of States: The Principle of *Uti Possidetis Juris* Today', *British Year Book of International Law*, 1996, vol. 67, pp. 130–1. Thus, in the dispute between Peru and Ecuador, Peru argued that the critical date was 1824, which was the real date of the end of colonial dependence of the area the subject of the dispute: St John, note 94, p. 117.

> arbitrations it is the award that is now determinative, even though it is based upon a view of the *uti possidetis juris* position. The award's view of the *uti possidetis juris* position prevails and cannot now be questioned juridically, even if it could be questioned historically. So for such a boundary the date of the award has become a new and later critical date.[286]

Furthermore, the Chamber declared that the date could be qualified if there was evidence to show that the parties had by acquiescence or recognition accepted a variation of the critical date.[287]

When the principle of the critical date was raised in Latin American boundary disputes, it was of limited value in any arbitral process. The boundary disputes between Argentina and Chile illustrate various aspects of the relevance of the principle of critical date to Latin American boundary disputes.

In the Boundary Treaty of 23 July 1881[288] between Argentina and Chile, the critical date of 1810 was effectively brought forward by the treaty to the date of the treaty. As the Tribunal in *The Beagle Channel Arbitration* noted, the effect of the treaty was to supersede and replace all previous territorial arrangements between the parties in relation to all outstanding and unresolved boundary issues.[289] This in effect created a new critical date of 1881 for the outstanding areas of dispute. However, this date was again altered for one area of disputation. Following the 1881 treaty an arbitral award was made in 1902, but further clarification of the boundary in the Palena region was necessary due to a geographical error in the 1902 award. In relation to the Palena region, the court noted in the 1966 award that 'there [was] obviously a sense in which the critical date [was] 1902 itself – or at the latest 1903, the date of the demarcation'. Argentina suggested that the critical date was 1941, while Chile argued that it was either 1945 or 1952. The court then noted that, given that it was its duty 'to say to what extent, if any, the course of the boundary between the territories of the Parties in the [Palena region] has remained unsettled since the 1902 Award, there is equally obviously a sense in which the critical date is the date of submission of the dispute to the Arbitrator, i.e., 1964'. In the end the court 'considered the notion of the critical date to be of little value' in the litigation and proceeded to examine all the evidence submitted to it 'irrespective of the date of the acts to which such evidence relate[d]'.[290]

In relation to the dispute over the Beagle Channel between Argentina and Chile, the majority of the arbitral tribunal determined a boundary line by reference to acts prior to the 1881 critical date, although it asserted that facts and

286 *Case Concerning the Land, Island and Maritime Frontier Dispute* (*El Salvador/Honduras*) [1992] ICJ Rep. 383, at 401.

287 Ibid.

288 72 BFSP 1103–5.

289 *The Beagle Channel Arbitration* (1977) 52 ILR 93, at 123–4.

290 *Argentine–Chile Frontier Case* (1966) 16 RIAA 109, at 166–7. See also *Eritrea/Yemen* (*Territorial Sovereignty*) (1998) 114 ILR 1, at 32.

events after 1881 confirmed and corroborated its conclusions.[291] However, Judge Gros disagreed with the majority on this point. Although he reached the same decision as the majority, he did so by excluding as irrelevant all facts and events after 1881, thereby effectively applying the critical date principle.[292] Similarly, in *El Salvador/Honduras*, although the critical date for the disputed boundary areas was 1821, facts and events after independence were relevant in determining the boundary line according to the principle of the *uti possidetis juris* of 1821, especially in relation to the dispute over the island of Meangeura.[293]

In the boundary dispute between Argentina and Paraguay the Treaty of Limits of 3 February 1876,[294] after defining certain parts of a boundary line, stipulated that the dispute over part of the El Chaco region would be referred to arbitration. The treaty made no reference to *uti possidetis* as the basis for the arbitrator's decision. In Article XI the treaty stipulated that if, after commencement of the arbitration proceedings, 'any act of ownership be committed prior to decision being given, such act shall have no value whatever, nor be considered in the discussion to constitute a fresh title'. By implication, any act prior to commencement of the arbitration proceedings could be relevant to the arbitrator's decision. Thus, 25 March 1878, the date Argentina presented its case to the arbitrator[295] and thereby the commencement date of the arbitration, became the critical date in accordance with the 1876 treaty.

The critical date, however, is not of relevance when the arbitral body is allocating a boundary according to principles of equity. In *Honduras Borders*, the Tribunal, after noting that a boundary line could not be determined according to the *uti possidetis* of 1821, stated:

> Subsequent developments in this region and the corresponding equities of the respective Parties demand, however, proper recognition in determining the definitive boundary which should be established between them in this territory according to equity and justice.[296]

The real significance of the dates of 1810 and 1821 lies not in the importance of the principle of critical date as defined above by Fitzmaurice. Rather, their real significance was that they represented the dates after which the Latin American states denied the right of occupation pursuant to the principle of *terra nullius*. Title

291 *The Beagle Channel Arbitration* (1977) 52 ILR 93, at 221.

292 Ibid., at 230, per Judge Gros.

293 See summary of the Chamber's decision in the separate opinion of Judge Torres Bernárdez in *Case Concerning the Land, Island and Maritime Frontier Dispute* (*El Salvador/Honduras*) [1992] ICJ Rep. 383, at 633. Thirlway comments that for the island of Meanguera the critical date, as defined by Fitzmaurice, clearly was not 1821, otherwise none of the extensive post-1821 evidence would have been admitted: Thirlway, note 101, p. 38.

294 68 BFSP 97–100.

295 Ireland, note 29, p. 32.

296 *Honduras Borders* (*Guatemala/Honduras*) (1933) 2 RIAA 1307, at 1341.

to territories occupied by colonial powers other than Spain and Portugal before the respective critical dates on the basis that they were *terra nullius* were recognised by the newly independent Latin American states. However, the principle of *uti possidetis* denied that any territory could be occupied by any colonial power after the critical dates. In this respect the critical dates of 1810 and 1821 were vital in Latin America's relations with the rest of the world, especially the European colonial powers.

4 The principle of *uti possidetis* in Asia and Africa

Prior to the wave of decolonisation in the wake of World War II, the application of the principle of *uti possidetis* as a basis for the resolution of post-decolonisation border disputes was essentially confined to the Americas. It was only with its use and further development in post-World War II Africa, and to a lesser extent Asia, that it was transformed into a general principle of international law in the context of post-decolonisation border disputes.

Uti possidetis in Asia

In the wave of decolonisation in Asia after World War II boundary disputes were the subject of only two arbitral decisions. Arbitration of Asian boundary disputes was not as prevalent as in the case of Latin America for two reasons. First, much of Asia was already composed of independent states with defined international boundaries. Second, there was a general reluctance in Asia to have disputes of any kind, including boundary disputes, resolved by arbitral proceeding. Alternative methods of dispute resolution were favoured.[1] Of the two cases, only the decision in *The Indo-Pakistan Western Boundary* (*Rann of Kutch*) *Case* (*India -v- Pakistan*)[2] (the *Rann of Kutch Arbitration*) saw the application to some degree of principles akin to *uti possidetis* as previously developed in Latin America.[3]

1 Gillian Triggs, 'Confucius and Consensus: International Law in the Asian Pacific', *Proceedings of the Australian and New Zealand Society of International Law, Fifth Annual International Law Conference*, 29 May–1 June 1997, Canberra, Centre for International and Public Law, Australian National University, 1997, pp. 21–4.

2 (1968) 50 ILR 2.

3 In the other case, *Case Concerning the Temple of Preah Vihear* (*Cambodia -v- Thailand*) (*Merits*) (1962) 33 ILR 48, at 70–1, the boundary dispute was determined on the principle of acquiescence to the provisions of a boundary treaty. Brownlie and Shaw contend that this case is one applying the *uti possidetis* principle: I. Brownlie, *Principles of Public International Law*, 5th edition, Oxford, Oxford University Press, 1998, p. 135; M. N. Shaw, 'The Heritage of States: The Principle of *Uti Possidetis Juris* Today', *British Year Book of International Law*, 1996, vol. 67, pp. 104–5. However, the case was one based upon the interpretation of a treaty and had nothing to do with *uti possidetis*: H. Thirlway, 'The Law and Procedure of the International Court of Justice 1960–1989, Part Seven', *British Year Book of International Law*, 1995, vol. 66, pp. 16.

In the *Rann of Kutch Arbitration* the dispute was between Pakistan and India over the boundary between what was in pre-independence times the colonial province of Sind, now part of Pakistan, and the vassal state of Kutch and other Native Indian States, now part of India. India and Pakistan submitted rival versions of the boundary line and it was the role of the *ad hoc* tribunal to determine the true boundary. This task was, by the terms of the Agreement of 30 June 1965, to be determined 'in the light of [India's and Pakistan's] respective claims and evidence produced'.[4]

The tribunal resolved the boundary dispute in two parts. The first and very small part of the disputed boundary was held to have been determined by an agreement between Sind and Kutch in 1914. The tribunal unanimously ruled that the agreement established that part of the boundary between India and Pakistan as at the date of independence of 15 August 1947.[5] However, the reasoning differed between the majority opinion of the tribunal Chairman and that of the third arbiter, Mr Bebler. The Chairman ruled that the principle of *uti possidetis* was inapplicable, except insofar as it applied to preclude a finding that any of the disputed territory was *terra nullius*.[6] However, in relation to the boundary line established by the 1914 agreement, he began by asking the question:

> Did there exist in the disputed region a recognized and well-established boundary at the time of the emergence of India and Pakistan as independent nations, and if so, what was the alignment?[7]

In answering the first part of this question in the affirmative by reference to the line established by the 1914 agreement, and further stating that the line could not be disturbed, the Chairman was in effect applying a principle akin to that of succession by a new state to the territory and boundaries of its predecessor state.

On the other hand, Mr Bebler ruled that the 1914 agreement created an international boundary between two independent states, namely Great Britain, as the colonial power in Sind, and the independent, although vassal, state of Kutch. The fact that the boundary was between a fully sovereign state, Britain, and a not fully sovereign state raised questions as to 'the modalities of application of the general principles of International Law governing boundaries, not determined by treaties, inasmuch as the Sind–Kutch boundary was an international boundary of a peculiar character'.[8] However, principles of acquiescence and recognition, as applied to the 1914 boundary agreement meant that it remained an international boundary which by international law bound India and Pakistan upon their gaining independence in

4 *The Indo-Pakistan Western Boundary* (*Rann of Kutch*) *Case* (*India -v- Pakistan*) (1968) 50 ILR 2, at 14–16. At 18, in a preliminary hearing, the tribunal ruled that the provisions of the 1965 agreement did not permit the use of principles of equity in the arbitration.

5 Ibid., at 474–5, per Chairman Mr Lagergren, and at 466, per Mr Bebler.

6 Ibid., at 470.

7 Ibid., at 474.

8 Ibid., at 409.

1947. In so ruling, Mr Bebler was applying the principle of succession by a new state to the territory of its predecessor.[9] Given that Mr Bebler ruled that the 1914 agreement created an international boundary and that, by implication, this was not the case of colonial boundaries, this was not an application of the principle of *uti possidetis juris*, although he had earlier in his opinion referred approvingly to the relevance of *uti possidetis* as a principle for resolving boundary disputes.[10]

As to the remainder of the boundary in dispute the Chairman's majority opinion ruled that there had been no existing boundary. Claims by the Rao of Kutch to the entire territory of the Rann, accompanied by British indifference to the territory, legitimated India's claim. However, the Chairman ruled that India's claim, in the circumstances, had to give way to Pakistan in regions where 'a continuous and for the region intensive Sind activity, meeting with no effective opposition from the Kutch side, is established'. In such regions Pakistan had a 'better and superior title'. Thus, the final boundary delimitation awarded about 90 per cent of the disputed region to India and the rest to Pakistan.[11] This part of the Chairman's opinion, in effect, applied the principle of *uti possidetis de facto* as applied in Latin America.

Mr Bebler dissented in relation to this part of the boundary. He ruled that there was a boundary line published by the British in 1871 and 1872 which was mutually recognised by the British and Kutch. Displays of Sind authority in the Rann were 'far from sufficient to disturb the recognized and depicted boundary'.[12] This boundary was an international boundary, and for the same reasons that the 1914 agreement created an international boundary binding India and Pakistan in 1947, so too did the boundary line published by the British in 1871 and 1872.

Uti possidetis in Africa

In the wave of decolonisation in Africa after World War II a principle akin to *uti possidetis juris* as applied in Latin America was adopted to settle international boundaries after decolonisation. This was most vividly confirmed by the actions of the

9 'According to the principle *res transit cum suo onere*, all rights and duties arising from treaties of the predecessor state concerning boundary lines . . . devolve on the successor state': R. Jennings and A. Watts, *Oppenheim's International Law*, Volume I, *Peace*, 9th edition, London, Longman, 1992, p. 213. 'Boundary agreements are *sui generis*. Unlike ordinary contractual arrangements, they create an objective judicial situation which continues independent of the existence of original signatory parties, provided, of course, that effective link between one or both of them and the succeeding state (one or both) can be established': A. O. Cukwurah, *The Settlement of Boundary Disputes in International Law*, Manchester, Manchester University Press, 1967, p. 108. Article 11 of the Convention on Succession of States in Respect of Treaties (1978) provides that a succession of states does not, as such, affect a boundary established by a treaty. In *Case Concerning the Territorial Dispute* (*Libyan Arab Jamahiriya/Chad*) [1994] ICJ Rep. 6, at 37, the Chamber said: 'A boundary established by treaty thus achieves a permanence which the treaty itself does not always enjoy. The treaty can cease to be in force without in any way affecting the continuance of the boundary.'

10 *The Indo-Pakistan Western Boundary* (*Rann of Kutch*) *Case* (*India -v- Pakistan*) (1968) 50 ILR 2, at 407–8.

11 Ibid., at 511–19.

12 Ibid., at 466–9.

Organisation of African Unity (OAU). Article 3(3) of the OAU Charter, adopted on 25 May 1963, stipulated that member states would 'respect . . . the territorial integrity of each State and its inalienable right to independent existence'.[13] This provision was only an indirect reference to the principle of *uti possidetis juris*. A more direct statement was made by a resolution in July 1964 at the OAU conference of Heads of State and Government in Cairo which stipulated that all member states 'pledge themselves to respect the borders existing on their achievement of national independence'.[14] In *Case Concerning the Frontier Dispute* (*Burkina Faso and Mali*) (the *Frontier Dispute Case*), the Chamber of the International Court of Justice observed that the OAU resolution on the intangibility of former colonial boundaries derived from the application of the principle of *uti possidetis juris*.[15]

As in Latin America, the constitutions of many of the new African states gave effect to the principle of *uti possidetis juris* by explicitly declaring that their boundaries were those of the respective former colonial entities. Thus, Article 1(2) of the Constitution of Lesotho of 1966 declared that the territory of Lesotho comprised that of the former colony of Basutoland.[16] The 1968 Constitution of the Kingdom of Swaziland in Article 1(2) had a similar provision as to the former protectorate of Swaziland.[17] The various independence Acts passed by the United Kingdom Parliament on the occasion of the independence of its African colonies usually referred to the relevant new independent state as having the territory of the appropriate British colonial entity.[18]

13 479 UNTS 70–89. According to Elias, who participated in the drafting of the Charter, the immediate reason for the adoption of Article 3(3) was the concern of a number of small states about the intentions of their larger neighbours, particularly in relation to the issue of boundaries: T. O. Elias, 'The Charter of the Organization of African Unity', *American Journal of International Law*, 1965, vol. 59, p. 248. The establishment of the OAU represented, as was often stated, the culmination of the pan-African dream. However, Article 3(3) was in some senses paradoxical, in that the pan-Africanists consistently regarded the colonial boundaries as obstacles that had to be removed as soon as possible. Yet Article 3(3) significantly reinforced those colonial boundaries: S. Chime, 'The Organization of African Unity and African Boundaries', in C. G. Widstrand (ed.), *African Boundary Problems*, Uppsala, The Scandinavian Institute of African Studies, 1969, p. 67.

14 The text of the 1964 OAU resolution is reproduced in I. Brownlie, *African Boundaries: A Legal and Diplomatic Encyclopaedia*, London, C. Hurst & Co, 1979, p. 11.

15 *Case Concerning the Frontier Dispute* (*Burkina Faso and Mali*) [1986] ICJ Rep. 554, at 565. See also *Case Concerning Kasikili/Sedudu Island (Botswana/Namibia)* (2000) 39 ILM 310, at 320, referring to the OAU resolution as 'an implementation of the principle of *uti possidetis juris*'.

16 The Lesotho Constitution of 1966 is reprinted in H. H. Marshall, *From Dependence to Statehood in Commonwealth Africa:* Volume I: *Southern Africa, Selected Documents, World War I to Independence*, London, Oceania Publications, 1980, pp. 419–98.

17 The Swaziland Constitution of 1968 is reprinted in Marshall, note 16, pp. 643–717.

18 See for example section 1 of the *Lesotho Independence Act 1966* (UK) reprinted in Marshall, note 16, p. 402; and section 1 of the *Botswana Independence Act 1966* (UK); section 1(1) of the *Gambia Independence Act 1964* (UK); section 1 of the *Ghana Independence Act 1957* (UK); section 1(3) of the *Kenya Independence Act 1963* (UK); section 1(1) of the *Uganda Independence Act 1962* (UK); section 1 of the *Zambia Independence Act 1964* (UK), all reprinted in *Materials on Succession of States in Respect of Matters Other Than Treaties*, New York, United Nations Publications, 1978, pp. 129, 189, 193, 246, 431, 468, respectively.

In Africa, as in Latin America, the application of *uti possidetis juris* was concerned with the problem of establishing the precise locations of the former colonial boundaries. Just as in Latin America, when the principle of *uti possidetis juris* was applied, there were problems ascertaining boundaries because of conflicting and incomplete documentary evidence. The *Frontier Dispute Case* was one case which required the International Court of Justice to undertake a painstaking analysis of a significant amount of documentation to resolve the boundary dispute between Burkina Faso and Mali. The Chamber referred to the problem when it said:

> The Chamber has to ascertain where the frontier lay in 1932 in a region of Africa little known at the time and largely inhabited by nomads, in which transport and communications were very sketchy. In order to identify this the Chamber has to refer to the legislative and regulative maps and sketch-maps which are sometimes of doubtful accuracy and reliability and which contradict one another; and to administrative documents which, having been drawn up for the purposes of a system of government which ceased to exist nearly 30 years ago, have had to be obtained from various collections of archives. . . . The case file shows inconsistencies and shortcomings. . . . [T]he Parties have informed the Chamber that they were unable to locate specific documents. . . . But even if those documents were located, the Chamber cannot exclude the possibility that a large body of archives from French West Africa administration, now dispersed among several countries, may contain further documents of considerable relevance.[19]

Divergences from the Latin American experience

Whether the principles that emerged from the two OAU meetings were derived from the Latin American experience with *uti possidetis* is debatable. The absence of the expression in both the OAU Charter and the 1964 resolution indicates that it was not. The adoption of the Declaration on the Granting of Independence to Colonial Countries and Peoples[20] in 1960 by the UN General Assembly, with its emphasis on the continued territorial integrity of colonial territories after independence, would appear to be the more likely inspiration for the 1964 OAU resolution.[21] If one accepts, as did the Court in the *Frontier Dispute Case*, that the OAU documents did derive from the Latin American experience with *uti possidetis*, it is clear that even though the OAU and post-colonial Latin America had similar concerns in relation to boundaries on independence, the African application of *uti possidetis* differed in some significant respects from its Latin American predecessor.

19 *Case Concerning the Frontier Dispute* (*Burkina Faso and Mali*) [1986] ICJ Rep. 554, at 587.

20 General Assembly Resolution 1514 (XV), 14 December 1960.

21 S. N. Lalonde, 'Uti Possidetis and Internal Administrative Boundaries', unpublished doctoral dissertation, University of Cambridge, 1997, pp. 129–34.

Terra nullius

In Latin America *uti possidetis* was primarily and fundamentally justified on the basis that it was concerned with excluding the further application of the doctrine of *terra nullius* to the Americas and thereby preventing further European colonisation of the region after the wars of independence from colonial rule. In Africa such a justification was never voiced. In Africa the primary and fundamental justification for the application of *uti possidetis* was, as observed by the Chamber in the *Frontier Dispute Case*, that of 'securing respect for the territorial boundaries at the moment when independence is achieved'.[22]

The Chamber indicated the concern that underpinned the need to maintain the sanctity of former colonial boundaries when it said:

> Its obvious purpose is to prevent the independence and stability of new States being endangered by fratricidal struggles following the withdrawal of the administering power.[23]

Later the Chamber said:

> [T]he maintenance of the territorial status quo in Africa is often seen as the wisest course, to preserve what has been achieved by peoples who have struggled for their independence, and to avoid a disruption which would deprive the continent of the gains achieved by much sacrifice. The essential requirement of stability in order to survive, to develop and gradually to consolidate their independence in all fields, has induced African States judiciously to consent to the respecting of colonial frontiers.[24]

One of the Chamber's members, Judge Bedjaoui, in a dissenting opinion in *Case Concerning the Arbitral Award of 31 July 1989* (*Guinea-Bissau -v- Senegal*),[25] (*Guinea-Bissau–enegal*) made explicit the nationalist concerns of independence leaders, when he said:

> Following the achievement of independence in close succession by one African country after another in the 1960s, a situation arose in which, on the one hand, several ethnic groups coexisted in one and the same State (poly-ethnic State) and, on the other hand, one and the same ethnic group found itself extending over two or more States (multinational ethnic group). It was only the

22 *Case Concerning the Frontier Dispute* (*Burkina Faso and Mali*) [1986] ICJ Rep. 554, at 566.

23 Ibid., at 565. See similar sentiments in *The Indo-Pakistan Western Boundary* (*Rann of Kutch*) *Case* (*India -v- Pakistan*) (1968) 50 ILR 2, at 408.

24 *Case Concerning the Frontier Dispute* (*Burkina Faso and Mali*) [1986] ICJ Rep. 554, at 567. See also *Case Concerning the Territorial Dispute* (*Libyan Arab Jamahiriya/Chad*) [1994] ICJ Rep. 6, at 92, per sep. op. Judge Ajibola.

25 (1989) 83 ILR 1.

> fear of the newly-independent African States that potentially explosive situations might cause the break-up of States that were fragile after colonial withdrawal which led the African leaders to proclaim the intangibility of land frontiers and to take the prudent step of a sort of renewal 'ratification' of the General Act of Berlin which, by its partition of Africa, was historically the origin of that situation.[26]

The irrelevance of concerns with the possible application of the doctrine of *terra nullius* to Africa is significant. In Latin America the purpose of denying the operation of *terra nullius* gave the principle of *uti possidetis* a vital connection to the principle of the same name in Roman law. In Roman law the principle granted possessory rights to the person in actual possession which was good against anyone except the true owner. The Roman law principle was thus concerned with the adjudication of competing claims to property. In Latin America, although the principle was adapted to claims to ownership rather than possession, it was nevertheless concerned with competing claims to ownership of territory. By denying the operation of *terra nullius* in their region, Latin American leaders were asserting superior claims to those of any potential colonial power with regards to the ownership of territory in Latin America, notwithstanding that much of the region had never actually been occupied by the former Spanish and Portuguese colonial masters. The notion of competing claims to Latin American territory preserved a vital principled link between the Roman law principle of *uti possidetis* and its Latin American reincarnation. In Africa there was no concern that new colonial masters would seek to occupy the continent and thus compete with the territorial claims of the newly independent states.

Critical date

The fact that the continued operation of *terra nullius* was not a justification for the application of *uti possidetis* in Africa, meant that the significance of the critical date principle varied markedly between Latin America and Africa.

In Africa the principle of the critical date referred to a point in time at which material facts in a dispute have occurred, after which the parties by their actions can no longer affect the issue. However, in Latin America it was significant in determining the dates of 1810 and 1821 as the dates after which the principle of *terra nullius* ceased to be recognised in respect of South and Central America. The Latin American states did not deny the title of colonial powers to territories in these regions occupied in accordance with the operation of the principle of *terra nullius* prior to the respective critical dates. In Africa because occupation pursuant to the principle of *terra nullius* was not a reality in the post-World War II era, the critical

26 Ibid., at 61. See also Y. Makonnen, *International Law and the New States of Africa: A Study of the International Legal Problems of State Succession in the Newly Independent States of Eastern Africa*, Addis Abeba, UNESCO, 1983, pp. 460–3.

date in this respect was irrelevant. In Africa the critical date was only of technical relevance in the sense that it was the date of independence of any given colony. That date was 'critical' only insofar as it meant that it was by reference to that date that the colonial borders were to be determined for the purposes of ascertaining a newly independent state's international borders. This difference in importance between the Latin American and African applications of the critical date is reflected in the fact that in Latin America the critical date was always 1810 or 1821, irrespective of when a state achieved independence. Thus, when Venezuela achieved independence from Gran Colombia in 1829, the critical date was 1810 and Venezuela's borders were those of the Captaincy-General of Venezuela as they existed in 1810. In Africa the critical date was simply the date of independence, whenever that occurred. In Africa the critical date principle never had the function of marking an end to the operation of occupation of African territory according to the principle of *terra nullius*.

Uti possidetis de facto

The African principle was specifically one of *uti possidetis juris*. Although in Latin America *uti possidetis juris* was often the case, in Africa it was the norm. In Africa *uti possidetis de facto* was, as a rule, effectively subordinate to *uti possidetis juris*. In Latin America the two principles were equal rivals. This is not to say that *uti possidetis de facto* was irrelevant in Africa. In Africa the word *effectivité* was used instead of *uti possidetis de facto*. In the *Frontier Dispute Case*, the Chamber noted that colonial *effectivités* were relevant in establishing the line according to *uti possidetis juris*. Colonial *effectivités* were described as 'conduct of the administrative authorities as proof of effective exercise of territorial jurisdiction in the region during the colonial period'.[27] This is, in effect, the principle of *uti possidetis de facto*, as is confirmed by Judge Torres Bernárdez in *Case Concerning the Land, Island and Maritime Frontier Dispute* (*El Salvador/Honduras*)[28] (*El Salvador/Honduras*), and Judge Ajibola in his separate opinion in *Case Concerning the Territorial Dispute* (*Libyan Arab Jamahiriya/Chad*)[29] (*Libya/Chad*). In this sense it is similar to the situations that arose in Latin American boundary disputes involving Venezuela and Colombia, and El Salvador and Honduras, discussed in the previous chapter. In the *Frontier Dispute Case*, the Chamber, in ruling on the relevance of 'colonial *effectivités*', said:

> Where the act corresponds exactly to law, where effective administration is additional to the *uti possidetis juris*, the only role of *effectivité* is to confirm the

27 *Case Concerning the Frontier Dispute* (*Burkina Faso and Mali*) [1986] ICJ Rep. 554, at 586.

28 [1992] ICJ Rep. 383, at 635.

29 [1994] ICJ Rep. 6. In this case, Judge Ajibola, at 87, after noting the difference between *uti possidetis juris* and *effectivités*, asked the rhetorical question: 'But does it matter seriously whether the principle is *uti possidetis juris* or *uti possidetis de facto* with regard to its application in Africa?' Apart from the issue that it raised, this question, in the context of the preceding discussion clearly implies that *uti possidetis de facto* and the principle of *effectivités* are one and the same thing.

> exercise of the right derived from a legal title. Where the act does not correspond to the law, where the territory which is the subject of the dispute is effectively administered by a State other than the one possessing the legal title, preference should be given to the holder of the legal title. In the event that the *effectivité* does not co-exist with any legal title, it must invariably be taken into consideration. Finally, there are cases where the legal title is not capable of showing exactly the territorial expanse to which it relates. The *effectivités* can then play an essential role in showing how title is interpreted in practice.[30]

The effect of this passage was summed up by Judge Ajibola in *Libya/Chad* when he said:

> The Judgment undoubtedly gave preference to *uti possidetis juris* as a legal right over actual or effective occupation as the yardstick for title to a territory. Nevertheless it does not deny the fact that effective occupation could be taken into consideration.[31]

It can, however, be noted that the practical relevance of *uti possidetis de facto* was considerably less in Africa than in Latin America. More reliable maps and lines were known in the former as compared with the latter. This was due to a number of factors. First, in Africa it was only the highest rank of administrative division, the colony, that achieved independence.[32] Lesser administrative divisions did not achieve independence. In Latin America it was not only the viceroyalty that achieved independence, but also its various internal divisions. Subordinate subdivisions of the primary administrative divisions were generally not as well delineated. Second, mapping techniques were more advanced in the nineteenth and twentieth centuries than in the period prior to Latin American independence. Third, there being a greater number of competing colonial powers in Africa and Asia as compared to Latin America, many of the African colonial boundaries were indeed international rather

30 *Case Concerning the Frontier Dispute* (*Burkina Faso and Mali*) [1986] ICJ Rep. 554, at 586–7. These views were endorsed in *Case Concerning the Land, Island and Maritime Frontier Dispute* (*El Salvador/Honduras*) [1992] ICJ Rep. 383, at 398.

31 *Case Concerning the Territorial Dispute* (*Libyan Arab Jamahiriya/Chad*) [1994] ICJ Rep. 6, at 89.

32 Attempts by colonial powers to create federations of a number of colonies with a view to those federations attaining independence as states rather than the relevant colonies gaining independence as states were uniformly rejected by the African leaderships in the relevant colonies. Thus, the Central African Federation of the British colonies of Northern Rhodesia (Zambia), Southern Rhodesia (Zimbabwe) and Nyasaland (Malawi) established in 1953 was disbanded in 1963, which was before the respective colonies achieved independence: J. Kendle, *Federal Britain: A History*, London, Routledge, 1997, pp. 136–3. However, upon achieving independence some African states joined into federations or confederations, with mixed success. The federation of Tanganyika and Zanzibar to form Tanzania in 1964 has survived although Zanzibar has on occasions threatened to secede: S. Y. Hameso, *Ethnicity and Nationalism in Africa*, Commack, Nova Science Publishers, 1997, pp. 126–7. On the other hand, the confederation of Senegal and Gambia in 1982, into

than internal administrative boundaries as in Spanish America. This meant that more accurate maps were likely to be produced. Put simply, doubts over the positioning of borders were not as prevalent in Africa as in Latin America.[33]

International colonial boundaries

Another difference between the Latin American and African applications of *uti possidetis* flows from the paramountcy of *uti possidetis juris* in Africa. This had its impact in Africa in relation to boundaries between former colonial entities where there had been different colonial powers before independence. In Africa, the principle of *uti possidetis juris* applied to former international boundaries between the various colonial powers just as it did to internal boundaries of colonial entities under the rule of a single power. The Chamber in the *Frontier Dispute Case* said of these international boundaries:

> By becoming independent, a new State acquires sovereignty with the territorial base and boundaries left to it by the colonial power. This is part of the ordinary machinery of State succession.[34]

Earlier in its judgement the Chamber said:

> There is no doubt that the obligation to respect pre-existing international frontiers in the event of a State succession derives from a general rule of international law, whether or not the rule is expressed in the formula *uti possidetis*.[35]

A similar approach was taken in the *Guinea–Guinea Bissau Maritime Delimitation Case*,[36] where an arbitral tribunal had to deal with a dispute between two states which had been colonies of different imperial powers. In relation to a Convention of 1886 between the two former colonial powers, the tribunal observed:

> It remained in force between France and Portugal until the end of the colonial period, and became binding between the successor States by virtue of the principle of *uti possidetis*.[37]

Senegambia, dissolved in 1989. An initiative commenced in the late 1940s that had the ultimate aim of federating the British colonies of Uganda, Kenya and Tanganyika and which was to some degree supported by these colonies after gaining independence with the establishment of the East African Community ultimately failed, the failure being formalised by its dissolution in 1987: E. W. Davies, *The Legal Status of British Dependent Territories: The West Indies and North Atlantic Region*, Cambridge, Cambridge University Press, 1995, pp. 106–8.

33 J. R. V. Prescott, *Political Frontiers and Boundaries*, London, Allen & Unwin, 1987, pp. 203–4; R. Y. Jennings, 'Closing Address', in C. Brölmann, R. Lefeber and M. Zieck (eds), *Peoples and Minorities in International Law*, Dordrecht, Martinus Nijhoff Publishers, 1993, p. 346.

34 *Case Concerning the Frontier Dispute* (*Burkina Faso and Mali*) [1986] ICJ Rep. 568, at 566.

35 Ibid.

36 (1985) 77 ILR 635.

37 *Guinea–Guinea Bissau Maritime Delimitation Case* (1985) 77 ILR 635, at 657.

This approach of applying *uti possidetis juris* to boundaries of colonies which had previously belonged to different colonisers can be criticised.[38] Preservation of these boundaries results from the rules relating to succession of new states to existing boundary treaties, not the principle of *uti possidetis juris*. The two principles are distinct, in that the former is concerned with the stability and continuation of existing international boundaries, whereas the latter is concerned with the creation of a new international boundary by the transformation of an old colonial administrative boundary.[39] It must be noted that in disputes between Brazil and the states which emerged from Spain's former colonial empire, the principle of *uti possidetis juris* was not applied. As already noted, the principle of *uti possidetis de facto* was applied in these disputes without exception. The principle of *uti possidetis juris* applied only, if at all, in disputes between former Spanish colonial entities.[40]

The Chamber's approach has the consequence, as Ratner observes, that in Africa the principle of *uti possidetis juris* 'entailed notions of treaty succession to address boundaries between different colonial powers'.[41]

Application to colonies only

A further difference between the application of *uti possidetis* in Latin America and Africa relates to the fact that in Africa it was the colony, as the highest rank of administrative division, that achieved independence. Almost universally, lesser administrative divisions did not achieve independence.[42] In the former Hispanic colonies in Latin America it was not only the viceroyalty, but also its various internal divisions that achieved independence. In some cases such as Bolivia, subdivisions across viceroyalty borders united to form a state. Although independence leaders in Hispanic America initially supported the idea that independence should have been based only on the higher order of colonial administrative units, this did not occur. Thus, the state of Gran Colombia progressively broke up after 1830 into the four states of Colombia, Venezuela, Ecuador and Panama. Similarly, the Federal Republic of Central America broke up into the five states of Costa

38 Tomaš Bartoš, '*Uti Possidetis, Quo Vadis?*', *Australian Year Book of International Law*, 1997, vol. 18, pp. 62–6.

39 Thirlway, note 3, pp. 15–6.

40 Lalonde, note 21, p. 139.

41 S. R. Ratner, 'Drawing a Better Line: *Uti Possidetis* and the Borders of New States', *American Journal of International Law*, 1996, vol. 90, p. 596. Heidi Jiminez takes a similar view claiming that the principle of *uti possidetis* was not applied in Africa, but rather the doctrine of state succession to treaties, although he also noted that *uti possidetis* was either akin to, or a prolongation of, the doctrine of state succession to boundary treaties: J. Klabbers and R. Lefeber, 'Africa: Lost Between Self-Determination and *Uti Possidetis*', in C. Brölmann, *et al.* (eds), note 33, p. 57.

42 One of the few exceptions was in British Cameroons where an internal administrative line established by the British in 1946 became an international border following separate plebiscites in the regions north and south of the 1946 line which resulted in the northern region joining Nigeria, and the southern region joining the Republic of Cameroon: M. A. Ajomo, 'The Nigeria/Cameroun Border Dispute: Implications at International Law', *Nigerian Current Law Review*, 1982, p. 137.

Rica, El Salvador, Guatemala, Honduras, and Nicaragua in 1838. The approach in Africa had the effect of precluding secession from colonies after independence, as is evidenced by the generally hostile attitude of African states to the attempted secessions of Katanga from Congo in 1960 and Biafra from Nigeria in 1967.

Uti possidetis *as a general international law principle*

The most significant difference between the African and pre-1986 Latin American experiences was the binding nature of *uti possidetis juris* in Africa as the applicable principle of international law in the resolution of all boundary disputes upon decolonisation. In pre-1986 Latin America the application of the principle of *uti possidetis juris* was dependent on agreement, usually by treaty, between the disputant states. In Africa, and in Latin America after 1986, the principle of *uti possidetis juris* was an obligatory rule of international law in judicial or arbitral proceedings concerned with boundary disputes, unless the relevant states specifically agreed that other principles should apply.[43] This transformation of *uti possidetis juris* into a 'time-hallowed principle'[44] of international law was the result of the decision of the Chamber in the *Frontier Dispute Case*.[45]

In ruling that *uti possidetis juris* was a rule of international law the Chamber made it clear that this was not a result of the African practice of respecting former colonial boundaries. It was not the case that the practice of African states contributed to the gradual emergence of a principle of customary law.[46] Rather, it was

43 There was no prohibition of states mutually agreeing by treaty to settle a boundary irrespective of what the boundary line was according to the *uti possidetis juris* rule. In *Case Concerning the Territorial Dispute* (*Libyan Arab Jamahiriya/Chad*) [1994] ICJ Rep. 6, at 23, the Chamber of the International Court of Justice said: 'There is nothing to prevent the parties from deciding by mutual agreement to consider a certain line as a frontier, whatever the previous status of that line.' It was on the basis of a treaty rather than on the basis of *uti possidetis juris*, that this case was determined, the Chamber holding, at 38, that the principle of *uti possidetis juris* was irrelevant.

44 *Case Concerning the Frontier Dispute* (*Burkina Faso and Mali*) [1986] ICJ Rep. 554, at 566.

45 In *Case Concerning the Territorial Dispute* (*Libyan Arab Jamahiriya/Chad*) [1994] ICJ Rep. 6, at 88, in a separate opinion, Judge Ajibola took the view that in dissenting opinions in *Case Concerning Sovereignty Over Certain Frontier Land* (*Belgium/Netherlands*) [1959] ICJ Rep. 209 Judges Armand-Ugon, at 240, and Moreno Quintana, at 255, both supported the view that the principle of *uti possidetis* should be treated as a general principle of international law. This view is overstated, given that neither of the two dissenting judges explicitly made such claims, although it could be inferred that the noting of the principle of *uti possidetis* in the context of a boundary dispute in Europe perhaps implies such a conclusion. A similar comment could be made in relation to the individual opinion of Judge M. Levi Carneiro in *The Minquiers and Ecrehos Case* (*France/United Kingdom*) [1953] ICJ Rep. 47, at 104–5, where mention was made of the *uti possidetis* principle and its interpretation and application by Brazil.

46 A different approach to this point was taken in *Case Concerning the Territorial Dispute* (*Libyan Arab Jamahiriya/Chad*) [1994] ICJ Rep. 6, in the separate opinion of Judge Ajibola, who, at 89, said: '[T]he *uti possidetis* principle should no longer be viewed as a principle limited in its application and scope to Latin America and African States, but one of general scope and universality which *has now finally emerged as a principle of customary international law*.' (Emphasis added.)

the application in Africa of a 'rule of general scope'.[47] Thus, the OAU statement of July 1964 on the intangibility of former colonial boundaries was merely 'declaratory rather than constitutive' in relation to this principle.[48] A consequence of this was that no challenge could be made to the application of the *uti possidetis juris* rule simply on the ground that independence was achieved before the OAU statement came into effect in 1964.[49]

The Chamber expressly declined to establish the basis upon which the *uti possidetis juris* rule was a 'firmly established principle of international law where decolonization is concerned'.[50] Technically the Chamber did not need to establish the basis for its claim. As it held, it was not necessary for the purposes of the case at hand to confirm that *uti possidetis juris* always applied after decolonisation. This was so because the parties themselves had by the Preamble of a Special Agreement of 16 September 1983 indicated that the Chamber was to rule on their boundary dispute on the basis of 'the principle of the intangibility of frontiers inherited from colonization'.[51] The Chamber interpreted this to mean that it was bound to apply the principle of *uti possidetis juris*.[52] In effect, the Chamber was following the practice of Latin American states before 1986 and applying *uti possidetis juris* because the disputant states stipulated that it be applied. Thus, it became immaterial as to whether *uti possidetis juris* was a general principle of international law to be applied wherever decolonisation occurred.

Nevertheless, the Chamber's failure to substantiate its assertion that *uti possidetis juris* was a firmly entrenched principle of international law is unfortunate.[53] No arbitral or judicial body had prior to this case made statements to that effect. The Chamber's lack of substantiation of itself raises doubts as to the validity of its assertion. However, there are good reasons to otherwise question the soundness of the Chamber's assertion.[54] The Chamber referred to the relevance of *uti possidetis juris* in Spanish America and held that the principle was not confined to that region but was rather a principle of general application. The Chamber then said that 'the principle of *uti possidetis*,[55] in the sense described above, fell to be applied'.[56] In effect, the Chamber ruled that in Spanish America, the principle of *uti possidetis juris* applied because it was, at that time, an existing general principle of international law. As the discussion of *uti possidetis* in the previous chapter has shown, in the context of Spanish America, this statement by the Chamber is wrong on two counts.

47 *Case Concerning the Frontier Dispute* (*Burkina Faso and Mali*) [1986] ICJ Rep. 554, at 565 and 566.
48 Ibid., at 566.
49 Ibid., at 567. See also *Case Concerning the Territorial Dispute* (*Libyan Arab Jamahiriya/Chad*) [1994] ICJ Rep. 6, at 90–1 per sep. op. Judge Ajibola.
50 *Case Concerning the Frontier Dispute* (*Burkina Faso and Mali*) [1986] ICJ Rep. 554, at 565.
51 Ibid., at 557.
52 Ibid., at 565.
53 For a critique of the Chamber's decision see Bartoš, note 38, pp. 55–60.
54 S. P. Sharma, *Territorial Acquisition, Disputes and International Law*, The Hague, Martinus Nijhoff Publishers, 1997, pp. 122–5.
55 The Chamber did not add the word '*juris*' to *uti possidetis* in this passage.
56 *Case Concerning the Frontier Dispute* (*Burkina Faso and Mali*) [1986] ICJ Rep. 554, at 565.

First, the principle of *uti possidetis juris* was not a principle of universal application in Spanish American boundary disputes. Rather than being *the* principle, it was *a* principle, adopted in resolving such disputes. The principle of *uti possidetis de facto* was often the basis of resolving boundary disputes. Second, when *uti possidetis juris* was adopted in Spanish America it was because the disputant states chose to do so, and not because of a universal principle that applied in the absence of the relevant states specifically providing otherwise. The experience of Spanish America, rather than confirming the views of the Chamber in the *Frontier Dispute Case*, points to the opposite conclusion.

Furthermore, doubts about the universal application of *uti possidetis juris* to boundary disputes following decolonisation were raised, at least implicitly, in the dissenting opinion of arbiter Bedjaoui in *Guinea-Bissau/Senegal*. In that case arbiter Bedjaoui, in ascertaining whether the principle of *uti possidetis juris* applied, thought it important to determine whether Guinea-Bissau agreed that the principle of *uti possidetis juris* applied. He said:

> This question is not superfluous because the *uti possidetis* principle for land frontiers has right from the start been under attack by certain African States. It must therefore be ascertained whether Guinea-Bissau was one of them.[57]

This passage implies that if Guinea-Bissau had been one of the states, such as Somalia and Morocco, which had questioned and opposed the principle of *uti possidetis*, such opposition would have been relevant in considering whether *uti possidetis* applied in its dispute with Senegal. If, however, the principle of *uti possidetis* was universal in application, it would be assumed that the question posed by arbiter Bedjaoui would simply be irrelevant, rather than, as he held, 'not superfluous'. The fact that Guinea-Bissau had not at any stage opposed the adoption of the principle of *uti possidetis*, and because the disputant states in *Guinea-Bissau/Senegal* expressly agreed that *uti possidetis* was to be the governing principle to be applied by the arbitral tribunal, meant it was unnecessary for arbiter Bedjaoui to further consider the issue. On the other hand, arbiter Bedjaoui did not exclude the possibility that *uti possidetis* may be a principle of general application in cases of boundary disputes following decolonisation. After stipulating that 'any reserve, hesitation, argument or questioning' regarding the applicability of the principle to the case at hand was irrelevant because both disputant states 'clearly stated their concurrence with this principle', arbiter Bedjaoui said:

> To my mind, this is an element of applicable law agreed by the Parties, *beyond any other consideration of general international law which might justify and impose the application of the principle in question.*[58] (Emphasis added)

57 *Case Concerning the Arbitral Award of 31 July 1989* (*Guinea-Bissau -v- Senegal*) (1989) 83 ILR 1, at 56.
58 Ibid., at 57.

Whatever one may make of arbiter Bedjaoui's opinion, it is hardly a clear endorsement of the views of the Chamber in the *Frontier Dispute Case*, of which he was, ironically, the President. Reservations about the Chamber's views in the *Frontier Dispute Case* were also expressed by Judge Lucharie in his separate opinion in that case, when he observed that:

> [F]rontiers of an independent State emerging from colonization may differ from frontiers of the colony which it replaces, and this may actually result from the exercise of the right of self-determination.[59]

Whatever the position may be on the question of the binding nature of *uti possidetis juris* in arbitral and judicial proceedings concerning boundary disputes, it is clear that in practice it was not always followed in Africa. This fact would tend to support the view that the principle is not one of such generality as stated in the *Frontier Dispute Case*. Thus, in the former German colony of Togo after World War I, the British and French divided the colony. In 1957 British Togoland merged with Ghana, rather than become a separate state.[60] In the British Cameroons the northern part voted for merger with Nigeria, while the southern part opted to join French Cameroon to form the Federal Republic of Cameroon.[61] British Northern Somaliland and Italian Southern Somalia united to form Somalia instead of remaining as two separate states.[62] The former Italian colony of Eritrea, which was administered by Britain after World War II, became a federal unit within Ethiopia in 1962, rather than an independent state.[63] However, Eritrean demands for independence were eventually successful, with Eritrea becoming an independent state in 1993 following a protracted war of secession from Ethiopia.[64] On the other hand, in 1962 the Belgian colony of Ruanda-Urundi dissolved into the two independent states of Rwanda and Burundi.[65] Finally, the colonial enclaves of Walvis Bay[66] and Ifni[67] did not

59 *Case Concerning the Frontier Dispute* (*Burkina Faso and Mali*) [1986] ICJ Rep. 554, at 653.

60 A. R. Sureda, *The Evolution of the Right of Self-Determination: A Study of United Nations Practice*, Leiden, A. W. Sijthoff, 1973, pp. 151–63. The secession of the former British Togoland from Ghana and allegations of irredentism by Togo (formerly French Togoland) has been a constant threat to the stability in the region and a source of difficulty in Ghana–Togo relations. See D. Brown, 'Borderline Politics in Ghana: The National Liberation Movement of Western Togoland', *Journal of Modern African Studies*, 1980, pp. 575–609.

61 Sureda, note 60, pp. 163–8.

62 Technically the union of the two Somali colonial territories was one of unification of independent states, as the unification was of two states that had only days before gained independence However, in practical terms it did amount to a non-application of the principle of *uti possidetis juris*.

63 Sureda, note 60, pp. 133–9.

64 R. Pateman, 'Eritrea Takes the World Stage', *Current History*, May 1994, vol. 93, no. 583, May 1994, pp. 228–31.

65 M. Shaw, *Title to Territory in Africa, International Legal Issues*, Oxford, Clarendon Press, 1986, pp. 113–14.

66 Ibid., pp. 137–40. Berat argues that the principle of *uti possidetis juris* was not applicable in the case

become independent but were integrated into the states of Namibia and Morocco respectively.[68]

Notwithstanding the above comments on the Chamber's view in the *Frontier Dispute Case*, it would appear that its ruling has gained acceptance, as is evidenced by the endorsement of those views by the Chamber in *El Salvador/Honduras*.[69]

Conclusion

The analysis of the principle of *uti possidetis* in this and the previous chapter leads to a number of conclusions that can be drawn from the application of this principle in Latin America, Asia and Africa.

First, the principle applied in cases of disputed boundaries between states in the wake of gaining independence from a colonial power. Although the disputes were between independent states, they were over the location of boundary lines determined by the former colonial power or powers. The purpose of the principle was to determine precisely where such boundary lines were in cases of disputes between states that emerged as the result of independence struggles or peaceful decolonisation. In Latin America the principle was directed at precluding the operation of the doctrine of *terra nullius* and preventing, or at least limiting, the occurrence of disputes between the newly independent states. In Africa the principle was directed solely at the latter of these two aims.

Second, the principle applied only if the disputant states agreed that it would. Consent was an absolute prerequisite. This was more evident in the case of Latin America, at least prior to 1986. In that year in the *Frontier Dispute Case* it was held that the principle of *uti possidetis juris* was an international law principle of general application in cases of boundary disputes following decolonisation. It must be noted that there are legitimate doubts as to whether the decision in the *Frontier Dispute Case* on this point is correct. However, even if the decision is accepted as correct, its effect was not to eliminate the requirement of consent. What it meant, especially in the context of African boundary disputes, was that the principle

of Walvis Bay because South Africa was not a member of the OAU and because the principle is not mandatory in any event: L. Berat, *Walvis Bay, Decolonization and International Law*, New Haven, CT, Yale University Press, 1990, pp. 166–7. Dugard, although not disagreeing that Walvis Bay properly belongs to Namibia, questions Berat's reasoning in relation to *uti possidetis juris*: J. Dugard, 'Book Review: Walvis Bay, Decolonization and International Law by Lynn Berat', *American Journal of International Law*, 1991, vol. 85, p. 753.

67 Shaw, note 65, pp. 135–6.

68 In relation to colonial enclaves Crawford is of the view that, if they are ethnically and economically parasitic upon a state, they do not constitute separate territorial units and thus have no right to self-determination: J. Crawford, *The Creation of States in International Law*, Oxford, Clarendon Press, 1979, p. 384. If so, no question of the application of the principle of *uti possidetis juris* can arise as such enclaves would not be able to emerge as independent states.

69 *Case Concerning the Land, Island and Maritime Frontier Dispute* (*El Salvador/Honduras*) [1992] ICJ Rep. 383, at 386–7. See also *Case Concerning the Territorial Dispute* (*Libyan Arab Jamahiriya/Chad*) [1994] ICJ Rep. 6, at 89, per sep. op. Judge Ajibola.

applied only if the disputant parties did not stipulate, as they were free to do, that other principles would apply. In Latin America other principles did apply. These included the principle of *uti possidetis de facto* and equity. On other occasions, states resorted to war to resolve boundary disputes and in effect applied the principle of *uti possidetis* as it had once applied to determine territorial rights following the end of war.

Third, the principle applied only to boundary disputes between states gaining independence from the same colonial power. Notwithstanding the decision in the *Frontier Dispute Case* to the contrary, it did not apply to cases involving boundary disputes where the disputant states gained independence from different colonial powers. In these cases the principle of state succession to international boundaries applied. In no case involving disputes between states which had different colonial masters was the principle of *uti possidetis juris* applied. Where such states did not feel bound by the principle of state succession to existing international boundaries, as in the case of Brazil, the principle of *uti possidetis de facto* was invariably applied.

An appreciation of the essential elements of the principle of *uti possidetis juris* is necessary before one can assess whether it can apply, or be adapted to apply, in cases of secession from an internationally recognised and independent federal state. In the case of Yugoslavia the principle was cited as justification for recognising the independence of Yugoslavia's republics within the limits of their existing internal federal borders. Whether this approach to the break-up of Yugoslavia was warranted or appropriate is a matter more fully explored in Chapter 7. However, before turning to this matter it is necessary to sketch Yugoslavia's historical background prior to its break-up in 1991, in particular the various changes to its internal borders that took place during that time. These issues are the focus of the next chapter. In Chapter 6 the evolution of the international community's policy, especially on the issue of post-secession borders, is traced, followed by an account of the various secessions that took place in Yugoslavia during the 1990s.

5 The national question and internal administrative borders in Yugoslavia, 1918–91

The secessions from the Socialist Federative Republic of Yugoslavia (SFRY), first of Slovenia and Croatia in late June 1991, and later of Macedonia, in late 1991, and Bosnia-Hercegovina, in early 1992, were all successful. International recognition as independent states and membership of the United Nations were granted to all four former Yugoslav republics. In all four cases recognition of statehood was within the bounds of Yugoslavia's internal republic borders established after World War II. Yugoslavia's other two republics did not seek international recognition as new states. Serbia and Montenegro[1] claimed to be the legal continuation of Yugoslavia after the secessions of the other four republics.[2]

To appreciate the historical, political and legal repercussions of the break-up of the SFRY in 1991 it is necessary to grasp the essentials of Yugoslavia's political and constitutional history. The turbulence of that history is indicated by the frequency of changes to Yugoslavia's name and constitutional structure. Yugoslavia, born in 1918 as the Kingdom of Serbs, Croats and Slovenes, was re-named the Kingdom of Yugoslavia in 1929. In the wake of the Kingdom's dismemberment during World War II, the Democratic Federative Yugoslavia emerged, to be renamed the Federative People's Republic of Yugoslavia in 1946, and then the SFRY in 1963. These name changes were not cosmetic, but rather reflected fundamental internal

1 In a referendum on 1 March 1992, 96 per cent of Montenegro's voters declared their support for 'Montenegro continuing to live in a common state of Yugoslavia as a sovereign republic and as an equal with other republics wishing to remain in Yugoslavia'. The referendum attracted 66 per cent of eligible voters, it being boycotted by Montenegro's Muslims, Albanians and some opposition parties: M. Andrejevich, 'Politics in Montenegro', in S. P. Ramet and L. S. Adamovich (eds), *Beyond Yugoslavia: Politics, Economics, and Culture in a Shattered Community*, Boulder, CO, Westview Press, 1995, p. 248. However, by late 1999 there was growing support within Montenegro for independence, with the Montenegrin government indicating that it was prepared to hold an independence referendum in the event that Montenegro's relationship with Serbia was not satisfactorily resolved.

2 The international community rejected this claim. Serbia and Montenegro were reconstituted as the Federal Republic of Yugoslavia (FRY) on 27 April 1992. On 31 October 2000 the United Nations (UN) Security Council recommended the FRY's admission to the UN: Security Council Resolution 1326 (2000), 31 October 2000. The UN General Assembly formally admitted the FRY to the UN on 1 November 2000: General Assembly Resolution 55/12, 1 November 2000.

structural changes in Yugoslavia's political landscape, including changes to the system of internal administrative borders. The same can be said of the various constitutions and constitutional changes that occurred during every decade of Yugoslavia's troubled history.

Yugoslavia's turbulent history represented an effort on the part of its political elites to find a workable constitutional structure to accommodate the aspirations of its multi-national population. This historical process, often referred to as the attempt to resolve Yugoslavia's national question, had, as an integral part of it, the establishment of acceptable internal administrative borders. The essence of the national question was a struggle between the forces that demanded either a centralist/unitary or a federalist constitutional order for Yugoslavia.

The inter-war Yugoslav Kingdom, 1918–41

The Kingdom of Serbs, Croats and Slovenes was established on 1 December 1918 and, as the name implies, reflected the multi-national character of the new state. At the start of the nineteenth century the territories of the future Yugoslavia, with the exception of Montenegro, were located within the confines of the Ottoman and Habsburg empires. The nineteenth century witnessed the evolution of Serb, Croat and Slovene nationalism. In each case it was the romantic nationalist ideas of Herder and Fichte that significantly influenced the leaders of each nation.[3]

The Serb national dream was the creation of a Serb nation-state that would incorporate Serbian territories in the Ottoman and Habsburg empires as well as Montenegro.[4] With the First and Second Balkan Wars of 1912 and 1913 this project had been essentially completed, at least insofar as the former Ottoman controlled lands were concerned. Indeed, it was the fear that Serbia would fully achieve its national dream at the expense of its South Slav possessions that drove Austria–Hungary towards seeking the military defeat of Serbia. The Sarajevo assassination of the heir to the Habsburg throne by a Bosnian Serb nationalist on 28 June 1914 provided Austria–Hungary with the excuse to provoke what it assumed would be the third Balkan War in as many years. Instead, Austria–Hungary's actions led to World War I and the collapse of its empire.

The Croats and Slovenes of the future Yugoslavia were predominantly located within the Austro-Hungarian empire. During the nineteenth century the most favoured goal towards the fulfilment of their nationalist aspirations was a revision of their status within the empire to create a third South Slav unit in the empire that

3 D. Heater, *The Theory of Nationhood: A Platonic Symposium*, London, Macmillan Press, 1998, pp. 125–6.

4 On the territorial space that formed part of the projected Serb state and the significance of such territories to Serb national consciousness see G. W. White, 'Place and its Role in Serbian Identity', in D. Hall and D. Danta (eds), *Reconstructing the Balkans: A Geography of the New Southeast Europe*, Chichester, John Wiley & Sons, 1996, pp. 39–52.

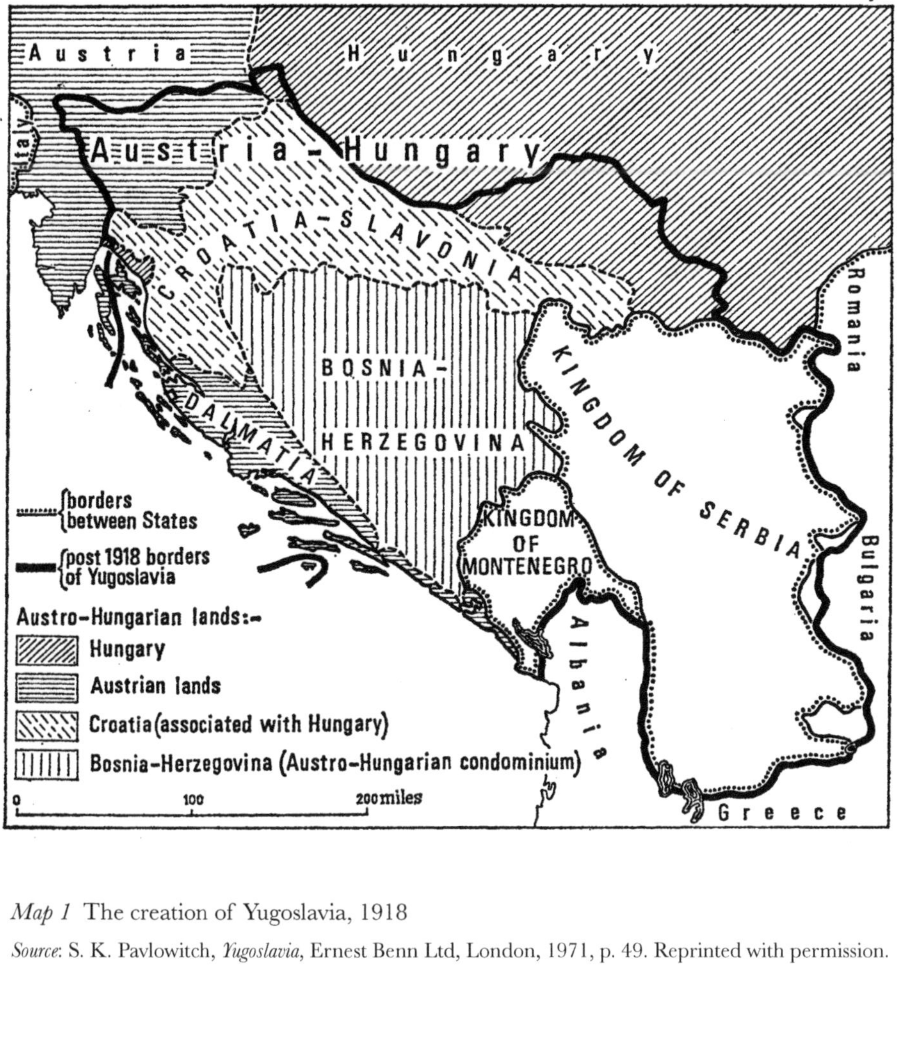

Map 1 The creation of Yugoslavia, 1918

Source: S. K. Pavlowitch, *Yugoslavia*, Ernest Benn Ltd, London, 1971, p. 49. Reprinted with permission.

would be equal to the existing German and Hungarian units.[5] It was only when the collapse of Austria–Hungary was inevitable as an outcome of World War I that this goal was abandoned. In its place the Croats and Slovenes sought union with Serbia and Montenegro. This arrangement was consummated by the proclamation, on 1 December 1918, of the Kingdom of Serbs, Croats and Slovenes under the aegis of Serbia's ruling dynasty.

5 A. C. Jenko, 'An Evolution of the Politics of Fragmentation: A Case Study of the Slovenes in Yugoslavia', unpublished doctoral dissertation, Boston University, 1993, pp. 71–141; N. I. Novosel, '*Regnum Regno*: Croatia's War Aims, 1914–1917', unpublished doctoral dissertation, Indiana University, 1986, pp. 12–41.

While it was agreed before its establishment that Yugoslavia would be a constitutional, democratic and parliamentary democracy, it was left to a future constituent assembly to establish whether the constitutional structure would be centralist/unitary or federalist. The Serbs overwhelmingly favoured centralism whereas the Croats and Slovenes favoured federalism. Serb political leaders were able to fashion a majority within the constituent assembly in favour of a centralist Constitution adopted on 28 June 1921.[6] The 1921 Constitution was a reflection of the official view that the Serbs, Croats and Slovenes were three tribes of one unified nation, namely the Yugoslavs. This approach was reflected in Article 3, which stipulated that the official language of the state was 'Serbo-Croato-Slovenian'.

In response the major Croat political party, the Croat Peasant Party (CPP), for most of the 1920s, boycotted the process of parliamentary democracy established by the 1921 Constitution. By the end of the decade Serb–Croat tensions had been exacerbated to such an extent that Yugoslavia's monarch, King Aleksandar, abrogated the 1921 Constitution and began a period of personal rule.

The oblast *internal administrative unit (1921–29)*

In terms of the Yugoslav Kingdom's internal administrative division, the 1921 Constitution established the *oblast* (district) as the basic political, economic and administrative unit in Yugoslavia (Article 95). By a ministerial decree, gazetted on 28 April 1922, the Kingdom was divided into 33 *oblasti*.[7] Given the official view of a unified Yugoslav nation, the state and regional entities that existed in the former Austro-Hungarian Empire were rejected as the basis of internal administrative divisions. It was argued that these former territorial units would, if maintained, encourage disunity and separatism.[8] The rationale underpinning *oblast* boundaries was the deliberate division of the state into a large, rather than small, number of administrative units, based upon 'natural, social and economic circumstances' (Article 95), without regard to former historical and cultural boundaries, thereby precluding 'tribalism'.[9] This intention was not completely realised. Bosnia-Hercegovina was divided into six *oblasti*, but Article 135 of the 1921 Constitution required the division to be completely within the framework of Bosnia-Hercegovina's historical boundaries as originally established during the Ottoman occupation of that region.[10] This constitutional provision was inserted as part of a package of concessions granted to the leading Muslim political party in Bosnia-Hercegovina for its support in voting for the

6 S. Jovanović, *Ustavno Pravo Kraljevine Srba, Hrvata i Slovenaca*, Belgrade, Službeni List SRJ, 1995, pp. 63–5.

7 Uredba o podeli zemlje na oblasti, 26 April 1922, in B. Petranović and M. Zečević (eds), *Jugoslovenski federalizam, Ideje i Stvarnost, Tematska zbirka Dokumenata, Prvi tom, 1914–1943*, Belgrade, Prosveta, 1987, pp. 192–4.

8 Jovanović, note 6, pp. 50–1.

9 Đ. Stanković, 'Administrativna podela Kraljevine SHS', *Istorijski glasnik*, 1981, no. 1–2, pp. 35–7.

10 B. Ž. Milojević, 'The Kingdom of Serbs, Croats, and Slovenes: Administrative Divisions in Relation to Natural Regions', *Geographical Review*, 1925, vol. 15, p. 82.

adoption of the 1921 Constitution, and it meant that the criteria for determining *oblast* boundaries as set out in Article 95 were ignored. A similar situation arose in the division of the territory of pre-war Serbia where *oblast* boundaries followed largely those of pre-World War I administrative units.[11] The administrative prefects of the *oblasti*, the *župani* (governors), were chosen by the King and had the task of administering the state's affairs in the *oblasti* (Article 95). *Oblast* assemblies passed regulations based upon the Constitution or other state laws (Article 99). However, due to political controversy surrounding the decree of 1922, it was only slowly implemented. Until the mid-1920s some areas were administered pursuant to the systems that existed before the creation of the Kingdom.[12]

The philosophy behind the *oblast* system reflected the programmes of the major Serb political parties. Serb politicians rejected federalism on largely practical grounds. Because the Serbs were the most territorially dispersed of Yugoslavia's constituent nations, it would have been impossible to create a Serb federal unit. In the view of Serb leaders, the adoption of federalism would have led to significant Serb minorities being subjected to domination by non-Serb national groups in other federal units.[13] Conversely, a unitary state based upon *oblast* local self-government was satisfactory for the Serbs, as such a state would not so divide them.

The banovina *internal administrative unit (1929–39)*

In his proclamation of personal rule on 6 January 1929, King Aleksandar asserted that parliamentarism, instead of strengthening the unity of the state, was increasingly threatening it, and that it was therefore his duty to do all he could to preserve the unity of the state and its peoples.[14] Aleksandar's personal rule formally came to an end, and was followed by a period of 'guided democracy', with the promulgation, on 3 September 1931, of a unitarist Constitution of the Kingdom of Yugoslavia. Aleksandar adopted a policy of integral Yugoslavism, the essential components of which were the establishment of a more effective centralised political system and the suppression of all forms of nationalistic expression. A key measure in this respect was a radical restructuring of the state at the very start of his personal rule into nine *banovine* (provinces), to replace the old division into 33 *oblasti*.[15] Theoretically the *banovine* were supposed to be responsive to both provincial needs and the principle of central government. Aleksandar argued that the *banovine* would preserve regional traditions while building national unity. To this effect the state was renamed the Kingdom of Yugoslavia on 3 October 1929.[16]

11 Ibid.

12 Stanković, note 9, p. 46.

13 B. Gligorijević, 'Unutrašnje (administrativne) granice Jugoslavije između dva svetska rata 1918–1941', *Istorija 20. Veka*, 1992, vol. 10, no. 1–2, p. 28.

14 Proklamacija Kralja Aleksandra, 6 January 1929, in Petranović and Zečević, note 7, pp. 293–4.

15 Zakon o nazivu i podeli Kraljevine na upravna područja, 3 October 1929, in Petranović and Zečević, note 7, p. 303.

16 Ibid.

Map 2 Yugoslavia's *banovina* borders, 1929–39

Source: A. N. Dragnich, *The First Yugoslavia: Search For a Viable Political System*, Stanford, CA, Hoover Institution Press, 1983, p. 82. Reprinted with permission.

During Aleksandar's personal rule all legislative authority was vested in the King. Under the 1931 Constitution legislative competence was shared between the King and the National Representation, a bicameral parliament containing a Senate and a National Assembly (Article 26). The 1931 Constitution maintained the system of *banovine*, established in 1929 (Article 83). The *banovine* provided for a degree of decentralisation, and were referred to as self-governing units (Article 84). Each *banovina* was headed by a *Ban* appointed by the King as the representative of the state (Article 85). Each *banovina* had a Council composed of elected members (Article 88). Each Council elected a *Banovina* Committee that acted as its executive organ (Article 89). The *banovine* had to act within the scope of competence permitted by law (Article 90) and were subject to the supervision of the central government (Article 92).

The administrative restructuring of the state was also accompanied by political reform in the form of the banning of all nationalist political parties, soon to be followed by the banning of all political parties. Any organisation based upon national interests was banned. Only a government-backed pan-Yugoslav political union could hope to succeed in national elections as was confirmed with the three elections held during the 1930s.

Aleksandar's policy of integral Yugoslavism failed. The suppression of nationalism met with bitter resistance. A significant segment of Serb leaders and the great majority of Croat leaders never accepted it. The policy led to the formation of more extreme nationalist organisations, such as the separatist Croat Ustaša movement. The Serb opposition was focused on the impact Aleksandar's policies had on abrogating political and civil liberties that they had fought for during most of the nineteenth century. Croats interpreted the suppression of nationalism as a mask for Serb hegemonism.[17]

The **Sporazum** *internal administrative system (1939–41)*

In October 1934 King Aleksandar was assassinated. Because his eldest son was still a minor, the royal prerogative passed to a Regency Council headed and dominated by Aleksandar's cousin, Prince Pavle. The Prince Regent saw a resolution of the Serb–Croat conflict as of paramount concern. He was also under considerable pressure from the United Kingdom and France to resolve Yugoslavia's internal problems so as to preserve its territorial integrity and prevent Nazi Germany from exploiting internal divisions and possibly dismembering it as had occurred in Czechoslovakia in 1938. This led to the *Sporazum* (Agreement) of 23 August 1939 negotiated between Pavle's government led by Dragiša Cvetković and the leader of the CPP, Vladko Maček.[18]

The *Sporazum* introduced a quasi-federal system in Yugoslavia by means of the

17 S. Trifković, 'The First Yugoslavia and Origins of Croatian Separatism', *East European Quarterly*, 1992, vol. 26, p. 362.

18 Sporazum Cvetković-Maček, 23 August 1939, in Petranović and Zečević, note 7, pp. 508–10.

creation of a federal Croatian *banovina*, whose territorial extent covered the two Croat-dominated Savska and Primorska *banovine* together with a number of bordering districts drawn from the Zetska, Vrbaska, Drinska and Dunavska *banovine*.[19] The precise extent of the Croatian *banovina* was to be determined when Yugoslavia was finally reorganised (Article 2).

By its terms the *Sporazum* granted the Croatian *banovina* extensive legislative competence. Matters relating to agriculture, commerce, industry, forests and mines, public works, social welfare, health, education, physical culture, justice and internal administration were the province of a revived Croatian *Sabor* (Articles 4–5). Executive authority in the *banovina* was entrusted to a *Ban*, who was appointed by the Crown and responsible to the Crown and a new Croatian assembly (Article 5). All other matters remained within the jurisdiction of the central government (Article 4). Definitive regulation of legislative competencies was deferred until the final reorganisation of the state (Article 6). The equality of Serbs, Croats and Slovenes within the Croatian *banovina* was recognised, as was the equality of major religious denominations (Articles 2–3).

The *Sporazum* failed to resolve the Serbo-Croat conflict. Its first problem was that it only applied a federal approach to part of Yugoslavia. Although it hinted at the extension of its provisions to the rest of Yugoslavia, the latter was still governed in accordance with the 1931 Constitution. The prospect of a future Slovenian *banovina* was the reason for Slovene support for the *Sporazum*.[20] However, extending federalism to the rest of Yugoslavia would have created significant problems in relation to federal borders, especially between Serbs and Croats in Bosnia and Hercegovina. The Croat political leadership sought the division of the rest of Yugoslavia into a number of *banovine*. Many Serb politicians demanded a single Serb *banovina* consisting of Yugoslavia minus the Croatian *banovina* as well as a new Slovenian *banovina*.[21] Furthermore, Serbs within the new Croatian *banovina* petitioned the authorities for their regions to be excluded from it. These Serb claims were unacceptable to Croat leaders, as they threatened a continuation of Serb supremacy in a federalised state. What the Croat leaders sought was the ascertainment of Croatian territory by application of nationalist and historical criteria, but the division of the rest of Yugoslavia by the application of geographic criteria.

The most significant aspect of the *Sporazum* was the rejection of the idea of a single Yugoslav people that was implicit in the 1921 and 1931 Constitutions and in Aleksandar's policy of integral Yugoslavism. The distinct national identity of the Croats was clearly recognised by the *Sporazum*. However, rather than resolving the Serbo-Croat conflict it only served to exacerbate it. It led to differences over the Croatian *banovina*'s final borders and the extension of the new arrangements to the rest of Yugoslavia. It also exacerbated more extreme sentiments amongst both

19 Gligorijević, note 13, p. 33.
20 Jenko, note 5, p. 257.
21 Nacrt uredbe o organizaciji srpske zemlje, in Petranović and Zečević, note 7, pp. 569–70.

Serbs and Croats. Maček's CPP found itself losing ground in Croatia to the separatist Ustaše movement. To the Ustaše the *Sporazum* was, at best, but a small step towards independence. Maček saw the *Sporazum* as a first step towards Croatia's quest for self-determination within the framework of a single Yugoslav state. Serb nationalist sentiment grew in opposition to the *Sporazum*. Many Serbs felt that too much had been conceded to the Croats. The ultimate expression of Serb nationalism was the military coup of 27 March 1941 which toppled Prince Pavle and installed King Aleksandar's son Petar, still a minor, to the throne. The coup leaders proclaimed internal factors as being the root causes for the coup, rather than dissatisfaction with Pavle's foreign policy which had led to Yugoslavia's adherence to the Tripartite Pact on 25 March 1941. The issue of what inspired the coup has long been a matter of historical controversy. It is indisputable, however, that the coup was essentially organised and supported by Serbs and reflected deep Serb nationalist sentiment. The direct consequence of the coup was the German-led Axis invasion of Yugoslavia, launched on 6 April 1941. The German invasion accentuated Croat dissatisfaction with the *Sporazum*. The lack of Croat resistance to the invading Germans and their evasion of the military call-up demonstrated 'complete [Croat] unwillingness to defend the agreement Maček had made on their behalf – or at least defend what it had become by the spring of 1941'.[22] The Axis invasion quickly resulted in the dismemberment of Yugoslavia in mid-April 1941. Yugoslavia was now drawn into World War II.

Of the three systems of internal administrative arrangements adopted during the life of the Kingdom of Yugoslavia, none resolved the nationalist dispute between the Serbs and Croats. The Croats saw the unitarist models contained in the 1921 and 1931 constitutions as harbingers of Serb hegemonism designed to obliterate Croat national identity and tradition. The quasi-federalist model contained in the 1939 *Sporazum* was seen by the Serbs as dividing much of the Serb nation into federal units where they would be minorities subject to assimilationist forces. They feared these forces would eventually deprive them of their Serb identity, and correspondingly reduce Serb influence in the Yugoslav state, which they saw as their own creation.

World War II and the first break-up of Yugoslavia, 1941–45

The March 1941 coup resulted in the Axis invasion and dismemberment of Yugoslavia which in turn unleashed a complex and multi-faceted war in Yugoslavia. Much of the fighting between various forces was motivated by nationalist hatred. This was most vividly exemplified in the Independent State of Croatia, established by the Axis powers and with the Ustaše movement installed in power. The

22 D. M. Mangham, '"Elusive Agreement": The Sporazum of 1939 and the Serb-Croat Dispute in the Context of the European Crisis', unpublished Master of Arts thesis, Rice University, 1992, p. 139.

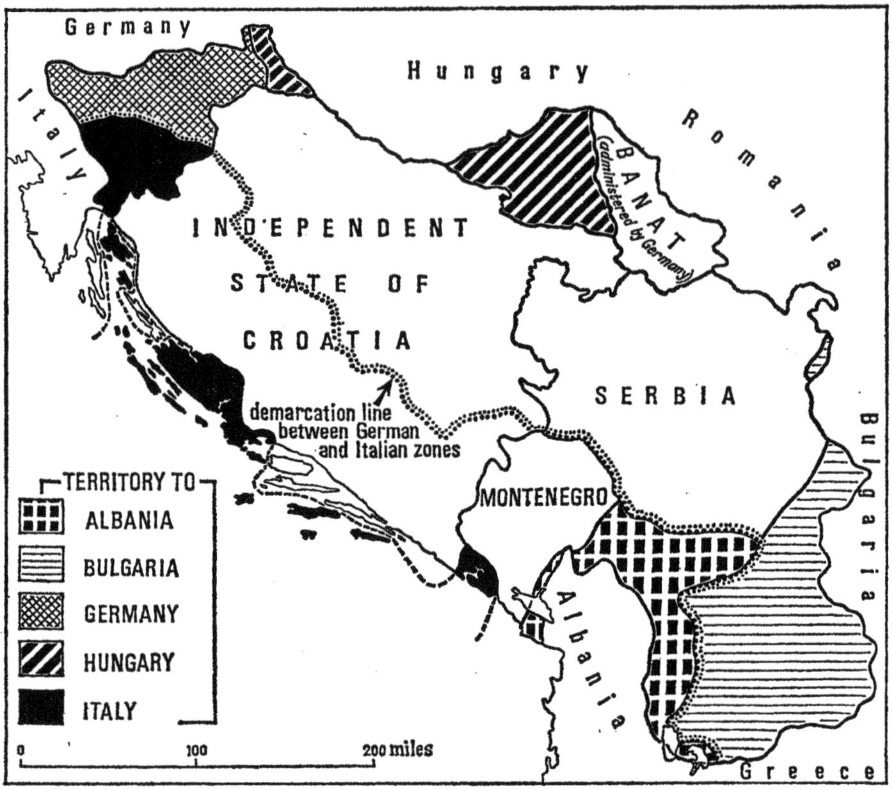

Map 3 The dismemberment of Yugoslavia during World War II, 1941–46

Source: S. K. Pavlowitch, *Yugoslavia*, London, Ernest Benn Ltd, 1971, p. 116. Reprinted with permission.

new Croat state incorporated traditional Croat lands dating back to the Austro-Hungarian Empire as well as Bosnia and Hercegovina. Approximately one-third of its population was Serb. A brutal policy of genocide against the Serbs, as well as the much smaller Jewish and Gypsy communities, was launched in mid-1941 with the aim of solving Croatia's 'Serb problem'.[23]

The most significant aspect of Yugoslavia's wartime experiences for present purposes is the different approaches to the question of the reconstruction of a united Yugoslavia after victory over the Axis forces. These different approaches came from the two major resistance movements, the Četniks and Partisans, which

23 M. Shelah, 'Genocide in Satellite Croatia During the Second World War', in M. Berenbaum (ed.), *A Mosaic of Victims: Non-Jews Persecuted and Murdered by the Nazis*, New York, New York University Press, pp. 74–9.

emerged in 1941 and which battled the foreign occupier and each other with a view to assuming power after the completion of the war.

The first resistance movement to emerge was the Četnik movement whose support was predominantly drawn from Yugoslavia's Serb population. Its initial political goal was the restoration of the monarchy and the pre-war unitary state structure. However, these goals changed by the end of the war to an acceptance of a federal state structure albeit with a dominant Serb unit.[24] Despite initial support from the Allies, in late 1943 the Četnik forces were abandoned in favour of their Partisan rivals. This led to the rise of the Partisans as the leaders of a reunited Yugoslavia that emerged in the wake of its liberation from Axis occupation by early 1945.

The Partisan movement, dominated by the Communist Party of Yugoslavia (CPY) and led by Josip Broz Tito, adopted a much more flexible and politically calculated approach to Yugoslavia's future structure. The essence of Partisan policy was equal treatment of all national groups in the face of Nazi occupation. The CPY's stress on the theme of 'brotherhood and unity' enabled it to eventually gain widespread support, even though initial support for the Partisans was overwhelmingly drawn from the Serbs. The Partisan leadership realised that only by appeals to the national identity of Yugoslavia's population would it succeed in attracting support. This in turn led the Partisans to introduce the Leninist concept of national self-determination into its political programme.[25] This necessitated a close identification of national and patriotic freedoms, which was a key factor in the appeal of the Partisan resistance.[26]

On 27 November 1942, the first session of the Antifascist Council of the People's Liberation of Yugoslavia (AVNOJ), an ostensibly multi-party 'partisan Parliament' organised by the CPY and convened at Bihać in Bosnia, declared itself the legitimate representative of the Yugoslav peoples.[27] At its second session held at Jajce in Bosnia, on 29–30 November 1943, AVNOJ proclaimed itself the supreme legislative and executive body of Yugoslavia. Furthermore, Yugoslavia was to 'be established on a democratic federative principle as a state of equal peoples'.[28] On 27 March 1944 the provisional government passed a law changing Yugoslavia's name to Democratic Federative Yugoslavia.[29] The law was never formally proclaimed as the provisional government was in the process of negotiating various agreements with the Royalist government-in-exile. As a result, on 7 March 1945,

24 M. Vesović and K. Nikolić, *Ujedinjene srpske zemlje: Ravnogorski nacionalni program*, Belgrade, Vreme Knjige, 1996, pp. 33–55, 56–71.

25 W. Connor, *The National Question in Marxist–Leninist Theory and Strategy*, Princeton, NJ, Princeton University Press, 1984, pp. 155–6.

26 P. Shoup, 'The Yugoslav Revolution: The First of a New Type', *Studies on the Soviet Union* (New Series), 1971, vol. 11, no. 4, p. 233.

27 Rezolucija o organizaciji AVNOJ, 27 November 1942, in Petranović and Zečević, note 7, p. 727.

28 Deklaracija Drugog zasedanja Antifašističkog Vijeća narodnog oslobođenja Jugoslavije, 29 November 1943, in Petranović and Zečević, note 7, pp. 795–6.

29 Zakon o imenu države i državnom grbu, 27 March 1944, in B. Petranović and M. Zečević (eds), *Jugoslovenski federalizam, Ideje i Strvarnost, Tematska zbirka dokumenata, Drugi tom, 1943–1986*, Belgrade, Prosveta, 1987, p. 10.

Tito was appointed the head of the government of a Yugoslav state which was the legal successor to the former inter-war Kingdom. However, the state was consistently referred to as the Democratic Federative Yugoslavia until it was renamed on 29 November 1945.

At its third session, held in Belgrade on 7–9 August 1945, AVNOJ was renamed the Provisional National Assembly.[30] On 21 August 1945 the Provisional National Assembly passed a Law on the Constituent Assembly for the purposes of electing a Constituent Assembly to prepare a new constitution for Yugoslavia.[31] The election for a new Constituent Assembly, held on 11 November 1945, resulted in an overwhelming victory for the Popular Front, headed by the CPY. When the Constituent Assembly convened on 29 November 1945, it immediately voted to proclaim the state's name as the Federative People's Republic of Yugoslavia (FPRY), formally ending the Kingdom of Yugoslavia. It also abolished the monarchy and declared Yugoslavia to be a federal republic, a community of equal peoples who had freely expressed their will to remain united within Yugoslavia.[32]

Although the CPY was officially committed to a policy of federalism in a reconstituted Yugoslavia, as a result of policies adopted at the second session of AVNOJ, administration of Partisan-controlled territory during the war was increasingly centralised in the hands of the CPY.[33] Throughout the war the CPY remained a highly centralised organisation. The war and revolution provided it with a new generation of cadres whose first loyalty was to the CPY and its essentially unitary approach to the national question.[34]

Tito's Yugoslavia, 1945–80

The victory of the Partisans coincided with a subsidence of nationalist expression within Yugoslavia. Many Yugoslavs welcomed the escape from the nationalistic mood of the war in which so many lives had been lost in the name of nationalism. Nationalist leaders had been forced to flee or were executed, leaving the forces of nationalism temporarily leaderless. Furthermore, the economic destruction of the war period left the state with new challenges to occupy the attention of its population. Official Yugoslav dogma asserted that the national question in Yugoslavia had been solved by the victory of the Partisans in World War II.[35] However,

30 Predlog rezolucije AVNOJa, 10 August 1945, Ukaz o zaključenju III zasedanja Privremene narodne skupštine Demokratske Federativne Jugoslavije, 26 August 1945, in Petranović and Zečević, note 29, pp. 193–4.

31 Zakon o Ustavotvornoj skupštini, 21 August 1945, in Petranović and Zečević, note 29, pp. 211–2.

32 Deklaracija o proglašenju Federativne narodne republike Jugoslavije, 29 November 1945, in Petranović and Zečević, note 29, pp. 228–30.

33 P. Shoup, *Communism and the Yugoslav National Question*, New York, Columbia University Press, 1968, pp. 72–4.

34 Ibid., pp. 91–2.

35 F. W. Hondius, *The Yugoslav Community of Nations*, The Hague, Mouton, 1968, p. 182, quoting Tito's claim that the national question had been solved by the Yugoslavs in the same way as it had been solved by Lenin and Stalin in the Soviet Union.

nationalism did persist. The non-Slavic minorities were a particular problem. Their association with the Axis forces during the war left them suspect in the eyes of the CPY, and they suffered many punitive acts. The effect of such actions was to reinforce the nationalist sympathies of these minorities. The campaign against the Catholic Church, for its role in Croatia during World War II, and the Serbian Orthodox Church, for its role as spokesman for Serb nationalism during the inter-war years, led to conflict between church and state, which quickly assumed nationalist overtones.[36]

The critical aspect of Yugoslavia's constitutional arrangements implemented during the period in which Tito was at the helm of the CPY – renamed as the League of Communists of Yugoslavia (LCY) in 1952 – was its federal structure.[37] This federal structure was the fundamental basis of the Partisan political programme during World War II which mandated that Yugoslavia was to consist of six republics, five of which were to be homelands for Yugoslavia's five constituent peoples, the Serbs, Croats, Slovenes, Macedonians and Montenegrins, with the sixth republic of Bosnia-Hercegovina, based upon historical borders, the home of Serbs, Croats and Slavic Muslims, the latter acquiring the status of a constituent nation only in the early 1970s. These provisions were justified on the principle of national self-determination and the equality of all of Yugoslavia's nations.[38] In addition to the republics, in 1946 it was resolved to create, within Serbia, the two autonomous sub-federal units of Kosovo-Metohija (renamed Kosovo in 1963) and Vojvodina.

This federal structure was sacrosanct, it being seen as one of the pillars of the communist Yugoslavia that emerged as a result of the Partisan struggle during World War II. Thus it appeared as a cardinal feature of all of communist Yugoslavia's constitutional documents, namely the 1946 Constitution adopted on 31 January 1946, the extensive amendments to that constitution by means of the Fundamental Constitutional Law of 13 January 1953, the 1963 Constitution adopted on 7 April 1963, and the 1974 Constitution adopted on 21 February 1974. However, in reality the Yugoslav state in the immediate post-World War II years was a highly centralised state due to political control exercised by the highly centralised CPY. In this respect the leadership role of Tito was crucial.

Despite its assertions to the contrary, the Partisan victory over its nationalist opponents in World War II did not resolve Yugoslavia's national question. By the 1960s nationalist sentiment had resurfaced and was most apparent in the debate over economic reform. The more prosperous republics of Slovenia and Croatia led the debate in demanding greater republic control over economic resources and a concomitant reduction of their subsidisation of the less economically advanced

36 Shoup, note 33, pp. 103–7.

37 For detailed analyses of these arrangements see P. Radan, 'Constitutional Law and the Multinational State: The Failure of Yugoslav Federalism', *University of New South Wales Law Journal*, 1998, vol. 21, pp. 185–203; Hondius, note 35.

38 Odluka Drugog zasedanja Antifašističkog Vijeća narodnog oslobođenja Jugoslavije o izgradnji Jugoslavije na federativnom principu, 29 November 1943, in Petranović and Zečević, note 7, pp. 800–1.

republics. The fall from power in 1966 of Aleksandar Ranković, Vice-President of Yugoslavia and leader of the opposition to such reforms, symbolised the victory of the Slovenian and Croatian reformers, and ushered in a short period of relatively overt nationalist sentiment, especially in Croatia where that republic's leadership was able mobilise large segments of its population in support of greater political decentralisation. It was only Tito's intervention, in 1971, that suppressed this growth in nationalism and rescued Yugoslavia from its most serious threat of political disintegration since World War II.

In constitutional terms, the 1963 Constitution was a significant stepping-stone in the trend towards extensive decentralisation of Yugoslavia's constitutional structure. This decentralisation was accompanied by a similar decentralisation within the LCY. The 1963 Constitution introduced the concept of the Yugoslav federation as being a 'community of nations' rather than a framework for some form of national integration. This constitution marked an emphatic rejection of the ideas of Yugoslavism and an all-Yugoslav culture that were briefly floated during the late 1950s. The process of decentralisation was completed by the adoption of the 1974 Constitution which saw the republics and autonomous provinces established as the major sources of political power. The key indicator of the supremacy of Yugoslavia's republics and autonomous provinces over federal institutions was the veto power they had over federal legislation.

The 1974 Constitution was bitterly resented by intellectual dissidents in Serbia. Dobrica Ćosić, a prominent Serb writer and party stalwart was expelled from the LCY in 1968 because of his opposition to the process of decentralisation, especially in relation to the advance in status of the autonomous province of Kosovo.[39] Mihailo Đurić, a professor of law at Belgrade university, took the view that the granting of significant powers to the republics meant that Yugoslavia was reduced to nothing more than a geographical concept, and that the republics were in effect independent states. In these circumstances he questioned the validity of republic borders, given that they were, with the exception of Slovenia, inadequate as borders for nation-states for the various Yugoslav nations. This was especially so for the Serbs with so many of them living outside Serbia. On this basis, Đurić claimed, the Serbs were the most disadvantaged of Yugoslavia's constituent nations.[40] Although not of great significance at the time, the ideas of Ćosić, and Đurić provided a conceptual basis for the Serb nationalism that emerged in the 1980s.

Significant Serb opposition to the 1974 Constitution did not arise during the 1970s because of the important role played by Tito. The 1974 Constitution made Tito Yugoslavia's President for life. His guiding hand was able to effectively control the republics by reaffirming the leading role of the LCY in Yugoslav society, its right to intervene in all aspects of Yugoslav life , and its monolithic unity. He was thus able to maintain the loyalty of republic political elites to himself and his

39 S. Đukić, *Čovek u svom vremenu, Razgovori sa Dobricom Ćosićem*, Belgrade, Filip Višnjić, 1989, pp. 185–200.

40 M. Đurić, 'Smišljenje smutnje', *Anali pravnog fakulteta u Beogradu*, 1971, vol. 19, no. 3, pp. 230–3.

vision of Yugoslavia. However, by the late 1970s the problems of maintaining such loyalty were becoming increasingly difficult. Even Tito sensed that Yugoslavia was facing a difficult future. In 1978, in response to a question from a long-time political collaborator about what was wrong with Yugoslavia and the Party, Tito replied: 'There is no Yugoslavia. . . . There is no party any more.'[41] Following his death in 1980, the system of a collective presidency of Yugoslavia established by the 1974 Constitution meant that no Yugoslav leader of Tito's stature was able to emerge. In such an environment, coupled with strained economic circumstances caused by a massive foreign debt, the role of the LCY declined, and the formal structures embodied in the 1974 Constitution facilitated the emergence of virulent republic-based nationalism.

The internal administrative borders of communist Yugoslavia

In relation to communist Yugoslavia's internal administrative borders established in 1946, although the second session of AVNOJ resolved that Yugoslavia would be a federation of republics, it did not pass any resolution relating to the borders between them. Republic borders were in fact determined by the leadership of the CPY from late 1945 to early 1946. The establishment of these borders was never the subject of any legal document or act of any state institution established by the 1946 Constitution.[42]

The borders of Yugoslavia's six republics were in essence determined at a meeting of the AVNOJ Presidency on 24 February 1945 along the following lines:

> Slovenia is taken in the borders of the former Dravska *banovina*; Croatia in the borders of the former Savska *banovina* with 13 districts of the former Primorska *banovina* and the Dubrovnik district of the former Zetska *banovina*; Bosnia-Hercegovina in the borders specified in the Berlin agreement; Serbia in the borders before the Balkan wars with districts taken from Bulgaria in the Treaty of Versailles; Macedonia – Yugoslav territories south of Kačanik and Ristovac; Montenegro in the borders before the Balkan wars with the Berane and Kotor districts and Plav and Gusinje.[43]

This decision relied largely on older historical borders, both as they existed in interwar Yugoslavia and in the former Austro-Hungarian and Ottoman empires.[44]

41 J. Ridley, *Tito: A Biography*, London, Constable, p. 409.

42 P. Radan, 'Yugoslavia's Internal Borders as International Borders: A Question of Appropriateness', *East European Quarterly*, 1999, vol. 33, p. 142; B. Lekić, 'Administrativne granice u Jugoslaviji posle Drugog Svetskog Rata', *Istorija 20. Veka*, 1992, vol. 10, no. 1–2, p. 145.

43 Quoted in K. Cavoški, *Na rubovima srpstva, Srpsko pitanje danas*, Belgrade, Tersit, 1995, p. 25.

44 Boban argues that at the second session of AVNOJ it was understood, although not explicitly stated, that republic borders would be set according to earlier, essentially historic, borders: L. Boban, *Hrvatske granice od 1918. do 1992. godine*, Zagreb, Školska Knjiga, 1992, p. 52.

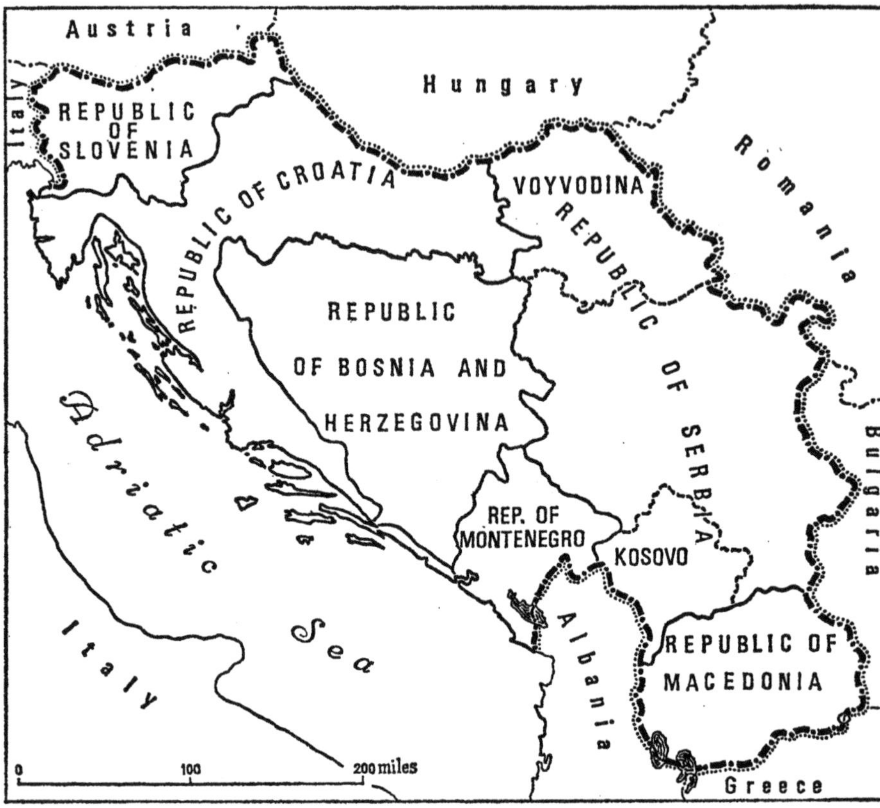

Map 4 Yugoslavia's internal administrative borders, 1946–91

Source: S. K. Pavlowitch, *Yogoslavia*, Ernest Benn Ltd, London, 1971, p. 228. Reprinted with permission.

In many respects the decision accepted borders that coincided with, either exactly or approximately, the borders claimed by the various nationalist movements of the nineteenth and early twentieth centuries.[45] This is most clearly evident in the cases of Slovenia and Bosnia-Hercegovina. Slovenia comprised those areas of Yugoslavia that were claimed by the Slovenes as their territories during the time of the Austro-Hungarian empire and which in interwar Yugoslavia were divided into two *oblasti* in 1922, and which later became the Dravska *banovina* in 1929. In addition, part of the Istrian peninsula gained by Yugoslavia from Italy after World War II was added to Slovenia. In the case of Bosnia-Hercegovina the borders were those

45 J. Pleterski, *Nacije-Jugoslavija-revolucija*, Belgrade, Izdavački Centar Komunist, 1985, p. 463.

established at the Congress of Berlin in 1878.[46] In interwar Yugoslavia under the *oblast* system, Bosnia-Hercegovina was to some extent kept intact, with the constitutional requirement that the six *oblasti* established there had to be within the borders established in 1878. It was only with the *banovina* system, and especially with the creation of the Croatian *banovina* in 1939, that Bosnia-Hercegovina's historic borders were not maintained in any sense at all.

In the case of Macedonia, borders approximated the claims of Macedonian nationalists to Macedonian territory within the confines of Yugoslavia. In the case of Montenegro, borders were very similar to those of the Montenegrin state as existed before its entry into World War I, although they were somewhat reduced in scope. On the other hand Montenegro included the Kotor district, which, prior to World War I, had been part of Dalmatia, ruled by the Habsburgs from Vienna. In the case of Croatia, apart from part of Vojvodina being allocated to Serbia, the rest of the republic, except for the Kotor district, essentially corresponded to the Croat medieval Triune Kingdom. To that was added the bulk of the Istrian peninsula gained from Italy after World War II. The Serbia–Croatia border in Vojvodina was the only border area in which any inter-republican commission was formed for the purposes of delimitation. The commission determined the border mostly on national criteria.[47]

In the case of Serbia, its borders were reduced in the south from those with which it entered World War I by the creation of Macedonia, but increased in the north by the addition of Vojvodina. Because the Serb population of Yugoslavia was so geographically dispersed, an even approximately homogeneous Serb national unit in Yugoslavia was impossible. The Serbs accepted this reality at that time.

In relation to Yugoslavia's internal administrative borders after World War II three matters need to be analysed. First is the question of why the CPY adopted these essentially historical borders. Second is the question of the significance that was attached to these borders. Third is the question of alterations to republic and autonomous province borders.

The reasons why essentially historic borders were adopted by the CPY are found in the nature of the Partisan political and military strategy during World War II. In its effort to gain popular support for its cause, the Partisan leadership recognised the importance of appealing to the nationalist sentiments of the population. In many cases this was a key factor in the Partisans' popular appeal. It was necessary to recognise the Macedonian nation to entice the Yugoslav Macedonians away from embracing Bulgaria. It was necessary to recognise the Montenegrin nation to secure their support and correspondingly reduce Četnik influence in the region. The support of the existing constituent nations of Yugoslavia, the Serbs, Croats and Slovenes, was also garnered by appealing to their senses of national

46 D. Rusinow, 'Yugoslavia's Disintegration and the Ottoman Past', in L. C. Brown (ed.), *Imperial Legacy: The Ottoman Imprint on the Balkans and the Middle East*, New York, Columbia University Press, 1996, pp. 95–6.

47 L. Dimić, 'Nekoliko dokumenata o privremenoj administrativnoj granici između jugoslovenskih republika Srbije i Hrvatske', *Istorija 20. Veka*, 1992, vol. 10, no. 1–2, pp. 231–46.

identity. In a socialist federation there was no reason to depart from essentially historical borders as the basis of internal administrative borders except where none had existed, as in the case of Macedonia. To do so would have risked alienating the popular support for the Partisans so carefully marshalled by appeals to popular nationalist sentiment. Furthermore, given that the federation was to be symbolic rather than substantive, internal administrative borders were of little practical consequence, especially since, in the minds of the CPY leadership, the national problem had been resolved by Partisan policies adopted during the war and revolution. The tightly disciplined and centralised CPY was to be the real power centre. No real power was to be granted to the republics.

The political reality of a centralised state in 1946 was the reason behind there being no Serb objections to the system of internal borders established at that time. However, further Serb acceptance of its republic borders was conditional upon the federation remaining centralised. In this there was a parallel with the circumstances prevailing in 1921. Serb leaders accepted the Yugoslav state established by the 1921 Constitution as long as it remained unitarist. It was the case that Serb dissatisfaction with Yugoslavia arose, in both the interwar period and the post-World War II period, when Yugoslavia moved away from these unitarist/centralist models.[48]

The significance, which was attached to republic borders in 1946, can be seen in a speech to the founding congress of the Communist Party in Serbia in May 1945 when Yugoslavia's first President, Josip Broz Tito, described them as 'only an administrative division'. He then went on to say:

> I do not want in Yugoslavia borders that will separate. As I have said 100 times, I want borders to be those that will unite our peoples.[49]

This comment was made in the context of rejecting claims that Serbia, on account of its republic borders, had been split apart. Tito explained that if Bosnia-Hercegovina and Serbia were equal republics with their own federal units, then the CPY had not split Serbia apart, but rather guaranteed the good fortune of Serbs (and Croats and Muslims) in Bosnia. In a speech later in May 1945 in Zagreb Tito repeated this theme when he said:

> Many do not yet understand what is the meaning of federative Yugoslavia. It does not mean the drawing of a border line between this or that federative unit. . . . No! Those border lines, as I see them, must be something like white veins in a marble staircase. The lines between federated states in a federal Yugoslavia are not lines of separation, but of union.[50]

48 M. Jovičić, *Državnost federalnih jedinica*, Belgrade, Naučna knjiga, 1992, p. 84.

49 Iz govora Generalnog Sekretara KPJ JB Tita na osnivačkom kongresu KP Srbije, 8 May 1945, in Petranović and Zečević, note 29, p. 159.

50 Quoted in Hondius, note 35, p. 180.

In the light of Tito's comments, Yugoslav internal federal borders were widely described, by the CPY, as being only 'formal' on account of Yugoslavia being a 'federal, undivided and joint state'.[51]

As to the alteration of internal federal borders, the 1946 Constitution declared that republic borders could not be altered without the consent of the relevant republics (Article 12). A similar provision was made in the 1963 Constitution, but it also provided that changes to republic borders required an agreement between the assemblies of the relevant republics (Article 109). The 1963 provisions were reaffirmed in the 1974 Constitution, with the added stipulation that they also applied to the borders of Serbia's two autonomous provinces (Article 5). What these provisions effectively meant was that internal federal borders were sacrosanct, as indeed they remained upon being delineated after World War II. Only minor adjustments to internal federal borders occurred in the decade thereafter.[52] The reason for the sacrosanct nature of these borders was the view that they were the achievement of the Partisan war and revolution. As such they were part of the underpinning of the entire constitutional and legal system and thus bound all future constitution-makers.

In addition to the republics the Yugoslav federal system established two autonomous units, Vojvodina and Kosovo-Metohija within the republic of Serbia. The establishment of these autonomous units was not a matter determined at the AVNOJ sessions, but rather in the lead-up to the 1946 Constitution. Vojvodina, with a relative majority Serb population, but with a strong Hungarian minority, was justified on grounds of its Hungarian population. Its borders were essentially based on historical borders dating back to the time of the Austro-Hungarian empire. Kosovo-Metohija was established along essentially national criteria on the basis of its majority Albanian population. This mixture of historical and national criteria for the establishment of autonomous units was confined to Serbia. If the criteria had been consistently applied to other republics, autonomy for Istria, within Croatia, would have been justified on historical criteria, and autonomy for the Serbs on the southern border regions of Croatia and the Albanians in western Macedonia would have been justified on national criteria.[53]

Nationalism and the beginning of the end of Yugoslavia, 1980–91

By the 1980s Yugoslav federalism in practice had been dramatically transformed from the practice of the late 1940s. In the terminology of Riker, the centralised federalism of the late 1940s had, as a legacy of the 1974 Constitution, been transformed into a peripheralised federal system.[54] With the restraining influence of

51 Lekić, note 42, pp. 147–8.

52 Ibid.

53 S. Samardžić, 'Yugoslav Federalism: Unsuccessful Model of a Multinational Community', *International Review of Sociology*, 1996, vol. 6, p. 250; Čavoški, note 43, pp. 32–6.

54 W. H. Riker, *Federalism, Origin, Operation, Significance*, Boston, Little, Brown & Co, 1964, pp. 5–8.

Tito gone, overt nationalism soon emerged for the first time since the mass Croat nationalist movement of the late 1960s–early 1970s. Its first outbreak was in the Albanian riots of 1981 which witnessed demands for constituent nation status for the Albanians and republic status for the autonomous province of Kosovo.[55] The Albanian demands ignited a Serb nationalist response. Kosovo was seen by many Serbs as the cradle of Serb civilisation. The Serb fixation on Kosovo could not countenance acceptance of Albanian demands. The 1981 riots in Kosovo were suppressed by federal authorities whose actions had the support of all the republics. Serbia's later demand for the reintegration of Kosovo into Serbia was opposed by a number of the republics, especially Slovenia. The reintegration of Kosovo into Serbia was achieved by amendments to Serbia's republic constitution in February 1989 and July 1990 which effectively revoked the legal basis for Kosovo's autonomy within Serbia. Kosovo's status reverted to that held under the 1946 Constitution. Kosovo's parliament was suspended and direct rule from Belgrade was imposed.[56]

The most significant document evidencing the revival of Serb nationalism was a draft Memorandum of the Serbian Academy of Sciences and Arts which was leaked to the media in 1986. The document called for the return to the centralised federalism of the immediate post-World War II era and for the reunification of Serbs within a reconstituted Yugoslav state ruled by the LCY. Although it firmly rejected the 1974 Constitution, it did not reject the idea of a Yugoslav state. Only at its end did the Memorandum concede that, if Yugoslavia's other nations did not accept the Serb solution of Yugoslavia's reintegration, the Serbs would have to consider other alternatives.[57] Serbia's aspirations to greater centralism coincided with demands for greater central control of the economy made by the international financial community which was pressing Yugoslavia over its massive foreign debt.[58]

The response to Serb calls for increased centralism was led by Slovenia, later to be joined by Croatia. The substance of their response was transformation of Yugoslavia into a confederation, or failing that, independence. The conflict between these rival conceptions as to Yugoslavia's future proved to be insoluble. This failure was symbolised by the collapse of the LCY at the Extraordinary Fourteenth Congress in January 1990. At the Congress Slovenia initiated proposals to transform the LCY into an organisation of equal League of Communist organisations which were free to join the LCY. This proposal to confederalise the LCY was rejected.[59] This rejection resulted in the Slovenian, and then the Croatian, delegations abandoning the Congress. In many ways this marked the political end of federal Yugoslavia. With the demise of the LCY at a federal level

55 A. Pavković, *The Fragmentation of Yugoslavia: Nationalism and War in the Balkans*, 2nd edition, London, Macmillan, 2000, pp. 86–7.

56 M. Vickers and J. Pettifer, *Albania: From Anarchy to Balkan Identity*, London, Hurst & Company, 1997, pp. 147–8.

57 Pavković, note 55, p. 89.

58 S. L. Woodward, *Balkan Tragedy: Chaos and Dissolution After the Cold War*, Washington, DC, Brookings Institution, 1995, p. 59.

59 Extraordinary LCY Congress, 30 January 1990, *BBC Summary of World Broadcasts*, EE/0675/C/1.

there was no force, except perhaps the Yugoslav Army, capable of keeping the republics together in one state. In republic elections across Yugoslavia in 1990 victory went to parties with nationalist platforms, whether led by nationalist dissidents, as in Croatia, or by communists, as in the case of Serbia. In the multi-national republic of Bosnia-Hercegovina no single party emerged victorious. Rather, a fragile power-sharing arrangement was reached by the three nationalist parties, representing the Muslims, Serbs and Croats, which had gained overwhelming support within their respective national constituencies.[60] Anti-nationalist, pro-Yugoslav parties gained only marginal support in all of these elections.[61]

In the first half of 1991 a series of summits between republic presidents failed to reach any compromise over Yugoslavia's future. These summits saw Serbia and Montenegro arguing for a centralised federal state. Slovenia and Croatia demanded the transformation of Yugoslavia into a confederation. This confederacy proposal, originally submitted in October 1990 as a draft for the constitutional restructuring of Yugoslavia, effectively amounted to the partition of Yugoslavia into several sovereign and independent states.[62] The presidents of Bosnia-Hercegovina and Macedonia argued for a compromise between these two alternatives that would allow republics to establish mutual relations of varying closeness. Some would establish federal links, others would establish confederal links.[63] Whilst these summits were in progress Slovenia and Croatia announced their intention to secede from Yugoslavia on 25 June 1991.

During this period of increased political tension there was greater international attention and concern over the fate of Yugoslavia. Although international leaders uniformly called for the continued integrity of Yugoslavia and condemned threats of secession, the international reaction to the deepening crisis in Yugoslavia was confined to such rhetoric. This was so despite the United States of America being well informed by its Central Intelligence Agency that any collapse of Yugoslavia was likely to be violent.[64] Symbolic of this attitude was the reaction of the USA to the escalating Yugoslav crisis. In a visit to Yugoslavia on 25–26 February 1990 Deputy Secretary of State Lawrence Eagleburger made it clear to Slovenian and Croatian leaders that the United States would not advocate the dismemberment of Yugoslavia, but by the same token it was not going to fight for Yugoslavia's unity.[65] Nearly sixteen months later Secretary of State James Baker visited Yugoslavia on

60 On the republican elections and results see Woodward, note 58, pp. 119–23; S. M. Tull, 'Ethnopolitics and Conflict in the Breakup of Yugoslavia: A Theory of Ethnic Mobilization', unpublished doctoral dissertation, University of Michigan, 1995, pp. 91–131.

61 L. J. Cohen, *Broken Bonds: Yugoslavia's Disintegration and Balkan Politics in Transition*, 2nd edition, Boulder, CO, Westview Press, 1995, p. 160.

62 R. M. Hayden, *Blueprints for a House Divided: The Constitutional Logic of the Yugoslav Conflicts*, Ann Arbor, University of Michigan Press, 1999, pp. 53–65.

63 Pavković, note 55, pp. 125–7.

64 W. Zimmermann, *Origins of a Catastrophe, Yugoslavia and Its Destroyers – America's Last Ambassador Tells What Happened and Why*, New York, Times Books, 1996, p. 84.

65 Ibid., p. 62.

21 June 1991.[66] Although Baker called for restraint on all sides and reiterated continued support for Yugoslavia's territorial integrity, it was also clear to all of Yugoslavia's republic leaders that the USA, and thus the rest of the international community, would not actively intervene in the crisis.[67] This amounted to giving the green light for the use of force against secessionist republics. On the other hand, the statements that the USA could live with the dismemberment of Yugoslavia was interpreted by the Slovenian and Croatian leaderships 'as a green light to push a secession program'.[68] Within days Slovenia and Croatia declared their independence.

Why did Yugoslavia's federation fail?

In seeking an explanation as to why the Yugoslav federation failed, it is important to appreciate that internal or domestic political factors cannot be considered in isolation from external or international factors. Despite Yugoslavia's internal problems and the parlous nature of its federalism, Yugoslavia's collapse was not anticipated by many observers and scholars. This was so because the bipolar international system militated against the collapse of states. However, with the changes to the international order that followed directly from the policies of *glasnost* and *perestroika* in the USSR in the 1980s, a new international order emerged. It was one in which preservation of the territorial integrity of states was not as important as it once had been. It was a time in which Yugoslavia would be allowed to break up if its internal political structure was incapable of maintaining the state's continued unity.

From the perspective of internal politics the reason for the failure of federalism in Yugoslavia is relatively simple. Federalism is, as Howse and Knop argue, an inadequate response to the forces of nationalism in multi-national states. The nation, as a group linked by a common history and culture and bound to a national ideal that the nation should be autonomous, united and distinct in its national homeland, focuses upon an individual's loyalty to the nation rather than the state as such. It

66 Ibid., pp. 135–8; J. A. Baker III, *The Politics of Diplomacy: Revolution, War and Peace, 1989–1992*, New York, G. P. Putnam's Sons, 1995, pp. 478–83.

67 In testimony before the US House of Representatives International Relations Committee on 12 January 1995, Baker conceded that the USA and the international community had not been strong enough in their support for Yugoslavia's territorial integrity. He said: '[I]t was Slovenia and Croatia who unilaterally declared independence. . . . They used force to seize their border posts. And that, indeed, triggered the civil conflict. . . . [T]he position of the United States with respect to maintaining the territorial integrity of Yugoslavia, was supported by 32 countries of the [CSCE]. Everyone supported that. And it was the right policy. And it's too bad we didn't stand up to that policy for longer than we did': Hearing by the House International Relations Committee, Chaired by: Representative Benjamin A. Gilman, Witness: James Baker, Former Secretary of State, 12 January 1995, Federal News Service Transcript (Lexis/Nexis). See also Baker, note 66, p. 635.

68 Zimmermann, note 64, p. 62. In his book, at 73, Zimmermann notes that in a meeting with Croatia's President Tuđman after the 1990 Croatian elections, Tuđman 'was relieved to hear' Zimmermann's statement that the USA 'favored the unity of Yugoslavia but wouldn't support the preservation of unity through force'.

has as its optimal goal a state, the nation-state. Thus, the territorial integrity of multi-national states is not a nationalist goal. Rather, for the nationalist the politics of secession and irredentism are legitimate means towards the desired goal of a nation-state. The right to a nation-state is usually justified on the basis of the romantic theory of the right of peoples to self-determination.[69]

On the other hand, federalism entails a division of competencies between the central authority and its constituent units. Nationalism, in seeking its own independent nation-state, does not envisage any sharing of competencies. The nationalist's ideal is for a unitary or centralised state. In seeking to accommodate nationalist groups within a multi-national state by means of creating federal units for each national group, the nationalist is accepting what is always the second-best alternative. Independent statehood is always the preferred objective. The creating of federal structures in such cases is likely to increase, rather than decrease, the level of dispute and conflict. The federal unit will always claim that the central authority is intruding on its legitimate interests and affairs. If the central authority seeks to exercise powers, it will be branded as hegemonistic and domineering. If it concedes to the federal unit, it will be seen as weak and ineffective, and ultimately unnecessary. Granting a federal unit strong social, political, legal and economic institutions only serves to make nationalism more, rather than less, of a force. The only factor that can keep a federation together in such circumstances is the presence of a centralised political party structure in which the party structure operating at the central authority level is able to control the party structure at the level of federal units. If there is only a single party operating in such a centralised party structure then the task of maintaining the federation is generally easier.[70]

Yugoslavia's history offers significant evidence in support of these arguments. The quasi-federalist *Sporazum* of 1939, rather than satisfying Croat demands, only served to increase them. Although the Croat political leadership was not in favour of secession at the time, there is little doubt that secession would have been demanded by them if the international circumstances were different. Similarly, the trend towards decentralisation of the 1960s facilitated the growth of nationalism and republic demands for greater rights, to such an extent that Yugoslavia's integrity was genuinely threatened in 1971. With the breakdown of central authority and fragmentation of the LCY during the 1980s, and with an international system without vested interests in preserving Yugoslavia, the latter came to a predictable end.

In granting substantial cultural,[71] social, political, economic and legal rights to

69 R. Howse and K. Knop, 'Federalism, Secession, and the Limits of Ethnic Accommodation: A Canadian Perspective', *New Europe Law Review*, 1993, vol. 1, pp. 271–89. A similar argument is advanced in W. Kymlicka, 'Is Federalism a Viable Alternative to Secession?', in P. B. Lehning (ed.), *Theories of Secession*, London, Routledge, 1998, pp. 112–13, 138–41.

70 Riker, note 54, pp. 129–36.

71 Wachtel argues that the devolution of political power in relation to cultural and educational matters from the 1960s onwards was a vital and necessary prerequisite to the nationalism that emerged in the 1980s, and concludes that '[a]lthough it was believed that giving the various nations more

various national groups within the framework of federal and sub-federal territorial units, Yugoslavia facilitated the nationalism, not only of the Croats, but also the Slovenes, Bosnian Muslims, Macedonians and Albanians. All these groups sought to secede from Yugoslavia within the confines of their territorial federal units. The only mechanism capable of keeping the forces of separatism in check was the LCY. With its increased fragmentation after Tito's death in 1980 and its ultimate collapse in 1990, it was only a matter of time before one of the republics declared its independence.

Given the geographical dispersion of Serbs within Yugoslavia it was not surprising that they favoured a centralised Yugoslavia that could serve as a guarantor of their equal treatment with members of Yugoslavia's other nations. However, the centralised form of state structure was consistently and, in the end, effectively, resisted by Yugoslavia's other nations. As far back as 1920, the eminent Serb constitutional lawyer and historian Slobodan Jovanović observed that pre-World War I Serbia was not the Prussia of the Balkans, as it had neither the military might nor the disciplined political tradition to dominate Yugoslavia as Prussia dominated the unified German state after 1871.[72]

Yugoslavia's history validates the thoughts of John Stuart Mill who in *Representative Government*, wrote:

> [In areas of mixed nationality sometimes] the different races come to feel towards each other as fellow countrymen; particularly if they are dispersed over the same tract of country. But if the era of aspiration to free government arrives before this fusion . . . [and the nationalities remain unreconciled], there is not only an obvious propriety, but, if either freedom or concord is cared for, a necessity, for breaking the connection altogether.[73]

At the heart of Mill's claim is the belief that in a multi-national state centralism which is opposed by one or more national groups is not a solution. This is illustrated by Yugoslavia's experiences for most of the interwar period and for the post-World War II period up to the mid-1960s. This is not to say that multinational states cannot survive. They can, and have, where the self-interest of national groups makes the continuation of the common state preferable to its dismemberment. This occurred on occasions in Yugoslavia, for example, in the very first years of her existence, and in the late 1930s. However, by 1991 such sentiment was largely absent in Yugoslavia. There was no political figure with real power who

autonomy would reduce centrifugal tensions within the country, this did not happen. Rather the separate nations of Yugoslavia simply demanded more and more autonomy at the expense of a rapidly weakening center': A. B. Wachtel, *Making a Nation, Breaking a Nation: Literature and Cultural Politics in Yugoslavia*, Stanford, CA, Stanford University Press, 1998, p. 226.

72 S. Jovanović, 'Je li federalizam kod nas mogućan', in R. Samardžić and Ž. Stojković (eds), *Sabrana dela Slobodana Jovanovića*, Vol 1, Belgrade, Bigz, p. 368.

73 Quoted from Representative Government, Chapter XVI, in J. S. Mill, *Utilitarianism – Liberty – Representative Government*, London, J. M. Dent & Sons Ltd, 1954, p. 366.

espoused the ideology of a perpetual and indissoluble Yugoslav federation. Yugoslavia's political history had not produced an equivalent to Abraham Lincoln. As a result, the secessionist demands of four of its republics led to the break-up of Yugoslavia. The course of Yugoslavia's secessions and the international response to them are the subjects of the next chapter.

6 The international response to and course of the Yugoslav secessions

As the political tensions unfolded in Yugoslavia from the late 1990s onwards the international community did not initially involve itself to a great degree. It was more pre-occupied with other major international problems, notably the impending collapse of the Soviet Union and the Gulf War against Iraq. Indeed, it was only after the secessions of Slovenia and Croatia in late June 1991 that any significant steps were taken to contain and control what had by then evolved beyond a political crisis into a military crisis of significant magnitude. The principal international institution involved in Yugoslavia's break-up, at least in the initial stages, was the European Community (EC).

The transformation of the international reaction to the Yugoslav secessions

In the months preceding the Slovenian and Croatian declarations of independence, the international community publicly voiced its opposition to secession and supported the continued territorial integrity of Yugoslavia. In a letter of 28 March 1991 to Yugoslav Prime Minister Ante Marković, President George Bush of the United States of America (USA) stated that 'the United States . . . will not encourage those who would break the country apart'.[1] A subsequent and detailed State Department Statement in May 1991 declared that 'the US will not encourage or reward secession', and reiterated US support for 'the territorial integrity of Yugoslavia within its present borders'.[2] On 21 June 1991, during a visit to Yugoslavia, US Secretary of State James Baker made it clear that the USA would not recognise the planned declarations of independence by Slovenia and Croatia. On the other hand, Baker made it clear that the USA would not condone the use of force to keep Yugoslavia together.[3] US policy was motivated by concerns that the

1 George Bush Letter to Prime Minister Marković of March 28, *Focus*, Special Issue (Belgrade), 14 January 1992, pp. 44–5.

2 US Statement on Yugoslavia, *Focus*, note 1, p. 73.

3 W. Zimmermann, *Origins of a Catastrophe, Yugoslavia and Its Destroyers – America's Last Ambassador Tells What Happened and Why*, New York, Times Books, 1996, pp. 133–8; J. A. Baker III, *The Politics of Diplomacy, Revolution, War and Peace, 1989–1992*, New York, G. P. Putnam's Sons, 1995, pp. 478–83.

break-up of Yugoslavia would encourage secessionist and disintegrative forces within the Union of Soviet Socialist Republics (USSR).[4]

The USSR, beset with its own centrifugal forces, supported Yugoslav unity. In April 1991, Soviet Foreign Minister Aleksandr Bessmertnykh remarked that Yugoslavia's territorial integrity was 'one of the essential preconditions for the stability of Europe'.[5]

The EC expressed views similar to those of the USA.[6] A high-powered delegation to Yugoslavia in late May 1991 supported Yugoslavia's integrity.[7] This approach was reinforced at a meeting of EC Foreign Ministers on 23 June 1991, which, in an issued statement, declared that the EC would not recognise any unilateral declaration of independence by either Slovenia or Croatia.[8] On 19 June the 35-member Conference of Security and Cooperation in Europe (CSCE), of which Yugoslavia was a member, issued a statement supporting Yugoslavia's integrity.[9] The principle underpinning these policy statements was derived from the Helsinki Final Act 1975 which stipulated that there could be no changes to international state borders except by consent.[10]

The Slovenian and Croatian declarations of independence in late June 1991 led to war in Yugoslavia. The first front was in Slovenia, but was short-lived and ended ten days later with the withdrawal of the Yugoslav People's Army (YPA). The second front was in Croatia. There the conflict was far more bloody and lasted until a successful cease-fire was negotiated in January 1992. Against this background of military conflict, management of the Yugoslav crisis at the international level passed, by general international consensus, to the EC. On 28 June 1991 the European Council issued a Statement in which earlier pronouncements of the EC and CSCE on Yugoslavia were reaffirmed. However, the Council Statement called for a moratorium of three months concerning the declarations of independence.[11] The Council's Statement was clearly equivocal. On the one hand it supported the earlier statements supporting the territorial integrity of Yugoslavia, but on the other hand it did not close the door on recognising the Slovenian and Croatian secessions. The door was left open by the call for the moratorium. The Statement was a compromise position, behind which lay deep divisions within the EC on the question of recognition of the seceding republics.

The division within the EC saw France and Spain in favour of maintaining a

4 R. Lukic and A. Barton, *Europe from the Balkans to the Urals: The Disintegration of Yugoslavia and the Soviet Union*, New York, Oxford University Press, 1996, pp. 244–5.

5 L. J. Cohen, *Broken Bonds: Yugoslavia's Disintegration and Balkan Politics in Transition*, 2nd edition, Boulder, CO, Westview Press, 1995, p. 218.

6 M. Lak, 'The Involvement of the European Community in the Yugoslav Crisis During 1991', *Yearbook of European Studies*, 1992, vol. 5, pp. 177–8.

7 Cohen, note 5, p. 219.

8 *The European Report*, 26 June 1991, no. 1688, p. 7.

9 Statement on Situation in Yugoslavia, in A. Bloed (ed.), *The Conference on Security and Co-operation in Europe: Analysis and Basic Documents, 1972–1993*, Dordrecht, Kluwer Academic Publishers, 1993, p. 818.

10 (1975) 14 ILM 1292–325.

11 *Europe*, 29 June 1991, no. 5523, p. 8.

federal Yugoslavia.[12] Germany and Belgium supported the other viewpoint favouring the possible recognition of Slovenia and Croatia in particular.[13] Thus, German Chancellor Helmut Kohl, soon after the European Council Statement of 28 June 1991, declared his support for the principle of self-determination.[14] Similarly, Belgian Prime Minister Wilfried Martens called upon the EC members 'to envisage the recognition of independence of Croatia and Slovenia, if, after a period of three months, it is not possible to organise the co-existence of the republics on a new legal basis in a peaceful manner'.[15]

The ambiguity of the EC position was further reflected in an EC Declaration on 5 July 1991, which asserted that as a result of the secessions of Slovenia and Croatia 'a new situation has arisen'. It also referred to settlement of the crisis on the basis of respect for international law. Particular reference was made to 'the right of peoples to self-determination' and the 'territorial integrity of States'.[16] According to the senior official dealing with Yugoslavia in Germany's Foreign Ministry, the explicit reference to the right of peoples to self-determination was included in the declaration at the insistence of Germany.[17] The tenor of this declaration was repeated in the Brioni Accord of 7 July 1991, which also provided for a moratorium of three months on implementation of the declarations of independence by Slovenia and Croatia.[18]

On 8 July 1991 European Commission President Jacques Delors, in a statement reflecting the pro-recognition view within the EC, asserted that the EC had not ruled out the possibility of recognising Slovenia and Croatia, and also stressed that there was no question of contesting a people's right to self-determination.[19]

On 27 August 1991 an EC Declaration on Yugoslavia stated, in reference to Croatia, that the EC was determined never to recognise changes to Croatia's frontiers which were brought about by force. This was a significant statement in that it appeared to accept Croatia as a subject of international law. Further, it made clear that the principles of territorial integrity applied not only to international borders, but also to the internal federal borders of an internationally recognised state.[20]

The 27 August 1991 Declaration by the EC also established the EC Conference on Yugoslavia. In due course former British Foreign Secretary Lord Carrington was appointed as its Chairman. The mandate given to Lord Carrington included two

12 A. Macleod, 'French Policy Toward the War in the Former Yugoslavia: A Bid for International Leadership', *International Journal*, 1997, vol. 52, pp. 245–6.

13 *The European Report*, 6 July 1991, no. 1691, p. 3.

14 *Europe*, 1–2 July 1991, no. 5525, p. 4. See also M. Libal, *Limits of Persuasion: Germany and the Yugoslav Crisis, 1991–1992*, Westport, CT, Praeger, 1997, pp. 15–16.

15 *Europe*, 5 July 1991, no. 5228, p. 4.

16 EC Declaration on the Situation in Yugoslavia, 5 July 1991, in S. Trifunovska (ed.), *Yugoslavia Through Documents: From its Creation to its Dissolution*, Dordrecht, Martinus Nijhoff Publishers, 1994, p. 310.

17 Libal, note 14, pp. 19–20.

18 Joint Declaration of the EC Troika and the Parties Directly Concerned with the Yugoslav Crisis, the So-Called 'Brioni Accord', 7 July 1991, in Trifunovska, note 16, p. 312.

19 *The European Report*, 10 July 1991, no. 1692, p. 2.

20 Declaration on Yugoslavia, 27 August 1991, in Trifunovska, note 16, pp. 333–4.

significant conditions. First, none of the six Yugoslav republics would be recognised as independent states unless there was an overall settlement reached that was acceptable to all six republics. Second, no changes could be made to borders except by peaceful agreement.[21] This latter point was made explicitly clear in the EC Declaration on the occasion of the opening of the Conference on Yugoslavia on 7 September 1991. The Declaration stated that the EC was 'determined never to recognise changes of *any* borders which have not been brought about by peaceful means and by agreement'[22] (emphasis added). On 18 October 1991 the Conference on Yugoslavia issued a framework for the peaceful settlement of the Yugoslav crisis in which it referred to the recognition of independence 'within the existing borders, unless otherwise agreed, of those republics wishing it'.[23] An amended framework issued on 1 November 1991 contained an identical provision.[24]

In a similar vein, a CSCE Statement of 3 September 1991 stressed that 'no territorial gains or changes within Yugoslavia brought about by violence are acceptable'.[25] This provision clearly implied the inviolability of Yugoslavia's internal borders, and was endorsed by the United Nations Security Council on 25 September 1991.[26] On 10 October 1991 a further CSCE Statement stipulated that its member states would 'never . . . recognize any changes of borders, whether external or internal, brought about by force'.[27] In a joint declaration of the EC, the USA and the USSR on 18 October 1991, it was stated that there could be no acceptance of changes to borders, internal or external, obtained by force, and that all such changes would be considered 'unacceptable in 1991 in the heart of Europe'.[28]

Given the impossibility of agreement between the Yugoslav republics on changing internal borders, the consequence of the EC approach was that if new international states were to emerge from Yugoslavia, these states would be based upon the republics of Yugoslavia, either as separate independent states, or as combinations of republics forming new states. This was confirmed by an EC declaration of 8 November 1991 which referred to the 'prospects of recognition and independence of those Republics wishing it'.[29]

It was at this stage that German political leaders assumed the initiative within the EC. Since July 1991, Germany had been manoeuvring behind the scenes to secure Western recognition of Slovenia and Croatia. German public opinion,

21 Lord Carrington, 'Turmoil in the Balkans: Developments and Prospects', *RUSI Journal*, 1992, vol. 137, no. 5, p. 1.

22 Declaration on the Occasion of the Ceremonial Opening of the Conference on Yugoslavia, 7 September 1991, in Trifunovska, note 16, pp. 343–5.

23 Peace Conference on Yugoslavia: Arrangements for General Settlement, Article 1.1(e), 18 October 1991, in Trifunovska, note 16, pp. 357–63.

24 Peace Conference on Yugoslavia: Treaty Provisions for the Convention, Article 1.1(e), 1 November 1991, in Trifunovska, note 16, pp. 370–8.

25 Statement on the Cease-Fire in Yugoslavia, 3 September 1991, in Bloed, note 9, p. 907.

26 Security Council Resolution 713 (1991), Preamble, 25 September 1991.

27 The Situation in Yugoslavia, 10 October 1991, in Bloed, note 9, p. 910.

28 Declaration on Yugoslavia, 18 October 1991, in Trifunovska, note 16, p. 356.

29 Declaration on the Suspension of the Trade and Cooperation Agreement With Yugoslavia, 8

especially of its managerial elite, supported recognition of the seceding republics.[30] Soon after the Slovenian and Croatian independence declarations, German leaders voiced opinions favouring international recognition of Slovenia and Croatia. Thus, on 29 June 1991, at an EC heads of state summit, Chancellor Kohl argued that the unity of Yugoslavia could not be maintained by force.[31] On 3 July 1991 German Foreign Minister Hans-Dietrich Genscher assured the Croat member of the Yugoslav Collective Presidency and its last President, Stipe Mesić, that Germany would intervene with leading states to gain support for the recognition of Slovenia and Croatia.[32] On 4 September 1991 Chancellor Kohl and Genscher, when addressing the German parliament, spoke of recognition of seceding republics based upon the right of self-determination. Genscher said: 'If those peoples of Yugoslavia who desire independence cannot realize it through negotiations, we will recognize their unilateral declarations of independence'.[33] In October 1991 Slovenenian politicians were assured by Bonn that recognition was 'only a matter of choosing the right moment and the right circumstances'.[34] The German recognition that the claims to statehood of the seceding republics were based upon the right of peoples to self-determination was reflected in an EC Declaration on the Situation in Yugoslavia of 6 October 1991. This Declaration was issued against the background of increased violence in Yugoslavia. The Declaration said:

> The right to self-determination of all peoples of Yugoslavia cannot be exercised in isolation from the interests and rights of ethnic minorities within the individual Republics. These can only be assured through peaceful negotiations for which the Conference on Yugoslavia, including its Arbitration Commission, has been convened.[35]

EC conditions for recognition of Yugoslavia's seceding republics

The culmination of Germany's diplomatic initiative on behalf of the seceding republics was the meeting of EC Foreign Ministers on 16 December 1991.[36] This

November 1991, in Trifunovska, note 16, p. 379. It can also be noted that on 4 October 1991, the Chairman of European Political Cooperation said that 'it would be necessary to formulate a political solution on the basis of the perspective of recognition of the independence of those republics wishing it': Meeting held at Ministry of Foreign Affairs, 4 October 1991, *Focus*, note 1, p. 169. This was the first formal statement of the possible recognition of the secessionist republics.

30 Cohen, note 5, p. 236.

31 R. Caplan, 'The European Community's Recognition of New States in Yugoslavia: The Strategic Implications', *Journal of Strategic Studies*, 1998, vol. 21, no. 3, pp. 24–45.

32 S. Mesić, *Kako smo srušili Jugoslaviju: Politički memoari*, Zagreb, Globus, 1992, p. 75.

33 Libal, note 14, pp. 44–5.

34 Cohen, note 5, p. 238.

35 EC Declaration on the Situation in Yugoslavia, 6 October 1991, in Trifunovska, note 16, pp. 351–2.

36 For accounts of the crucial EC meeting see Libal, note 14, pp. 83–5; H-D. Genscher, *Rebuilding a*

meeting issued a Declaration inviting Yugoslavia's republics to submit applications for recognition to the EC by 23 December 1991.

In an application for recognition, a republic had to state whether:

- it wished to be recognised as an independent state;
- it agreed to accept the commitments of EC Guidelines on recognition;
- it agreed to accept obligations respecting human rights of national or ethnic minorities;
- it supported the continued efforts of the UN and EC to resolve the Yugoslav crisis.

Finally, an applicant for recognition had to have constitutional and political assurances in place to the effect that it had no territorial claims towards any neighbouring EC member state.[37] This last condition was inserted to allay Greece's fears of alleged territorial claims by Macedonia to Greek Macedonia.[38]

The EC Guidelines on recognition, after specifically confirming 'the principle of self-determination', went on to stipulate the following requirements as pre-conditions for recognition of Yugoslavia's seceding republics:

- respect for the provisions of the UN Charter, the Final Act of Helsinki[39] and the Charter of Paris,[40] especially with respect to the rule of law, democracy and human rights;[41]
- guarantees for the rights of ethnic and national minorities;
- respect for the inviolability of all frontiers, which could only be changed by peaceful agreement;
- commitment to settle by agreement or arbitration all questions concerning state succession and regional disputes;

House Divided: A Memoir by the Architect of Germany's Reunification, New York, Broadway Books, 1998, pp. 513–15.

37 Declaration Concerning the Conditions for Recognition of New States, 16 December 1991, in Trifunovska, note 16, pp. 431–2.

38 It was ironic that the EC required applicants for recognition to have constitutional and political assurances of this type in place, given that one EC member, Ireland, had provisions in its constitution that explicitly referred to territorial ambitions against another state, the United Kingdom. Article 2 of the Irish Constitution of 1937 stipulates: 'The national territory consists of the whole of the island of Ireland, its islands and the territorial waters'. Article 3 makes reference to 'pending the re-integration of the national territory'. By the terms of the Northern Ireland Peace Agreement of 10 April 1998, Ireland agreed to repeal Articles 2 and 3 of its Constitution. A new Article 3 stipulates that Irish unification is the aim of the Irish nation, but that it can only be achieved by peaceful means and with the democratically expressed consent of both Ireland and Northern Ireland.

39 (1975) 14 ILM 1292–325. It is ironic that respect for the Helsinki Final Act was one of the pre-conditions for recognition, given that the Slovenian and Croatian unilateral declarations of independence and forceful seizure of border posts were, as noted by US Secretary of State, James A. Baker, 'all in violation of the Helsinki Accords': Baker, note 3, p. 635.

40 (1991) 30 ILM 190–228.

41 Because of the essentially European nature of these two documents it is arguable that the EC guidelines on recognition are of relevance only in Europe and not to other parts of the world.

- acceptance of all relevant commitments with regard to disarmament and nuclear non-proliferation as well as to security and regional stability.[42]

Each application received by the EC was to be referred to the Arbitration Commission, headed by French lawyer Robert Badinter (the Badinter Commission), which had been established pursuant to the EC Declaration of 27 August 1991. The Badinter Commission was part of the framework of the Conference on Yugoslavia with the function of resolving difficulties between 'the relevant authorities' (not specifically identified).[43] It consisted of five members, all being presidents of constitutional courts of EC member states.[44] The decision to set up the Badinter Commission was subsequently endorsed by both the USA and USSR.[45]

The Badinter Commission was to make recommendations to the EC in time for an EC meeting on 15 January 1992 when decisions on recognition would be made. Applications for recognition were received for consideration from Slovenia, Croatia, Bosnia-Hercegovina and Macedonia. Serbia and Montenegro did not make applications on the basis that they regarded themselves as being the continuation of Yugoslavia.

The EC Declaration of 16 December 1991 formally confirmed the switch in policy by the international community away from insisting on the maintenance of Yugoslavia's territorial integrity and towards legitimising secession, albeit within the confines of Yugoslavia's internal republic borders.[46] What was left to be determined was whether individual seceding republics complied with the conditions for recognition. Against this background, it is appropriate to detail the course and results of the various secessions within Yugoslavia.

42 Guidelines on Recognition, 16 December 1991, in Trifunovska, note 16, pp. 431–2. Kingsbury makes the pertinent observation that 'outside the declarations of the CSCE, which are not legally binding, there were no international treaties that set forth in detail the meaning of – let alone the means of realizing and ensuring – the rule of law, democracy, or rights of ethnic groups, national groups, or minorities. Indeed these latter categories have not been fully defined': B. Kingsbury, 'Claims by Non-State Groups in International Law', *Cornell International Law Journal*, 1992, vol. 25, pp. 505–6.

43 Declaration on Yugoslavia, 27 August 1991, in Trifunovska, note 16, p. 334. See also S. Terrett, *The Dissolution of Yugoslavia and the Badinter Arbitration Commission: A Contextual Study of Peace-Making in the Post-Cold War World*, Aldershot, Ashgate, 2000, pp. 119–41.

44 The EC Declaration of 27 August 1991 envisaged that two of the five members would be appointed by unanimous decisions of the Presidency of Yugoslavia, but as no such appointments were forthcoming, the three EC nominees from France, Germany and Italy, appointed the other two members from Spain and Italy: M. Ragazzi, 'Conference on Yugoslavia Arbitration Commission: Opinions on Questions Arising from the Dissolution of Yugoslavia, Introductory Note', 31 ILM 1488.

45 Declaration on Yugoslavia, 18 October 1991, in Trifunovska, note 16, pp. 356–7.

46 The EC policy in favour of recognition was opposed by Lord Carrington, Javier Perez de Cuellar, the Secretary-General of the United Nations, and Cyrus Vance, the Secretary General's Personal Envoy on Yugoslavia: J. Williams, *Legitimacy in International Relations and the Rise and Fall of Yugoslavia*, London, Macmillan Press, 1998, p. 127; L. Silber and A. Little, *Yugoslavia: Death of a Nation*, revised and updated edition, New York, Penguin Books, 1997, pp. 199–200.

The secession of Slovenia

Slovene aspirations to statehood can be traced back to World War II. Nationalist sentiment was strong within the ranks of Slovene Partisans during the war. According to Milovan Đilas, a senior Partisan official:

> In no other Yugoslav land, among no other Yugoslav people, was there such keen awareness, such enthusiasm over the creation of one's own state. . . . The cult was Slovenia itself, a unanimous surge toward statehood as the crowning fulfilment of nationalism and the beginning of socialism.[47]

The first overt stirrings of Slovenian nationalism in the post-World War II era occurred in the mid-1960s. At the Sixth Congress of the League of Communists of Slovenia in 1968, various speakers spoke of Slovenia's sovereignty and statehood. In the next few years the Slovenian government of Stane Kavčić sought a more independent position for Slovenia as a means of opening it up to non-Yugoslav markets. However, these efforts failed and this period of Slovene nationalism subsided with Kavčić's removal from office in 1972 as part of Tito's crackdown on nationalism throughout Yugoslavia.[48]

In the mid-1980s Slovenian calls for independence resurfaced. In March 1987, in the literary journal *Nova Revija*, a diverse group of Slovene intellectuals formulated a Slovene national programme. Their call was for an independent Slovenia as the realisation of the Slovene right to self-determination.[49] France Bučar, later president of the Slovenian Assembly, wrote at the time that, 'Yugoslavia should not be a state any more, but simply a sum of sovereign nation-states'.[50] The need for an independent Slovenia was deemed a necessary prerequisite to the integration of Slovenia into a united Europe. Integration of Slovenia into Europe through the medium of the Yugoslav state would, it was argued, not adequately secure Slovene interests and national identity. Only an independent Slovenia could properly protect Slovene concerns in the process of European integration.[51] As one of the *Nova Revija* contributors, Dimitrij Rupel, later wrote:

47 M. Djilas, *Wartime*, London, Martin Secker & Warburg, 1977, p. 340.

48 P. Vodopivec, 'Slovenes and Yugoslavia, 1918–1991', *East European Politics and Societies*, 1992, vol. 6, pp. 234–6.

49 Ibid., p. 238.

50 L. Sekelj, *Yugoslavia: The Process of Disintegration*, New York, East European Monographs, 1993, p. 247.

51 V. Hribar, 'Slovene Statehood', *Nationalities Papers*, 1993, vol. 21, pp. 43–9; D. Rupel, 'Slovenia and the World', *Review of International Affairs*, 5 February 1991, vol. 42, no. 980, pp. 12–15; D. Rupel, 'Slovenia in Post-Modern Europe', *Nationalities Papers*, 1993, vol. 21, pp. 51–9; T. Peršak, 'A Slovene State as a Vital Condition for Existence and Survival', in N. Grafenauer (ed.), *The Case of Slovenia*, Ljubljana, Nova Revija, 1991, pp. 95–8. This sentiment was often stated by Slovenian leaders in the march towards secession. Thus on 6 December 1990, President Milan Kučan, in addressing the Slovenian National Assembly, said: 'The creation of the Slovene national state, which is a historical necessity, is not our ultimate goal. ... We see it as a means and a way of Slovenia forging new

> The core of the Slovene confrontation with the Yugoslav state was that, at the moment of European integration, Yugoslavs wanted to lead us to such a solution as would set Yugoslavia, and not Slovenia, side by side with European nation-states. I have frequently stated that Slovenia is willing to 'renounce' its sovereignty to Brussels and Strasbourg, but not Belgrade. . . . In order for Slovenia to become a democratic and European country, [Yugoslavia] needed to be ruthlessly destroyed.[52]

Slovenia's communist leadership initially rejected the *Nova Revija* national programme. However, political developments in Yugoslavia soon led to the adoption of the *Nova Revija* programme by the Slovenian communists led by President Milan Kučan.[53] The rise of Slobodan Milošević to the Presidency of Serbia in 1987 saw the emergence of a Serb communist politician eager to extend his authority across Yugoslavia. In his campaign to achieve his goal Milošević was prepared to mobilise Serb nationalism that had been on the rise since the Albanian riots in Kosovo in 1981 and which had found its programme articulated in the 1986 draft Memorandum prepared by the Serbian Academy of Sciences and Arts. The Milošević campaign spurred Slovenia's communist leadership to acceptance of the *Nova Revija* national programme.[54]

Implementation of the *Nova Revija* agenda commenced on 27 September 1989 when the Slovenian Assembly passed various amendments to its republic constitution, including a provision giving the Republic of Slovenia the 'complete and undeniable right' to 'self-determination, including the right of secession' (Amendment X). This amendment was justified by reference to Article 1 of the International Covenant on Economic, Social and Cultural Rights, adopted by the General Assembly of the United Nations in December 1966.[55] The substantive amendments to the constitution were justified on the basis of this right to self-determination. Thus, Slovenia's sovereignty was asserted by an amendment that stipulated that Slovenia had the right to invalidate federal legislation in defence of its rights and sovereignty (Amendments XLVI and LXII), and that only Slovenian republic authorities could declare a state of emergency in Slovenia (Amendment

integrations and links, either within the framework of Yugoslavia, or within the wider European framework': Milan Kucan Addresses Slovene Assembly on Independence Plebiscite, *BBC Summary of World Broadcasts*, EE/0942/B/1, 8 December 1990.

52 Rupel, 'Slovenia in Post-Modern Europe', note 51, pp. 57, 58. For similar comments by F. Bučar, see Zimmermann, note 3, pp. 70–1, where Zimmermann also concludes that in their 'drive to separate from Yugoslavia' the Slovenians 'bear considerable responsibility for the bloodbath that followed their secession'.

53 D. Rupel, 'Slovenia's Shift from the Balkans to Central Europe', in J. Benderly and E. Kraft (eds), *Independent Slovenia: Origins, Movements, Prospects*, New York, St Martin's Press, 1994, pp. 186–8.

54 J. Drnovsek, 'Riding the Tiger: The Dissolution of Yugoslavia', *World Policy Journal*, 2000, vol. 17, no. 1, p. 59.

55 R. M. Hayden, *The Beginning of the End of Yugoslavia: The Slovenian Amendment Crisis of 1989*, Pittsburgh, The Carl Beck Papers in Russian and East European Studies, no. 1001, Centre for Russian and East European Studies, University of Pittsburgh, 1992, pp. 8–9.

LXIII). Furthermore, Slovenia asserted that it alone had the right to regulate its affairs with other international states and organisations (Amendment XCIX). These amendments amounted to the application of the nullification doctrine, first espoused by South Carolina in the early 1830s in its conflict with the federal government of the USA, by which a federal unit asserted its supremacy over the central authority in areas assigned to the legislative competence of the central authority.[56] On 5 October 1990 the Slovenian Assembly enacted further amendments to the Slovenian constitution which had the effect of invalidating all of Yugoslavia's constitutional laws which were inconsistent with the Slovenian constitution.[57] In effect Slovenia was asserting its independence and seeking to transform Yugoslavia into a confederation.[58]

In January 1990[59] and October 1991[60] the Constitutional Court of Yugoslavia declared the amendments to Slovenia's constitution unconstitutional. The references in the amendments to self-determination and secession were declared unconstitutional because the Slovene nation could not act unilaterally in this respect. The consent of all of Yugoslavia's nations and republics was required. The nullification provisions were unconstitutional on the grounds that federal laws, in accordance with Article 270 of Yugoslavia's 1974 Constitution, applied across the entire territory of Yugoslavia and could not be negated by unilateral action of a single republic.[61] As to the state of emergency amendment, this was

56 The most thorough accounts of the South Carolina nullification crisis are in W. W. Freehling, *Prelude to Civil War: The Nullification Controversy in South Carolina 1816–1836*, New York, Oxford University Press, 1992; W. W. Freehling, *The Road to Disunion: Secessionists at Bay, 1776–1854*, New York, Oxford University Press, 1990, pp. 211–286; R. E. Ellis, *The Union at Risk: Jacksonian Democracy, States' Rights, and the Nullification Crisis*, New York, Oxford University Press, 1987. For analyses of South Carolina's nullification doctrine see D. F. Houston, *A Critical Study of Nullification in South Carolina*, New York, Longmans, Green, & Co, 1896, esp. pp. 16–32; L. Hartz, 'South Carolina vs. The United States', in D. Aaron (ed.), *America in Crisis: Fourteen Crucial Episodes in American History*, New York, Alfred A. Knopf, 1952, pp. 73–89; D. F. Ericson, *The Shaping of American Liberalism: The Debates Over Ratification, Nullification and Slavery*, Chicago, University of Chicago Press, 1993, pp. 75–113.

57 E. Marko-Stockl and J. Marko, 'Republic of Slovenia, Chronology', in A. P. Blaustein and G. H. Flanz (eds), *Constitutions of the Countries of the World*, Volume XVII, Release 92–6, entry on 'Slovenia', Dobbs Ferry, Oceania Publications, 1992, p. xvii; D. Nečak, 'A Chronology of the Decay of Tito's Yugoslavia 1980–1991', in Grafenauer, note 51, p. 198.

58 P. Nikolić, *Od raspada do beznađa i nade, Svedočanstvo o jednom vremenu*, Belgrade, Filip Višnjić, 1997, pp. 28–9.

59 *Mišljenje Ustavnog suda Jugoslavije o suprotnosti amandmana IX–XC na ustav SR Slovenije s ustavom SFRJ*, 18 January 1990, Službeni List SFRJ, 23 February 1990, vol. 46, no. 10, p. 593.

60 *Mišljenje USJ o suprotnosti ustavnom zakona za sprovođenje ustavnog amandmana XCVI na ustav Republike Slovenije i ustavnog zakona za sprovođenje ustavnih amandmana XCVI i XCVII na ustav Republike Slovenije u oblasti narodne odbrane ca ustavom SFRJ*, 2 October 1991, in M. Buzadžić, *Secesija bivših jugoslovenskih republika u svetlosti odluka Ustavnog suda Jugoslavije, Zbirka dokumenata s uvodnom raspravom*, Belgrade, Službeni List SRJ, Belgrade, 1994, p. 77; *Mišljenje USJ o suprotnosti ustavnog amandmana XCIX na ustav Republike Slovenije s ustavom SFRJ*, 2 October 1991, in Buzadžić, above, p. 80.

61 *Mišljenjee USJ o suprotnosti ustavnom zakona za sprovođenje ustavnog amandmana XCVI na ustav Republike Slovenije i ustavnog zakona za sprovođenje ustavnih amandmana XCVI i XCVII na ustav Republike Slovenije u oblasti narodne odbrane ca ustavom SFRJ*, 2 October 1991, in Buzadžić, note 60, p. 79.

unconstitutional because the power to declare a state of emergency over all or part of Yugoslavia was vested in the Presidency of Yugoslavia by virtue of a number of articles in Yugoslavia's 1974 Constitution. This also could not be negated by the unilateral act of one republic.[62] As to the amendment relating to Slovenia's relations with other international states and organisations, this was declared unconstitutional on the ground that these matters were the exclusive domain of the federal authorities and could not be unilaterally altered by the act of one republic.[63] Thus, all the amendments conflicted with the provisions of Yugoslavia's 1974 Constitution, and because republic constitutions could not conflict with the federal constitution, they were all unconstitutional.

The Court rulings were ignored by the Slovenian leadership. On 2 July 1990, the Slovenian Assembly overwhelmingly adopted a Declaration on the Sovereignty of the Republic of Slovenia,[64] basing the republic's claim to sovereignty on 'the Slovene nation's right to self-determination' (Article 1). The Declaration restated the nullification doctrine in relation to the application of federal laws in Slovenia (Articles 2, 3, 4), and finally stipulated that a new constitution for Slovenia be proclaimed within one year (Articles 5, 6). The Yugoslav Constitutional Court in January 1991[65] declared the nullification articles void on the grounds that they conflicted with provisions in Yugoslavia's 1974 Constitution to the effect that federal laws applied across the entire federation (Article 270), including Slovenia. As to Article 1, the Constitutional Court ruled that it was not inconsistent with the 1974 Constitution as it expressed the constitutionally guaranteed right of all nations to self-determination, including the right of secession. However, this aspect of the decision is difficult to reconcile with the provisions of the 1974 Constitution. In its ruling the Court confirmed Slovenia's declaration of sovereignty. The 1974 Constitution clearly did not vest sovereignty in the republics, but in 'the people' (Article 3). To concede sovereignty to a republic pursuant to a unilateral declaration by one republic in effect amounted to a constitutional amendment without following the procedures for such an amendment stipulated in the 1974 Constitution.

On the day following the Declaration, Dimitrij Rupel, later Slovenia's Foreign Minister, announced that 'Yugoslavia no longer exists'.[66] Slovenian Prime Minister Lojze Peterle stated that the sovereignty declaration did not mean independence as yet, but would lead to independence unless Yugoslavia was re-organised into a confederation.[67] Entry into such a confederation was viewed as being a voluntary act

62 *Mišljenje Ustavnog suda Jugoslavije o suprotnosti amandmana IX–XC na ustav SR Slovenije s ustavom SFRJ*, 18 January 1990, Službeni List SFRJ, 23 February 1990, vol. 46, no. 10, pp. 594–5.

63 *Mišljenje USJ o suprotnosti ustavnog amandmana XCIX na ustav Republike Slovenije s ustavom SFRJ*, 2 October 1991, in Buzadžić, note 60, p. 80.

64 Deklaracija o suverenosti države Republike Slovenije, 2 July 1990, in Buzadžić, note 60, pp. 241–2.

65 *Odluka o ocenjivanju ustavnosti deklaracije o suverenosti države Republike Slovenije*, 10 January 1991, Službeni List SFRJ, 5 April 1991, vol. 47, no. 23, p. 452.

66 Hayden, note 55, p. 24.

67 Cohen, note 5, p. 121.

based upon 'the inalienable and unexpendable right of every nation to self-determination'.[68] In the meantime plans were initiated for a new Slovenian constitution which would define Slovenia as a 'sovereign state', rather than as a 'Yugoslav federal unit'.[69]

On 6 December 1990 the Slovenian Assembly passed a law stipulating that a plebiscite be held on the questions of whether Slovenia should become an independent state, and if the result was in favour of independence, whether independence should be declared within six months of the plebiscite,[70] The plebiscite was justified 'on the basis of the permanent and inalienable right of the Slovene people to self-determination'. The Assembly further declared that if the result of the plebiscite was for 'a sovereign and independent Slovenia', Slovenia would 'strive to become, as soon as possible, a member of the United Nations Organization and other international bodies'.[71] The plebiscite was held on 23 December 1990. Approximately 88.5 per cent of the 93.2 per cent of citizens who

68 Ibid., p. 179.

69 L. J. Cohen, 'Post-Federalism and Judicial Change in Yugoslavia: The Rise of Ethno-Political Justice', *International Political Science Review*, 1992, vol. 13, p. 309.

70 B. Bučar, 'The International Recognition of Slovenia', in D. Fink-Hafner and J. R. Robbins (eds), *Making a New Nation: The Formation of Slovenia*, Aldershot, Dartmouth, 1997, pp. 34–5.

71 The Assembly resolution is reproduced in Grafenauer, note 51, pp. 171–2. In January 1991 the Constitutional Court of Yugoslavia ruled that implementation of the Slovenian Assembly resolution to become an independent and sovereign state could not proceed on the ground that such action would result in a unilateral alteration to Yugoslavia's international and internal borders in violation of the 1974 Constitution: *Rešenje o obustavi izvršenja pojedinačnih akata i radnji preduztih na osnovu čl. 4. i 10. zakona o plebicitu o samostalnosti i nezavisnosti Republike Slovenije kojima organi Republike Slovenije preuzimaju ustavom SFRJ utvrđena prava i dužnosti federacije ili kojima se jednostrano menja granica SFRJ, odnosno granica između republika*, 8 January 1991, Službeni List SFRJ, 18 January, 1991, vol. 47, no. 4, p. 64. This decision was confirmed in November 1991: *Odluka o oceni ustavnosti odredaba čl. 4. i 10. zakona o plebicitu o samostalnosti i nezavisnosti Republike Slovenije*, 7 November 1991, Službeni List SFRJ, 28 February, 1992, vol. 48, no. 14, pp. 189–90. Buzadžić takes a similar view in his comments on the plebiscite conducted in Bosnia-Hercegovina in early 1992. He was of the view that whilst a republic could organise plebiscites on matters within the competence of the republic, a plebiscite on sovereignty or secession could not be organised. This was so because it would infringe the competency of federal institutions to deal with matters relating to Yugoslavia's, composition, borders and territory: Buzadžić, note 60, pp. 275–84. The reasoning of Yugoslavia's Constitutional Court can be contrasted with that of the Russian Constitutional Court concerning the Autonomous Province of Tartarstan in Russia. There the Court declared as impermissible an attempt to hold a sovereignty plebiscite in Tartarstan because it would have the effect of disrupting the unity of the Russian Federation. Such unity was protected by international law, via various treaties and UN General Assembly resolutions that guaranteed Russia's territorial integrity: M. Suski, *Bringing in the People: A Comparison of Constitutional Forms and Practices of the Referendum*, Dordrecht, Martinus Nijhoff Publishers, 1993, p. 247. Similar reasoning was adopted by the Court in 1995 in the Chechnya Case: P. Gaeta, 'The Armed Conflict in Chechnya Before the Russian Constitutional Court', *European Journal of International Law*, 1996, vol. 7, pp. 564–6. Thus, the Russian Court relied on international law, whereas the Yugoslav Court relied on domestic constitutional law to arrive at the same result, namely that the holding of plebiscites on sovereignty or independence was impermissible.

voted expressed support for Slovenia's secession should that be deemed necessary. Three days later the Slovene Assembly adopted a declaration on the republic's sovereignty.[72]

On 20 February 1991 the Slovenian Assembly passed a resolution by which Slovenia disassociated itself from Yugoslavia and other republics. The disassociation, as opposed to secession, was justified 'on the basis of the permanent and inalienable rights of self-determination of the Slovene nation, which is one of the basic principles of international law'.[73] This resolution was pronounced unconstitutional by Yugoslavia's Constitutional Court.[74] The Court ruled that the provisions on self-determination and secession in the preamble to Yugoslavia's Constitution of 1974 had no normative status and thus could not be the basis for secession. The only way in which secession could occur would be by legislation passed by the federation through its appropriate and constitutionally sanctioned organs. Furthermore, the resolution on disassociation amounted to a violation of Yugoslavia's territorial integrity as guaranteed by Article 5 of the 1974 Constitution.

On 9 May 1991 the Slovenian Assembly approved that the Yugoslav Prime Minister be notified that Slovenia would secede from Yugoslavia no later than 26 June 1991.[75] Secession was effected on 24 June 1991 by two acts of the Slovenian Assembly, one proclaiming Slovenia an independent state,[76] and another providing for the enforcement of Slovenia's independence.[77] These acts were accompanied by a formal Declaration of Independence[78] which declared Slovenia 'an independent state . . . no longer . . . a part of the Socialist Federal Republic of Yugoslavia' as of 25 June 1991.

The first act of the Slovenian Assembly declared that the borders of the independent Slovenian state were the same as the borders of Slovenia as existed in Yugoslavia (Article II). Slovene constitutional lawyers argued that this flowed from international law principles and practice as evidenced by the application of the principle of *uti possidetis* in Latin America, the resolution of the Organisation of African States on the inviolable nature of borders following decolonisation, and

72 Slovene Assembly Session Republic of Slovenia Proclaimed Independent, *BBC Summary of World Broadcasts*, EE/0959/B/1, 1 January 1991.

73 Resolution of the Assembly of the Republic of Slovenia on the Proposal for the Disunion of the Socialist Federal Republic of Yugoslavia by Mutual Consent, 20 February 1991, *Focus*, note 1, p. 14; Slovene Assembly Adopts Resolution on Separation, *BBC Summary of World Broadcasts*, EE/1003/B/1, 22 February 1991.

74 *Odluka o ocenjivanju ustavnosti rezolucije o predlogu za sporazumno razdruživanje Socialističke Federativne Republike Jugoslavije*, 2 October 1991, Službeni List SFRJ, 13 December 1991, vol. 47, no. 89, p. 1426.

75 S. P. Ramet, 'Slovenia's Road to Democracy', 45, *Europe–Asia Studies*, 1993, vol. 45, p. 873.

76 Constitutional Act of the Assembly of the Republic of Slovenia, 24 June 1991, *Focus*, note 1, pp. 97–9.

77 Constitutional Law on the Enforcement of the Constitutional Act on the Autonomy and Independence of the Republic of Slovenia, 24 June 1991, *Focus*, note 1, 100–7.

78 Slovenia's Declaration of Independence, 24 June 1991, in *Focus*, note 1, pp. 92–6.

finally, the provisions of the Helsinki Final Act to the effect that borders could only be altered by peaceful means.[79] The Declaration of Independence further stated that 'Slovenia expects legal recognition from all countries which respect the democratic principles and right of all nations to self-determination.' Independence was based on 'the fundamental principles of natural law, namely the right of the Slovene nation to self-determination, . . . the principles of international law and the Constitution of the Republic of Slovenia, and on the basis of the absolute majority vote in the plebiscite held on December 23, 1990'. Slovenia's Foreign Affairs Minister Dimitrij Rupel justified Slovenia's secession in the following words:

> The main reason behind the Slovene nation's will to achieve independence and its own state does not lie in the fact that we are fed up with suffering all of Yugoslavia's woes, but in the fact that we have – as do all the nations of the world – the inalienable right to self-determination. Yet this right is non-existent if it cannot be realised.[80]

The response of Yugoslavia's federal authorities to Slovenia's Declaration of Independence was to declare it (and Croatia's declaration of independence of the following day) unconstitutional and illegal.[81] In due course this was confirmed by Yugoslavia's Constitutional Court which held that the two acts passed by the Slovenian Assembly and the formal independence declaration were unconstitutional.[82] The Court's reasoning referred to, *inter alia*, violations of provisions in Yugoslavia's 1974 Constitution that stipulated that Slovenia was a part of Yugoslavia (Article 2), guaranteed Yugoslavia's territorial integrity (Article 5), and ensured Yugoslavia's international borders which could only be altered by legislation passed by the Federal Assembly (Article 283).

Military intervention by the YPA aimed at suppressing Slovenia's secession was short-lived, and ended with the Brioni Accord of 7 July 1991 which led to the withdrawal of the YPA.[83] The success of Slovenia's drive for independence was all but assured. International recognition was not immediate. The Brioni Accord

79 B. Bučar, 'Međunarodni aspekti jugoslovenske reforme i osamostaljenja Slovenije', *Međunarodna Politika*, 1 June 1991, vol. 52, no. 988, p. 4.

80 D. Rupel, 'Slovenia – A New Member of the International Community', in Grafenauer, note 51, p. 89.

81 Stands and Conclusions of the SFRY Presidency Concerning the Situation in Yugoslavia, 27 June 1991, in Trifunovska, note 16, p. 305.

82 *Odluka o ocenjivanju ustavnosti osnovne ustavne povelje o samostalnosti i nezavisnosti Republike Slovenije*, 16 October 1991, Službeni List SFRJ, 13 December 1991, vol. 47, no. 89, p. 1422; *Odluka o ocenjivanju ustavnosti zakona za sprovođenje osnovne ustavne povelje o samostalnosti i nezavisnosti Republike Slovenije*, 16 October 1991, Službeni List SFRJ, 13 December 1991, vol. 47, no. 89, p. 1423; *Odluka o ocenjivanju ustavnosti deklaracije povodom nezavisnosti*, 9 October 1991, Službeni List SFRJ, 13 December 1991, vol. 47, no. 89, p. 1427.

83 The Brioni Accord was claimed as a triumph by the EC. However, Slovenia's President Kučan and Serbia's President Milošević in January 1991 had a series of meetings and reached agreement on Slovenia's departure from the Yugoslav federation: Silber and Little, note 46, p. 166.

stipulated a moratorium for three months on the implementation of Slovenia's declaration of independence.[84] On 8 October 1991, after the expiration of the moratorium, Slovenia formally seceded from Yugoslavia. Following the EC invitation of 16 December 1991 to Yugoslav republics to submit applications for international recognition, Slovenia duly submitted an application. On 23 December 1991, a new Slovenian Constitution was proclaimed.[85] The constitution was declared to proceed, *inter alia*, from 'the basic and permanent right of the Slovene nation to self-determination' (Preamble). Slovenia was declared to be 'a state of all its citizens based upon the permanent and inviolable right of the Slovene nation to self-determination' (Article 3). On 11 January 1992, the Badinter Commission, after noting that a plebiscite on independence had been held in Slovenia, recommended recognition of Slovenia.[86] The EC recognised Slovenia on 15 January 1992.[87] This was followed by over 50 other states recognising Slovenia in the ensuing days. On 18 May 1992 the UN Security Council recommended Slovenia's admission to the UN.[88] The UN General Assembly formally admitted Slovenia to the UN on 22 May 1992.[89]

The secession of Croatia

In the post-World War II period, the first significant nationalist movement in Croatia emerged during the so-called 'Croatian Spring' of the late 1960s and early 1970s. Secessionist sentiment was widespread at that time as exemplified in the words of one nationalist leader, Dražen Budiša, who wrote:

> On the agenda, first and foremost, is the question of national emancipation in the political sense. The essence of that emancipation is that, free of centralism and unitarism, the Yugoslav community be transformed into a community of sovereign nation-states.[90]

However, following the purge of Croatia's liberal leadership by Tito in early 1972, Croat nationalism remained dormant until the late 1980s. Claims to secession based upon self-determination only became official republic policy with the electoral victory

84 Joint Declaration of the EC Troika and the Parties Directly Concerned with the Yugoslav Crisis, the So-Called 'Brioni Accord', 7 July 1991, in Trifunovska, note 16, pp. 311–15.

85 Reproduced in B. Milinković (ed.), *Novi ustavi na tlu bivše Jugoslavije*, Belgrade, Međunarodna Politika, 1995, pp. 89–125.

86 *Opinion No. 7 on International Recognition of the Republic of Slovenia by the European Community and its Member States*, 11 January 1992, (1992) 31 ILM 1512.

87 Statement by the Presidency on the Recognition of Yugoslav Republics, 15 January 1992, in Trifunovska, note 16, p. 501.

88 Security Council Resolution 754 (1992), 18 May 1992.

89 General Assembly Resolution 46/236, 22 May 1992.

90 Quoted in M. Šuković, 'Činjenice za osvjetljavanje i razumijevanje koncepcije federacije u Ustavu SFRJ iz 1974', in D. Grbić (ed.), *Filozofija i društvo VI, Teorijske pretpostavke razumevanja raspada Jugoslavije*, Belgrade, Institut za filozofiju i društvenu teoriju, 1994, p. 264.

of Dr Franjo Tuđman and his Croatian Democratic Union (CDU) in late April and early May 1990. The CDU election platform, in the words of Tuđman, was centred around the 'struggle to establish an independent, sovereign and democratic Croatia'.[91] Tuđman did not explicitly call for the secession of Croatia, but rather for a new Yugoslav confederation or 'alliance of states'.[92] A crucial part of implementing this platform was reform of Croatia's existing republic constitution of 1974.

In July 1990 the process of constitutional reform was initiated. In that month the existing republic constitution was amended. The amendments enshrined the Croat literary language as the official language in Croatia, adopted a new national emblem that resembled the one used by the Ustaše state during World War II, and removed the requirement for a two-thirds majority vote in the Croatian assembly on issues relating to national relations within Croatia.[93] According to Tuđman, the effect of these amendments was to make Croatia 'a politically and economically sovereign state'.[94] The process of constitutional reform culminated in the promulgation of a new constitution on 22 December 1990.[95] The 1990 Constitution was in essence a declaration of Croatia's independence as a state. A key provision of the new constitution was Part I (Historical Foundations) in which it was, *inter alia*, stated:

> [T]he Republic of Croatia is hereby established as the national state of the Croat nation and a state of members of other nations and minorities who are its citizens: Serbs, Muslims, Slovenes, Czechs, Slovaks, Italians, Hungarians, Jews and others.

This provision was a significant departure from the 1974 Croatian Constitution which stipulated that Serbs and Croats were constituent nations and equal in status. The 1990 Constitution was directed at the establishment of a Croat nation-state,[96] and effectively relegated the Serbs, who accounted for 12.2 per cent of the population,[97] to the status of a minority,[98] The important consequence of this

91 Interview: Dr Franjo Tuđman, *Danas*, Nova Serija, Broj 73, Zagreb, 31. svibnja (May), 1994, p. 8.

92 C. Cviic, 'Croatia's Violent Birth', *Current History*, November 1993, vol. 92, no. 577, p. 374.

93 R. L. Hislope Jr, 'Nationalism, Ethnic Politics, and Democratic Consolidation: A Comparative Study of Croatia, Serbia and Bosnia-Hercegovina', unpublished doctoral dissertation, Ohio State University, 1995, pp. 170–1.

94 R. Hayden, *Blueprints for a House Divided: The Constitutional Logic of the Yugoslav Conflicts*, Ann Arbor, University of Michigan Press, 1999, p. 47.

95 Reproduced in Milinković, note 85, pp. 39–68.

96 T. Z. Kuzmanović, 'Croatia's Constitution: A Blueprint for Democracy in Croatia', *Journal of Croatian Studies*, 1991–92, vol. 32–3, p. 166.

97 According to the 1991 census the Serbs of Croatia amounted to 12.2 per cent of the population. The Croats amounted to 77.9 per cent of the population: R. Petrović, 'The National Composition of Yugoslavia's Population, 1991', *Yugoslav Survey*, 1992, vol. 33, no. 1, p. 7. According to Tuđman, the percentage of Croats in Croatia's population qualified Croatia to be called 'nationally homogenous', that is, a nation-state: F. Tudjman, *Nationalism in Contemporary Europe*, Boulder, CO, East European Monographs, 1981, p. 148.

98 S. Trifunovska, 'Political and Security Aspects of Minorities in Croatia', in S. Trifunovska (ed.), *Minorities in Europe: Croatia, Estonia and Slovakia*, The Hague, TMC Asser Press, 1999, pp. 22–4.

change in status of the Serbs was, according to repeated statements by Tuđman, that the Serbs as a minority had no right to self-determination.[99]

In his speech to the Croatian *Sabor* (Assembly) at the time of the promulgation of the Constitution, Tuđman referred to the occasion as 'a confirmation of the national sovereignty of the Croat nation'. He went on to state that the 'ultimate aim of the Croat nation' was 'for the Republic of Croatia to achieve as soon as possible full, internationally recognised, state sovereignty'. Croatia was 'against supporting Yugoslavia in the present or some third form', and proposed the transformation of Yugoslavia 'into an alliance or perhaps several alliances of sovereign Yugoslav states'. The justification for this approach according to Tuđman, was to 'ensure the right of the Croat nation to self-determination'.[100] Tuđman's speech reflected his long-held views that the Croat nation had the right to self-determination pursuant to Yugoslavia's 1974 Constitution, and that the right included a right of secession.[101]

The Constitution further stated that Croatia would remain part of Yugoslavia 'until a new agreement is reached by the Yugoslav republics, or until the Croatian *Sabor* decides otherwise' (Article 140). If Croatia was in any way endangered, threatened or disadvantaged within Yugoslavia, Croatia would make appropriate decisions protecting its interests (Article 140). Such actions would be justified 'on the basis of the right of self-determination and the sovereignty of the Republic of Croatia'.[102]

On 21 February 1991 the *Sabor* passed an act supplementing the constitution which invoked the nullification doctrine in relation to the application of federal laws in Croatia and the declaring of a state of emergency in Croatia.[103] These provisions were declared unconstitutional by Yugoslavia's Constitutional Court in July 1991 on the same grounds as the similar Slovenian amendments were declared unconstitutional.[104]

Following receipt of the Slovene Assembly's disassociation resolution of 20 February 1991, the *Sabor* passed a resolution on 21 February 1991 endorsing the process of the disassociation of Yugoslavia. The *Sabor* based the resolution on 'the inalienable and inexpendable right of the Croat nation to self-determination, including the right of secession and association with other nations and states'.[105]

99 At a press conference on 22 March 1994, Tuđman reaffirmed his views that the Serbs of Croatia, as a minority, had no right to self-determination: *Newsletter 29*, Republic of Croatia, Ministry of Foreign Affairs, Information Department, 31 March 1994; S. Markotich, 'Ethnic Serbs in Tudjman's Croatia', *RFE/RL Research Report*, 24 September 1993, vol. 2, no. 38, p. 30.

100 Tuđman's speech is reprinted in *Izvješća Hrvatskog Sabora*, Zagreb, no. 15, 22. prosinca (December) 1990, pp. 7–18, with quotations at pp. 8, 14 and 15.

101 F. Tuđman, *Bespuća povijesne zbiljnosti, Rasprava o povijesti i filozofija zlosilja*, Zagreb, Nakladni Zavod Matice Hrvatske, 1990, p. 454.

102 Cohen, note 5, pp. 130–1, 176, and 193.

103 The Constitutional Act Supplementing the Constitutional Act for the Implementation of the Constitution of the Republic of Croatia, 21 February 1991, in Trifunovska, note 16, pp. 280–1.

104 *Mišljenje USJ o suprotnosti odredaba Čl. 9A, 9B i 9C ustavnog zakona za provedbu ustava Republike Hrvatske sa ustavom SFRJ*, 10 July 1991, in Buzadžić, note 60, p. 86.

105 Croatian Resolution on Acceptance of the Process of Disunion, 21 February 1991, *Focus*, note 1, pp. 17–20.

The resolution also called for an agreement-based separation of Yugoslavia's republics into several independent states within the framework of existing republic borders. This resolution was declared unconstitutional by the Yugoslav Constitutional Court on the ground that the resolution effectively amounted to Croatia's secession from Yugoslavia.[106] The Court's reasoning was the same as in its ruling which declared Slovenia's disassociation resolution unconstitutional.

On 19 May 1991 an independence plebiscite was held in which 93 per cent of those voting supported the creation of a 'sovereign and independent' Croatia.[107] The timing of independence was left to the government to determine in accordance with Article 140 of the Croatian Constitution.

On 25 June 1991 the Croatian Assembly passed a Constitutional Decision[108] and a Declaration[109] relating to Croatia's independence. In the Constitutional Decision Croatia's independence was based upon the 'Inalienable, unconsumable, indivisible and untransferable right of the Croatian nation to self-determination, including the right of disassociation'. In the Declaration reference was made to the 1974 Yugoslav Constitution granting to 'the Republic of Croatia the right to self-determination including secession'. Both documents referred to Croatia's international borders being existing republic borders and those parts of Yugoslavia's international borders relevant to Croatia. The Declaration also emphasised Croatian claims to independence as deriving from an unbroken period of Croatian statehood going back some thirteen centuries. The Declaration confirmed that Croatia was going to take immediate steps to seek international recognition. Both the Constitutional Decision and the Declaration of Independence were subsequently declared unconstitutional and void by Yugoslavia's Constitutional Court in October 1991 and November 1991 respectively.[110] The Court's reasoning was much as it had been when it declared Slovenia's independence declaration and enabling legislation unconstitutional.

The secession of the Republic of Serb Krajina from Croatia

The process of constitutional change in Croatia during 1990 had a dramatic impact on Croatia's Serb population. As Ignatieff observed, 'in Yugoslavia, [the Serbs] were a protected constitutional nation. In an independent Croatia, they

106 *Odluka a ocenjivanju ustavnosti rezolucije o prihvaaćnju postupka za razdruživanje SFRJ i o mogućim udruživanju u savez suverenih republika,* 2 October 1991, Službeni List SFRJ, 29 November 1991, vol. 47, no. 86, p. 1364.

107 Cohen, note 5, p. 212.

108 Constitutional Decision on the Sovereignty and Independence of the Republic of Croatia, 25 June 1991, in Trifunovska, note 16, pp. 299–301.

109 Declaration on the Establishment of the Sovereign and Independent Republic of Croatia, 25 June 1991, in Trifunovska, note 16, pp. 301–4.

110 *Odluka o ocenjivanju ustavnosti ustavne odluke o suverenosti i samostalnosti Republike Hrvatske,* 16 October 1991, in Buzadžić, note 60, p. 156; *Odluka o ocenjivanju ustavnosti deklaracije o proglašenju suverene i samostalne Republike Hrvatske,* 13 November 1991, in Buzadžić, note 60, p. 159.

were reduced to a national minority in a state with a genocidal past.'[111] Serb concerns were raised even before the 1990 elections that had swept Tuđman and the CDU into power. Opinion polls conducted prior to the election confirmed that the majority of Croatia's Serbs strongly opposed any confederalisation of Yugoslavia and rejected the idea of Croatia's secession from Yugoslavia.[112] The centre of Serb reaction was in Knin and within the ranks of the Serbian Democratic Party (SDP) led by Dr Jovan Rašković.

On 25 July 1990, in the wake of that month's amendments to Croatia's constitution, the SDP organised a rally of Croatia's Serbs at Srb.[113] The rally formalised the creation of the Serb National Council as the representative body of Croatia's Serbs[114] and endorsed a Declaration of Sovereignty and Autonomy of the Serb People.[115] The Declaration asserted the right of Croatia's Serbs to self-determination, including the right of secession, based upon the status of Serbs as a constituent nation within Croatia, with rights to sovereignty equal to that of the Croats. On the basis of this sovereignty the Declaration demanded autonomy for the Serbs of Croatia. The extent of that autonomy was dependent upon whether Yugoslavia remained a federation or became a confederation. In the former case rights to cultural autonomy were asserted. In the latter case wider rights of autonomy were claimed, including political and territorial autonomy. In the months leading up to the proclamation of the Croatian Constitution in December 1990, Rašković, a moderate who favoured some form of negotiated autonomy agreement for the Serbs of Croatia, asserted that, if Croatia seceded from Yugoslavia, the Serb regions of Croatia would secede from Croatia.[116] In October 1990 Rašković was ousted from his leadership position by the more militant Dr Milan Babić. Babić's political agenda was consistently directed to the secession of Serb majority areas from Croatia.[117] These areas on Croatia's borders with Bosnia-Hercegovina and Serbia were, in most cases, formerly part of the historical Military Frontier. They were home to approximately half of Croatia's Serb population. Most of Croatia's other Serbs were scattered over various parts of Croatia and especially in its capital Zagreb.

The Serb National Council proceeded to organise a plebiscite which was held between 19 August and 2 September 1990. The result was an overwhelming endorsement of a proposal for Serb autonomy within Croatia.[118] In the wake of the plebiscite a Declaration of Serb Autonomy was issued on 30 September

111 M. Ignatieff, *Blood and Belonging: Journeys into the New Nationalism*, New York, Farrar, Straus & Giroux, 1993, p. 47.
112 Cviic, note 92, p. 374.
113 Hislope, note 93, p. 208.
114 M. Dakić, *Srpska Krajina, Istorijski temelji i nastanak*, Knin, Iskra, 1994, p. 52.
115 Deklaracija o suverenosti i autonomiji srpskog naroda, 25 July 1990, in S. Radulović, *Sudbina Krajine*, Belgrade, Dan Graf, 1996, pp. 123–4.
116 R. Dmitrović, 'Povratak Krajine: Hrvatska i njen novi ustav', *NIN*, 20 December 1990, no. 2086, p. 13.
117 For a discussion of the differing views of Rašković and Babić see Hislope, note 93, pp. 167–81.
118 Of 756,781 votes, 756,549 were in favour of autonomy: Dakić, note 114, p. 52.

1990.[119] The Declaration claimed Serb autonomy over Croatian territory where Serbs lived or which was historically Serb. In anticipation of the proclamation of the new Croatian Constitution on 22 December 1990, Croatia's Serbs in the Knin region proclaimed, on 21 December 1990, the formation of the Serb Autonomous District of Krajina (SAD Krajina) centred on Knin.[120] A further two autonomous districts of, first, Slavonija, Baranja and Western Srem, and second, Western Slavonija, were formed soon thereafter.[121]

In the wake of the Croatian *Sabor* resolution of 21 February 1991, endorsing Croatia's disassociation from Yugoslavia, SAD Krajina passed a resolution on the disassociation of SAD Krajina from Croatia on 28 February 1991.[122] The resolution was justified on the basis of 'the internationally recognised right of people to self-determination' as well as provisions in Yugoslavia's 1974 Constitution prescribing 'the equality of all the Yugoslav nations'. The resolution stipulated that SAD Krajina wished to remain in Yugoslavia and had no objections to 'the right of the Croat people to separate from the Yugoslav state within the bounds of their ethnic space'. The resolution was formalised on 18 March 1991 by a decision of SAD Krajina to separate from Croatia and remain within Yugoslavia.[123]

On 1 April 1991 SAD Krajina resolved to attach itself to the Republic of Serbia.[124] A plebiscite on the question was planned but Serbia's President Milošević rejected such a course of action.[125] The plebiscite question was rephrased, and on 12 May 1991 the Serbs of SAD Krajina overwhelmingly voted in favour of SAD Krajina remaining in Yugoslavia.[126] On 30 April 1991 the SAD Krajina Assembly was constituted. Dr Milan Babić was elected President.[127] Following Croatia's Declaration of Independence on 25 June 1991, its formal secession on 8 October 1991, and the imminence of EC recognition of Croatia in January 1992, the three Serbian autonomous districts in Croatia merged and declared their own independent state on 19 December 1991, under the name of

119 Proglašena srpska autonomija, 30 September 1990, in Dakić, note 114, p. 70.

120 Dakić, note 114, pp. 52–3.

121 Ibid., p. 52.

122 Rezolucija o razdruživanju Republike Hrvatske i SAO Krajine, 28 February 1991, in Radulović, note 115, pp. 131–2.

123 Odluka o odvajanje od Republike Hrvatske, 18 March 1991, in Dakić, note 114, p. 74.

124 Odluka o prisajedinjenju SAO Krajine Republici Srbiji, 1 April 1991, in Radulović, note 115, p. 133.

125 The reasons for Milošević's acting in this way are a matter of speculation. However, it can confidently be suggested that his actions were partly determined by his official policy of keeping Yugoslavia together. Milošević had attacked the Slovenian and Croatian declarations on sovereignty as unconstitutional and as leading to Yugoslavia's dismemberment. If he had endorsed Krajina's accession to Serbia, he would have been accused of breaking up Yugoslavia.

126 Radulović, note 115, pp. 30–1. It should be noted that even after separating from Croatia, Krajina's aim was always of linking up into one state with Serbia, Montenegro and the Serb regions of Bosnia-Hercegovina. Krajina as an independent state was always viewed as the less favoured option.

127 Dakić, note 114, p. 54.

the Republic of Serb Krajina.[128] By the terms of its Constitution, Krajina was declared to be 'a nation-state of the Serb nation and the state of all citizens' living in Krajina (Article 1). The Preamble to the Constitution firmly based Krajina's claim to statehood on the right to self-determination of its Serb population.

Following Croatia's declaration of independence, the EC-brokered Brioni Accord of 7 July 1991 called for a moratorium on Croatia's secession. Unlike Slovenia, the moratorium did not lead to a resolution of the dispute over Croatia's future. On the contrary, a bitter war erupted between Croatia's fledgling armed forces and the armed forces of Krajina, backed by the YPA. The intensity of the fighting led to UN Security Council Resolution 713 on 25 September 1991 which imposed 'a general and complete embargo on all deliveries of weapons and military equipment to Yugoslavia'.[129] Resolution 713 also authorised the Secretary-General to offer his assistance in seeking to resolve the crisis in Yugoslavia.[130] On 8 October 1991 former US Secretary of State Cyrus Vance was appointed by the Secretary-General as his Personal Envoy for the purposes of assisting the Secretary-General to fulfil his obligations under Resolution 713.[131] On the same day, following the expiration of the three-month moratorium provided for in the Brioni Accord, Croatia formally seceded from Yugoslavia, reiterating the basis of independence as the 'inalienable right of the Republic of Croatia to self-determination'.[132]

Following the EC announcement on its recognition policy on 16 December 1991, Croatia applied for recognition. The EC refused to accept an application submitted by the Republic of Serb Krajina.[133] On 11 January 1992, the Badinter Commission, after noting that a plebiscite on independence had been held in Croatia, recommended that, with one exception, Croatia met the conditions of recognition. The exception related to Croatia's constitutional law provisions on the rights of national minorities which were, in the opinion of the Badinter Commission, inadequate to meet the EC conditions on recognition.[134]

128 Ibid., pp. 56–7. Krajina's 1991 Constitution is reproduced in Milinković, note 85, pp. 281–308.

129 Security Council Resolution 713 (1991), para. 6, 25 September 1991.

130 Ibid., para. 3.

131 Report of the Secretary-General Pursuant to Paragraph 3 of Security Council Resolution 713 (1991), para.5, S/23169, 25 October 1991.

132 Croatian Assembly Declares Secession from Yugoslavia, 8 October 1991, *Focus*, note 1, pp. 178–80. The *Sabor* decision was declared unconstitutional by the Yugoslav Constitutional Court in December 1991 on the grounds that Croatia's break with Yugoslavia would be a unilateral, and thus unconstitutional, alteration of Yugoslavia's international borders, and further that Croatia, as a constituent unit of the Yugoslav federation could not act independently in relation to political, economic and other forms of relations with other international states, as this was, by virtue of Yugoslavia's 1974 Constitution, the responsibility of the Yugoslav federal authorities: *Odluka o ocenjivanju ustavnosti odluke Sabora Republike Hrvatske o raskidu državnopravne veze sa SFRJ*, 25 December 1991, Službeni List SFRJ, 21 February 1992, vol. 48, no. 12, p. 163.

133 S. L. Burg and P. S. Shoup, *The War in Bosnia-Herzegovina: Ethnic Conflict and International Intervention*, New York, M. E. Sharp Inc., 1999, p. 96.

134 *Opinion No. 5 on International Recognition of the Republic of Croatia by the European Community and its Member States*, 11 January 1992, (1992) 31 ILM 1503.

Nevertheless, Croatia was recognised by the EC on 15 January 1992, on the basis of a hurried assurance, obtained from President Tuđman on 13 January 1992, that Croatia's minority Serb population would be granted special autonomous status.[135] This assurance was deemed sufficient to meet the objection of the Badinter Commission to recognition.[136] On 18 May 1992 the UN Security Council recommended Croatia's admission to the UN.[137] The UN General Assembly formally admitted Croatia to the UN on 22 May 1992.[138]

Running parallel to the process of obtaining recognition of Croatia were the efforts of Cyrus Vance to broker a lasting cease-fire in Croatia. This was eventually achieved on 2 January 1992.[139] This was soon after followed by an agreement which provided for UN peacekeeping forces in Croatia to patrol the three United Nations Protected Areas (UNPAs) of Krajina, Western Slavonija and Eastern Slavonia.[140] The so-called Vance Plan was formally approved by the UN Security Council on 21 February 1992.[141] Babić, who opposed the plan, was replaced as President of the Republic of Serb Krajina by Goran Hadžić on 26 February

135 B. Vukas, 'The Legal Status of Minorities in Croatia', in Trifunovska, note 98, p. 52; Libal, note 14, p. 86. In May 1992 Croatia amended its constitution in relation to the position of its minorities. These amendments were considered adequate for the Badinter Commission, on 4 July 1992, to withdraw its reservations expressed in *Opinion No. 5*: Comments on the Republic of Croatia's Constitutional Law of 4 December 1991, as last amended on 8 May 1992, (1992) 31 ILM 1505, at 1505–7. However, the UN Human Rights Committee remained unsatisfied with Croatia's provisions on minority rights: S. Tierney, 'In a State of Flux: Self-Determination and the Collapse of Yugoslavia', *International Journal on Minority and Group Rights*, 1999, vol. 6, p. 213.

136 The recognition of Croatia posed difficulties for the EC, on account of Germany's decision on 19 December 1991 to recognise Croatia, with implementation of the decision to be delayed to 15 January 1992. The German concern with the Serb minority in Croatia was allayed by a report commissioned by the German government and prepared by Christian Tomuschat in late November 1991 to the effect that Croatia's constitutional law provisions on minorities were 'of exemplary significance to the further development of the protection of minorities in Europe'. Genscher's account of Germany's action on this matter is misleading in that he asserts that the Badinter Commission recommended the recognition of Croatia and that Germany's recognition of 19 December 1991, based upon the Tomuschat report, was vindicated: Genscher, note 36, pp. 515–16. Libal is closer to the truth when he states that the Badinter Commission gave a qualified 'yes' to recognition of Croatia: Libal, note 14, p. 86.

137 Security Council Resolution 753 (1992), 18 May 1992.

138 General Assembly Resolution 46/238, 22 May 1992.

139 Accord Implementing Ceasefire Agreement of 23 November 1991, 2 January 1992, in Trifunovska, note 16, pp. 468–70.

140 The plan was originally presented to the UN Security Council by the Secretary-General on 11 December 1991: Report of the Secretary-General Pursuant to Security Council Resolution 721 (1991), Annex III, S/23280, 11 December 1991, in D. Bethlehem and M. Weller (eds), *The 'Yugoslav' Crisis in International Law: General Issues*, Part I, Cambridge, Cambridge University Press, 1997, p. 479. In the implementation of the plan the UN forces were deployed into four sectors: Sector East (Eastern Slavonia UNPA), Sector West (Western Slavonia UNPA), Sector North (northern part of Krajina UNPA) and Sector South (southern part of Krajina UNPA): Further Report of the Secretary-General Pursuant to Security Council Resolution 749 (1992), S/23844, 24 April 1992, in Bethlehem and Weller, above, p. 506.

141 Security Council Resolution 743 (1992), para. 2, 21 February 1992.

1992. The UNPAs corresponded closely to the territory under the control of Croatia's Serbs, who in turn were dependent for survival on support from Serbia and the YPA.[142]

From early 1992 to May 1995 the UN presence in Croatia, in general terms, preserved the status quo established by the Vance Plan. Serbs remained largely in control of the territories within the UNPAs. However, Croatia was determined to reclaim full control of these territories from the Serbs at any cost.[143] By early 1995 Croatia, despite the UN arms embargo, had considerably improved its military position *vis-à-vis* the Serbs in Croatia. Serbia's support for Krajina was dwindling in the wake of the economic sanctions which had been imposed against Serbia, Montenegro and the Serbs of Croatia and Bosnia-Hercegovina by the UN Security Council in May 1992.[144] In two short offensives, first in the Western Slavonia UNPA in May 1995, and then in the Krajina UNPA in August 1995, Croat forces easily regained the territories from Serb forces which had no support from Serbia.[145] The Croatian military campaigns resulted in a mass exodus of over 150,000 Serbs from the areas captured by Croatian forces.[146] As for the Eastern Slavonia UNPA, it was to be progressively handed over to Croatia pursuant to the Basic Agreement of the Region of Eastern Slavonia, Baranja and Western Srem negotiated on 12 November 1995 as a prelude to the Dayton Accords relating to Bosnia-Hercegovina.[147] With these Croatian victories the secession of the Republic of Serb Krajina was effectively suppressed.[148]

142 P. Shoup, 'The UN Force: A New Actor in the Croatian-Serbian Crisis', *RFE/RL Research Report*, 27 March 1992, vol. 1, no. 13, pp. 17–22.

143 R. Holbrooke, *To End a War*, New York, Random House, 1998, p. 45.

144 Security Council Resolution 757 (1992), paras. 3–11, 30 May 1992.

145 Silber and Little, note 46, pp. 353–60.

146 D. Mirković, 'Croatian Liberation of Western Slavonia and Krajina', *Peace Research*, 1998, vol. 30, no. 1, p. 16.

147 Basic Agreement on the Region of Eastern Slavonia, Baranja and Western Sirmium, 12 November 1995, (1995) 35 ILM 186–7. Following the Basic Agreement of 12 November 1995, on 15 January 1996 the UN Security Council established a civilian and military transitional administration under the name 'United Nations Transitional Administration for Eastern Slavonia, Baranja and Western Sirmium' (UNTAES): Security Council Resolution 1037 (1996), 15 January 1996. The UNTAES mandate was twice extended: Security Council Resolutions 1079 (1996), 15 November 1996, 1120 (1997), 14 July 1997. It was terminated on 15 January 1998 and the region handed over to Croatian administration. A small force of UN civilian police monitors remained for a further nine months: Security Council Resolution 1145 (1997), 19 December 1997.

148 Krajina's main backer, Serbia, refused to formally recognise Krajina. Serbia's Assembly rejected a proposal to that effect on 27 December 1991, and instead adopted a 'Declaration on the Inalienable Right of the Serbian People to Self-Determination'. The Declaration committed Serbia to care for Serbs beyond the borders of Serbia and asserted that the Krajina secession was an act of self-defence against the unilateral secession of Croatia: Serbian Assembly Adopts Declaration on Self-Determination of Serbs, *BBC Summary of World Broadcasts*, EE/1265/C1/1, 30 December 1991.

The secession of Bosnia-Hercegovina

The movement towards the secession of Bosnia-Hercegovina can be traced to the aftermath of multiparty elections in that republic held on 18 November 1990. In that election three recently formed nationalist parties representing and reflecting the multi-national composition of Bosnia-Hercegovina emerged as the main winners. No party was able to gain an absolute majority. The three parties were the Party of Democratic Action (PDA), formed on 26 May 1990, as the political party of 'Yugoslav citizens who belong to the Muslim cultural-historical circle',[149] the Serbian Democratic Party (SDP), formed on 27 July 1990, as the party for 'renewing the political life of the Serb people in Bosnia-Hercegovina',[150] and the Croat Democratic Union (CDU), formed on 6 September 1990, with the major aim of 'assuring the right of the Croat people to self-determination to the right of secession and the statehood and sovereignty of the Republic of Bosnia-Hercegovina'.[151] The Bosnian Muslims accounted for 43.7 per cent, the Serbs 31.4 per cent and the Croats 17.3 per cent, of the republic's population.[152] In the election these three nationalist parties secured nearly 80 per cent of the total votes cast. Each of the three nationalist parties attracted at least 84 per cent of the votes from their respective national constituencies.[153] These votes were distributed between the three parties in proportions that approximated very closely to the population strengths of the three national groups within Bosnia-Hercegovina.[154]

The result of the election led to a power-sharing arrangement between the three parties in which a Bosnian Muslim was to head the seven-person collective presidency, a Serb to be the president of the republic's National Assembly, and a Croat to be Prime Minister of the republic's government. Ministerial positions within the government were distributed between the parties in proportion to the numbers of seats in the National Assembly. In practice this power-sharing arrangement resulted in each national group installing its own people in ministries under their control and excluding members of other national groups. Thus, government ministries in effect became instruments of the relevant parties controlling them. A similar process was evident in the *opštine* (local government units), where the majority party in any given *opština* gained control to the exclusion of the other two parties.[155]

149 From the PDA programme in M. Lazarević (ed.), *Stranke u Jugoslaviji*, Belgrade, Novinska Agencija Tanjug, 1990, p. 40.

150 From the SDP programme in Lazarević, note 149, p. 43.

151 From the CDU programme in Lazarević, note 149, p. 45.

152 Petrović, note 97, p. 4.

153 R. M. Hayden, 'Constitutional Nationalism and the Logic of the Wars in Yugoslavia', *Problems of Post-Communism*, 1996, vol. 43, no. 5, pp. 31–2.

154 S. L. Burg, 'Bosnia Herzegovina: A Case of Failed Democratization', in K. Dawisha and B. Parrott (eds), *Politics, Power, and the Struggle for Democracy in South-East Europe*, Cambridge, Cambridge University Press, 1997, pp. 127–35.

155 R. M. Hayden, 'Constitutional Nationalism in the Formerly Yugoslav Republics', *Slavic Review*, 1992, vol. 51, p. 661.

The party leaderships also agreed that any legislation dealing with the status of any of the three national groups could only be passed if the three parties unanimously agreed to such legislation.[156] This political arrangement was in conformity with Bosnia-Hercegovina's republic constitution of 1974 as amended by a series of amendments adopted on 31 July 1990. Amendment LIX resulted in Bosnia-Hercegovina being declared 'a democratic sovereign state of equal citizens, the nations of Bosnia and Hercegovina – Muslims, Serbs and Croats and members of other nationalities who live within it'.[157] Proportional representation of the three constituent nations to all of the republic's governmental institutions was guaranteed by Amendment LXI.[158] The effect of the 1990 amendments and a supplementary constitutional law for their implementation was summarised by Hayden as follows:

> The amended Constitution . . . required participation by representatives of the 'nations and nationalities' in governmental organs at all levels, in proportion to their respective numbers in the population, and also required special, two-thirds majorities to pass legislative provisions challenged as violating the principles of national equality, even after such legislation had obtained unanimous consent in the Council for Questions of the Establishment of Equality of Nations and Nationalities of Bosnia and Hercegovina in the republican parliament.[159]

On 30 January 1991, following the examples of Slovenia and Croatia, the PDA proposed that the National Assembly of Bosnia-Hercegovina adopt a Declaration of State Sovereignty and Indivisibility of the Republic of Bosnia and Hercegovina.[160] The CDU was supportive, but the SDP strongly opposed the proposal. The SDP argued that the declaration was superfluous as Bosnia-Hercegovina had, by the constitutional amendment of July 1990, been declared a sovereign state, with the Muslims, Serbs and Croats as its constituent nations.[161] The SDP interpreted the proposal as merely a stepping-stone towards secession. SDP fears were confirmed in February 1991 when the PDA–CDU coalition proposed that the National Assembly declare that republic laws prevailed over any inconsistent federal laws.[162] The SDP was able to prevent adoption of the proposal. The PDA leadership nevertheless persisted in its efforts to have such a

156 Hislope, note 93, p. 305.

157 Quoted in R. M. Hayden, 'Bosnia's Internal War and the International Criminal Tribunal', *Fletcher Forum of World Affairs*, 1998, vol. 22, no. 1, p. 54.

158 Ibid.

159 Hayden, note 94, p. 91.

160 In a pre-election speech in September 1990, PDA leader Alija Izetbegović said that 'if the threat that Croatia and Slovenia leave Yugoslavia is carried out, Bosnia will not remain in a truncated Yugoslavia': quoted in Burg and Shoup, note 133, p. 47.

161 Nikolić, note 58, p. 80.

162 R. Kumar, *Divide and Fall? Bosnia in the Annals of Partition*, London, Verso, 1997, p. 43.

declaration adopted by the National Assembly, even though it clearly failed to attract the unanimity required by the post-election agreement of the three nationalist political parties. In April 1991 Alija Izetbegović, the PDA leader and republic president, indicated he would seek passage of the declaration despite SDP opposition.[163]

The formal declarations of secession by Slovenia and Croatia in late June 1991 and the eruption of hostilities in Yugoslavia led the PDA–CDU coalition in Bosnia-Hercegovina to persist in its efforts to secure the passage of a sovereignty declaration through the National Assembly. The Slovenian and Croatian declarations of secession prompted the PDA and CDU to propose that the National Assembly assess 'disassociation' from Yugoslavia as a legitimate expression of the right to self-determination. Izetbegović told the Assembly on 10 July 1991 that if Croatia left, Bosnia-Hercegovina would not remain in Yugoslavia.[164]

On 10 October 1991 a PDA–CDU Memorandum on the Sovereignty of Bosnia-Hercegovina[165] was submitted to the National Assembly. The Memorandum reaffirmed the republic's sovereignty as already stipulated in the republic's constitution. It also stipulated Bosnia-Hercegovina's support for the continuation of the Yugoslav federation, but only on the condition that Serbia and Croatia remained within the federation. Furthermore, the Memorandum stipulated that the participation of the republic's representatives to Yugoslavia's federal institutions was conditional upon participation of representatives from all other federal units. Decisions made by federal institutions which did not involve participation from all federal units would be regarded as not binding on Bosnia-Hercegovina. The Memorandum also asserted that the future of the republic was properly to be determined by the National Assembly on the basis of a majority vote of delegates, and that such a vote would be an expression of the will of the majority of the republic's citizens. The Memorandum was rejected by the SDP, who proceeded to boycott the National Assembly. On 15 October 1991 the rump National Assembly adopted the Memorandum on a majority vote of delegates present.[166]

The SDP argued that the Memorandum was unconstitutional on the basis that it did not have the support of the necessary two-thirds of the National Assembly as required by the republic's constitution.[167] In effect the Serbs adopted the same

163 Continuing Conflict Over Bosnia-Hercegovina Declaration of Independence, *BBC Summary of World Broadcasts*, EE/1006/B/1, 26 February 1991.

164 Extraordinary Session of Bosnian Assembly Discusses Mobilisation; Brioni Accord, *BBC Summary of World Broadcasts*, EE/1122/B/1, 12 July 1991.

165 Memorandum, in Buzadžić, note 60, pp. 263–4.

166 The vote in the National Assembly was by a majority of 142 of the total number of delegates (including the Serbs who boycotted the vote) of 240: Hayden, note 157, p. 56.

167 Hayden, note 94, p. 94. Burg and Shoup comment that the adoption of the Memorandum 'hardly reflected the kind of consensus necessary to make a constitution meaningful' and that it 'appeared to reflect the efforts of one or two groups to impose their will on a third': Burg and Shoup, note 133, p. 79.

position *vis-à-vis* republic institutions in Bosnia-Hercegovina as did the majority of the republic's National Assembly *vis-à-vis* Yugoslavia's federal institutions.[168] The position of the SDP in relation to the status of Bosnia-Hercegovina was further evidenced in its own proposal put before the National Assembly.[169] This proposal sought the continuation of the republic within the existing Yugoslav federation. However, in the event that Croatia seceded and obtained international recognition, there would be held in Bosnia-Hercegovina separate plebiscites within each of its three constituent national groups to establish if they wanted to remain within Yugoslavia, or establish their own states, or join with other states. This proposal argued that the possible partition of the republic on national lines was based upon the right of each constituent nation to self-determination, including the right of secession.

Following the EC declaration of 16 December 1991 which stipulated the conditions upon which Yugoslav republics would be granted international recognition as independent states, Bosnia-Hercegovina's initial application was rejected by the EC on 15 January 1992. The Badinter Commission's recommendation was that Bosnia-Hercegovina could not be recognised because the 'will of the peoples of Bosnia and Hercegovina' had not been ascertained as to whether they were in favour of the republic becoming 'a sovereign and independent State'. *Opinion No. 4* concluded with a statement that the decision not to recommend recognition could be reviewed following a plebiscite which established the will of 'all the citizens [of Bosnia-Hercegovina] without distinction' to seek independence.[170]

With the SDP still boycotting the National Assembly, the PDA–CDU coalition voted for a plebiscite to be held on 29 February–1 March 1992. The resolution in favour of the plebiscite was passed in the early hours of the morning of 25 January 1992 without the presence of Serb deputies in the National Assembly. The resolution was passed after a marathon session of the Assembly on 24 January 1992 in which all three major national groups had participated and which had resulted in an apparent agreement on the republic's political–territorial reorganisation. However, Izetbegović rejected the agreement and called for a resolution for a plebiscite to be held. The response of the Serb speaker of the Assembly was, at 3.30 a.m. on 25 January 1992, to pronounce the day's session closed, with the Assembly to reconvene at 10.00 a.m. on the same day. An hour after the speaker's ruling an SDA member took to the podium in the Assembly and called for a vote on the plebiscite proposal. It was adopted in the absence of the Serb delegates. This vote was unconstitutional on the basis that it did not have the required two-thirds majority.[171]

The plebiscite question put to the voters was: 'Are you for a sovereign and

168 Hayden, note 157, p. 56.

169 Resolution on the Position of Socialist Republic of Bosnia-Hercegovina in Resolving the Yugoslav Crisis, *Focus*, note 1, pp. 183–4.

170 *Opinion No. 4 on International Recognition of the Socialist Republic of Bosnia and Herzegovina by the European Community and its Member States*, 11 January 1992, (1992) 31 ILM 1501.

171 Hayden, note 94, pp. 96–7.

independent Bosnia and Hercegovina, a state of equal citizens, nations of Bosnia and Hercegovina – Muslims, Serbs, Croats and other nations that live in it?'[172] The great majority of Serbs in the republic heeded the call of the SDP to boycott the plebiscite. Of the 63.4 per cent of the population that voted, 99.4 per cent voted in favour of independence. Given the Serb boycott of the plebiscite, this meant that 62.7 per cent of the total electorate in the republic voted for independence.[173] On 3 March 1991 the Republic of Bosnia-Hercegovina formally declared its independence. Notwithstanding the view of the Badinter Commission in *Opinion No. 4* that the 'will of the peoples' in favour of independence be required before recognition be granted, the EC granted recognition on 6 April 1992, despite the fact that only the Muslims and Croats can be said to have voted in support of independence.[174] On the following day the USA recognised Bosnia-Hercegovina, as well as Slovenia and Croatia.[175] On 20 May 1992 the UN Security Council recommended Bosnia-Hercegovina's admission to the UN.[176] The UN General Assembly formally admitted Bosnia-Hercegovina to UN membership on 22 May 1992.[177]

The secession of the Serb Republic from Bosnia-Hercegovina

The PDA–CDU proposal for a sovereignty declaration of 30 January 1991 and Izetbegović's determination for the National Assembly to adopt it without Serb support drew a response from the SDP. On 26 April 1991 fourteen Serb-controlled *opštine* centred around Banja Luka created the Community of Bosanska Krajina. This entity, and others that followed, were ostensibly promoted as a means to ensure the economic vitality of the regions, but in fact were a mechanism to establish Serb organs of authority which would promote Serb interests at the local level. In September 1991 these entities were transformed into four Serbian Autonomous Districts (SADs), namely the SAD Hercegovina (12 September), SAD

172 Buzadžić, note 60, p. 275.

173 M. Andrejevich, 'More Guns, Less Butter in Bosnia and Hercegovina', *RFE/RL Research Report*, 13 March 1992, vol. 1, no. 11, p. 14.

174 EC Declaration on Recognition of Bosnia and Hercegovina, 6 April 1992, in Trifunovska, note 16, p. 521. See also Hayden, note 94, p. 95; M. Barutciski, 'Politics Overrides Legal Principles: Tragic Consequences of the Diplomatic Intervention in Bosnia-Hercegovina (1991–1992)', *American University Journal of International Law and Policy*, 1996, vol. 11, p. 777. In opinions delivered after recognition, the Badinter Commission effectively rejected its own views in *Opinion No. 4* by speaking of Bosnia-Hercogvina's recognition being justified on the basis of a majority vote of the population of the republic in favour of independence: *Opinion No. 8 of the Arbitration Commission of the Peace Conference on Yugoslavia* (1992) 31 ILM 1521 at 1523; *Opinion No. 11 of the Arbitration Commission of the Peace Conference on Yugoslavia* (1993) 32 ILM 1587 at 1588.

175 President Bush's Statement, 7 April 1992, in Trifunovska, note 16, p. 521.

176 Security Council Resolution 755 (1992), 20 May 1992.

177 General Assembly Resolution 46/237, 22 May 1992. Although Bosnia-Hercegovina's independence from Yugoslavia was recognised by the international community on the basis of support for independence from only two of its three constituent nations, any future division of Bosnia-Hercegovina would only be accepted by the international community 'if that were the desire of each of a majority of the three ethnic groups at some future date': Holbrooke, note 143, p. 364.

Bosnian Krajina (16 September), SAD Romanija (17 September) and SAD North-Eastern Bosnia (19 September).[178] The SADs provided the bases for a future single Serb entity in Bosnia-Hercegovina in the event that the republic sought to secede from Yugoslavia. The SDP perceived this as the only adequate response to the reality of being outvoted by the PDA–CDU coalition in the National Assembly.[179] The SDP feared that the PDA–CDU coalition would eventually vote for the secession of Bosnia-Hercegovina from Yugoslavia, with the result that the PDA would, on the basis of the relative majority population of Muslims in the republic, seek to establish a unitary state dominated by the Muslims.[180] Izetbegović's visit to Turkey in July 1991, where he sought Bosnia-Hercegovina's admission to the Organisation of Islamic States only served to reinforce Serb apprehensions.[181]

Following the adoption of the Declaration on Sovereignty by the National Assembly on 15 October 1991, the SDP began to organise the secession of Serb regions in the republic. On 24 October 1991 the Serb deputies who had left the republic's National Assembly[182] established their own Assembly of the Serb People in Bosnia-Hercegovina.[183] On the same day this Assembly declared that, based upon the right of the Serbs in Bosnia-Hercegovina to self-determination, the Serbs of Bosnia-Hercegovina would remain in a united Yugoslav state with Serbia, Montenegro and any other parts of Yugoslavia which had the same objective.[184] The Assembly sought ratification of its declaration by means of a plebiscite of the Serbs of Bosnia-Hercegovina held on 9–10 November 1991. Approximately 85 per cent of eligible voters participated in the plebiscite with 98 per cent voting to endorse the Assembly declaration.[185]

178 J. Gow, *Triumph of the Lack of Will: International Diplomacy and the Yugoslav War*, New York, Columbia University Press, 1997, p. 34.

179 Hislope, note 93, pp. 305–6.

180 Serb apprehensions were, in part, driven by the fact that Izetbegović was a devout Muslim and author of *The Islamic Declaration*, first published in 1970. Republished in 1990, *The Islamic Declaration* was interpreted as a manifesto for a unitary Muslim-dominated state of Bosnia-Hercegovina. Furthermore, the increase in the relative numbers of Muslims in Bosnia-Hercegovina compared with Serbs and Croats indicated that the Muslims would become an absolute majority of the population within another generation. The Muslims accounted for 39.5 per cent of the population in 1981. By 1991 the figure had increased to 43.7 per cent, while the percentages for Serbs and Croats had decreased during the same period: Petrović, note 97, p. 4. These demographic trends also alarmed many Serbs.

181 Silber and Little, note 46, p. 213.

182 The Serb deputies consisted of the SDP deputies together with a handful of Serb deputies from minor parties represented in the National Assembly: R. Kuzmanović, *Konstitutivni akti Republike Srpske*, Banja Luka, Glas srpski, 1994, pp. 19–20.

183 Odluka o osnivanju Skupštine Srpskog naroda u Bosni i Hercegovini, 24 October 1991, in Kuzmanović, note 182, pp. 117–19.

184 Odluka o ostajanju srpskog naroda Bosne i Hercegovine u zajedničkoj državi Jugoslaviji, 24 October 1991, in Kuzmanović, note 182, pp. 121–2.

185 Hislope, note 93, pp. 313–14. In *Opinion No. 4* the Badinter Commission asserted that the Serb referendum was 'outside the institutional framework' of Bosnia-Hercegovina's Constitution: *Opinion No. 4 on International Recognition of the Socialist Republic of Bosnia and Herzegovina by the European Community and its Member States*, 11 January 1992, (1992) 31 ILM 1501 at 1503. The relevant provision of the

Following Bosnia-Hercegovina's request to the EC for recognition as an independent state, the Assembly of the Serb People in Bosnia-Hercegovina, on 9 January 1992, declared the formation of the Republic of Serb People in Bosnia-Hercegovina based upon the four established SADs.[186] On 12 August 1992 this Republic was renamed the Serb Republic (*Republika Srpska*), and for convenience will hereafter be referred to by that name. The declaration justified itself on the basis of the 'right of the Serb nation [in Bosnia-Hercegovina] to self-determination'. It referred to the November 1991 plebiscite as giving the declaration legitimacy. The declaration cited the insistence of the Muslim–Croat coalition in seeking international recognition for Bosnia-Hercegovina as the immediate reason for the proclamation of the Serb Republic, which thereafter became, according to the declaration, a federal unit within the Yugoslav federation. The declaration envisaged the necessary partition of Bosnia-Hercegovina on the grounds that the territorial integrity of Bosnia-Hercegovina was, since the reconstruction of Yugoslavia during and immediately after World War II, only guaranteed for as long as it remained a federal unit within the Yugoslav federation. The partition of Bosnia-Hercegovina was to take place by agreement with the Muslims and Croats whose rights to self-determination on this issue would be respected. A later declaration of the Assembly on 12 August 1992 referred to plebiscites as being the basis for partition.[187]

On 28 February 1992 the Serb Republic proclaimed its Constitution.[188] The Constitution's Preamble asserted that the Serb Republic was based upon 'the inalienable and unassignable natural right of the Serb nation to self-determination'. The Serb Republic was declared to be 'a state of the Serb people' (Article 1), whose borders were Serb majority areas of Bosnia-Hercegovina as well as those regions where the Serbs became a minority as the result of genocide against the Serbs (Article 2). This latter provision was a reference to the Ustaše genocide against the Serbs during World War II. The Serb Republic was declared a part of the Yugoslav federation (Article 3), although it was permitted to enter into relationships with state entities established by Bosnia-Hercegovina's constituent nations (Article 4). The proclamation of this Constitution effectively marked the Serb Republic's secession from Bosnia-Hercegovina in anticipation of the expected recognition of the latter as an independent state following the plebiscite

'institutional framework', only partially quoted by the Commission, stated that citizens exercised their powers 'through representatives in assemblies of social-political communities, by referendum, *in public meetings and other forms of personal declaration of opinion*'. The italicised words were not cited in *Opinion No 4*. Hayden argues that the Serb plebiscite was legitimate as it came within 'other forms of personal declaration': Hayden, note 94, p. 96.

186 Declaracija o proglašenju Republike Srpskog Naroda Bosne i Hercegovine, 9 January 1992, in Kuzmanović, note 182, pp. 123–9.

187 Deklaracija o državnom i političkom uređenju države, Article I, 12 August 1992, in Kuzmanović, note 182, pp. 131–4.

188 The Serb Republic's 1992 Constitution is reproduced in Milinković, note 85, pp. 249–79.

conducted on 29 February–1 March 1992. The Serb Republic formally declared its independence as a state on 7 April 1992.[189]

Croat and Muslim autonomous communities in Bosnia-Hercegovina

Although the CDU allied itself with the PDA against the SDP, Muslim–Croat relations were tense. The CDU also had apprehensions about an independent Bosnia-Hercegovina becoming a unitary state dominated by the Muslims. Although the CDU voted in favour of the sovereignty declaration on 15 October 1991, it followed the example of the SDP and established two autonomous Croat districts in Bosnia-Hercegovina in areas with majority Croat populations. In November 1991 the Croat Community of Herceg-Bosna centred on Mostar and the Croat Community in the Sava Valley in north-eastern Bosnia was established.[190] These Croat entities were ostensibly justified on the grounds of the Bosnia-Hercegovinian government's failure to protect the state against Serb territorial aspirations in the newly recognised state. In fact, the moves represented the desires of significant numbers of Croats in Bosnia-Hercegovina, supported by Croatia's government, to create a Croat statelet as a preliminary to the partition of Bosnia-Hercegovina between Croatia and Serbia.[191] In mid-1993 a bitter military conflict erupted between Bosnia-Hercegovina's Muslims and Croats, the latter supported by Croatia. It lasted until an uneasy peace was restored in March 1994.

In response to significant pressure from the USA, the Muslim–Croat conflict was resolved by the Washington Agreements signed on 18 March 1994. The first of the agreements was a Proposed Constitution of the Federation of Bosnia and Hercegovina.[192] This Constitution created federal units within the state, based upon territories with majority Muslim and Croat populations (Article 1(1)). This provision, as was conceded by the US State Department, effectively disenfranchised the non-

189 Nikolić, note 58, p. 88.

190 Kumar, note 162, pp. 47–8; X. Bougarel, 'Bosnia and Hercegovina – State and Communitarianism', in D. A. Dyker and I. Vejvoda (eds), *Yugoslavia and After: A Study in Fragmentation, Despair and Rebirth*, London, Longman, 1996, p. 101. In September 1992 the Constitutional Court of Bosnia-Hercegovina declared that the establishment of the Croat Community of Herceg-Bosna was unconstitutional on the basis that it was established in violation of the republic's Constitution and laws relating to local municipalities. The Court recognised that the Croat Community of Herceg-Bosna had elements of statehood, such as an executive, administrative and judicial authorities, and armed forces, but maintained that because of the unconstitutional manner in which it was established, it was an illegal entity: Croatian Hercegbosna Community Proclaimed Illegal by Constitutional Court, *BBC Summary of World Broadcasts*, EE/1487/C1/1, 16 September 1992.

191 A. Hoare, 'The Croatian State Project to Partition Bosnia-Hercegovina 1990–1994', *East European Quarterly*, 1997, vol. 31, pp. 128–30. Tuđman's views that Bosnia-Hercegovina should have been part of a Croatian federal unit were voiced well before he came to power: Tudjman, note 97, pp. 112–15.

192 Constitution of the Federation of Bosnia and Hercegovina, 18 March 1994, (1994) 33 ILM 740–84.

Muslims and non-Croats in the territories covered by these proposed federal units.[193] The international community and the government of Bosnia-Hercegovina were now officially sanctioning the division of that state into nationally defined territorial units. The Serb-controlled areas were left to be determined by subsequent agreements as part of a final settlement of the war in Bosnia-Hercegovina (Article 1(2)). The Republic of Bosnia-Hercegovina which had been recognised internationally in April 1992 was to be renamed the Federation of Bosnia and Hercegovina.[194] The second part of the Washington Agreements was a confederation treaty between Croatia and the transformed Federation of Bosnia and Hercegovina.[195]

Within the ranks of the Muslims of Bosnia-Hercegovina divisions emerged once war erupted after its international recognition in early April 1992. The Serb Republic gained early military success and soon controlled approximately 70 per cent of Bosnia-Hercegovina. Serb control was in the eastern parts of Bosnia and Hercegovina and a large part of western Bosnia, with the two parts connected by a narrow corridor through the Brčko region in northern Bosnia. Serb military success drove a wedge between the Muslims concentrated in the north-western corner of Bosnia centred on the town of Bihać and the remainder of the Muslims located in central Bosnia. Following divisions within the Muslim leadership ranks over military and political strategy, Muslims in the north-west, led by Fikret Abdić, proclaimed the Autonomous Province of Western Bosnia (APWB) on 27 September 1993.[196] The APWB demand for autonomy was not aimed at secession, but at recognition as a separate administrative unit within Bosnia-Hercegovina.[197] Its Constituent Assembly declared that it would 'merge with the Republic of Bosnia on the basis of equitable decision making'.[198] Abdić established cease-fire agreements with Croatia and the leaders of the Serbs and Croats in Bosnia-Hercegovina and traded extensively with Croatia as he sought the survival of his fledgling statelet against the Muslim armed forces loyal to Izetbegović.[199] Following

193 Hayden, note 153, p. 28.

194 For a critical analysis of the complex constitutional structure of the Constitution see R. M. Hayden, 'The Constitution of the Federation of Bosnia and Herzegovina: An Imaginary Constitution for an Illusory "Federation"', *Balkan Forum*, 1994, vol. 2, no. 3, pp. 77–91.

195 Preliminary Agreement Concerning the Establishment of a Confederation Between the Federation of Bosnia and Herzegovina and the Republic of Croatia, 18 March 1994, (1994) 33 ILM 605–18.

196 B. O'Shea, *Crisis at Bihac: Bosnia's Bloody Battlefield*, Phoenix Mill, Sutton Publishing, 1998, p. 22. On 29 September 1993 the Constitutional Court of Bosnia-Hercegovina declared the APWB an illegal and unconstitutional entity, on much the same grounds as its earlier ruling on the Croat Community of Herceg-Bosna: Constitution Does Not Permit Autonomous Provinces, Court Rules, *BBC Summary of World Broadcasts*, EE/1806/C, 29 September 1993.

197 M. Heinrich, 'Moslems Declare Autonomous Province in Maverick Enclave', *The Reuter Library Report*, 27 September 1993; Croatian Radio Reports Abdic's Appeal for Support for Western Bosnian Autonomy, *BBC Summary of World Broadcasts*, EE/1804/C, 27 September 1993.

198 Constituent Assembly Adopts Constitutional Provisions, *BBC Summary of World Broadcasts*, EE/1808/C, 1 October 1993.

199 Bougarel, note 190, pp. 106–7; E. O'Ballance, *Civil War in Bosnia, 1992–94*, New York, St Martin's Press, 1995, pp. 216–18.

a brief loss of APWB territory to forces loyal to the central government of Bosnia-Hercegovina, Abdić's forces, assisted by Bosnian Serb forces, recovered the lost territory in late 1994. On 26 July 1995, APWB was proclaimed as the Republic of Western Bosnia, thereby transforming the earlier autonomy movement into a push for secession.[200]

The secession of the Republic of Western Bosnia was suppressed within weeks of its proclamation following a successful Muslim–Croat military offensive in western Bosnia against the Abdić forces and those of the Serb Republic. This offensive, accompanied by a major bombing of strategic Serb positions throughout Bosnia-Hercegovina by NATO during August and September 1995, eventually led to the cessation of hostilities in Bosnia-Hercegovina by October 1995.[201] This then led to the Dayton Peace Accords initialled on 21 November 1995 and formally signed in Paris on 14 December 1995.[202]

The Dayton Peace Accords provided for a new constitution for Bosnia-Hercegovina, effectively superseding the 1994 constitution established under the Washington Agreements. The major feature of the new constitutional structure was the creation of two 'entities' within Bosnia-Hercegovina, as the state was now renamed, namely the Federation of Bosnia and Hercegovina and the Serb Republic (Annex 4, Article I(3)). In addition, each 'entity' was granted 'the right to establish special parallel relationships with neighbouring states consistent with the sovereignty and territorial integrity of Bosnia and Hercegovina' (Annex 4, Article III(2)(a)). These provisions effectively continued the process of the division of Bosnia-Hercegovina into nationally defined territorial units commenced by the Washington Agreements in 1994.[203] In effect, Bosnia-Hercegovina became a UN

200 Rebel Muslims Declare Separate Republic in Western Bosnia, *Xinhua News Agency*, Item No. 0726053, 26 July 1995.

201 International intervention in Bosnia prior to the NATO bombing campaign was focused mainly on humanitarian assistance, coupled with diplomatic efforts by a joint EC (renamed the European Union as from 1 November 1993) and UN International Conference on the Former Yugoslavia (ICFY). The ICFY proposed a number of alternative peace plans, none of which attracted the support of all three national groups in Bosnia-Hercegovina. The UN Security Council passed a number of resolutions that affected, but did not stop, military hostilities. These included imposition of a 'no-fly' zone over Bosnia-Hercegovina: Security Council Resolution 781 (1992), 9 October 1992; the establishments of 'safe areas': Security Council Resolution 819 (1993), 16 April 1993; Security Council Resolution 824 (1993), 6 May 1993; and the establishment of an international tribunal to prosecute persons guilty of serious violations of international humanitarian law committed on the territory of the former Yugoslavia as from 1 January 1991: Security Council Resolution 808 (1993), 22 February 1993; Security Council Resolution 827 (1993), 25 May 1993. Military intervention by the international community prior to the NATO bombings of August and September 1995, was confined to a number of minor NATO bombings, all targeted against the armed forces of the Serb Republic.

202 The General Framework Agreement for Peace in Bosnia and Herzegovina, 14 December 1995, (1996) 35 ILM 89–169. In the official texts of the Dayton Accord, the Serbian *Republika Srpska* is used rather than 'the Serb Republic'.

203 Hayden, note 153, p. 28; R. M. Hayden, 'Imagined Communities and Real Victims: Self-Determination and Ethnic Cleansing in Yugoslavia', *American Ethnologist*, 1996, vol. 23, p. 792.

military protectorate, divided into three nationalist entities with three separate armies, three separate police forces and possessed of 'a national government that exists mostly on paper and operates at the mercy of the entities'.[204]

The secession of Macedonia

The movement towards Macedonia's secession from Yugoslavia can be traced to the amendment of its republic constitution in 1989. Prior to that time the constitution had declared Macedonia to be 'a state of the Macedonian people and the Albanian and Turkish minorities'. This was a reflection of Macedonia's population in which, according to the 1991 census, Macedonians accounted for 64.6 per cent, Albanians 21.0 per cent, and Turks 4.8 per cent, of the population.[205] The 1989 amendment redefined Macedonia as 'the national state of the Macedonian nation'.[206]

Following Macedonia's first multi-party elections in November 1990 the fragile nature of the multi-national republic was clearly exposed. The Macedonian nationalist coalition of the Internal Macedonian Revolutionary Organisation and the Democratic Party for Macedonian National Unity won 31.7 per cent of the seats in Macedonia's parliament, followed by the Social Democratic Union of Macedonia (the renamed League of Communists for Macedonia) with 25.8 per cent of seats, and the Party for Democratic Prosperity/Peoples' Democratic Party, supported by Macedonia's Albanians, which gained 25.8 per cent of seats. This parliament elected Kiro Gligorov as Macedonia's President on 27 January 1991.[207] Gligorov had held various high positions in Yugoslavia during the Tito era and was disposed towards maintaining Yugoslavia.

In the wake of earlier Slovenian and Croatian moves toward sovereignty and independence, Macedonia's Assembly adopted a Declaration on the Sovereignty of the Socialist Republic of Macedonia on 25 January 1991.[208] The Declaration asserted the right of the Macedonian people to self-determination, including the right of secession (Article 1), and stipulated that Yugoslavia's 1974 Constitution should only be applied within Macedonia as long as it was not contrary to Macedonia's republic constitution (Article 2). In the event that Yugoslavia's problems were not resolved by agreement, Macedonia's Assembly would proclaim a law which would resolve other constitutional–legal aspects of Macedonia's sovereignty

204 J. M. B. Lyon, 'Will Bosnia Survive Dayton?', *Current History*, March 2000, vol. 99, no. 635, p. 110.

205 Petrović, note 97, p. 8.

206 G. H. Flanz, 'Macedonia, Chronology, 1920–1993', in A. P. Blaustein and G. H. Flanz (eds), *Constitutions of the Countries of the World*, Volume XI, Release 93–7, entry on 'Macedonia', Dobbs Ferry, Oceania Publications, 1993, p. xvi.

207 D. M. Perry, 'The Republic of Macedonia: Finding Its Way' in Dawisha and Parrott, note 154, pp. 233–4.

208 Deklaracija o suverenosti Socijalističke Republike Makedonije, 25 January 1991, in Buzadžić, note 60, pp. 260–1; Macedonian Assembly Adopts Declaration on Sovereignty, *BBC Summary of World Broadcasts*, EE/0982/B/1, 29 January 1991.

(Article 7). This Declaration meant that Macedonia, while still favouring a restructured Yugoslavia, left open the right to secede in the event it was felt necessary in the interests of the republic.

Yugoslavia's Constitutional Court ruled the Declaration as being unconstitutional on the basis that it, as a whole, 'brought into question the territorial integrity of [Yugoslavia]'. In particular the nullification principle in Article 2 infringed Article 270 of Yugoslavia's 1974 Constitution which stipulated that federal laws applied to all of Yugoslavia's territory.[209]

Macedonia's move toward independence was triggered by the Slovenian and Croatian secessions in June 1991 and the realisation that it was unlikely that these two republics would remain in the Yugoslav federation. On 8 September 1991 a plebiscite was held in Macedonia. Voters were asked: 'Are you in favour of a sovereign and autonomous Macedonia with the right to join a future alliance of sovereign states of Yugoslavia?' Albanians in Macedonia largely boycotted the plebiscite, meaning that only 72.16 per cent of voters actually voted. The plebiscite question was answered in the affirmative by 95.26 per cent of those who voted.[210]

On the basis of the plebiscite results, the Macedonian Assembly passed a Declaration on the Sovereignty and Independence of the Republic of Macedonia on 17 September 1991.[211] On 17 November 1991 a new Macedonian Constitution was proclaimed.[212] The Constitution's Preamble referred to 'the historical fact that Macedonia is established as a national state of the Macedonian people in which full equality as citizens, and permanent co-existence with the Macedonian people, is provided for Albanians, Turks, Vlachs, Romanies and other nationalities living in the Republic of Macedonia'.

Following the 16 December 1991 Declaration by the EC, Macedonia submitted its application for international recognition. On 6 January 1992 Macedonia amended its constitution to include stipulations that Macedonia had no territorial claims against neighbouring states (Amendment I), and that its borders could only be changed in accordance with its constitution (Amendment II).[213] On 11 January 1992, the Badinter Commission, after noting that a plebiscite on independence had been held in Macedonia, recommended recognition.[214] However, the EC did not extend recognition to Macedonia because of Greece's continued concerns about possible irredentist claims by Macedonia as well as Greece's refusal to accept Macedonia's use of the word 'Macedonia' in its name. This action prevented

209 *Odluka o ocenjivanju ustavnosti deklaracije o suverenosti Socialističke Makedonije*, 28 January 1991, Službeni List SRJ, vol. 1, no. 4, p. 61.

210 Results of the Referendum held on September 8, 1991, in Trifunovska, note 16, p. 345.

211 Declaration on the Sovereignty and Independence of the Republic of Macedonia, 17 September 1991, in Trifunovska, note 16, pp. 345–7.

212 This constitution was foreshadowed in the 25 January 1991 Declaration on Sovereignty (Article 3). Macedonia's 1991 Constitution is reproduced in Milinković, note 85, pp. 127–57.

213 Flanz, note 206, p. xviii.

214 *Opinion No. 6 on the Recognition of the Socialist Republic of Macedonia by the European Community and its Member States*, 11 January 1992, (1992) 31 ILM 1507.

widespread recognition of Macedonia. By September 1992 only a handful of states recognised Macedonia. These included Bulgaria, Russia, Belarus, Lithuania, Croatia, Slovenia and the Philippines.[215] The UN Security Council recommended Macedonia's admission to the UN under the provisional name of the Former Yugoslav Republic of Macedonia (FYROM) on 7 April 1993.[216] The UN General Assembly admitted FYROM to the UN on 8 April 1993.[217] Over the next year all EC member states, except Greece, recognised FYROM. The USA recognised it on 9 February 1994.[218] It was only in September 1995, following diplomatic intervention by the USA, that Greece and FYROM reached an Interim Accord which provided for mutual recognition.[219]

The 1995 Interim Accord resolved one of Macedonia's major problems following its declaration of independence. Its other major problem was its sizeable Albanian minority which was concentrated in western Macedonia. On 11–12 January 1992 Macedonia's Albanians held a plebiscite on territorial and political autonomy. The Albanian demand was for equality with Macedonians as a constituent nation of Macedonia.[220] Macedonian–Albanian relations have consistently been tense since (and before) Macedonia's secession from Yugoslavia.[221] Given Serbia's problem with its Albanian minority in Kosovo, the problem of Albanian minorities had the potential to ignite further conflict in the southern Balkans. With this and Greece's ongoing problems with Macedonia in mind, the UN Security Council authorised the deployment of UN peacekeepers to Macedonia in December 1992 as a preventive measure against conflict.[222] Successive Security Council resolutions extended this mission to 28 February 1999.[223] A veto by China

215 S. P. Ramet, 'The Macedonian Enigma', in S. P. Ramet and L. S. Adamovich (eds), *Beyond Yugoslavia: Politics, Economics, and Culture in a Shattered Community*, Boulder, CO, Westview Press, 1995, p. 221.

216 Security Council Resolution 817 (1993), 7 April 1993.

217 General Assembly Resolution 47/225, 8 April 1993.

218 M. C. R. Craven, 'What's in a Name? The Former Yugoslav Republic of Macedonia and Issues of Statehood', *Australian Year Book of International Law*, 1995, vol. 16, p. 206.

219 Greece–The Former Yugoslav Republic of Macedonia: Interim Accord and Memorandum on Practical Measures Related to the Interim Accord, 13 September 1995, (1995) 34 ILM 1461–81.

220 D. Hall, *Albania and the Albanians*, London, Pinter Reference, 1994, p. 212.

221 M. Vickers and J. Pettifer, *Albania: From Anarchy to a Balkan Identity*, London, Hurst & Co, 1997, pp. 166–80.

222 Security Council Resolution 795 (1992), 11 December 1992.

223 Originally the UN Macedonia mission was part of the United Nations Protection Force (UNPROFOR) which was established by the UN on 21 February 1992: Security Council Resolution 743 (1992), 21 February 1992. The UN mission in Macedonia continued under the umbrella of UNPROFOR until 31 March 1995. On that day the mission was separated from UNPROFOR and named United Nations Preventive Deployment Force (UNPREDEP): Security Council Resolution 983 (1995), 31 March 1995. Subsequent Security Council resolutions extended the life of UNPREDEP until 28 February 1999: Security Council Resolutions 1027 (1995), 30 November 1995; 1058 (1996), 30 May 1996; 1082 (1996), 27 November 1996; 1110 (1997), 28 May 1997; 1140 (1997), 27 November 1997; 1142 (1997), 4 December 1997; 1186 (1998), 21 July 1998.

on any extension of the UN mission in Macedonia[224] led to its replacement by a mission under the auspices of NATO.[225]

The secession of the Republic of Kosovo from Serbia

In Yugoslavia's 1946 Constitution the Kosovo-Metohija region in southern Serbia was constituted as the Autonomous Region of Kosovo-Metohija within the Republic of Serbia (Article 2). In the 1963 Constitution the region was elevated in status to that of an autonomous province (Article 111). By constitutional amendment (No. VII) in 1968 it was renamed the Socialist Autonomous Province of Kosovo. This name, and its status as an autonomous province, were retained in both the Yugoslav (Article 2) and Serbian republic (Article 1) constitutions. The creation of the autonomous province was officially justified on the basis of its significant Albanian population, which according to the 1948 Yugoslav census accounted for 68.4 per cent of its population. By the time of the 1991 census the figure had grown to 81.6 per cent.[226] Throughout the post-World War II period the Serb population in Kosovo declined in relative terms as against the Albanian population for a number of reasons, including the much higher birth-rate of the latter and the emigration of the former in the late 1960s and throughout the 1980s. Although Kosovo's poor economic circumstances contributed to this Serb emigration, the major contributing factor was a policy of systematic discrimination against Kosovo's Serbs engineered by the local Albanian political leadership that emerged following the devolution of power to the autonomous province of Kosovo in the late 1960s.[227] By the late 1980s it was estimated that less than 10 per cent of the province's population were Serbs.

Albanian political demands, based upon the right to self-determination,[228] for elevation of the province to the status of a republic first emerged in the late 1960s. Amendments to Yugoslavia's 1963 Constitution in the late 1960s and early 1970s significantly transformed the status of Kosovo (as well as that of the Autonomous Province of Vojvodina within Serbia). Prior to that time the autonomous provinces were constituent units of the Republic of Serbia, and Serbia's republic constitution defined their autonomous rights and duties. By the early 1970s the autonomous provinces were effectively transformed into constituent units of the Yugoslav federation on an almost equal footing with republics. However, the autonomous provinces were not formally granted the title of republic and Kosovo formally

224 Press Release SC/6648, 25 February 1999.

225 D. Perry, 'Macedonia's Quest for Security and Stability', *Current History*, March 2000, vol. 99, no. 635, p. 134.

226 B. Cani and C. Milivojević (eds), *Kosmet ili Kosova*, Belgrade, NEA, 1996, p. 251.

227 M. Blagojević, 'The Migration of Serbs from Kosovo during the 1970s and 1980s: Trauma and/or Catharsis', in N. Popov (ed.), *The Road to War in Serbia: Trauma and Catharsis*, Budapest, Central European University Press, 2000, pp. 224–30.

228 B. Petranović and M. Zečević, *Jugoslovenski federalizam, Ideje i stvarnost, Tematska zbirka dokumenata, Drugi tom, 1943–1986*, Belgrade, Prosveta, 1987, p. 552.

remained a constituent part of Serbia as was confirmed by Yugoslavia's 1974 Constitution (Articles 1 and 2), the 1974 Constitution of Serbia (Article 1) and the 1974 Constitution of Kosovo (Article 1).

After 1974 Serbia's republic leadership, on a number of occasions, sought constitutional amendments to reintegrate Kosovo into Serbia and thereby remove the province's *de facto* republic status. These efforts failed because Serbia could not get the unanimous support of Yugoslavia's other republics for the necessary constitutional amendment.[229] During the 1980s continued Albanian demands for republic status for Kosovo eventually triggered unilateral action by Serbia, in the form of the reform of Serbia's republic constitution, towards curtailment of the rights of the autonomous provinces. Amendments to Serbia's constitution proclaimed on 28 March 1989[230] and a new republic constitution proclaimed on 28 September 1990[231] negated the constitutional benefits gained by Kosovo and Vojvodina dating back to the constitutional reform of the late 1960s and early 1970s.

The Preamble to the 1990 Constitution emphasised Serbia's origins in the 'centuries-long struggle of the Serb nation' and to their determination 'to create a democratic state of the Serb people'. The Constitution then declared the republic's territory to be 'undivided' (*jedinstvena*) (Article 4). Kosovo, now renamed 'the Autonomous Province of Kosovo and Metohija', was stated to have a 'form of territorial autonomy' (Article 6). The limited legislative scope of the autonomous province was required to function within the republic constitution (Article 109). Legislation could only be passed by the provincial assembly with the prior approval of Serbia's National Assembly (Article 110). The new Serbian Constitution effectively reversed the *de facto* republic status of Kosovo enjoyed since 1974 and pursuant to which Serbia was precluded from intervening in Kosovo's internal affairs.[232] Kosovo's place within Serbia reverted to that under the 1946 Yugoslav Constitution in which the status of Serbia's autonomous province and region was determined by Serbia's republic constitution (Article 103).

As to Serbia's position within the Yugoslav federation, Article 72 of its 1990 Constitution stipulated:

> The Republic of Serbia regulates and secures:
> 1. the sovereignty, independence and territorial totality of the Republic of Serbia and her international status and relations with other states and international organisations.

This provision was in conflict with the Yugoslav Constitution of 1974 and thus unconstitutional,[233] and paralleled Slovenia's earlier sovereignty declaration of 2 July 1990.

229 V. Pešić, 'The War for Ethnic States', in Popov, note 227, pp. 31–2.
230 Službeni Glasnik Socialističke Republike Srbije, 11/1989.
231 Službeni Glasnik Republike Srbije, 1/1990.
232 M. Vickers, *Between Serb and Albanian: A History of Kosovo*, London, Hurst & Co, 1998, pp. 178–9.
233 Nikolić, note 58, p. 79. Serbia's reaction to charges that provisions in the 1990 Constitution were

On the other hand the 1990 Constitution reaffirmed Serbia as a continuing unit within the Yugoslav federation (Article 135). However, it also invoked the nullification doctrine in relation to federal acts which interfered with Serbia's position of equality or endangered her interests. In these circumstances Serbia would undertake acts to protect her interests (Article 135). The 1990 Constitution also empowered the Serbian government 'to maintain contacts with Serbs living outside of the Republic of Serbia, with the aim of protecting their national and cultural-historical independence' (Article 72). This provision implied that if a Yugoslav republic with a sizeable Serb population seceded, it would be faced with possible border and territorial disputes with Serbia.

The initial Albanian response to the curtailment of Kosovo's autonomy following the 1989 constitutional amendments and new constitution in 1990 in Serbia was to intensify the demand for republic status within the Yugoslav federation. On 2 July 1990 Kosovo's provincial assembly issued a Declaration of Independence.[234] The Declaration was not one of secession from Yugoslavia, but rather from Serbia. It demanded that Kosovo be recognised 'as an independent and equal unit' within the 'Yugoslav Federation-Confederation' on the basis of equality with other such units. This demand was based upon 'the sovereign right of the people of Kosovo, including the right to self-determination'. The Declaration further asserted that the Albanians were a people (*narod*) just like the Serbs and other peoples of Yugoslavia, and not a minority. Finally, the Declaration declared inoperative the March 1989 amendments to Serbia's Constitution.[235]

On 19 February 1991, Yugoslavia's Constitutional Court ruled that the Declaration was unconstitutional.[236] The Court ruled that a change in the status of Kosovo to a republic could not be achieved without amendments to the constitutions of Yugoslavia and Serbia. Furthermore, it was held that declaring Kosovo an equal federal unit within Yugoslavia meant alteration of Serbia's territorial extent and borders and this could not be done, in accordance with Article 4 of Yugoslavia's 1974 Constitution, without Serbia's consent. Finally, the Court ruled that as Albanians were not a constituent nation within Yugoslavia's 1974 Constitution, they could not, as a minority, rely on that Constitution's provisions relating to self-determination for the purpose of proclaiming Kosovo a federal unit within Yugoslavia.

Serbia's response to the Declaration was to dissolve Kosovo's assembly and government on 5 July 1990.[237] This action was endorsed by the Presidency of

unconstitutional was that they were justified and defensive responses to earlier violations of the federal constitution by Slovenia and Croatia: Cohen, note 69, p. 311.

234 Ustavna deklaracija o Kosovu kao samostalnoj i ravnopravnoj jedinici u okviru federacije (konfederacije) Jugoslavije kao ravnopravnog subjekta sa ostalim jedinicama u federaciji (konfederaciji), 2 July 1990, in Buzadžić, note 60, pp. 259–60.

235 Cohen, note 69, p. 310.

236 *Odluka o ocenjivanju ustavnosti ustavne deklaracije o Kosovu kao samostalnoj i ravnopravnoj jedinici u okviru federacije (konfederacije) Jugoslavije kao ravnopravnog subjekta sa ostalim jedinicama u federaciji (konfederaciji)*, 19 February 1991, Službeni List SFRJ, 20 May 1991, vol. 47, no. 37, pp. 618–9.

237 Law Terminating Work of SAP Kosovo Assembly and the Executive Council, 5 July 1990, in M. Weller, *The Crisis in Kosovo 1989–1999: From the Dissolution of Yugoslavia to Rambouillet and*

Yugoslavia on 11 July 1990. The Kosovo Presidency resigned in protest. On 7 September 1990 the majority of delegates from the dissolved Kosovo assembly met in the town of Kačanik and issued the Kačanik Resolution.[238] The Resolution reaffirmed the right of the Albanian people to self-determination and reiterated the essential demands of the 2 July 1990 Declaration concerning Kosovo's status as an equal member of the Yugoslav federation, referring to the latter as a 'community of Yugoslav peoples'.

On the same date as the Kačanik Resolution the dissolved Kosovo assembly proclaimed the Constitution of the Republic of Kosovo.[239] The Constitution was justified as an expression of the right of the Albanian people to 'self-determination to the point of secession' (Preamble). Kosovo was declared to be 'the state of the Albanian people and members of other nations and national minorities that are its citizens' (Article 1). Other relevant provisions were virtually identical to provisions in Serbia's Constitution proclaimed three weeks later. Kosovo's territory was declared to be 'indivisible' (*jedinstvena*) (Article 8). Kosovo was declared to be a 'state' and as such a member of the 'Yugoslav community' (Article 2). Kosovo's sovereignty, independence and territorial integrity were expressed in almost identical terms to Article 72 of Serbia's 1990 Constitution (Article 95). The Kosovo Constitution effectively marked Kosovo's secession from Serbia, although not from Yugoslavia.

On 24 May 1991, an Assembly of the Republic of Kosovo elected Ibrahim Rugova as president of Kosovo. Rugova was the leader of the Democratic League of Kosovo which was established in December 1989.[240] Plans were initiated for the holding of a plebiscite on Kosovo's sovereignty and independence. The plebiscite was held on 26–30 September 1991. Of the 87 per cent of Kosovo's eligible voters who voted, 99.87 per cent voted in favour of Kosovo's sovereignty and independence.[241] Despite the plebiscite results, leaders of Kosovo's political parties indicated that Kosovo would remain within Yugoslavia if Yugoslavia's federation was preserved. However, they indicated that, if Slovenia and Croatia seceded from Yugoslavia, Kosovo would not remain part of what remained of the federation.[242] In the light of decisions by Slovenia and Croatia in early October 1991 to proceed with secession, Kosovo declared its independence on 18 October 1991 and began to seek international recognition, especially from the EC.[243] This was not forthcoming. Given that

the Outbreak of Hostilities, Cambridge, Documents and Analysis Publishing Ltd, 1999, pp. 61–2.

238 Kačanička rezolucija, 7 September 1990, in Cani and Milivojević, note 226, pp. 265–6.

239 The Kosovo Constitution is reproduced in Weller, note 237, pp. 65–72.

240 Vickers and Pettifer, note 221, p. 150.

241 Central Board of Kosova for the Conduct of the Referendum Result, 7 October 1991, in Weller, note 237, p.72.

242 E. Biberaj, 'Kosova: The Balkan Powder Keg', in P. Janke (ed.), *Ethnic and Religious Conflicts: Europe and Asia*, Aldershot, Dartmouth, 1994, pp. 12–13.

243 Letter (Chairman of the Republic of Kosovo), 21 December 1991, in S. Trifunovska, *Former Yugoslavia Through Documents: From its Dissolution to the Peace Settlement*, The Hague, Martinus Nijhoff Publishers, 1999, pp. 767–9; Letter from Dr Rugova to Lord Carrington, Peace Conference on Yugoslavia, 22 December 1991, in Weller, note 237, p. 81.

the EC was only prepared to grant recognition to republics of Yugoslavia, and not its autonomous provinces, Kosovo's application for recognition was not even accepted by the EC for consideration by the Badinter Commission.[244] On 24 May 1992 Albanians in Kosovo took part in elections to elect an assembly and a president pursuant to its constitution. Rugova was elected president and his party gained 96 of the 130 assembly seats.[245]

The only state to recognise Kosovo's independence was Albania on 22 October 1991.[246] The situation in Kosovo since its secession has remained tense, with periodic outbursts of violence and civil unrest. Serbia's police rule in the province was originally met with passive resistance from the Albanians. However, with the emergence of the militant Kosovo Liberation Army (KLA) in early 1998 the level of hostility increased dramatically. The KLA's emergence revealed factionalism within the ranks of Kosovo's Albanians over the means by which independence should be sought. In mid-1998 fierce fighting broke out between Yugoslavia's police and armed forces, on the one hand, and the KLA, on the other, over control of Kosovo's territory. This led to increased international concern over the region. International reaction focused on condemning both sides to the conflict for the use of force, a rejection of Albanian claims to independent statehood, and demands for genuine autonomy for Kosovo.[247]

In October 1998, following a sustained counter-offensive by Yugoslavia's forces against the KLA and following threats of air strikes against Yugoslavia by NATO, Yugoslavia agreed to reduce its military presence in Kosovo[248] and to allow the introduction of 'verifiers' from the Organisation of Security and Coooperation in Europe (OSCE).[249] As Yugoslav forces pulled out of Kosovo, KLA forces reoccupied those areas vacated by Yugoslav forces. Both sides to the conflict claimed the other was guilty of provocations and massacres. In early 1999 both sides were summoned to Rambouillet castle near Paris by the so-called Contact Group (the USA, France, the United Kingdom, Germany, Russia and Italy) to secure a three-year interim agreement on autonomy prepared by the Contact Group. The KLA–Kosovo Albanian delegation reluctantly agreed to the so-called Rambouillet Accord,[250] but Yugoslavia refused to sign.[251] This refusal, coupled with continued

244 Burg and Shoup, note 133, p. 96.

245 *Kosova Daily Report*, 26 May 1992, no. 119; 29 May 1992, no. 122.

246 Declaration (Republic of Albania), 22 October 1991, in Trifunovska, note 243, pp. 766–7.

247 Security Council Resolutions 1160 (1998), 31 March 1998; 1199 (1998), 23 September 1998; 1203 (1998), 24 October 1998.

248 T. Judah, 'Kosovo's Road to War', *Survival*, 1999, vol. 41, pp. 13–14.

249 Agreement on the OSCE Kosovo Verification Mission, 16 October 1998, (1999) 38 ILM 24–7.

250 Interim Agreement for Peace and Self-Government in Kosovo, 23 February 1999, in Weller, note 237, pp. 453–69.

251 For an account of the talks in Rambouillet by an adviser to the Kosovo Albanian delegation see M. Weller, 'The Rambouillet Conference on Kosovo', *International Affairs*, 1999, vol. 75, pp. 211–51. MccGwire argues that the Rambouillet conference 'was set up to fail' so that NATO would on the eve of its fiftieth birthday celebrations demonstrate its continued relevance and establish its right to act without the endorsement of the United Nations: M. MccGwire, 'Why Did

unrest in Kosovo led to NATO launching air strikes against Yugoslavia on 24 March 1999.

The NATO bombing campaign, launched without UN Security Council authorisation, lasted 78 days, and led to Yugoslavia agreeing to terms that differed only slightly from the Rambouillet Accord. This agreement, confirmed by the UN, led to the deployment of UN security forces.[252] Although the territorial integrity of the Federal Republic of Yugoslavia was formally confirmed, a *de facto* partitioning of Kosovo from the Federal Republic of Yugoslavia occurred with Kosovo becoming, in effect, a UN military protectorate.[253]

Conclusion

With the exception of Bosnia-Hercegovina, for all the secessions of and within Yugoslavia's republics, it was explicitly claimed that they were justified on the basis of the right of peoples to self-determination. This is apparent from the various declarations of independence and constitutions adopted by the seceding entities. Bosnia-Hercegovina was a special case due to the absence from that republic of a dominant national group. However, self-determination was still a significant factor. The political programmes and actions of each of its three major political parties were manifestations of the right of the respective nations to self-determination. The Serbs and Croats sought the partition of Bosnia-Hercegovina and the incorporation of their territories into their respective mother states of Serbia and Croatia. The Muslim aim of a unitary Bosnia-Hercegovina was in essence a demand for a state to be dominated by the relative majority Muslim population. None of the three parties achieved their goals. However, the Dayton Peace Accords of 1995 essentially partitioned Bosnia-Hercegovina into two defined federal units, the Serb Republic and Muslim–Croat Federation. Although the Croat entities created during the war were explicitly abolished by the Dayton Peace Accords, effective control of the Muslim–Croat Federation remained divided between Croats and Muslims.[254] This, combined with the Serb Republic, effectively partitioned Bosnia-Hercegovina into three nationally defined units. From this perspective, the Serbs and Croats came closest to achieving their goals based upon claims to self-determination. Apart from the continued territorial integrity of

We Bomb Belgrade?', *International Affairs*, 2000, vol. 76, pp. 12–4. See also Hayden, note 94, pp. 170–5; R. Fisk, 'The Trojan Horse that "Started" a 79–Day War', *The Independent*, 26 November 1999.

252 Security Council Resolution 1244 (1999), 10 June 1999.

253 L. J. Cohen, 'Kosovo: "Nobody's Country"', *Current History*, March 2000, vol. 99, no. 635, pp. 117–23. By late 1999 leading US officials in the administration of President Clinton were of the view that Kosovo's secession from Yugoslavia was inevitable: J. Smith, 'US Officials Expect Kosovo Independence; Secession Increasingly is Seen as Inevitable', *The Washington Post*, 24 September 1999.

254 In a referendum organised by the major Croat political party in Bosnia in November 2000, 70 per cent of Bosnian Croats supported greater autonomy for Bosnia's Croat population: *RFE/RL Newsline*, 13 November 2000, vol. 4, no. 220, Part II.

Bosnia-Hercegovina, the Bosnian Muslims gained very little from the Dayton Peace Accords.

The Bosnia-Hercegovina established by the Dayton Peace Accords can be compared to the Yugoslavia of the 1970s. The loose federal structures of the 1974 Yugoslav Constitution provided a legal framework for the break-up of Yugoslavia after the unifying presence of Tito departed. Similar federal structures are now in place in Bosnia-Hercegovina, with an international civil and military presence acting as a guarantor of its territorial integrity. If and when that international guarantor departs, Bosnia-Hercegovina will face the same pressures that Yugoslavia faced in the late 1980s and early 1990s. The same uncertainty awaits Kosovo.

All the demands for secession based upon self-determination invoked the romantic theory of self-determination. All these demands defined 'a people' in terms of a nation. This was made explicitly clear in the various declarations, constitutional amendments and new constitutions that accompanied the secession processes. This led to what Hayden has defined as 'constitutional nationalism'. By this he meant 'a constitutional and legal structure that privileges the members of one ethnically defined nation over other residents in a particular state'.[255] Hayden goes on to note that a consequence of this is that constitutional nationalism 'envisions a state in which sovereignty resides with a particular nation (*narod*), the members of which are the only ones who can decide fundamental questions of state form and identity'.[256]

The international community's reaction to these secessionist demands was to recognise the secessions of Yugoslavia's republics, but not those within the republics. Thus, the republics of Slovenia, Croatia, Bosnia-Hercegovina and Macedonia were recognised, whereas the Republic of Serb Krajina, the Serb Republic, the Republic of Western Bosnia, and Kosovo were not. International recognition of the four seceding republics was seen by the international community as the application of the right of peoples to self-determination. This is clear from the EC Guidelines on the Recognition of States issued on 16 December 1991 which were stated in a document that confirmed the attachment of the EC 'to the principles of the Helsinki Final Act and the Charter of Paris, in particular to the principle of self-determination'.[257] Furthermore, the importance that the Badinter Arbitration Commission attached to the holding of plebiscites in the seceding republics to determine the 'will of the people' is indicative of self-determination being the basis upon which recognition was granted. As Cassese has observed, the Commission elevated the plebiscite to the status of 'a basic requirement for the *legitimation of secession*'.[258]

255 Hayden, note 155, p. 655.

256 Ibid., p. 656.

257 Guidelines on Recognition, 16 December 1991, in Trifunovska, note 16, pp. 431–2.

258 A. Cassese, *Self-Determination of Peoples: A Legal Reappraisal*, Cambridge, Cambridge University Press, 1995, p. 272. Hillgruber recognises the significance of self-determination to the process of recognition of the seceding Yugoslav republics. However, he denies that the EC recognised a right of secession. Rather, he argues that self-determination merely required plebiscites to establish the

Cassese also asserts that the recognition of the seceding republics was 'a realisation of the *political principle* of self-determination'.[259] This assertion cannot be accepted. The EC Guidelines explicitly refer to self-determination in the context of the Helsinki Final Act and the Charter of Paris, which themselves rely on the UN Charter and other international documents that Cassese recognises establish the right of peoples to self-determination as a non-derogable norm of international law (*jus cogens*).[260]

The international recognition of the right of the Yugoslav republics to their independence within existing internal federal borders was underpinned in a number of rulings made by the Badinter Arbitration Commission. These rulings concerned the question of whether Yugoslavia was the victim of secession or dissolution, the scope of the right of peoples to self-determination and the principle of *uti possidetis juris*. These rulings are the subject of critical analysis in the next chapter.

will of the populations of the separate republics for independence: C. Hillgruber, 'The Admission of New States to the International Community', *European Journal of International Law*, 1998, vol. 9, pp. 508–9.

259 A. Cassese, 'Self-Determination of Peoples and the Recent Break-up of the USSR and Yugoslavia', in R. St John Macdonald (ed.), *Essays in Honour of Wang Tieya*, Dordrecht, Martinus Nijhoff Publishers, 1994, p. 139.

260 Cassese, note 258, pp. 133–40.

7 The Badinter Commission

Secession, self-determination and *uti possidetis*

Prior to making its recommendations on the recognition of Yugoslavia's republics, the Badinter Commission made three crucial rulings. These were important as they provided a basis upon which recognition of Yugoslavia's secessionist republics within internal federal borders was recommended. The first ruling related to whether Yugoslavia was the subject of secession or whether it was in the process of dissolution. The second related to the scope of self-determination. The third related to the relevance of *uti possidetis juris* to cases outside the context of decolonisation. Each of these rulings needs to be analysed in detail.

Yugoslavia: secession or dissolution?

On 29 November 1991 the Badinter Commission handed down *Opinion No. 1 of the Arbitration Commission of the Peace Conference on Yugoslavia*[1] (*Opinion No. 1*). This opinion was in response to a question put to it on the issue of whether the Socialist Federative Republic of Yugoslavia (SFRY) was experiencing secession of a number of republics or whether it was in the process of 'disintegration or breaking-up'.[2]

1 (1992) 31 ILM 1494.

2 Serb commentators on the Badinter Arbitration Commission have argued that Lord Carrington exceeded his authority in passing on the question in that form to the Commission. By the terms of an EC declaration on 3 September 1991 the Chairman of the Conference on Yugoslavia was to 'transmit to the Arbitration Commission the issues submitted for arbitration': EC Declaration on Yugoslavia, 3 September 1991, in *Focus*, Special Issue (Belgrade), 14 January 1992, p. 145. The question that Serbia submitted for transmission to the Commission was: 'Is secession legal from the standpoint of the United Nations Charter and other relevant rules of international law?': M. Kreća, *The Badinter Arbitration Commission: A Critical Commentary*, Belgrade, Jugoslovenski pregled, 1993, pp. 7–9, 28; M. Pavlović and N. Popović, *Secesija u režiji velikih sila, Od očuvanja do nametanja mira u građanskom ratu u prethodnoj SFR Jugoslvaiji*, Belgrade, Institut za političke studije, 1996, pp. 114–15. It can be noted that Serbia's question was very similar to the second question of the Canadian government's reference to the Supreme Court of Canada in relation to the possible secession of Quebec. The Supreme Court ruled that in international law there was a right of secession from a state in certain and defined, but limited, circumstances. If the secession did not fall within these defined circumstances, the question of its validity would be determined by the relevant state's domestic laws. If it was not permitted by that state's domestic laws it would, in the opinion of the Supreme Court, be unlikely that international law would recognise the validity of the secession. In

The Badinter Commission ruled that the SFRY was 'in the process of dissolution' on the basis of three factors. First, there was reference to the plebiscites on sovereignty and independence held prior to *Opinion No. 1* in Slovenia, Croatia and Macedonia, as well as the sovereignty resolution of the Assembly of Bosnia-Hercegovina on 15 October 1991. Second, was the finding that federal institutions such as the Federal Presidency, the Federal Assembly, the Constitutional Court and the Yugoslav People's Army had ceased to 'meet the criteria of participation and representativeness inherent in a federation'. Third, was the fact that federal authorities and the republics had been unable to enforce respect for any of the numerous cease-fires that had been negotiated by the European Community (EC) and the United Nations (UN), but which had broken down soon after being negotiated.

In *Opinion No. 8 of the Arbitration Commission of the Peace Conference on Yugoslavia*[3] (*Opinion No. 8*) handed down on 4 July 1992, the Badinter Commission ruled that the process of dissolution was 'now complete and that SFRY no longer exists' and 'that it no longer [has] legal personality'.[4] In support of that conclusion the Badinter Commission referred to the following factors. First, there was the plebiscite on sovereignty and independence in Bosnia-Hercegovina in late February 1992. Second, there was the view that Serbia and Montenegro had since constituted themselves as a new state, the Federal Republic of Yugoslavia (FRY). Third, there was the fact that most of the states seceding from the SFRY had recognised each other and, in the cases of Slovenia, Croatia and Bosnia-Hercegovina, gained widespread international recognition and admission to membership of the UN. This supported the assertion that the authority of the federal state was not exercised over the territories of the seceding republics, which were now sovereign and independent. Fourth, was the fact that the new states accounted for the 'greater part of the territory and population' of the SFRY. Fifth, was the view that federal bodies in the SFRY no longer existed. Sixth, was the fact that a number of UN Security Council Resolutions and a European Council Declaration on Yugoslavia of 27 June 1992 had referred to 'the former' Yugoslavia. Finally, there was the generally accepted view that the FRY could not automatically continue the UN membership of the SFRY.[5]

The significance of the finding in *Opinion No. 1* that the SFRY was 'in the process of dissolution' was that, in subsequently granting recognition to the SFRY's republics, the EC would not be seen to be sanctioning secession. Rather, it would

the context of Canada, the circumstances in Quebec and the provisions of Canadian constitutional law led the Supreme Court to conclude that a unilateral secession by Quebec would not be valid under either Canada's domestic law or international law: *Reference re: Secession of Quebec* (1998) 161 DLR (4th) 385.

3 (1992) 31 ILM 1521.

4 In September 1992, the UN Security Council took the view that the SFRY had ceased to exist: Security Council Resolution 777 (1992), 19 September 1992.

5 It could be added that another contributing factor to the dissolution of the SFRY was the demand by the EC and the rest of the international community that the SFRY not use force to preserve its territorial integrity and statehood: A. Whelan, 'The Liberty of Peoples – Ireland, the EC and Eastern Europe', in A. Whelan (ed.), *Law and Liberty in Ireland*, Dublin, Oak Tree Press, 1993, p. 95.

be recognising new states that emerged from the ruins of a state 'in the process of dissolution'.[6] This had the further consequence that the normal requirements for recognition of statehood would not be applied as rigorously as they would have been had the situation been one of secession.[7] Furthermore, because the SFRY was in the process of dissolution, the Badinter Commission later ruled that existing republic borders had to be maintained as future international borders on the basis, *inter alia*, of the principle of *uti possidetis juris*.[8] However, as will be shown below, the recognition of new states from the SFRY was recognition of states that seceded from the SFRY. It was not recognition of new states that emerged from the debris of a SFRY that had dissolved or was in the process of dissolution. On the other hand, *Opinion No. 1* and *Opinion No. 8* had significant implications for issues related to state succession, which would not have been so prevalent had there been a continuity of the SFRY in the form of the remaining republics of Serbia and Montenegro.[9]

The question that needs to be asked is whether the Badinter Commission was justified in concluding that the SFRY was in a process of dissolution and that it eventually ceased to exist. According to Oppenheim, a state ceases to exist, *inter alia*, 'when a state breaks up so that its whole territory henceforth comprises two or more states'. Oppenheim also observes that whether the situation is one of two or more new states replacing the old state or 'whether one of them constitutes a continuation, much diminished, of the original state is not always easy to answer'.[10] However, as Crawford points out, there is 'the presumption – in practice a strong one . . . in favour of the continuance, as against the extinction of an established state'.[11]

On the issue of whether the SFRY was 'in the process of dissolution' it must be questioned whether the expression has any legal meaning. According to Craven:

6 C. Hillgruber, 'The Admission of New States to the International Community', *European Journal of International Law*, 1998, vol. 9, p. 508. According to Williams, the SFRY was the first case in which a 'predecessor state . . . dissolved into a number of independent states, with none of these states being considered the continuing state': P. R. Williams, 'The Treaty Obligations of the Successor States of the Former Soviet Union, Yugoslavia, and Czechoslovakia: Do They Continue in Force?', *Denver Journal of International Law and Policy*, 1994, vol. 23, p. 16.

7 M. C. R. Craven, 'The European Community Arbitration Commission on Yugoslavia', *British Year Book of International Law*, 1995, vol. 66, p. 378.

8 *Opinion No. 3 of the Arbitration Commission of the Peace Conference on Yugoslavia* (1992) 31 ILM 1499, at 1500.

9 It must be recognised that the international community's decision to view the situation in the SFRY as one of dissolution rather than secession was essentially politically motivated. In the view of the State Department of the United States of America (USA) it was 'politically unpalatable' to interpret the events in the SFRY as instances of secession: E. D. Williamson and J. E. Osborn, 'A US Perspective on Treaty Succession and Related Issues in the Wake of the Breakup of the USSR and Yugoslavia', *Virginia Journal of International Law*, 1993, vol. 33, p. 270.

10 R. Jennings and A. Watts, *Oppenheim's International Law, Volume I, Peace*, 9th edition, London, Longman, 1992, p. 207.

11 J. Crawford, *The Creation of States in International Law*, Oxford, Clarendon Press, 1979, p. 417.

> Dismemberment . . . is merely descriptive of a form of extinction following the disassociation of various territorial units. As such, it can only really be attributed to a situation *ex post facto* once the lack of continuity of the State has been finally determined. If the issue is simply whether or not a State continues to exist, it makes no sense to speak of dismemberment as a process.[12]

In *Opinion No. 8* the Badinter Commission recognised that, at the date of *Opinion No. 1*, despite the SFRY being 'in the process of dissolution' it 'was at that time still a legal international entity'.[13] On this basis Craven is justified in asserting that the Badinter Commission should have refrained from offering its view that the SFRY was in the process of dissolution in November 1991.[14]

Notwithstanding the introduction of the concept of a state in the process of dissolution, an examination of the bases upon which the Badinter Commission ruled that the SFRY was in such a process and eventually ceased to exist needs to be undertaken to ascertain if a case for the rebuttal of the presumption against extinction was established.

Plebiscites

The reference to the holding of plebiscites on sovereignty and independence as a basis for finding that a state was in the process of dissolution and heading towards extinction is novel. None of the standard authorities and texts on international law and state-creation refer to plebiscites in this context. If the plebiscite results are accepted at face value, all they establish is that various sections of the population in particular territorial units in the SFRY agreed that the republics should be sovereign and independent.[15] Plebiscites can confirm that certain segments of the population of a particular territorial unit desire to secede. The loss of territory and population may indicate the extinction of a state if it is of such an extent that not even a core or nucleus of the state remains. However, the holding of a plebiscite does not of itself establish anything as to the continuation or existence of a state.

However, even if one accepts that plebiscites of the type conducted in the SFRY's republics were of relevance, one must closely analyse them and assess their legal and political legitimacy. First, all the plebiscites within the SFRY were unconstitutional. In January 1991, the Constitutional Court of the SFRY ruled that the Slovenian Assembly Resolution to hold a plebiscite in December 1990 was unconstitutional on the ground that the sovereignty and independence of Slovenia

12 Craven, note 7, p. 369. Craven uses the word 'dismemberment' to mean the same thing as 'dissolution' in *Opinion No. 1*.

13 *Opinion No. 8 of the Arbitration Commission of the Peace Conference on Yugoslavia* (1992) 31 ILM 1521, at 1522.

14 Craven, note 7, p. 369.

15 In the context of domestic Canadian law, the Supreme Court of Canada has held that a plebiscite in favour of secession 'in itself and without more, has no direct legal effect, and could not in itself bring about unilateral secession': *Reference re: Secession of Quebec* (1998) 161 DLR (4th) 385, at 424.

pursuant to the plebiscite would result in a unilateral alteration to the international and internal borders of the SFRY.[16] Similarly, the passage of the resolution to hold a plebiscite by the National Assembly of Bosnia-Hercegovina without the presence or support of the Serb deputies at the time the vote was taken, made such a resolution unconstitutional under that republic's constitution.[17]

Second, the political legitimacy of the plebiscites must be questioned. All of them were conducted in highly volatile political circumstances where nationalist passions had been inflamed and, in the cases of Macedonia and Bosnia-Hercegovina, against the background of war that had erupted on the territory of the SFRY.[18] Furthermore, these plebiscites were conducted in an environment where there was no opportunity to present the case against sovereignty and independence. The media were under the control and influence of the republic authorities responsible for initiating the plebiscites. Voters were not presented with anything approaching a balanced debate on the merits or otherwise of alternative views. Nor were there any official state documents and materials forwarded to all voters outlining the cases for the 'Yes' and 'No' vote.

Third, one must question whether all of those who voted 'Yes' did so with the actual desire that their republic become an independent state. This is particularly relevant to the Croatian and Slovenian plebiscites. The questions put to the voters in both republics were ones that sought support for sovereignty and independence. However, in Slovenia, its sovereignty and independence were to come about only if a restructured Yugoslav state could not be negotiated. In this respect the Slovenian plebiscite mirrored the plebiscite in Quebec in October 1995. In Quebec, voters were asked: 'Do you agree that Quebec should become sovereign, after having made a formal offer to Canada for a new Economic and Political Partnership, within the scope of the Bill respecting the Future of Quebec and of the agreement signed on 12 June 1995?'[19] It has been shown that a vote for the sovereignty of Quebec was not always understood as a vote for independent statehood. Between one-quarter and one-third of Quebec voters favouring sovereignty believed that it meant that Quebec would remain a province of Canada.[20]

16 *Rešenje o obustavi izvršenja pojedinačnih akata i radnji preduztih na osnovu čl. 4. i 10. zakona o plebicitu o samostalnosti i nezavisnosti Republike Slovenije kojima organi Republike Slovenije preuzimaju ustavom SFRJ utvrđena prava i dužnosti federacije ili kojima se jednostrano menja granica SFRJ, odnosno granica između republika*, 8 January 1991, Službeni List SFRJ, 18 January 1991, vol. 47, no. 4, p. 64. This decision was confirmed in November 1991: *Odluka o oceni ustavnosti odredaba čl. 4. i 10. zakona o plebicitu o samostalnosti i nezavisnosti Republike Slovenije*, 7 November 1991, Službeni List SFRJ, 28 February 1992, vol. 48, no. 14, p. 189.

17 R. M. Hayden, 'Bosnia's Internal War and the International Criminal Tribunal', *Fletcher Forum of World Affairs*, 1998, vol. 22, no. 1, p. 59.

18 'Hasty referendum votes often represent a tyrannical majority's grab for power, especially if they are orchestrated by a nationalist movement in an atmosphere of rising ethnic tension': D. Callahan, *Unwinnable Wars, American Power and Ethnic Conflict*, New York, Hill & Wang, 1997, p. 35.

19 K. McRoberts, *Misconceiving Canada: The Struggle for National Unity*, Toronto, Oxford University Press, p. 226.

20 Ibid., p. 230; S. Contenta, 'Sovereignists Scramble for a Game Plan, Federal Offensive Finds PQ in State of Disarray and Confusion', *The Toronto Star*, 21 September 1997.

No analysis has been done on what voters understood when they cast their votes in the Slovenian or Croatian plebiscites. The Quebec experience suggests that there may have been a significant number who voted 'Yes', but who did not believe or wish such a vote to be a vote for statehood independent of the SFRY. For a plebiscite to have legitimacy in the context of secession it should be a clear expression of the democratic will of those voting. As the Supreme Court of Canada remarked in its consideration of the validity of a possible unilateral secession of Quebec from Canada:

> The [plebiscite] result, if it is to be taken as an expression of the democratic will, must be free of ambiguity both in terms of the question asked and in the terms of the support it achieves.[21]

Participation and representativeness

The second factor that indicated that the SFRY was in the process of dissolution according to the Badinter Commission was the assertion that various federal institutions had ceased to 'meet the criteria of participation and representativeness in a federation'. Earlier the Commission had noted that 'the existence of the [federal] State implies that the federal organs represent the components of the Federation and wield effective power'. This was no doubt true in a general sense, but two comments must be made. First, the reason for any lack of participation and representativeness in the SFRY was the abandonment of the representative positions by delegates from the seceding republics as and when declarations of independence were made. Second, under the 1974 Constitution of the SFRY no federal organs were representatives of the republics (Articles 291, 362 and 397). Republics were not directly represented in federal bodies. All federal officials were required by oath to defend the sovereignty and territorial integrity of the SFRY (Article 397). As such they could not receive directions from, or directly represent, the republics or autonomous provinces.[22] The implications of this argument by the Badinter Commission are startling. If the abandonment of representative positions in federal institutions is evidence of the dissolution of a state, the secession of thirteen states from the United States of America (USA) in 1861 would have meant that the USA was, at that point of time, in a process of dissolution. At the time, President Abraham Lincoln adamantly rejected this proposition.[23] Hurst Hannum has observed as follows:

> In effect the Commission is attempting to create a new rule of international law: If a state is founded on . . . federal principles, then it is sufficient for a

21 *Reference re: Secession of Quebec* (1998) 161 DLR (4th) 385, at 424.

22 M. Kreća, 'Succession and the Continuity of Yugoslavia', *Jugoslovenska revija za međunarodno pravo*, 1992, vol. 33, no. 2–3, pp. 183–4.

23 Hayden, note 17, p. 51.

> constituent republic to cease participating in the federal government in order to deprive the state as a whole of recognition as a state by the international community.[24]

Craven correctly observes that the mere lack of representativeness or participation in government cannot lead to the conclusion that a state has ceased to exist. What is crucial

> is the notion of control . . . which concerns the *de facto* authority exercised by the government over the people. . . . [S]o long as a government continues to wield power over its territory, any lack of representativeness will be of little consequence as far as its continuity is concerned'.[25]

It is not disputed that the SFRY, and later the FRY, had control over Serbia and Montenegro at all times. On this basis it cannot be said that the SFRY was in the process of dissolution.

On the other hand, if one accepts the argument on the lack of representativeness, then an inconsistency is revealed within *Opinion No. 1* and *Opinion No. 8*. In these two opinions the Badinter Commission accepted the sovereignty resolution of the Assembly of Bosnia-Hercegovina of 15 October 1991 and the plebiscite on independence in late February 1992 as evidence that the SFRY was in the process of dissolution. Yet both of these events could be challenged on the ground that they were unrepresentative actions and in violation of the consensus provisions that had been reached by the leaders of the three major national parties after the 1990 republic elections. In other words, if the SFRY lacked legitimacy on the basis of the absence of representativeness and participation, then so too did the sovereignty resolution and plebiscite in Bosnia-Hercegovina.[26]

Collapse of cease-fires

Much the same can be said of the third factor mentioned in *Opinion No. 1*. The fact that cease-fires could not be enforced by federal authorities in the SFRY cannot be seen as a factor towards establishing the dissolution of a state. If this view of the

24 H. Hannum, 'Self-Determination, Yugoslavia, and Europe: Old Wine in New Bottles?', *Transnational Law and Contemporary Problems*, 1993, vol. 3, p. 64.

25 Craven, note 7, p. 367; R. Etinski, 'Has the SFR of Yugoslavia Ceased to Exist as a Subject of International Law?', in R. Petković, *International Law and the Changed Yugoslavia*, Belgrade, Institute of International Politics and Economics, 1995, p. 24.

26 Kreća, note 22, p. 186. According to Barutciski, in relation to Bosnia-Hercegovina, 'the international community proceeded to recognize the independence of a state that had ceased to exist in any meaningful way. The constitutional crisis left a parliament that no longer represented the three constituent nations and a government that no longer functioned legally': M. Barutciski, 'Politics Overrides Legal Principles: Tragic Consequences of the Diplomatic Intervention in Bosnia-Hercegovina (1991–1992)', *American University Journal of International Law and Policy*, 1996, vol. 11, p. 783.

Badinter Commission is accepted as correct, then it can only lead to secessionist groups having a vested interest in starting military hostilities and then perpetuating them by either refusing to negotiate cease-fires or by deliberately ignoring and violating them after they have been negotiated. This procedure would contribute to the extinction of states and thus facilitate secession. This does not mean that state impotence cannot eventually lead to a conclusion that a state has ceased to exist. However, as Crawford observes, 'a State can continue to exist . . . even if its government is reduced to relative impotence'.[27] This is currently confirmed by the example of Somalia where state and government authority is essentially lacking in an atmosphere of widespread anarchy.[28] Yet Somalia is still recognised as a state and its membership of the UN is not doubted. But, Somalia's existence as a state could eventually come into question. Somalia's extinction would arise when it is 'proved . . . by the continuance of anarchy so prolonged as to render reconstitution impossible or in a high degree improbable'.[29] It could not be said that this stage had been reached with the SFRY by November 1991, nor by January 1992 when the EC extended recognition to two of the SFRY's seceding republics.

The FRY Constitution

The fourth factor that the Badinter Commission saw as evidence that the SFRY had ceased to exist was the adoption of a new Yugoslav constitution and the renaming of the SFRY as the FRY on 27 April 1992.[30] Why a new constitution and name should make for a new state rather than the continuation of the remnants of an existing state is not made clear.[31] As Crawford observes, 'merely altering the municipal constitution and form of government', does not alter the existence of the state – it 'remains the same'.[32] From the time of its establishment in 1918 to the time it had, according to the Badinter Commission, ceased to exist, the Yugoslav state had had five constitutions and five different names. Throughout that time the existence and continuity of this Yugoslav state were never questioned or in doubt because of these constitutional and name changes.[33] The FRY Constitution of 1992 clearly implied that the FRY was not a new state, but rather the continuation of the SFRY.[34] Thus, the Preamble referred to the 'unbroken continuity of

27 Crawford, note 11, p. 411.

28 V. Jovanović, 'The Status of the Federal Republic of Yugoslavia in the United Nations', *Fordham International Law Journal*, 1998, vol. 21, pp. 1726–7, where the author also refers to Afghanistan and Albania as instances of states that should, on the precedent of the SFRY, have been declared to have ceased to exist.

29 W. E. Hall, *A Treatise on International Law*, 8th edition, London, Oxford University Press, 1924, p. 21.

30 The FRY Constitution is reproduced in B. Milinković, *Novi ustavi na tlu bivše Jugoslavije*, Belgrade, Međunarodna Politika, 1995, pp. 7–38.

31 Declaration, 27 April 1992, in *Constitution of the Federal Republic of Yugoslavia*, Belgrade, Ministry of Information of the Republic of Serbia, 1992, p. 57.

32 Crawford, note 11, p. 405; Hall, note 29, p. 21.

33 Etinski, note 25, p. 27.

34 This point was also stressed in a joint statement by representatives of Serbia and Montenegro

Yugoslavia'. This was further implied by reference in the Preamble to the Federal Assembly of the SFRY adopting and proclaiming the new constitution.[35] The continuity of the Yugoslav state, notwithstanding the new constitution, was expressly confirmed by the Declaration of the Joint Session of the Federal Assembly of the SFRY and the Assemblies of Serbia and Montenegro which accompanied the proclamation of the new constitution (Article 1).

International recognition of seceding republics

The fifth factor referred to by the Badinter Commission as evidencing the SFRY's extinction was the fact that the seceding republics had recognised each other and that Slovenia, Croatia and Bosnia-Hercegovina had also received widespread international recognition from other states and membership of the UN. However, this does not evidence the SFRY's extinction. It in fact refers to the reduction in the SFRY's territorial scope and population. Furthermore, the mutual recognition by the seceding republics was held to be unconstitutional by the Constitutional Court of the SFRY on the grounds that the SFRY's membership, territory and borders were altered in violation of Yugoslavia's 1974 Constitution (Articles 1, 2 and 5).[36]

Loss of territory and population

The loss of the 'greater part of the territory and population' of the SFRY is the sixth factor said by the Badinter Commission to evidence the extinction of that state. However, as Crawford observes:

> It is established that the acquisition or loss of territory does not *per se* affect the continuity of the State. This may be so even where the territory acquired or lost is substantially greater in area than the original or remaining territory. The presumption is particularly strong where the constitutional system of the State prior to acquisition or loss continues in force.[37]

Later Crawford observes that with changes to population the 'same considerations apply' as with territorial changes.[38]

issued on 12 February 1992, which detailed the basic structure of the constitution adopted in April: Basic Principles of the Organization and Operation of Yugoslavia as a Joint State, 12 February 1992, *Yugoslav Survey*, 1992, vol. 33, no. 1, pp. 43–4.

35 Pavle Nikolić, *Od raspada do beznađa i nade, Svedočanstvo o jednom vremenu*, Belgrade, Filip Višnjić, 1997, p. 203.

36 *Odluka o ocenjivanju ustavnosti odluke o priznanju Republike Slovenije kao suverene i samostalne države*, 29 January 1992, in M. Buzadžić, *Secesija bivših jugoslovenskih republika u svetlosti odluka Ustavnog suda Jugoslavije*, *Zbirka dokumenata s uvodnom raspravom*, Belgrade, Službeni List SRJ, 1994, pp. 165–6.

37 Crawford, note 11, p. 404.

38 Ibid., p. 405.

The four seceding republics in the SFRY accounted for 60.1 per cent of its territory and, based upon 1988 estimates, 55.8 per cent of its population.[39] By way of comparison, the secession of Bangladesh from Pakistan resulted in a loss of 15.2 per cent of Pakistan's territory and 56 per cent of its population.[40] In the case of the USA, the Louisiana Purchase of 1803 increased the territorial extent of that state by 97 per cent over what it had been prior to that date.[41] In neither of these cases was there any suggestion that Pakistan and the USA had ceased to exist by virtue of the dramatic changes to their territory or population. In accordance with Crawford's statement of principle it is suggested that the SFRY could not be said to have ceased to exist simply because of its loss of territory and population. As Crawford observes:

> [A] State may be said to continue as such as long as the same governmental system continues to exist with respect to a significant part of a territory and population: its constitutional system need not be the same, as long as it is in fact independent as defined.[42]

In the same vein Hall writes:

> The identity of a state . . . is considered to subsist so long as a part of the territory which can be recognised as the essential portion through the preservation of the capital or of the original territorial nucleus, or which represents the state by continuity of government, remains either as an independent residuum or as the core of an enlarged organisation.[43]

Non-existence of Yugoslav political institutions

The seventh factor upon which the Badinter Commission, in *Opinion No. 8*, based its conclusion that the SFRY had ceased to exist was the claim that 'the common

39 Based upon data in B. McFarlane, *Yugoslavia, Politics, Economics and Society*, London, Pinter Publishers, 1998, p. xviii.

40 A. Heraclides, *The Self-Determination of Minorities in International Politics*, London, Frank Cass & Co, 1991, p. 149.

41 Based upon data in the *Hammond United States Atlas*, Gemini edition, Maplewood, Hammond Inc, 1989, p. U-16.

42 Crawford, note 11, p. 403. An approach consistent with this view was taken by the UN when India continued its membership of the UN and its existence after the 1947 partition that created Pakistan: T. D. Musgrave, *Self-Determination and National Minorities*, Oxford, Clarendon Press, 1997, p. 202.

43 Hall, note 29, p. 22. In relation to Hall's reference to 'the original territorial nucleus' it can be said that most of Serbia as it existed in 1991 was the Serbia that existed at the outbreak of World War I and prior to the formation of Yugoslavia. That Serbia formed the nucleus of the Yugoslav state formed in 1918 is confirmed by the fact that Serbia, as part of the victorious Allies, liberated large areas of Austria–Hungary that became part of the Yugoslav state: S. Avramov and M. Kreća, *Međunarodno javno pravo*, 14th edition, Belgrade, Savremena administracija, 1996, p. 101. Furthermore, there is support, although not unanimous, that the new Yugoslav state was a legal successor to Serbia: *Ivancevic -v- Artukovic* (1954) 211 F 2d 565, at 570–4; Etinski, note 25, pp. 44–6; Crawford, note 11, p. 409.

federal bodies on which all the Yugoslav bodies were represented no longer exist'.[44] No evidence to support this claim was referred to by the Commission. Nor could the Commission have referred to such evidence because it did not exist. Federal bodies of the SFRY did exist and function. Thus, the Collective Presidency of the SFRY was involved in negotiations and gave its consent to the deployment of UN peacekeepers in Croatia in early 1992.[45] As noted above, the Federal Assembly of the SFRY adopted the FRY Constitution of 27 April 1992. Federal institutions of the SFRY did not cease to exist on the adoption of the FRY Constitution of 27 April 1992. By the terms of the Constitutional Law for the Implementation of the Constitution of the FRY, adopted by the Federal Assembly of the SFRY on 27 April 1992,[46] federal bodies of the SFRY were to continue to function during the period of transition and until the new federal institutions under the 27 April 1992 Constitution were constituted. Thus, the Collective Presidency of the SFRY functioned until 15 July 1992, and the federal government of the SFRY functioned until 14 July 1992.[47] It is clear that the Badinter Commission had no basis upon which to conclude that federal bodies of the SFRY had ceased to exist. On the contrary, they functioned for a time after the date of *Opinion No. 8*. What is true is that these federal bodies did not have representatives from the seceding republics. However, the voluntary abandonment of these federal bodies by representatives of the seceding republics did not mean that they had ceased to exist.

References to 'the former' Yugoslavia

The eighth factor referred to by the Badinter Commission as evidence of Yugoslavia's extinction were references in a number of UN and EC documents to 'the former' SFRY. UN Security Council Resolutions 752[48] and 757[49] do make such references in their preambular and substantive parts. However, it must be noted that these two resolutions were passed after the adoption of the name of the FRY on 27 April 1992, when, for the time being the FRY was, according to its constitution, constituted by Serbia and Montenegro (Article 2). After 27 April 1992 it became necessary to make a distinction between the territorial scope of the SFRY and the FRY in the Security Council Resolutions. It is clear that the resolutions, in referring to 'the former' SFRY, are referring to the territory of the SFRY as it

44 *Opinion No. 8 of the Arbitration Commission of the Peace Conference on Yugoslavia* (1992) 31 ILM 1521, at 1523.

45 For details of the negotiations leading to the deployment of UN peacekeepers in Croatia see Further Report of the Secretary-General Pursuant to Security Council Resolution 721 (1991), S/23513, 4 February 1992.

46 Službeni List SRJ, 27 April 1992, vol. 1, no. 1.

47 M. B. Milojević, 'Mišljenja Arbitražne komisije o Jugoslaviji', *Anali Pravnog Fakulteta u Beogradu*, 1993, vol. 41, no. 5, p. 570.

48 Security Council Resolution 752 (1992), 15 May 1992.

49 Security Council Resolution 757 (1992), 30 May 1992.

existed before the outbreak of hostilities in June 1991. Thus, in Resolution 752 the Security Council called upon:

> all parties and others concerned to ensure that forcible expulsions of persons from the areas where they live and any attempts to change the ethnic composition of the population, anywhere in the former Socialist Federal Republic of Yugoslavia, cease immediately.[50]

This is a clear reference to the geographical extent of the SFRY, not a statement about its existence.[51] A similar conclusion can be drawn from an analysis of the European Council Declaration of 27 June 1992 (the Lisbon Declaration).[52] Two of the references were to 'the territory of the former Yugoslavia' in the context of the violence and displaced persons on the territory of the SFRY. The other references were to 'the peoples of the former Yugoslavia' and the 'problems of the former Yugoslavia', both indicative of a reference to the peoples and problems of the territory known as the SFRY, rather than that of the peoples and problems of the territory of the FRY, the latter also being mentioned within the Lisbon Declaration.

The FRY not the successor to the SFRY

The final basis upon which the Badinter Commission ruled that the SFRY had ceased to exist was the reference to the view that the FRY's claim to be the successor to the SFRY had not been generally accepted by the international community. This stemmed from statements to that effect in UN Security Council Resolution 757 and the Lisbon Declaration. However, it must be observed that neither of these documents resolved that the FRY was not the successor to the SFRY. Indeed, the Lisbon Declaration specifically entertained the possibility that the FRY could be the successor to the SFRY. On this point the Lisbon Declaration stated the following:

> The Community and its member States do not recognize the new federal entity comprising Serbia and Montenegro as the successor State of the former Yugoslavia until the moment a decision has been taken by the qualified international organisations.[53]

If, as the Lisbon Declaration contemplates, the FRY could possibly be accepted as the continuation of and successor to the SFRY, then it is logically impossible to conclude that the SFRY had ceased to exist at that time.

50 Security Council Resolution 752 (1992), Paragraph 6, 15 May 1992.

51 It was not until two months after *Opinion No. 8* that the Security Council made a clear statement that the SFRY had 'ceased to exist': Security Council Resolution 777 (1992), 19 September 1992.

52 European Council Declaration on the Former Yugoslavia, 27 June 1992, in S. Trifunovska (ed.), *Yugoslavia Through Documents: From its Creation to its Dissolution*, Dordrecht, Martinus Nijhoff Publishers, 1994, pp. 625–6.

53 Ibid., p. 626.

On the basis of the above analysis it is suggested that none of the factors mentioned by the Badinter Commission, of themselves, point to the SFRY being in the process of dissolution, as at the date of *Opinion No. 1*, or as having ceased to exist, as at the date of *Opinion No. 8*. Some factors are either irrelevant or have to be rejected as irrelevant because of their implications. Those that could be relevant do not rebut the strong presumption in favour of the continuation, rather than extinction, of a state. Even if the factors are considered collectively the same conclusion must be drawn. Even substantial changes to territory, population and government do not necessarily point to the extinction of a state.[54] In support of this proposition, Crawford cites the radical distribution of Poland's populations and territory as well as the revolutionary changes to its constitutional and political system after World War II which did not affect the continuity of the Polish state.[55]

It should also be noted that the declarations of independence by the seceding republics all referred to the process of separating themselves from the SFRY. None of them expressed their independence declarations in the context of the dissolution of the SFRY. All of them were consistent with the SFRY remaining a state from which the seceding republics were severing their ties.[56] Indeed, in 1996 the FRY entered into agreements for the normalisation of relations with Macedonia, Croatia and Bosnia-Hercegovina in which each of the latter three states accepted the state continuity of the FRY. Jovanović argues that these agreements evidence the acceptance by these three states of the FRY as a continuation of the SFRY, and by implication that their existence was pursuant to secession from, and not dissolution of, an existing state.[57]

The appropriate conclusion to be drawn on the question of whether the SFRY was in the process of dissolution at the time when the Badinter Commission issued its recommendations on international recognition of four of the SFRY's republics, is that the SFRY was a state whose existence was beyond doubt and which had not come to an end. Accordingly, recognition of the republics was recognition of states following secession from the SFRY rather than recognition of new states arising from the debris of a near-failed state.[58]

Self-determination

On 11 January 1992, in *Opinion No. 2 of the Arbitration Commission of the Peace Conference on Yugoslavia*[59] (*Opinion No. 2*), the Badinter Commission had to give its advice on the following question put to it by the Chairman of the Conference on Yugoslavia, Lord Carrington:

54 Crawford, note 11, p. 417.
55 Ibid., p. 409. However, Crawford, at p. 410, questions the validity of this conclusion.
56 D. O. Lloyd, 'Succession, Secession, and State Membership in the United Nations', *New York University Journal of International Law and Politics*, 1994, vol. 26, p. 790; Etinski, note 25, pp. 22–3; Jovanović, note 28, pp. 1722–3.
57 Jovanović, note 28, pp. 1731–2, 1735.
58 Musgrave, note 42, p. 203.
59 (1992) 31 ILM 1497.

> Does the Serbian Population in Croatia and Hercegovina, as one of the constituent peoples of Yugoslavia, have the right to self-determination?[60]

The Badinter Commission advised as follows:

> 1. The Commission considers that international law as it currently stands does not spell out all the implications of the right to self-determination. However, it is well established that, whatever the circumstances, the right to self-determination must not involve changes to existing frontiers at the time of independence (*uti possidetis juris*) except where the States concerned agree otherwise.
> 2. Where there are one or more groups within a State constituting one or more ethnic, religious or language communities, they have the right to recognition of their identity under international law.[61]

The Badinter Commission went on to hold that the Serb population of Croatia and Bosnia-Hercegovina had to be granted all the rights accorded to minority groups under international law, including the right of an individual member of the Serb minority population to belong to the national, religious or language group of that individual's choice.

The Badinter Commission also asserted that self-determination cannot result in changes to borders 'at the time of independence'. This assertion should be interpreted as meaning that borders as they exist at the time of independence cannot be changed, either then or thereafter, except by agreement. Alternatively, it could be interpreted to mean that borders cannot be changed at the time of independence except by agreement, but leaves open the question of changes without mutual agreement thereafter. This latter interpretation must be rejected as it is clearly inconsistent with the tenor of *Opinion No. 2*.

If the borders of Croatia and Bosnia-Hercegovina could not, on the basis of the right of their Serb minorities to self-determination, be changed on or after independence, the question that must be asked is: How could the borders of the SFRY have been changed by the exercise of the right to self-determination by groups forming sections of the SFRY's population? These groups were minorities in the context of the SFRY in that none of them was the largest national group within that state, just as the Serbs were not the largest national group in either Croatia or Bosnia-Hercegovina. If the borders of Croatia and Bosnia-Hercegovina were sacrosanct at the time of independence, it must be asked why the international borders of the SFRY were not sacrosanct. In this context, Hannum has suggested the following:

60 The question posed by Lord Carrington was a reformulation of a question that Serbia had sought him to transmit to the Commission, and which sought an answer to whether a nation or a federal unit was entitled to self-determination: Pavlović and Popović, note 2, pp. 114–15.

61 *Opinion No. 2 of the Arbitration Commission of the Peace Conference on Yugoslavia* (1992) 31 ILM 1497, at 1498.

> To ensure equity, minorities in a new state founded to preserve ethnic or cultural homogeneity should be granted the same rights of self-determination that were asserted by the seceding population. Legitimate self-determination can only be exercised on the basis of the consent of all involved parties, not just those who wish to separate. If neither international law nor politics offers a mechanism through which minorities trapped within a new ethnic state may rejoin their former state, or at least, create an autonomous region within their new home, rejection of the new borders by force may be seen as the only alternative.[62]

The question of why the Croats and Bosnian Muslims of Croatia and Bosnia-Hercegovina could change the international borders of the SFRY is not addressed by the Badinter Commission in *Opinion No. 2*. In seeking an answer to this question it cannot be argued that the borders of the SFRY were irrelevant because that state was in the process of dissolution. As already noted, this process did not commence until 29 November 1991, some time after Croatia became an independent state in international law on 8 October 1991. One could perhaps mount this argument in the case of Bosnia-Hercegovina, given that it did not become an independent state in international law until 6 March 1992.[63] At this time the SFRY was, according to the Badinter Commission, in the process of dissolution, but not yet extinct. However, that would result in treating Croatia and Bosnia-Hercegovina differently, which was not the case in *Opinion No. 2*. Thus, given that the independence of republics of the SFRY was not a case of the dissolution or extinction of a state,

62 H. Hannum, 'The Specter of Secession, Responding to Claims for Ethnic Self-Determination', *Foreign Affairs*, 1998, vol. 77, no. 2, p. 17. Higgins recognises that in cases such as Yugoslavia, where internal federal borders were sacrosanct and federal authorities were condemned for the use of force to suppress secession, it meant that force could not be used to protect a state's international borders. This, she asserts, means that 'the seceding state has the legal initiative'. She goes on to conclude 'that the mere repetition of the formula that boundaries may not be changed by force does not begin to provide serious normative guidance to most of the issues that face us today in the context of secessionism': R. Higgins, 'Postmodern Tribalism and the Right to Secession' in C. Brölmann, R. Lefeber and M. Zieck (eds), *Peoples and Minorities in International Law*, Dordrecht, Martinus Nijhoff Publishers, 1993, p. 34. Franck raises this issue as follows: '[W]hy should international law approve the formal right of Croatia to secede from the Yugoslav Federation while denying a similar right of secession to the Serbian regions of Croatia? What justice would be served if international law were to recognize Quebec's right to secede, but no right for the Ungava native peoples' region to secede from Quebec? If international law recognizes a *right* of secession, can it be fairly limited . . . to the subordinate units – provinces – of a federal parent state?' Later Franck suggests that minorities in newly created states can secede provided this is done without external assistance and peacefully: T. M. Franck, *Fairness in International Law and Institutions*, Oxford, Clarendon Press, 1995, pp. 160, 167. Kofman suggests that such minorities could secede if they are territorially concentrated and/or if there is evidence of a strong likelihood that their minority and individual rights will be violated: D. Kofman, 'Secession, Law, and Rights: The Case of Former Yugoslavia' *Human Rights Review*, 2000, vol. 1, no. 2, p. 13.

63 *Opinion No. 11 of the Arbitration Commission of the Peace Conference on Yugoslavia* (1993) 32 ILM 1587, at 1588.

but rather one of secession, there appears to be no justification for insisting that the borders of the republics of Croatia and Bosnia-Hercegovina remain sacrosanct while not extending that same right to the borders of the SFRY. From this it follows that if a minority group in Croatia or Bosnia-Hercegovina is not, pursuant to the right to self-determination, permitted to alter borders, then neither should minority groups within the SFRY have been permitted, pursuant to the right to self-determination, to alter the borders of that internationally recognised state.

Given that *Opinion No. 2* deals with the Serbs of Croatia and Bosnia-Hercegovina as a minority, it could be argued that the comments of the Badinter Commission on self-determination only relate to minorities and not to peoples. The consequence would be that a people, in the exercise of its right to self-determination, could change the borders of an existing state. It could then be argued that the Croats and Bosnian Muslims were peoples and not minorities, on the basis of their status as constituent nations under the 1974 Constitution of the SFRY. It would thus follow that the Croats and Bosnian Muslims, as peoples rather than minorities, could, in the exercise of their rights to self-determination, change the borders of the SFRY.

For such an argument to prevail it must be established that the Croats and Bosnian Muslims were not minorities in the SFRY and that their status differed from that of the Serbs of Croatia and Bosnia-Hercegovina. However, this cannot be established. The Serbs had the same constitutional status under the 1974 Constitution of the SFRY as did the Croats and Bosnian Muslims, namely that of constituent nations. Under the republic constitution of Bosnia-Hercegovina the Serbs, Croats and Bosnian Muslims were recognised as equal and constituent nations of that republic. In Croatia, under its republic constitution of 1974 the Serbs and Croats were equal and constituent nations of that republic. The 1990 amendments to Croatia's constitution relegated the Serbs to the status of a minority. However, this amendment was clearly unconstitutional. It was not considered by the Constitutional Court of the SFRY, but its lack of constitutionality is clear. Pursuant to the 1974 Constitution of the SFRY the Serbs were a constituent nation. Furthermore, republic constitutions could not be inconsistent with the federal constitution (Article 206). The relegation of the Serbs to the status of a minority was a clear violation of this requirement, and therefore unconstitutional.

It follows that as Croats, Bosnian Muslims and Serbs were constituent nations within the SFRY, one could not discriminate between their rights to self-determination. If the Croats and Bosnian Muslims of Croatia and Bosnia-Hercegovina, in the exercise of the right to self-determination, had the right to their own states at the expense of the borders of the SFRY, then logically the Serbs of Croatia and Bosnia-Hercegovina, in the exercise of their right to self-determination, had the same right at the expense of the borders of Croatia and Bosnia-Hercegovina.

It could be argued that the Serbs of these two republics had no right to self-determination on the basis that these Serbs, as a fraction of a people, cannot have a right to self-determination independent of the rest of that people living elsewhere in the SFRY. The Badinter Commission, in *Opinion No. 4 on the International Recognition of the Socialist Republic of Bosnia and Herzegovina by the European Community and Its Members*[64] (*Opinion No. 4*), suggests that a fraction of a people can exercise the right of self-determination independently of the rest of the people. In *Opinion No. 4* the Badinter Commission recommended that the population of Bosnia-Hercegovina had to indicate its will for independence by means of a plebiscite in which that republic's population would vote. This meant that a fraction of the Serb people, together with fractions of the Croat and Bosnian Muslim peoples, could exercise the right of self-determination by voting for the independence of Bosnia-Hercegovina. Thus, a fraction of a people can exercise the right of self-determination independently of the rest of that people.[65]

A further observation in relation to *Opinion No. 2* relates to the statement that international law 'does not spell out *all* the implications of the right to self-determination' (emphasis added.) This is not an objectionable statement. However, international law does spell out, and quite clearly, some of the implications of the right to self-determination. One of them, as detailed in the Declaration on Friendly Relations, is that a people, in the realisation of its right to self-determination, has, in principle, the right to establish a sovereign and independent state, that is, the right of secession. One of the issues relating to self-determination is the question of whether a minority is a people and thus whether a minority is entitled to secede from a state. The Badinter Commission in *Opinion No. 2* makes significant comments that are consistent with the view that a minority is a people, but on the other hand, denies that a minority can secede from a state.

The implication that a minority is a people according to the Badinter Commission flows from its application of common Article 1 of the two international covenants on human rights of 1966. According to Article 1 ' all peoples have the right of self-determination'. It was by virtue of Article 1 that the Serbs of Croatia and Bosnia-Hercegovina obtained their rights as stipulated in *Opinion No. 2*. Because these rights flowed from the right of peoples to self-determination provided for in Article 1, the Serbs of Croatia and Bosnia-Hercegovina must have been a people. This conclusion of the Badinter Commission accords with arguments discussed in Chapter 3 to the effect that a minority is a people for the purposes of self-determination.

However, *Opinion No. 2* circumscribed the rights of the Serbs, and in particular effectively excluded their right of secession. But, if the Serbs of Croatia and Bosnia-Hercegovina were peoples, then, according to international law, they would, in principle, have had the right of secession. To the extent that it circumscribes the right of a people, *Opinion No. 2* of the Badinter Commission contradicts the unambiguous provisions of the Declaration on Friendly Relations as to the right of a people to establish its own sovereign and independent state. On this basis the views of the Badinter Commission on this aspect of *Opinion No. 2* should be rejected.

64 (1992) 31 ILM 1501.

65 J. C. Duursma, *Fragmentation and the International Relations of Micro-States: Self-Determination and Statehood*, Cambridge, Cambridge University Press, 1996, p. 72.

The most significant aspect of the Badinter Commission's analysis of self-determination is its rejection of the meaning of 'a people' consistent with the classical theory of self-determination. On this theory, the population of the SFRY would have been a people. None of the individual nations or republics of the SFRY would have constituted a people. However, by endorsing the independence claims of the various republics of the SFRY, the Badinter Commission was, in the view of some commentators, endorsing the meaning of people largely consistent with the romantic theory of self-determination. As Musgrave has observed:

> The European Community and the United States considered the exercise of popular sovereignty within the constituent republics of . . . Yugoslavia as amounting to acts of self-determination. However, these exercises of popular sovereignty did not occur within the defined territorial limits of the state as a whole, nor amongst its entire population, but only within particular areas of the state and amongst particular sections of its total population. . . . The response of the European Community and the United States to the situation in Yugoslavia indicated that particular sections of the state's population, within a particular part of that state's territory, could unilaterally create a state of its own, which would then be recognized by the international community on the basis that an act of self-determination had occurred. Moreover, although Western states emphasized that self-determination must occur within the frontiers of a constituent republic and amongst its entire population regardless of ethnic criteria, the exercise of popular sovereignty within the constituent republics of . . . Yugoslavia was in reality an act of self-determination by a particular ethnic group.[66]

Although the definition of a people as the total population of a state was rejected by the EC and the Badinter Commission, the meaning of people based upon the nation was not accepted in its entirety. Instead the population of a sub-state territorial unit was deemed to be a people. On the basis that the concept of territoriality is present here, this could be seen as consistent with the classical theory of self-determination. However, in reality it is closer to the romantic theory of self-determination. This stems from the fact that the republics, as relevant sub-state units within the SFRY, were dominated by one particular national group. The secessions of the republics were acts of self-determination in the romantic sense. The actions of the Slovenes, Croats and Muslims in seeking to secede from the SFRY within the bounds of internal federal borders, were actions that paralleled those of the Germans in the nineteenth century. They were nations in search of their own states.

66 Musgrave, note 42, pp. 123–4. See also Hayden, note 17, pp. 52–3; V. Đerić, 'Right to Self-Determination: Criteria for Determining "Self"', *Jugoslovenska revija za međunarodno pravo*, 1995, vol. 42, pp. 232–6; J. Williams, *Legitimacy in International Relations and the Rise and Fall of Yugoslavia*, London, Macmillan Press, 1998, p. 120.

The Badinter Commission's rejection of the classical theory of self-determination and implicit acceptance of the romantic theory of self-determination is also indicated, as discussed above, by its implicit recognition of the Serbs of Croatia and Bosnia-Hercegovina as a people. The implication of this is that the different national groups within the SFRY were all peoples.

Borders on secession – *uti possidetis juris*

What was crucial to the early recognition of the secessions from the SFRY was the acceptance of the principle that the SFRY's internal borders would be international borders of the new nation-states. The Badinter Commission in *Opinion No. 2* referred to the principle of *uti possidetis juris* as the legal basis of these new international borders. The Commission's comments on the principle of *uti possidetis juris* are arguably the most far-reaching of all comments made in any of the opinions issued by the Commission.

Although the principle of *uti possidetis juris* is mentioned in *Opinion No. 2*, the more detailed discussion of it by the Badinter Commission is in *Opinion No. 3 of the Arbitration Commission of the Peace Conference on Yugoslavia*[67] (*Opinion No. 3*) handed down on 11 January 1992. In *Opinion No. 3* the Badinter Commission had to respond to the following question put to it by Lord Carrington:

> Can the internal boundaries between Croatia and Serbia and between Bosnia and Hercegovina and Serbia be regarded as frontiers in terms of public international law?

In answering that question, the Badinter Commission noted that the situation in the SFRY required that, in the circumstances of the emergence of new states from the debris of the SFRY that was in the process of dissolution, both the external and internal borders of the SFRY had to be respected and could not be changed by force. For convenience this ruling is hereafter referred to as 'the Badinter Borders Principle'.[68]

In the case of the SFRY's external borders the Badinter Borders Principle flowed from various international instruments including the UN Charter and the Helsinki Final Act. In relation to the SFRY's internal borders, they became protected international borders pursuant to the international law principles of respect for the territorial status quo and *uti possidetis*, and could only be altered by agreement. The Badinter Commission also observed that its conclusions as to the SFRY's internal borders were bolstered by Article 5 of the SFRY Constitution of 1974.

The Badinter Commission's ruling in *Opinion No. 3* needs to be analysed on the following points:

67 (1992) 31 ILM 1499.

68 Bartoš refers to the same as '*Uti possidetis modernis*': T. Bartoš, '*Uti Possidetis, Quo Vadis?*', *Australian Year Book of International Law*, 1998, vol. 18, p. 71.

- whether the Badinter Border Principle applies to the borders of new states which are the result of secession from a state, or the dissolution of a state, or both;
- whether the Badinter Border Principle is justified on the basis of the international law principle of respect for the territorial status quo;
- whether the Badinter Borders Principle is justified on the basis of the international law principle of *uti possidetis*;
- whether Article 5 of the 1974 Constitution of the SFRY justifies the conclusion reached in *Opinion No. 3* that the Badinter Borders Principle applies to the break-up of Yugoslavia.

Secession or dissolution or both?

A cursory reading of *Opinion No. 3* suggests that the Badinter Border Principle applies only to cases of dissolution of states. This flows from a reference to *Opinion No. 1* at the beginning of *Opinion No. 3*, as well as the fact that *Opinion No. 3* was delivered in the context of the SFRY being, in the view of the Badinter Commission, in the process of dissolution. However, a closer analysis of *Opinion No. 3*, read in conjunction with *Opinion No. 11 of the Arbitration Commission of the Peace Conference on Yugoslavia*[69] (*Opinion No. 11*), handed down by the Badinter Commission on 16 July 1993, reveals that in the case of the SFRY the Badinter Borders Principle was applied in the context of secession, and not the dissolution of a state.

In *Opinion No. 3*, the Badinter Commission observed that the Badinter Borders Principle applies once a situation has reached the stage of 'the creation of one or more independent states'.[70] In *Opinion No. 11* the Badinter Commission referred to the dates upon which the various former Yugoslav republics became independent states. The first independent states were Croatia and Slovenia, who gained that status on 8 October 1991, followed by Macedonia which became independent on 17 November 1991.[71] In the same opinion the Badinter Commission asserted that the process of dissolution in the SFRY had commenced on 29 November 1991.[72] Thus, the states of Croatia and Slovenia were created before the process of the dissolution of the SFRY had commenced. Consequently, these three states arose as the result of secession. On this basis the Badinter Borders Principle was applied to cases of states emerging as the result of secession.

While it is clear that, in the context of the fragmentation of the SFRY, the Badinter Borders Principle was applied to cases of secession, *Opinion No. 3* did not

69 *Opinion No. 11 of the Arbitration Commission of the Peace Conference on Yugoslavia* (1993) 32 ILM 1587, at 1588.

70 *Opinion No. 3 of the Arbitration Commission of the Peace Conference on Yugoslavia* (1992) 31 ILM 1499, at 1499.

71 *Opinion No. 11 of the Arbitration Commission of the Peace Conference on Yugoslavia* (1993) 32 ILM 1587, at 1587–9.

72 Ibid., at 1587.

necessarily rule out its application to cases of dissolution of states. There is support for the view that it applies to both situations. In 1992 the government of the Canadian province of Quebec commissioned a report, prepared by five international law experts, on the question of Quebec's international borders in the event of its secession from Canada, hereafter referred to as 'the Quebec Report'.[73] The Quebec Report stated that in such circumstances Quebec's provincial borders would automatically become international borders. The report relied heavily upon the decision of the Badinter Commission in *Opinion No. 3*. On the question of whether the Badinter Borders Principle applies to cases of secession or dissolution of a state, the Quebec Report asserted the following:

> [I]n cases of secession or dissolution of States, pre-existing administrative boundaries must be maintained to become borders of the new States and cannot be altered by the threat or use of force, be it on the part of the seceding entity or of the State from which it breaks off.[74]

On the other hand, it has been argued that the Badinter Borders Principle does not apply to cases of secession and that it is confined to cases of dissolution of states. In the context of a possible unilateral secession of the province of Quebec from Canada, the Canadian government has asserted that there 'is neither a paragraph nor line in international law that protects Quebec's territory [and that] international experience demonstrates that the borders of the entity seeking independence can be called into question'.[75] The Canadian government has asserted that the Badinter Borders Principle only applies to cases of dissolution of states and not to those of secession and has cited the case of the break-up of the SFRY as support for this view.[76] This assertion is based upon an acceptance of the proposition that the fragmentation of the SFRY was a case of dissolution and not of secession by its constituent republics. The Canadian government has expressed the view that the Badinter Borders Principle would only apply in the case of the dissolution of Canada, a process that could be triggered by the unravelling of that state following a unilateral secession of Quebec.[77]

73 T. Franck *et al.*, The Territorial Integrity of Quebec in the Event of the Attainment of Sovereignty (the Quebec Report), 8 May 1992, para. [2.47]. This English translation was obtained on the Internet in December 1997 at http://www.mri.gouv/qc.ca/etiqaeso.html. Alain Pellet was the principal author of the report. He was also an international law consultant to the Badinter Commission.

74 Ibid. In a similar vein Duursma has suggested that 'it serves no legal purpose to distinguish between secession, dissolution, separation or disintegration': Duursma, note 65, p. 89.

75 Letter to Mr Lucien Bouchard, 11 August 1997, in S. Dion, *Straight Talk: Speeches and Writings on Canadian Unity*, Montreal and Kingston, McGill-Queen's University Press, 1999, p. 191. Dion restated this position in, Letter to Mr Bernard Landry, August 1997, in Dion, above, p. 195.

76 Letter to Mr Bernard Landry, 28 August 1997, in Dion, note 75, p. 199.

77 Personal communication to the author by Canada's Minister for Intergovernmental Affairs, Stéphane Dion, at the Jerusalem Conference in Canadian Studies, Hebrew University of Jerusalem, 30 June 1998.

It is arguable that the stance of the Canadian government is not endorsed by the decision of the Supreme Court of Canada in *Reference re: Secession of Quebec*.[78] Although the focal rulings in this case were that a unilateral secession of Quebec would be illegal, both under Canadian constitutional law[79] and international law,[80] the decision has implications relating to Quebec's borders in the event of secession occurring.[81] The Court recognised that a unilateral secession, even though illegal, could be successful if recognised by the international community.[82] Although the Court made no direct statement on borders in this context, it implied that Quebec's recognition would be within the scope of its existing territorial borders. Furthermore, the Court implied that Quebec's independence would be the product of secession from, rather than the dissolution of, Canada. The first implication flows from the fact that the Court never spoke in terms of part of Quebec seceding unilaterally and obtaining international recognition. Rather, it referred to the 'unilateral secession by Quebec',[83] and of action to achieve that goal undertaken by the 'National Assembly, legislature or government of Quebec'.[84] The second implication stems from the fact that there is nothing in the Court's judgment that suggests that a unilateral declaration of independence by Quebec would be anything other than secession from Canada. Nothing in the judgment suggests that such unilateral action by Quebec would mean the dissolution of Canada. The inevitable conclusion to be drawn from these implications is that, in the event of international recognition of a unilateral declaration of independence by Quebec, the Supreme Court of Canada assumes that it will be a case of secession and that the Badinter Borders Principle will apply.

On the other hand, it can be argued in support of the view of the Canadian government, that there is a significant difference between cases of secession and dissolution of a state. In a case of secession the former sovereign state remains in existence, whereas in a case of dissolution the former sovereign state ceases to exist. This distinguishing factor may justify a different approach to the question of borders following the creation of new states. As a matter of logic, in the case of dissolution of a sovereign state, either new states emerge or parts of the dissolved state become parts of pre-existing states, thereby filling the vacuum created as a result of dissolution. Internal borders of the former sovereign state may be a sound basis for the borders of these successor states. In cases of secession no such

78 (1998) 161 DLR (4th) 385.

79 Ibid., at 403–31.

80 Ibid., at 432–45.

81 The Court did rule that the secession of Quebec could be legally achieved by means of a negotiated constitutional amendment, and that the issue of Quebec's borders would be legitimate matter in such negotiations. Thus, in the case of a legal secession of Quebec its international borders would not automatically be its existing provincial borders: P. Radan, 'The Supreme Court of Canada and the Borders of Quebec', *Australian International Law Journal*, 1998, p. 171.

82 *Reference re: Secession of Quebec* (1998) 161 DLR (4th) 385, at 432, 449.

83 Ibid., at 444.

84 Ibid., at 432.

vacuum arises. If secession is successful, the sovereign state from which secession is achieved does not cease to exist. Ultimately, the only issue in such a secession is the territorial extent of the new state that is the result of secession. In cases of a federation there is no reason to insist in all cases that the new state's territorial extent should be that of a particular federal unit of the state from which secession has taken place. This is particularly so in cases where a significant minority opposes secession and wishes to remain part of the state from which secession is sought. Just as in the case of secession from a non-federal state, the territorial extent of the new state is ultimately a political question which will be resolved either (preferably) by negotiation or by force.[85]

Although the Badinter Commission did not explicitly deal with the question of whether the principles governing the determination of the borders of new states arising out of secession differ from those governing cases of dissolution of states, the view of the Canadian government on the future borders of an independent Quebec shows clearly that the issue is not without its practical implications, and is more than merely an academic question. In the context of the fragmentation of the SFRY the Badinter Commission opinions do not offer clear guidance on the answer to this question. On the one hand, the Commission asserted that it was dealing with a case of the dissolution of the SFRY. On the other hand, on the basis of its own finding of facts, the Commission was, as established above, dealing with cases of secession from the SFRY.

However, the more significant question is whether the Badinter Borders Principle itself can be justified at all, irrespective of whether it applies to circumstances of secession and/or dissolution of states. In *Opinion No. 3* the Badinter Commission gave a legal justification for the Badinter Borders Principle based upon two international law principles and Article 5 of the 1974 Constitution of the SFRY. The following sections of this chapter critically evaluate this reasoning as well as other justifications that have been suggested in support of the Badinter Commission's conclusions.

The principle of territorial status quo

The first of the international law principles relied upon by the Badinter Commission as a basis for the Badinter Borders Principle was that of respect for the territorial status quo of existing internationally recognised states. This principle is of

85 Crawford suggests that the use of force in cases of secession appears to be exempt from the prohibition against the use of force contained in Article 2(4) of the Charter of the United Nations: Crawford, note 11, pp. 268–70. Crawford implies that force used in such cases is confined to the use of force by the state from which secession is sought and the secessionists. However, as is illustrated by the case of the secessionist aspirations of the autonomous province of Kosovo-Metohija from the Federal Republic of Yugoslavia, the use of force by a third party to the dispute, in this case the member states of NATO in 1999, indicates that the implication in Crawford's suggestion may no longer be applicable.

undoubted validity. It is reflected in various provisions in international treaties and documents protecting the territorial integrity of states, the inviolability of international borders,[86] and the doctrine of the stability of borders. In relation to the principles of territorial integrity and the inviolability of international borders, they do not provide any justification for the Badinter Borders Principle. This is because these principles only apply to international states, and not to federal sub-units of such states.[87]

As to the doctrine of the stability of borders, the International Court of Justice in *Case Concerning the Temple of Preah Vihear*[88] observed as follows:

> In general, when two countries establish a frontier between them, one of the primary objects is to achieve stability and finality. This is impossible if the line so established can, at any moment, and on the basis of a continuously available process, be called into question, and its rectification claimed, whenever any inaccuracy by reference to a clause in the parent Treaty is discovered. Such a process could continue indefinitely, and finality would never be reached so long as possible errors still remain to be discovered. Such a frontier, far from being stable, would be completely precarious.[89]

However, the stability of borders principle relates only to international borders.[90] The question of the stability of internal state borders is not a matter within the ambit of international law. Furthermore, the stability of borders principle is dependent on there being a treaty establishing a border. In *Case Concerning the Territorial Dispute (Libyan Arab Jamahiriya/Chad)* Judge Shahabuddeen, in his separate opinion, stated:

> The principle of the stability of boundaries, as it applies to a boundary fixed by agreement, hinges on there being an agreement for the establishment of a boundary; it comes into play only after the existence of such an agreement is established and is directed to giving proper effect to the agreement. It does not operate to bring into existence a boundary agreement where there was none.[91]

In the light of these observations, the stability of borders principle was not a sound justification for the protection of the SFRY's internal federal borders

86 Charter of the United Nations, Article 2(4); Declaration on Principles of Law Concerning Friendly Relations and Co-operation Among States in Accordance With the Charter of the United Nations, General Assembly Resolution 2625 (XXV), Principle V, 24 October 1970; Final Act of Helsinki, Principle VIII, 1 August 1975.

87 Bartoš, note 68, p. 73.

88 *Case Concerning the Temple of Preah Vihear (Cambodia -v- Thailand) (Merits)* (1962) 33 ILR 48.

89 Ibid., at 72. See also *Case Concerning the Territorial Dispute (Libyan Arab Jamahiriya/Chad)* [1994] ICJ Rep. 6, at 37; R. Y. Jennings, *The Acquisition of Territory in International Law*, Manchester, Manchester University Press, 1963, p. 70.

90 Kreća, note 2, p. 35.

91 *Case Concerning the Territorial Dispute (Libyan Arab Jamahiriya/Chad)* [1994] ICJ Rep. 6, at 45.

following secession, for the following reasons. First, the SFRY's internal borders were not international borders. Second, even if it is accepted that upon international recognition these internal federal borders became international borders, the stability of borders principle would still be irrelevant. This is because the principle requires that the borders be determined by treaty or agreement. In the case of the SFRY internal federal borders were not the subject of any legal document or act of any state or republic institution.[92] They were established by the inner sanctum of the Communist Party of Yugoslavia following World War II.[93] Thus, nothing even analogous to a border treaty or agreement was ever entered into in relation to the internal borders of the SFRY.

The principle of uti possidetis juris

The second international law principle relied upon by the Badinter Commission in *Opinion No. 3* was that of *uti possidetis*. As to the principle of *uti possidetis* being a basis for the Badinter Borders Principle, the Badinter Commission stated the following in *Opinion No. 3*:

> *Uti possidetis*, though initially applied in settling decolonization issues in America and Africa, is today recognized as a general principle, as stated by the International Court of Justice in the case between Burkina Faso and Mali (Frontier Dispute, (1986) ICJ Reports 554 at 565): 'Nevertheless the principle is not a special rule which pertains to one specific system of international law. It is a general principle, which is logically connected with the phenomenon of the obtaining of independence, wherever it occurs. Its obvious purpose is to prevent the independence and stability of new States being endangered by fratricidal struggles'.[94]

However, it must be noted that the Badinter Commission selectively quoted from the decision in the *Frontier Dispute Case*.[95] Immediately after the passage from the *Frontier Dispute Case* quoted by the Badinter Commission, the International Court of Justice added the words: 'provoked by the challenging of frontiers following the withdrawal of the administering power'.[96]

92 B. Lekić, 'Administrativne granice u Jugoslaviji posle Drugog Svetskog Rata', *Istorija 20. Veka*, 1992, vol. 10, no. 1–2, 145.

93 K. Čavoški, *Half a Century of Distorted Constitutionality in Yugoslavia*, Belgrade, Center for Serbian Studies, 1997, p. 7.

94 *Opinion No. 3 of the Arbitration Commission of the Peace Conference on Yugoslavia* (1992) 31 ILM 1499, at 1500.

95 Bernárdez refers to the 'misrepresentations of the reasoning' of the *Frontier Dispute Case*: S. T. Bernárdez, 'The "Uti Possidetis Juris Principle" in Historical Perspective', in Konrad Ginther *et al.* (eds), *Völkerrecht zwischen normativem Anspruch und politischer Realität: Festschrift für Karl Zemanek zum 65. Geburtstag*, Berlin, Duncker & Humbolt, 1994, p. 435.

96 *Case Concerning the Frontier Dispute (Burkina Faso and Mali)* [1986] ICJ Rep. 554, at 565.

These omitted words clearly indicate that the principle of *uti possidetis juris* applied in the context of decolonisation. This point is made quite explicitly in other parts of the *Frontier Dispute Case* judgment. Earlier in the same paragraph as that quoted from by the Badinter Commission, the International Court of Justice said:

> Although there is no need, for the purposes of the present case, to show that this is a firmly established principle of international law where decolonization is concerned, the Chamber wishes to emphasize its general scope.[97]

Later in its judgment the Court said:

> *Uti possidetis*, as a principle which upgraded former administrative delimitations, established during the colonial period, to international frontiers, is therefore a principle of a general kind which is logically connected with this form of decolonization wherever it occurs.[98]

The Court's reference to the generality of the principle of *uti possidetis juris* was to indicate that it was not confined in its application to decolonisation in 'one specific system of international law',[99] namely that of Latin America, but rather that it applied to decolonisation wherever it occurred.[100]

Nothing in the decision in the *Frontier Dispute Case* suggests that the principle of *uti possidetis* applies to cases of secession from internationally recognised states.[101] Rather, the whole tenor of the decision indicates that the principle is confined to decolonisation. The principle is not, as claimed by the Badinter Commission, recognised as a general principle applicable to all cases of independence. As Bernárdez has written:

> As a principle of international law the uti possidetis rule is simply not concerned with the question of the definition of title to territory and boundaries in such types of succession as transfer of a territory of a State, separation from a State, dissolution of a State, [and] uniting of States.[102]

Shaw has defended the Badinter Commission's interpretation of the *uti possidetis juris* principle on the basis that the International Court of Justice in the *Frontier*

97 Ibid.

98 Ibid., at 566.

99 Ibid., at 565.

100 Kreća, note 2, pp. 36–7.

101 Ibid., p. 36; Craven, note 7, p. 388; S. R. Ratner, 'Drawing a Better Line: *Uti Possidetis* and the Borders of New States', *American Journal of International Law*, 1996, vol. 90, p. 614.

102 Bernárdez, note 95, p. 434. Craven refers to the Badinter Commission's 'novel extension of the *uti possidetis* principle outside the context of decolonization': Craven, note 7, p. 386. See also Musgrave, note 42, pp. 234–5; Hannum, note 24, p. 957; Ratner, note 101, p. 614; R. A. Falk, *Human Rights Horizons: The Pursuit of Justice in a Globalizing World*, New York, Routledge, 2000, pp. 115–16.

Dispute Case did not need to discuss the principle of *uti possidetis juris* because it was binding upon it by virtue of the Special Agreement between Burkina Faso and Mali. The fact that the Court did discuss the principle of *uti possidetis juris* in some detail is viewed by Shaw as indicating that the Court viewed it as applying beyond the context of decolonisation.[103] However, Shaw's analysis cannot be sustained for two reasons.

First, it ignores the explicit and repeated references by the Court to *uti possidetis juris* applying specifically in the context of decolonisation. Second, although it was not strictly necessary for the Court to analyse the principle of *uti possidetis juris* because the Special Agreement between Burkina Faso and Mali clearly indicated the basis upon which their border dispute was to be resolved, the Court did so in order to establish the generality of the principle's application to decolonisation beyond the region of Latin America. The discussion on the generality of the principle of *uti possidetis juris* was clearly in relation to its generality in the context of decolonisation. There is nothing in the Court's judgment to justify the references to the generality of the principle as extending to cases involving secession from independent and internationally recognised states.

It has been suggested that in the case of the SFRY the application of the *uti possidetis juris* principle was justified on the basis that its fragmentation amounted to a form of decolonisation, and furthermore, that there was an agreement by its republics that internal federal borders were to be future international borders. A closer analysis of the facts reveals that both of these suggestions are without merit.

The suggestion that the SFRY represented a form of colonisation by Serbia *vis-à-vis* the seceding republics, and that therefore the principle of *uti possidetis juris* was appropriate to the 'decolonisation' of the SFRY,[104] cannot be sustained for the following reasons. First, colonialism has been consistently understood by the United Nations (UN) as applying to 'overseas' colonies, and does not apply to states that may have been constituted as the result of territorial expansion into adjacent areas, such as the USSR.[105] Thus, in 1960 the UN General Assembly decided that the process of decolonisation pursuant to the right to self-determination related to 'territory which is geographically separate and is distinct

103 M. N. Shaw, 'Peoples, Territorialism and Boundaries', *European Journal of International Law*, 1997, vol. 8, p. 497.

104 M. A. Hill, 'What the Principle of Self-Determination Means Today', *ILSA Journal of International and Comparative Law*, 1995, p. 131. For a neo-colonialist account of Yugoslav history see A. Bebler, 'Yugoslavia's Variety of Communist Federalism and Her Demise', *Communist and Post-Communist Studies*, 1993, vol. 26, pp. 72–86. The neo-colonialism argument in relation to Canada and Quebec has been rejected by the Canadian Supreme Court: *Reference re: Secession of Quebec* (1998) 161 DLR (4th) 385, at 442. See also T. C. Carey, 'Self-Determination in the Post-Colonial Era: The Case of Quebec', *ASILS International Law Review*, 1977, vol. 1, pp. 67–70. It has been suggested that the secession of Bangladesh can be justified as an example of neo-colonialism: Crawford, note 11, p. 161.

105 P. Kunig, 'Decolonization', in R. Wolfrum (ed.), *United Nations Law, Politics and Practice*, vol. 1, new revised English edition, Dordrecht, Martinus Nijhoff Publishers, 1995, p. 390.

ethnically and/or culturally from the country administering it'.[106] Second, according to ordinary usage, 'colony' means territory which a state has made legally dependent without conferring the same legal status upon the indigenous population as upon the population of its own territory.[107] In the case of the SFRY this was manifestly not the case. Lands not forming part of pre-World War I Serbia all made the decision to seek unification with Serbia after World War I to form the Yugoslav state, and in all subsequent Yugoslav constitutions all citizens were subject to the same provisions.[108]

The suggestion that there was agreement by the various Yugoslav republics that there would be no unilateral changes to borders and that this implicitly invoked the principle of *uti possidetis juris*,[109] is based upon a statement made by a representative of the Chairman of the EC Conference on Yugoslavia following a meeting which was attended by the Presidents of Serbia and Croatia and the Defence Minister of the SFRY at the Hague on 4 October 1991.[110] The Hague Statement noted that agreement had been reached between the parties aimed at providing a peaceful political solution to the Yugoslav crisis. A twin-track policy approach was agreed to. Its first provision was for certain measures to be taken in relation to the military circumstances on the ground. Secondly, there was a political aspect which stipulated:

> It was agreed that the involvement of all parties concerned would be necessary to formulate a political solution on the basis of the perspective of recognition of the independence of the republics wishing it, at the end of the negotiating process conducted in good faith. The recognition would be granted in the framework of a general settlement, and have the following components:
> a. A loose association or alliance of sovereign or independent republics.
> b. Adequate arrangements to be made for the protection of minorities including human rights guarantees and possibly special status for certain areas.
> c. No unilateral changes to borders.[111]

The Hague Statement was made by the responsible EC representative who had acted as Chairman of the meeting. It was not the subject of a formally executed document. Nor was the meeting that led to the Statement attended by representatives from the other republics of the SFRY, namely Slovenia, Bosnia-Hercegovina,

106 General Assembly Resolution 1541(XV), 15 December 1960. This definition is sometimes referred to as the 'salt-water' theory of colonialism: R. Emerson, *From Empire to Nation: The Rise to Self-Assertion of Asian and African Peoples*, Cambridge, MA, Harvard University Press, 1962, p. 310; B. Neuberger, *National Self-Determination in Postcolonial Africa*, Boulder, CO, Lynne Reiner Publishers, 1986, p. 84.

107 Kunig, note 105, p. 390.

108 R. McCorquodale, 'Self-Determination Beyond the Colonial Context and Its Potential Impact on Africa', *African Journal of International and Comparative Law*, 1992, vol. 4, p. 601.

109 J. Gow, *Triumph of the Lack of Will: International Diplomacy and the Yugoslav War*, New York, Columbia University Press, 1997, pp. 55–6.

110 Meeting Held at Ministry of Foreign Affairs, The Hague, 4 October 1991, *Focus*, note 2, p. 169.

111 Ibid.

Montenegro and Macedonia. In the absence of a formally executed document, it cannot be said that the Hague Statement was legally binding upon the republics whose delegates were at the meeting. Nor was it legally binding upon those republics not represented at the meeting. On 18 October 1991, five of the SFRY's republics signed the so-called Carrington Draft Convention by which they agreed that a general settlement of the crisis would involve 'recognition of the independence, within the existing borders, unless otherwise agreed, of those republics wishing it'.[112] Significantly, Serbia refused to sign this document.

Even if the Hague Statement is accepted as having legal effect as from 4 October 1991, it would no longer have been legally binding by the end of 1991, by which time four republics had made application for international recognition by the EC in the wake of the meeting of EC Foreign Ministers on 16 December 1991 which had issued guidelines for international recognition for any Yugoslav republic seeking such recognition. Recognition was clearly not within the 'framework of a general settlement' that required 'a loose association or alliance of sovereign and independent states' as required by the Hague Statement. This effectively meant a violation of the Hague Statement and would have discharged any republic from further compliance with its terms. In effect, as at the end of 1991, there was no basis upon which it could be argued that there was in place a legally binding agreement to the effect that the republics of the SFRY had agreed that pre-secession internal federal borders would be future international borders. Accordingly, there was no basis to argue that the Yugoslav republics had adopted the principle of *uti possidetis juris*.

Indeed, the move by the EC to recognise the republics effectively ruled out the possibility of any general settlement on the Yugoslav crisis being negotiated without the use of force or coercion. This has been conceded by Lord Carrington who later noted that the EC decision on recognition 'changed the whole nature of the Conference [on Yugoslavia, removing] the one real instrument to keep the parties engaged in the negotiating process', namely the prospect of recognition.[113]

A final comment on the issue of whether the principle of *uti possidetis juris* is a justified basis for the Badinter Borders Principle relates to the function of the principle of *uti possidetis juris* in the context of border disputes following decolonisation. In Latin America and Africa the function of *uti possidetis juris* was to provide a mutually agreeable means of resolving disputes that were fundamentally different to the disputes that arose in the context of the secessions of republics from the SFRY. In

112 Trifunovska, note 52, p. 357.

113 Lord Carrington, 'Turmoil in the Balkans: Developments and Prospects', *RUSI Journal*, 1992, vol. 137, no. 5, p. 1. Similar concerns were voiced by UN Secretary-General Xavier Perez de Cuellar. Given that the Secretary-General's views against premature recognition of the seceding republics were endorsed by the UN Security Council, the EC's decision to recognise has been described by Damrosch as 'legally suspect' and 'a derogation from the authority of UN organs in the sphere of international peace and security': quoted in S. L. Burg and P. S. Shoup, *The War in Bosnia-Herzegovina: Ethnic Conflict and International Intervention*, New York, M. E. Sharp Inc., 1999, pp. 94–5.

Latin America and Africa, when the principle of *uti possidetis juris* was applied, there was no dispute that the former colonial borders would be future international borders. The principle of *uti possidetis juris* was applied in the arbitration process to resolve differences between neighbouring states who could not agree on the exact location of colonial border lines.

In the SFRY there was never any dispute about the location of the exact border lines between the various republics at the time of secession. What was in dispute was the question of whether these lines should be future international borders. Agreement that existing colonial borders were to be international borders was a pre-condition to the application of *uti possidetis juris* in the decolonisation context in Latin America and Africa. The principle of *uti possidetis juris* was not relevant to the resolution of a dispute as to whether existing colonial borders should be future international borders. Thus, in the context of the SFRY, the principle of *uti possidetis juris* was of no relevance, given that the issue in dispute was not the location of internal federal borders, but rather, whether they should be future international borders. If the internal federal borders of the SFRY were to be future international borders, the principle of *uti possidetis juris* was irrelevant because the location of those borders was not in dispute.

Article 5 of the SFRY Constitution of 1974

Apart from principles of international law, the Badinter Commission sought to justify the relevance of the Badinter Borders Principle by reference to Article 5 of the SFRY's 1974 Constitution. The Commission said that the Badinter Borders Principle:

> applies all the more readily to the Republics since the second and fourth paragraphs of Article 5 of the Constitution of the SFRY stipulated that the Republics' territories and boundaries could not be altered without their consent.[114]

In referring to Article 5 the Badinter Commission was again guilty of selective quoting. Article 5 stipulated as follows:

> 1 The territory of the [SFRY] is indivisible (*jedinstvena*) and consists of the territories of its socialist republics.
> 2 A republic's territory cannot be altered without the consent of that republic, and the territory of an autonomous province – without the consent of that autonomous province.
> 3 A border of the SFRY cannot be altered without the concurrence of all republics and autonomous provinces.

114 *Opinion No. 3 of the Arbitration Commission of the Peace Conference on Yugoslavia* (1992) 31 ILM 1499, at 1500.

> 4 A border between republics can only be altered on the basis of their agreement, and in the case of a border of an autonomous province – on the basis of its concurrence.

In relying on paragraphs 2 and 4 of Article 5, the Badinter Commission ignored the provisions of paragraphs 1 and 3. In doing so it was justifying the division of the SFRY and the alteration of its international borders in violation of paragraphs 1 and 3. Furthermore, it can be argued that the territorial integrity of republics and the sanctity of their borders referred to in paragraphs 2 and 4 of Article 5 only applied in the context of the Yugoslav state whose own territorial integrity and borders remained in place. A republic seeking to violate the provisions of paragraphs 1 and 3 of Article 5 could hardly reap the guarantees contained within paragraphs 2 and 4. Consequently, Article 5 provides no support for the application of the Badinter Borders Principle to the fragmentation of the SFRY.[115]

Based upon the above analysis of the reasoning of the Badinter Commission in *Opinion No. 3* it can be concluded that neither the international law principles of respect for the territorial status quo and *uti possidetis*, nor the provisions of Article 5 of the 1974 Constitution of the SFRY, provide any justification for the Badinter Borders Principle.

Is the Badinter Commission approach appropriate?

Even if one rejects the legal reasoning of the Badinter Commission, it is nevertheless legitimate to question whether or not there are other reasons justifying the Badinter Borders Principle. It has been suggested that, apart from the reasoning of the Badinter Commission in *Opinion No. 3*, such other reasons do exist.

In the Quebec Report its authors took the view that international practice in the wake of recent secessions supported the Badinter Borders Principle approach.[116] The Quebec Report referred to statements by international organisations made in the context of the break-ups of the SFRY and the USSR. Included in this list is reference to the EC guidelines for recognition of former republics of the USSR and the SFRY announced on 16 December 1991.[117]

However, the Quebec Report fails to note that the EC issued a statement on 31 December 1991 in the context of the USSR and recognition of its republics which stated:

> Recognition shall not be taken to imply acceptance by the European Community and its Member States of the position of any of the republics concerning territory which is the subject of a dispute between two or more republics.[118]

115 Kreća, note 2, pp. 39–40.

116 Franck, note 73, para. [2.47].

117 Guidelines on Recognition, 16 December 1991, in Trifunovska, note 52, pp. 431–2.

118 Recognition of Former Soviet Republics, *Bulletin of the European Communities Commission*, 1991, no. 12, p. 121.

This statement clearly indicates that internal federal borders are not automatically to be taken as international borders following secession or the dissolution of an internationally recognised state.

It can also be noted that there has been considerable condemnation of the approach taken by the EC in recognising the former Yugoslav republics as independent states within existing federal borders. No convincing reasons were given for the maintenance of internal borders as international borders, apart from the unacceptability of the use of force to change them.[119] Lord Owen, the former Co-Chairman of the Steering Committee of the International Conference on the Former Yugoslavia, has expressed the view that sticking 'unyieldingly' to internal borders was a 'folly' and that the EC's rejection of a Belgian proposal to redraw borders was incomprehensible, with the consequence that:

> [t]he refusal to make these borders negotiable greatly hampered the EC's attempt at crisis management in July and August 1991 and subsequently put all peacemaking from September 1991 onwards within a straitjacket that greatly inhibited compromises between parties to the dispute.[120]

France's President François Mitterand also expressed criticism of the decision to recognise the seceding Yugoslav republics before questions of borders had been resolved.[121] What these statements show is that the international practice referred to in the Quebec Report amounted to bad practice.

One of the authors of the Quebec Report, Malcolm Shaw, has argued that the application of the principle of *uti possidetis juris* to both colonial and non-colonial cases is justified by the common concern 'to minimize threats to peace and security, whether internal, regional or international, by establishing an acceptable rule of the appropriate territorial framework for the creation of new States and thus entrenching, at least, territorial stability at the critical moment'.[122] Shaw's justification cannot be accepted for a number of reasons.

First, it is questionable whether threats to peace and security have been

119 Williams, note 66, p. 121.

120 D. Owen, *Balkan Odyssey* , London, Victor Gollancz, 1995, p. 33. See also S. R. Ratner, 'Ethnic Conflict and Territorial Claims: Where Do We Draw a Line?', in D. Wippman (ed.), *International Law and Ethnic Conflict*, Ithaca, NY, Cornell University Press, 1988, p. 114.

121 W. R. Roberts, 'The Tragedy that Could Have Been Averted', in R. G. C. Thomas and H. R. Friman (eds), *The South Slav Conflict: History, Ethnicity, and Nationalism*, New York, Garland Publishing, 1996, p. 370. Craven, while giving qualified support to the approach of the Badinter Commission, nevertheless doubted 'whether in the long term it is a technique which will provide a permanent and pacific settlement to the underlying territorial disputes': Craven, note 7, p. 388.

122 M. N. Shaw 'The Heritage of States: The Principle of *Uti Possidetis Juris* Today', *British Year Book of International Law*, 1996, vol. 67, p. 111.

minimised to an extent that would warrant such a justification.[123] In Latin America, war and threats of war were often the basis of settling border disputes. The most significant such wars have been the War of the Pacific (1879–83) and the Chaco War (1932–35), both discussed in Chapter 3. These wars, rather than the principle of *uti possidetis*, resolved border disputes. In Africa, the principle of *uti possidetis juris*, as reflected in the 1964 resolution of the OAU, has not prevented violent conflict. Such conflicts include the failed secessionist wars relating to Katanga from the Congo (1960–63)[124] and Biafra from Nigeria (1967–70),[125] the successful war of secession of Eritrea from Ethiopia (1974–93),[126] and the ongoing secessionist war of Southern Sudan from Sudan.[127] In addition there have been many border disputes such as those between Somalia and Ethiopia,[128] Nigeria and Cameroon,[129] and more recently, Ethiopia and Eritrea.[130]

In the case of the SFRY the insistence on maintaining internal federal borders not only failed to preclude or minimise violence after the secessions of Slovenia and Croatia, and later Bosnia-Hercegovina and Macedonia, but only served to prolong it. Robert Hayden has correctly observed that to maintain former internal federal borders as inviolable international borders where a large proportion of the population rejects them leads to the international community having to support a war of conquest in support of such borders. The consequences of such a war are either the forced imposition of these borders upon the rebel population, or its forced expulsion.[131] This observation is amply illustrated in the cases of the Serb populations of Croatia and Bosnia-Hercegovina. In the former case the great

123 '[A] stable world order may not always be achieved by a rigorous application of the principle of uti possidetis': J. Klabbers and R. Lefeber, 'Africa: Lost between Self-Determination and *Uti Possidetis*', in C. Brölmann, R. Lefeber and M. Zieck (eds), note 62, p. 38. See also M. Freeman, 'National Self-Determination, Peace and Human Rights', *Peace Review*, 1998, vol. 10, pp. 158–9.

124 On the Katanga secession see A. Heraclides, note 40, pp. 58–79.

125 On the Biafra secession see C. R. Nixon, 'Self-Determination: The Nigeria/Biafra Case', *World Politics*, 1971–72, vol. 24, pp. 473–97; Heraclides, note 40, pp. 80–106.

126 On the Eritrea secession see R. Iyob, *The Eritrean Struggle for Independence: Domination, Resistance, Nationalism, 1941–1993*, Cambridge, Cambridge University Press, 1995; Heraclides, note 40, pp. 177–95.

127 On the Southern Sudan secession see A. M. Lloyd, 'The Southern Sudan: A Compelling Case for Secession', *Columbia Journal of Transnational Law*, 1994, vol. 32, pp. 419–54; Heraclides, note 40, pp. 107–28.

128 See W. M. Reisman, 'Somali Self-Determination in the Horn: Legal Perspectives and Implications for Social and Political Engineering', in I. M. Lewis (ed.), *Nationalism and Self-Determination in the Horn of Africa*, London, Ithaca Press, 1983, pp. 151–73; R. Greenfield, 'Towards an Understanding of the Somali Factor', in P. Woodward and M. Forsyth (eds), *Conflict and Peace in the Horn of Africa: Federalism and Its Alternatives* Aldershot, Dartmouth, 1994, pp. 103–13.

129 This dispute has been referred to the International Court of Justice. On the background to this dispute see N. J. Bekong, 'International Dispute Settlement: Land and Maritime Boundary Between Cameroon and Nigeria – Origins of the Dispute and Provisional Measures', *African Journal of International and Comparative Law*, 1997, vol. 9, pp. 287–310.

130 M. Plaut, 'On the Map', *The World Today*, 1998, vol. 64, no. 7, pp. 191–2.

131 Hayden, note 17, p. 49. See also Ratner, note 120, p. 114; Williams, note 66, pp. 140–1.

majority of Serbs were expelled from Croatia, especially as the result of the two Croatian military offensives in mid-1995.[132] These offensives were carried out in violation of existing UN Security Council resolutions and with the tacit support of the United States of America, the world's only superpower.[133] In the case of Bosnia-Hercegovina, the UN authorised a NATO bombing campaign against the Serbs in August–September 1995 which was directed at forcing the Serbs to submit to negotiations to end the war on the condition that Bosnia-Hercegovina's republic borders were accepted as its international borders, albeit with a *de facto* partition of that state into separate Muslim–Croat and Serb 'entities'.[134] What all these cases do is to call into question whether the principle of *uti possidetis juris* does minimise threats to peace and security or whether it is a cause of such threats.[135]

Second, Shaw refers to *uti possidetis* as establishing an 'appropriate' border rule. What he fails to amplify is the question of 'appropriate to whom?' The litany of wars and threats of war that the principle of *uti possidetis* has failed to prevent indicates that in each of these disputes one of the sides deemed the principle of *uti possidetis* inappropriate. In the case of Africa, the commitment of leaders to the 1964 OAU resolution can be questioned, even though it has often been proclaimed. It must be recalled that in 1958, at the First All-African Peoples' Conference in Accra, a resolution was passed denouncing colonial boundaries as artificial, particularly where they cut across ethnic lines, and calling for the abolition or adjustment of such boundaries based upon the true wishes of the people.[136] Morocco and Somalia refused to accept the OAU resolution of 1964. In 1969, at an OAU meeting, Tanzania's President Nyerere criticised the OAU's emphasis on the inviolability of borders when he said:

132 L. Silber and A. Little, *Yugoslavia: Death of a Nation*, revised and updated edition, New York, Penguin Books, 1997, pp. 353–60; D. Mirkovic, 'Croatian Liberation of Western Slavonija and Krajina', *Peace Research*, 1998, vol. 30, no. 1, pp. 14–24.

133 W. Bert, *The Reluctant Superpower: United States Policy in Bosnia, 1991–95*, New York, St Martin's Press, 1997, pp. 222–3; G. Elich, 'The Invasion of Serbian Krajina', in R. Clark *et al.* (eds), *NATO in the Balkans*, New York, International Action Center, 1998, p. 131.

134 In his memoirs, Richard Holbrooke, the US Assistant Secretary of State for European and Canadian Affairs, concedes that the NATO action was aimed at forcing the submission of the Serbs. During the NATO campaign and the parallel ground offensive by forces from Croatia and the Muslim–Croat coalition in Bosnia-Hercegovina, Holbrooke said to the Croatian Defence Minister, Gojko Šušak: 'Gojko, I want to be absolutely clear. Nothing we said today should be construed to mean that we want you to stop the rest of the offensive, other than Banja Luka. Speed is important. We can't say so publicly, but please take Sanski Most, Prijedor, and Bosanski Novi. And do it quickly, before the Serbs re-group!': R. Holbrooke, *To End a War*, New York, Random House, 1998, p. 166.

135 Craven, note 7, p. 388; J. Castellino, *International Law and Self-Determination, The Interplay of the Politics of Territorial Possession with Formulations of Post-Colonial 'National' Identity*, The Hague, Martinus Nijhoff Publishers, 2000, pp. 140–1.

136 A. O. Cukwurah, 'The Organization of African Unity and African Territorial and Boundary Problems: 1963–1973', *Indian Journal of International Law*, 1973, vol. 13, pp. 179–92; Y. Makonnen, *International Law and the New States of Africa: A Study of the International Legal Problems of State Succession in the Newly Independent States of Eastern Africa*, Addis Abeba, UNESCO, 1983, p. 459.

> The OAU is not a trade union of African heads of State. . . . [W]e must be even more concerned about peace and justice in Africa than we are about the sanctity of the boundaries we inherited.[137]

Despite the official stance of the OAU in support of former colonial borders and against secession, various secessionist attempts in Africa have attracted reasonable levels of support from various African states. According to Neuberger, 'the degree of rejection [of secession by the OAU] is often vastly exaggerated'.[138] Furthermore, in 1977 the Secretary-General of the OAU made it clear that the principle of *uti possidetis* was not sacrosanct and could be overruled, especially on the basis of the right to self-determination.[139]

In more recent times the inappropriateness of many of Africa's borders is increasingly being recognised. The OAU resolution of 1964 has been criticised as mistaken and short-sighted.[140] In the 1990s state borders in Africa came increasingly under siege for a variety of reasons, including nationalism. Herbst believes '[t]here is no reason to believe that many African citizens have a stronger commitment to their states than the people in the Soviet Union or Yugoslavia did'.[141] As McCorquodale observes, 'the principle of *uti possidetis* . . . is a principle for *governments* to support their own sovereignty and their own interests and is not a principle in the *peoples'* interests'.[142] It is thus not surprising that Mazrui sees many changes to the borders of African states, with nationalism a key ingredient in many of them.[143]

137 Quoted in Carey, note 104, p. 66. Nyerere's comments were made in the context of Tanzania's recognition of Biafra. Nyerere's defence of Biafra's secession was based on the principles that included the right to secede being made a basic constitutional right: Neuberger, note 106, pp. 78–9.

138 Ibid., pp. 80–1, referring to the states in Africa which supported secessionist attempts in the Congo, Ethiopia, Sudan, Angola, Ghana and Nigeria.

139 Klabbers and Lefeber, note 123, p. 63.

140 S. Y. Hameso, *Ethnicity and Nationalism in Africa*, Commack, Nova Science Publishers, 1997, pp. 70–4; J. A. M. Cobbah, 'Towards a Geography of Peace in Africa: Redefining Sub-State Self-Determination Rights', in R. J. Johnston, D. B. Knight and E. Kofman (eds), *National Self-Determination and Political Geography* , London, Croom Helm, 1988, pp. 70–86; M. wa Mutua, 'Why Redraw the Map of Africa: A Moral and Legal Inquiry', *Michigan Journal of International Law*, 1995, vol. 16, pp. 1113–76. In the case of Nigeria it has been argued that partition along national lines is the only basis to reduce human rights violations and ensure citizen participation in the governing processes for Nigeria's multi-national population: O. Oko, 'Partition or Perish: Restoring Social Equilibrium in Nigeria Through Reconfiguration', *Indiana International and Comparative Law Review*, 1998, vol. 8, pp. 317–79. On the other hand Ezetah argues that an expanded notion of self-determination leading to a loose federation based upon 'ethno-cultural autonomy' is the appropriate solution to Nigeria's problems. Ezetah suggests this is necessary because 'the principle of *uti possidetis* in Africa may well have become a necessary evil': C. R. Ezetah, 'International Law of Self-Determination and the Ogoni Question: Mirroring Africa's Post-Colonial Dilemma', *Loyola of Los Angeles International and Comparative Law Journal*, 1997, vol. 19, p. 855.

141 J. Herbst, 'Challenges to Africa's Boundaries in the New World Order', *Journal of International Affairs*, 1992, vol. 46, p. 24.

142 McCorquodale, note 108, p. 607.

143 A. A. Mazrui, 'The Bondage of Boundaries', *The Economist*, Special Supplement, 11 September 1993, p. 28.

Shaw's justification of the principle of *uti possidetis* is indicative of the view of liberal internationalists who maintain that states can function within any borders. But as Ratner points out:

> [A]s much as liberal internationalists should cherish the idea of diverse peoples living together, we cannot, as John Chipman points out, 'impose a cosmopolitan diktat'. Instead, we must acknowledge that certain new states are not currently able or willing to guarantee the human rights of minorities in discrete territories, and must consider alternatives to leaving those groups at the mercy of new governments. Cosmopolitanism must remain the goal, not only because people can then identify themselves beyond real or imagined blood lines, but also because many minorities live within areas where border changes are not feasible. But in certain instances account may have to be taken of the need to avoid leaving peoples in new states where they do not wish to be or that will not treat them with dignity.[144]

A further reason why the Badinter Borders Principle is inappropriate in cases of secession is that it does not provide any solutions to secession involving non-federal or unitary states. This is illustrated by *Opinion No. 2*[145] of the Badinter Commission where it was held that the rights to self-determination of the Serb minorities in Croatia and Bosnia-Hercegovina did not extend to include the right to alter the borders of Croatia and Bosnia-Hercegovina by means of secession. This has significant implications for states dealing with minority groups. A state is unlikely to agree to federal or other decentralised state structures if by so doing it creates a basis for secession which could be avoided if the state remains a unitarist structure. If it is accepted that a federal or other decentralised state structure is a possible way of satisfying minority demands and thereby maintaining the unity of a state,[146] unitary states are unlikely to agree to such federalisation if it means that a federal unit could, on the basis of the Badinter Commission's opinions, legitimately secede.[147]

This is amply illustrated by the case of Croatia before the military operations of 1995 which led to the forced expulsion of most of its Serb minority. During 1994, leaders of the Serb People's Party in Croatia floated a proposal for a new constitutional arrangement within Croatia's internationally recognised borders as a

144 Ratner, note 101, p. 617.

145 *Opinion No. 2 of the Arbitration Commission of the Peace Conference on Yugoslavia* (1992) 31 ILM 1497.

146 Opinion on whether federal structures in fact do reduce the risk of secession is divided. See M. Hechter, *Containing Nationalism*, Oxford, Oxford University Press, 2000, pp. 139–49; A. Buchanan, 'Federalism, Secession, and the Morality of Inclusion', *Arizona Law Review*, 1995, vol. 37, pp. 55–7; R. Bauböck, 'Why Stay Together? A Pluralist Approach to Secession and Federation', in W. Kymlicka and W. Norman, *Citizenship in Diverse Societies*, Oxford, Oxford University Press, 2000, pp. 366–94.

147 M. Weller, 'The International Response to the Dissolution of the Socialist Federal Republic of Yugoslavia', *American Journal of International Law*, 1992, vol. 86, p. 606; H. Hannum, 'Rethinking Self-Determination', *Virginia Journal of International Law*, 1993, vol. 34, p. 39; Bartoš, note 68, pp. 85–6.

means of resolving the status of the republic's Serbs. The proposal envisaged clearly defined federal territorial units for the Serbs of Croatia.[148] This proposal was met with hostility within Croatia and was rejected on the basis that it would eventually lead to the secession of these units from Croatia, on the same basis that Croatia had seceded from the SFRY.[149] Similarly, Turkey has consistently rejected demands for a federation of Turkish and Kurdish federal units in Turkey on the ground that such a constitutional arrangement would be the first step towards secession of the Kurdish unit.[150] However, as Rich has observed, if a national group with its own federal unit is entitled to secede within the borders of that federal unit, it would be strange that secession be limited to such federal units and not extended to national groups within unitary states.[151]

A final reason why the principle of *uti possidetis juris* is inappropriate in cases of secession or dissolution lies in the different function of internal administrative borders as opposed to international borders. As Ratner observes:

> [G]overnments establish interstate boundaries to separate states and peoples, while they establish or recognize internal borders to unify and effectively govern a polity.[152]

According to the International Court of Justice, in the context of internal colonial boundaries in Spanish America:

> [I]t has to be remembered that no question of international boundaries could ever have occurred to the minds of those servants of the Spanish Crown who established administrative boundaries.[153]

148 The proposal as outlined by Milan Djukić, the leader of the Serb People's Party, was largely modelled on the constitutional arrangements for the Aaland Islands of Finland where the Swedish population of the islands has a considerable degree of autonomy pursuant to the Act on the Autonomy of Aaland 1991. Djukić publicly outlined his views in a newspaper interview: 'Srpskih Je Škola u Zagrebu Bilu i Prije, Pa Nema Razloga Da Ih Opet Ne Bude!', *Globus* (Zagreb), 8. travnja (April) 1994. The concept of a federal structure was also suggested by some opposition leaders in Croatia. On the Aaland autonomy arrangements see H. Hannum, *Autonomy, Sovereignty, and Self-Determination: The Accommodation of Conflicting Rights*, revised edition, Philadelphia, University of Philadephia Press, 1996, pp. 370–5.

149 See for example, 'Hrvatska Je Država Konstantna Vrijednost: Interview: Veselin Pejinović', *Danas*, Nova Serija, Broj 87 (Zagreb), 6 rujna. (September) 1994; 'Refederaliziranu Hrvatsku Ne Mogu Ni Zamisliti! Interview: Damir Zorić', *Danas*, Nova Serija, Broj 89, (Zagreb), 20 rujna (September) 1994; Tihomir Dujmović, 'Što Nam to Govore', *Nedeljna Dalmacija*, Broj 1222 (Split), 30 rujna (September) 1994.

150 J. Laber, 'The Hidden War in Turkey', *The New York Review of Books*, 23 June 1994, vol. XLI, no. 12.

151 R. Rich, 'Recognition of States: The Collapse of Yugoslavia and the Soviet Union', *European Journal of International Law*, 1993, vol. 4, p. 61.

152 Ibid 602. See also Shaw, note 103, p. 490.

153 *Case Concerning the Land, Island and Maritime Frontier Dispute* (*El Salvador/Honduras*) [1992] ICJ Rep. 383, at 388. See also *Dubai–Sharjah Border Arbitration* (1981) 91 ILR 543, at 579.

In the *Dubai–Sharjah Border Arbitration* the arbitral tribunal observed as follows:

> [O]ne cannot attribute the same value to a boundary which has been settled under a treaty, or as the result of an arbitral or judicial proceeding, in which independent interested Parties have had a full opportunity to present their arguments, as to a boundary which has been established by way of an administrative decision emanating from an authority which could have failed to take account of the Parties' views and arising from a situation of inherent inequality. In the first hypothesis, except in the case of nullity, the principles of *pacta sunt servanda* or of *res judicata* could be invoked to prevent the boundary so settled being called into question. In the second hypothesis, the boundary would have been established in the majority of cases, in the interests of the administering authority, on the basis of other than legal criteria, and according to the needs of a particular political or economic context.[154]

Ratner demonstrates that one of the significant reasons for the establishment and subsequent alterations of internal borders is the role such borders play in the process of integrating a state. He refers to the changes to Quebec's original borders within Canada as an example of this process.[155] Because Quebec claims it is entitled to secede within the bounds of its existing internal borders, Ratner legitimately poses the question of whether Quebec secessionists, in the case of Quebec's secession from Canada, can 'have their cake and eat it, too'. These borders, which significantly increased the size of Quebec, were given to it as part of its integration process into Canada.[156] A similar process was at play in the case of the SFRY. Its internal borders established after World War II, according to Milovan Đilas, were never intended to be international borders.[157] According to the Yugoslav leader Josip Broz Tito, internal republic borders were 'only an administrative division' having the function of unifying, rather than separating, the state.[158] If secession

154 *Dubai–Sharjah Border Arbitration* (1981) 91 ILR 543, at 579.

155 Ratner, note 101, p. 603; Bartoš, note 68, pp. 86–8.

156 Ratner, note 101, p. 607. At the time of Canada's formation Quebec was approximately one-third of its present area. Extensions to its territory were carried out in 1898 and 1912. These extensions comprised land overwhelmingly populated by Aboriginal peoples. Aboriginal peoples in Quebec argue that if the Canadian government allowed those territories added to Quebec in 1898 and 1912 to become part of an independent Quebec without their consent, it would be a violation of Canadian government obligations and undertakings to the Aboriginal peoples as set out in the James Bay and Northern Quebec Agreement of 1975. On these territorial extensions and the 1975 agreement see Grand Council of the Crees, *Sovereign Injustice: Forcible Inclusion of the James Bay Crees and Cree Territory into a Sovereign Quebec*, Toronto, ECW Press, 1995, pp. 199–217, 249–95. At the time of the 1995 sovereignty referendum in Quebec, the Inuit and Cree peoples organised their own referenda. The vote in both was over 95 per cent against Quebec sovereignty: R. A. Young, *The Struggle for Quebec: From Referendum to Referendum?*, Montreal and Kingston, McGill-Queen's University Press, 1999, pp. 29–30.

157 Owen, note 120, pp. 34–5.

158 'Iz govora Generalnog Sekretara KPJ JB Tita na osnivačkom kongresu KP Srbije' (8 maj 1945),

was seen as a possibility at the time when internal borders were being drawn, it is likely that different lines would have been drawn. Yet when four republics seceded from the SFRY the ruling of the Badinter Arbitration Commission allowed them, in Ratner's words, to 'have their cake and eat it, too'.

Conclusion

The opinions of the Badinter Commission have met with a mixed reaction. Some have endorsed its conclusions with varying degrees of enthusiasm.[159] Others have been critical on the basis that the Commission has inappropriately applied or analysed the principle of *uti possidetis juris* or self-determination.[160] The above analysis has extensively criticised the reasoning of the Badinter Commission and is in general agreement with the assessment of Marc Weller who has written:

> Overall, the generally very brief opinions of the Commission are likely to attract considerable and probably hostile scholarly interest. They are underpinned by the shallowest legal reasoning and do not appear destined to assist the international community greatly when addressing the potentially dangerous problem of secession in the future.[161]

in B. Petranović and M. Zečević (eds), *Jugoslovenski federalizam, Ideje i stvarnost, Tematska zbirka dokumenata, Drugi tom, 1943–1986*, Belgrade, Prosveta, 1987, pp. 158–9; F. W. Hondius, *The Yugoslav Community of Nations*, The Hague, Mouton, 1968, p. 180.

159 An international law consultant to the Badinter Commission has described the opinions as 'balanced and impartial': A. Pellet, 'The Opinions of the Badinter Arbitration Committee, A Second Breath for the Self-Determination of Peoples', *European Journal of International Law*, 1992, vol. 3, p. 181. See also M. Rady, 'Self Determination and the Dissolution of Yugoslavia', *Ethnic and Racial Studies*, 1996, vol. 19, p. 387; R. Mullerson, 'The Continuity and Succession of States By Reference to the Former Soviet USSR and Yugoslavia', *International and Comparative Law Quarterly*, 1993, vol. 42, pp. 485–7; G. J. Naldi, 'Separatism in the Comoros: Some Legal Aspects', *Leiden Journal of International Law*, 1998, vol. 11, pp. 249–51; S. Terrett, *The Dissolution of Yugoslavia and the Badinter Arbitration Commission: A Contextual Study of Peace-Making in the Post-Cold War World*, Aldershot, Ashgate, 2000, pp. 281–2. Kofman suggests that the application of the Badinter Borders Principle will depend upon the degree of autonomy and constitutional powers of the relevant administrative sub-state unit. The greater the degree, the firmer the application of the principle should be: Kofman, note 62, p. 13.

160 Ratner, note 101, pp. 613–14; S. N. Lalonde, 'Uti Possidetis and Internal Administrative Boundaries', unpublished doctoral dissertation, Cambridge University, 1997, pp. 205–6; M. Pomerance, 'The Badinter Commission: The Use and Misuse of the International Court of Justice's Jurisprudence', *Michigan Journal of International Law*, 1998, vol. 20, pp. 50–7; Bartoš, note 68, pp. 71–88; C. Antonopoulos, 'The Principle of *Uti Possidetis Iuris* in Contemporary International Law', 1996, *Revue Hellénique de Droit International*, vol. 49, no. 1, pp. 81–6.

161 M. Weller, 'International Law and Chaos', *Cambridge Law Journal*, 1993, vol. 52, p. 8.

Notwithstanding Weller's assessment, the opinions of the Badinter Commission have been cited by commentators as being of relevance in relation to existing secessions such as Cyprus[162] and Kosovo,[163] as well as possible future secessions from the United Kingdom,[164] South Africa[165] and Canada.[166]

162 Z. M. Necatigil, *The Cyprus Question and Turkish Position in International Law*, 2nd edition, Oxford, Oxford University Press, 1993, pp. 231–3.

163 M. Paunović, 'Serbia's Borders are Inviolable', *Review of International Affairs*, 15 April 1998, vol. 49, no. 1067, pp. 1–4.

164 C. Drew, 'Independence through Devolution – Scotland, Self-determination and the Badinter Paradox', 1996, *Juridical Review*, no. 2, pp. 161–4.

165 J. Dugard, 'Secession: Is the Case of Yugoslavia a Precedent for Africa?', *African Journal of International and Comparative Law*, 1993, vol. 5, pp. 163–75.

166 Franck, note 73, paras. 2.46, 3.20–3.21.

8 Conclusion

The break-up of the Socialist Federative Republic of Yugoslavia in the 1990s has attracted a plethora of historical, political and legal analyses. This volume of studies reflects the reality that the importance of this event extends well beyond its importance to those most directly affected by it, namely, the peoples of the former Yugoslavia. The wider significance of Yugoslavia's break-up lies in what it tells us about the causes of secession and how individual states and the wider international community should deal with such a potentially destabilising occurrence.

Given the significance of Yugoslavia's break-up it is not surprising that this extensive array of works has generated vigorous, and often heated, debate over Yugoslavia's break-up and its causes, course and implications. Thus, within the field of political theory there has been much written about the theoretical justifications for secession. However, as Pavković has observed, few political theorists have been able to find a theoretical basis to explain the successful and unsuccessful secessions that occurred in the former Yugoslavia. The former Yugoslavia is 'too hard a case' for secession theories.[1]

This book represents a contribution to the analysis of the break-up of former Yugoslavia from an international law perspective. Its focus has been upon the interplay of two rules of international law aimed at resolving the question of international borders of new states following secession from an existing internationally recognised state. These two rules are those of the right of peoples to self-determination and *uti possidetis juris*. Both of these international law rules have been analysed in detail.

In relation to self-determination, the major focus of attention was on the meaning of a 'people'. This was necessary because the right of self-determination allows, *inter alia*, a people to establish a sovereign and independent state. If a people have the right to a state, the meaning of people is of crucial importance in determining whether the right to self-determination encompasses secession from an internationally recognised state. A detailed analysis of relevant international instruments concluded that a nation, as understood in the romantic theory of self-determination, is a people. Given that most states in the international system are

1 A. Pavković, 'Recursive Secessions in Former Yugoslavia: Too Hard a Case for Theories of Secession?' *Political Studies*, 2000, vol. 48, pp. 485–502.

multi-national, *prima facie*, such national groups have the right of secession.

The romantic theory interpretation of a people is not universally accepted. Some scholars argue that the provisions on the territorial integrity of states in many international documents, combined with international practice in the context of post-World War II decolonisation, mean that a people is defined as the population of a territorial entity, such as a state or colony. This interpretation is consistent with the classical theory of self-determination. However, an interpretation of relevant international documents does not, on balance, support this classical theory interpretation of a people. There is greater support in these texts for a romantic theory interpretation of a people. This is particularly so in the context of the Friendly Relations Declaration, with its clear implication of the right of secession.

As for state practice in the context of decolonisation, it has been argued that, because independent statehood was gained within the confines of existing colonial borders, the population of a colony was a people, rather than a number of peoples. However, this assertion fails to account for the fact that the Declaration on Colonialism makes no explicit statement defining peoples in this way. On balance the Declaration is more consistent with a people being defined on the basis of the romantic theory of self-determination. Furthermore, there were a number of instances in which decolonisation did not take place within the confines of existing colonial borders. On the other hand, even if a classical theory interpretation of people is accepted in the context of decolonisation, it is not necessarily applicable in the context of secession from an independent state.

If a nation is a people, then, in principle, such a nation has the right to secession pursuant to the right to self-determination. This right is not an absolute right and is subject to two important qualifications. First, a people cannot secede from an independent state if the latter does not discriminate against that people. This is clear from provisions of the Declaration on Friendly Relations and the Fiftieth Anniversary Declaration. Second, the exercise of a people's right to self-determination can only lead to statehood if that people satisfy the criteria for recognition as a state. The criteria of a permanent population, defined territory, government, and international capacity, as stipulated in the Montevideo Convention of 1933, represent the basic prerequisites to statehood. If a people is unable to meet these criteria, its right to self-determination would need to be expressed in other ways.

If a people can meet the criteria for independent statehood, the critical question that arises in cases of secession is that of borders. In the context of the break-up of Yugoslavia, great reliance was placed on the principle of *uti possidetis juris* as the basis for determining the borders of the states that emerged as the result of secession. In international law this principle provides a basis for determining borders of new states following decolonisation. Where the principle applies, existing colonial borders become international state borders at the time of independence. This meaning of the principle of *uti possidetis juris* had its first application in the context of the decolonisation of Latin America. It was later applied in the context of Africa's decolonisation. A critical aspect of *uti possidetis juris* is that its application is confined to the process of decolonisation. Furthermore, its application requires that the disputant states agree that the principle applies as the basis for the determination of their international border. If the relevant states do not agree to the application of *uti possidetis juris*, it is irrelevant. In Latin America *uti possidetis juris* was not always adopted by states with border disputes. Other means, including war, resolved border conflicts. In Africa, there was general, but not universal, endorsement of *uti possidetis juris* by means of the Cairo resolution on borders adopted by the Organisation of African Unity in 1964.

In an effort to manage the crisis surrounding the break-up of Yugoslavia, the international community placed great reliance on the rules of self-determination and *uti possidetis juris*. However, the application of these international law rules was misguided and flawed. If international law on the right of a people to self-determination means that a nation can secede from a state in the exercise of its right to self-determination, then the break-up of Yugoslavia should not have proceeded on the basis of Yugoslavia's republics being able to form states within the confines of existing internal administrative borders. This is so because of the multi-national composition of the populations of most of Yugoslavia's republics. The birth of a new state as a result of secession cannot be based upon an internal political unit of the parent state if members of other nations in that unit do not wish to form part of the new state. In these circumstances international law requires that the new state must be based upon territory occupied by members of that nation seeking secession, irrespective of existing internal administrative borders.

In the context of Yugoslavia, the international community determined that the peoples of Yugoslavia were, for the purposes of self-determination, six in number and that they equated to the populations of Yugoslavia's six federal republics. Given that five of these republics had multi-national populations, this approach violated international law, which provides, as has been argued, that a people is not defined as the population of a territorial unit. Rather, it is, or at least includes, a nation. The approach of the international community also conflicted with what the population of Yugoslavia understood to be the meaning of peoples. Yugoslavia's 1974 Constitution recognised that its population was made up of a mixture of groups defined on the basis of national identity rather than on the basis of residence or domicile within a territorial unit. The Constitution referred to the population of Yugoslavia as being its constituent nations and nationalities (Article 1). Although the Constitution stated that only Yugoslavia's nations, and not nationalities (Introductory Part, Section I), had the right to self-determination, under international law both nations and nationalities would qualify as peoples for the purposes of the right to self-determination.

A proper understanding and application of the right of a people to self-determination in the case of Yugoslavia would have led to new states emerging with borders based upon nationality rather than pre-existing republic borders. This would have meant the partitioning of all republics with the exception of Slovenia. It is not necessarily the case that all of Yugoslavia's nations would have satisfied the criteria for, or even have desired, independent statehood. Thus, the Albanians in Kosovo and Macedonia may have preferred association with, or incorporation into, a greater Albanian state as their preferred means of realising their right to self-determination.[2]

The manner in which self-determination was applied in Yugoslavia was reinforced by the adoption of the principle of *uti possidetis juris* to validate existing internal federal borders as international borders following secession. This application of *uti possidetis juris* in the context of Yugoslavia was unwarranted. Yugoslavia was not a case of decolonisation, nor did the disputants in the conflict agree that their respective borders be determined by the principle of *uti possidetis juris* or some adaptation of that principle. On its proper understanding the principle of *uti possidetis juris* is irrelevant to border issues following secession. The principle of *uti possidetis juris* is a means by which disputed border lines are determined in circumstances where the disputant parties agree that an existing colonial border should be the border, but cannot agree on the location of colonial borders as at the date of independence. Such disputes arise because of uncertain, conflicting or inadequate documentary evidence relating to the location of colonial borders at the time of independence. Where the principle of *uti possidetis juris* applies, an arbitral body is required to determine the location of the relevant colonial border based upon the evidence. In the case of Yugoslavia the location of borders was not in dispute. Rather, the dispute was whether existing internal administrative borders should be international borders.

To insist that, in cases of secession from a federal state, internal administrative borders should automatically become international borders is to create a new rule of international law. To justify the application of this rule as an application of the principle of *uti possidetis juris* amounts to an unprincipled extension of the principle that applies in cases of ascertaining international borders following decolonisation. Such a new rule has no connection with its alleged progenitor. For this reason this book has referred to this new rule of international law as the 'Badinter Borders Principle', given that its origins lie in the opinions of the Badinter Arbitration Commission.

More fundamentally, irrespective of whether the Badinter Borders Principle is or is not based upon the principle of *uti possidetis juris*, it is, for a number of reasons, in political and practical terms, as the case of Yugoslavia illustrates, too simplistic and inflexible. First, it failed to take into account that Yugoslavia's internal administrative borders were always contentious and never the subject of widespread support from its various national groups. If they were contentious as internal administrative borders, it was inevitable that they would be even more so in the context of the break-up of Yugoslavia. This is especially so, given that these borders were never determined with the prospect that they would ever serve as future international borders. Second, the expectation that the application of the Badinter Borders Principle would bring about an end to the fighting which had erupted soon after the secessions of Slovenia and Croatia in late June 1991 was a

2 These means of self-determination are explicitly provided for in the Declaration on Friendly Relations.

false expectation.[3] This is amply evidenced by the facts that violent conflict continued throughout much of the 1990s and only came to an uneasy end after the truces imposed by the Dayton Peace Accords in November 1995 and the conclusion of NATO's air strikes against the Federal Republic of Yugoslavia in June 1999. Although the Dayton Peace Accords maintained the territorial integrity of Bosnia-Hercegovina, the reality is the *de facto* partition of that former Yugoslav republic. Its borders have been preserved, but in name only.[4] In reality the Dayton Peace Accords reflect the application of the principle of *uti possidetis* as once applied in international law following the termination of war much more than in its application in the context of resolving border disputes following decolonisation. Much the same can be said following the NATO air strikes campaign against the Federal Republic of Yugoslavia which had the result of coercing the latter to accept the *de facto* secession of Kosovo.

In dealing with secession from federal states a more flexible approach is required. The over-riding concerns in such cases are two-fold. The first concern should be the greatest possible minimisation of violence.[5] The second concern should be that recognition of independence not be granted to any secessionist movement unless the latter has convinced the international community that it has in place, and will honour, international norms on human and minority rights.

In some situations the recognition of statehood within existing internal federal borders will be appropriate. The case of Slovenia, because of its homogeneous Slovene population, is a case in point. However, in cases where the impulse for secession is driven by nationalist ideology, and where federal borders cut across national lines, more sophisticated measures need to be undertaken to ascertain international borders. At a time of revolutionary transformation of the kind that occurred with the break-up of Yugoslavia, the right of nations to self-determination should be recognised. As the Commission of Jurists indicated in the Aaland Islands dispute, these are the circumstances in which the principle of national self-determination can have a major role in the creation of new states.[6] In applying this principle, internationally supervised plebiscites in contested areas could be organised. Common-sense limitations based upon geography would need to be taken into consideration

3 M. Glenny, *The Fall of Yugoslavia: The Third Balkan War*, 3rd edition, London, Penguin Books, 1996, pp. 190–1.

4 Morrison summarises the constitutional structure established by the Dayton Accords as follows: 'This new Bosnian constitution makes the American Articles of Confederation of two centuries ago look like a centralized, unitary form of government. . . . [T]he constitution produces a much looser confederation than that of any other geographic unit that purports to be a single nation-state': F. L. Morrison, 'The Constitution of Bosnia-Herzegovina', *Constitutional Commentary*, 1996, vol. 13, pp. 145, 157.

5 According to Hannum, 'the only legitimate goal consistent with the present international order is ensuring that separation or unity occurs without disturbing international peace': H. Hannum, 'The Specter of Secession, Responding to Claims for Ethnic Self-Determination', *Foreign Affairs*, 1998, vol. 77, no. 2, p. 14.

6 D. F. Orentlicher, 'Separation Anxiety: International Responses to Ethno-Separatist Claims', *Yale Journal of International Law*, vol. 23, p. 35.

together with plebiscite results.[7] It may even be necessary to facilitate orderly and voluntary transfers of parts of the population.[8] The aim of such measures would be to establish borders which would result in the maximum number of persons being located on their preferred side of the line, while at the same time achieving this end without the violence that led to the same result in the case of Yugoslavia.[9]

Some may suggest that the above approaches amount to condoning the creation of new nationally homogeneous states and legitimising a form of 'ethnic cleansing'. However, such criticisms are misguided. They assume that a nationally homogeneous state is in itself a bad thing. The exploration of this assumption is beyond the scope of this book, but it can be noted that it has long attracted a spectrum of views amongst international lawyers, political scientists and philosophers.[10] Ratner is correct to point out that, while the ideal of liberal internationalists is laudable, there must be a recognition that the idea of diverse peoples living in one state is not always possible and that 'in certain instances account may have to be taken of the need to avoid leaving peoples in new states where they do not wish to be or that will not treat them with dignity'.[11] He also notes that redrawing borders along national

7 S. R. Ratner, 'Drawing a Better Line: *Uti Possidetis* and the Borders of New States', *American Journal of International Law*, 1996, vol. 90, pp. 622–3; H. Hannum, 'Rethinking Self-Determination', *Virginia Journal of International Law*, 1993, vol. 34, p. 56; V. P. Nanda, 'The New Dynamics of Self-Determination: Revisiting Self-Determination as an International Law Concept: A Major Challenge in the Post-Cold War Era', *ILSA Journal of International and Comparative Law*, 1992, vol. 3, pp. 451–2. Frowein suggests that plebiscites in border regions would have been appropriate in relation to Croatia and Bosnia-Hercegovina: J. A. Frowein, 'Self-Determination as a Limit to Obligations Under International Law', in C. Tomuschat (ed.), *Modern Law of Self-Determination*, Dordrecht, Martinus Nijhoff Publishers, 1993, p. 217. In relation to territorial disputes, the holding of plebiscites is not required by international law, nor is it a necessary corollary of the right to self-determination: V. Rudrakumuran, 'The "Requirement" of Plebiscite in Territorial Rapprochement', *Houston Journal of International Law*, 1989, vol. 12, pp. 35–7.

8 For a sustained defence of the necessity of planned population transfers see C. Kaufmann, 'Possible and Impossible Solutions to Ethnic Civil Wars', *International Security*, 1996, vol. 20, pp. 136–75; C. Kaufmann, 'Intervention in Ethnic and Ideological Civil Wars: Why One Can Be Done and the Other Can't', *Security Studies*, 1996, vol. 6, pp. 96–101. Fuller is of the view that population transfers are 'regrettable but inevitable': G. E. Fuller, 'Redrawing the World's Borders', *World Policy Journal*, 1997, vol. 14, p. 20. See also J. Tullberg and B. S. Tullberg, 'Separation or Unity? A Model For Solving Ethnic Conflicts', *Politics and Life Sciences*, 1997, vol. 16, no. 2, p. 239; J. Goldblat, 'The Balkan Imbroglio: A Way to Solve the Problem', *Security Dialogue*, 1999, vol. 30, p. 383.

9 Franck has argued that in dealing with secessionist claims, international law needs to replace both the principles of *uti possidetis* and the classical theory of self-determination with rules 'that evince more context-sensitive principles'. He suggests that parties to such claims be required to negotiate in good faith, obey humanitarian law and respect the principles of proportionality in an environment that precludes most external interventions: T. M. Franck, 'Friedmann Award Address', *Columbia Journal of Transnational Law*, 1999, vol. 38, pp. 1–8.

10 See G. Binder, 'The Case for Self-Determination', *Stanford Journal of International Law*, 1993, vol. 29, pp. 223–70; D. Miller, *On Nationality*, Oxford, Clarendon Press, 1995; M. Viroli, *For Love of Country: An Essay on Patriotism and Nationalism*, Oxford, Clarendon Press, 1995.

11 Ratner, note 7, p. 617. See also M. Barutciski, 'Politics Overrides Legal Principles: Tragic Consequences of the Diplomatic Intervention in Bosnia-Hercegovina (1991–1992)', *American University Journal of International Law and Policy*, 1996, vol. 11, pp. 785–91.

lines can in some cases assist in the process of facilitating the growth of democracy. More persons will belong to and be part of states to which they feel a sense of commitment, and they are more likely to have a positive attitude towards participation in that state's political processes.[12] However, even if the assumption that nationally homogeneous states are not desirable is accepted, the application of the Badinter Borders Principle will not necessarily avoid such a result. If the seceding federal unit is nationally homogeneous, a nationally homogeneous state will emerge. Slovenia serves as an illustration.

More importantly, in the case of a multi-national unit within a federation in which a majority national group resolves that the federal unit will secede, recognition of that unit within existing federal borders is, on the evidence of the secessions and recognition of Croatia and Bosnia-Hercegovina, likely to facilitate violent 'ethnic cleansing'.[13] The result will be either a nationally homogeneous state, or a *de facto* partition of the state along national lines. Croatia serves as an example of the former and Bosnia-Hercegovina is an example of the latter. Ironically, it was international intervention in the form of economic sanctions against the Serbs, the arming of Croat and Bosnian Muslim forces, and NATO air strikes against the military forces of the Serbs of Croatia and Bosnia-Hercegovina, which facilitated such results.[14] These measures led to the international community condoning what Richard Holbrooke defined as 'a milder form of ethnic cleansing'[15] of the Serbs from the Krajina region of Croatia, resulting in a nationally homogeneous nation-state in Croatia.[16] The insistence on preserving former internal borders as

12 S. R. Ratner, 'Ethnic Conflict and Territorial Claims: Where Do We Draw a Line?', in D. Wippman (ed.), *International Law and Ethnic Conflict*, Ithaca, NY, Cornell University Press, 1988, pp. 122–3. For a contrary view see R. Schaeffer, *Warpaths, The Politics of Partition*, New York, Hill & Wang, 1990, pp. 253–63.

13 R. M. Hayden, *Blueprints for a House Divided: The Constitutional Logic of the Yugoslav Conflicts*, Ann Arbor, University of Michigan Press, 1999, p. 163.

14 In the latter stages of the military Croat and Bosnian Muslim military offensive against the Serbs of Bosnia in the latter half of 1995, American Assistant Secretary of State for European and Canadian Affairs, Richard Holbrooke, in a note to Secretary of State Warren Christopher, summed up the military position as follows: 'I suspect that the most dramatic phase of the offensive is coming to an end, and that the recent fluidity of the front lines will gradually be replaced by a return to relatively stable front line . . . Contrary to many press reports and other impressions, the [Muslim–Croat] Federation military offensive has so far helped the peace process. This basic truth is perhaps not something we can say publicly right now . . . In fact, the map negotiation, which always seemed to me to be our most daunting challenge, is taking place right now on the battlefield, and so far, in a manner beneficial to the map. In only a few weeks, the famous 70%-30% division of the country has gone to around 50–50, obviously making our task easier': R. Holbrooke, *To End a War*, New York, Random House, 1998. pp. 167–8.

15 Ibid., p. 160. Holbrooke, at p. 73, also recounts how one of his aides observed that Croatia's forces had been 'hired' by the United States as their 'junkyard dogs', and that it was 'no time to get squeamish' over the methods employed by the Croatian forces.

16 Hayden suggests that the number of Serbs in Croatia by late 1995 had been reduced to 90,000 from the 1991 figure of 570,000: R. M. Hayden, 'Constitutional Nationalism and the Logic of the Wars in Yugoslavia', *Problems of Post-Communism*, 1996, vol. 43, no. 5, p. 31.

continuing international borders also led to the 'ethnic cleansing' of the Serb population from western Bosnia. However, international intervention on the side of the Croats and Bosnian Muslims was not unlimited and meant that the latter were prevented from 'ethnically cleansing' the Serbs from eastern Bosnia, with the result that the territorial gains made by the Serbs as a result of 'ethnic cleansing' in the earlier phases of the war in Bosnia-Hercegovina were consolidated, thereby enabling the *de facto* three-way partition of that state along national lines.[17] This *de facto* partition was essentially achieved as a result of force and before the Dayton Peace Accords of late 1995.[18] The only significant area in Bosnia-Hercegovina that changed hands after the Dayton Peace Accords was the Grbavica district of Sarajevo, which had been under Serb control during hostilities. In the immediate aftermath of the Dayton Peace Accords over 90 per cent of Grbavica's Serbs fled and the area passed to Bosnian Muslim control.[19]

In the case of Kosovo, NATO air strikes against the Serbs of the Federal Republic of Yugoslavia (FRY), aimed at reversing the expulsions of Kosovo Albanians by Serbs, resulted in the Kosovo Albanians being allowed to expel Kosovo's Serb population.[20] Although the territorial integrity of the FRY has been formally preserved, the NATO presence in Kosovo has facilitated a *de facto* partition of the state and the creation of a nationally homogeneous Kosovo.[21]

The consequences of the international community's adherence to the Badinter

17 In the case of Bosnia senior Serb political and military leaders (Radovan Karadžić, Momčilo Krajišnik and General Ratko Mladić) as well as a number of lesser military figures were indicted by the International Criminal Tribunal for the Former Yugoslavia on charges of war crimes. A lesser number of Croat and Bosnian Muslim military figures were similarly indicted. In the case of Croatia, the Serb political leader, Milan Martić, was also indicted on charges of war crimes. However, no Croat political or military leaders have been indicted in relation to the mass expulsion of Serbs in 1995: R. Bonner, 'War Crimes Panel Finds Croat Troops "Cleansed" the Serbs', *The New York Times*, 21 March 1999. The War Crimes Tribunal for former Yugoslavia was established by the Security Council of the United Nations in May 1993: Security Council Resolution 827 (1993), 25 May 1993.

18 In October 1999 Croatian President Franjo Tuđman called for the formal creation of a separate Croat entity in Bosnia-Hercegovina: 'Croatian President Talks to Foreign Reporters About Domestic International Issues', *BBC Worldwide Monitoring*, 19 October 1999.

19 L. Sell, 'The Serb Flight from Sarajevo: Dayton's First Failure', *East European Politics and Societies*, 2000, vol. 14, pp. 179–202.

20 During the NATO bombing campaign against Yugoslavia in 1999, Yugoslavia's President, Slobodan Milošević, and a number of senior Yugoslav political and military leaders, were indicted by the International Criminal Tribunal for the Former Yugoslavia on charges of war crimes in relation to the activities of Serb forces in Kosovo.

21 '[I]n the states in the former Yugoslavia . . . where democracy has not taken root, the assumption that post-independence borders must coincide with pre-independence lines has meant only expulsions and refugee crises, ethnic cleansing within the state, or even, . . . genocide': Ratner, note 12, pp. 123–4. According to Mayall, '[t]he refusal to countenance secession under any circumstances [in the case of Croatia] had predictably gruesome results': J. Mayall, 'Sovereignty, Nationalism, and Self-Determination', *Political Studies*, 1999, vol. 57, p. 486. See also Barutciski, note 11, pp. 784–5; A. Hoare, 'A Rope Supports a Man Who is Hanged – NATO Air Strikes and the End of Bosnian Resistance', *East European Politics and Societies*, 1998, vol. 12, pp. 217–19.

Borders Principle were disastrous for Yugoslavia. Any insistence upon its application in future secessions elsewhere could also be similarly disastrous. The possible secession of Quebec from Canada is worth noting in this context.

In 1998 the Supreme Court of Canada ruled that a unilateral secession of Quebec would be unconstitutional under Canadian constitutional law and would not be permitted under international law. In particular the Court ruled that, under Canada's constitution, the secession of Quebec could only be achieved by means of a negotiated constitutional amendment. As to international law, the Court ruled that there was no discrimination against the peoples of Quebec such as to give rise to the right of secession as an expression of the right to self-determination.[22] As to the issue of the borders of a future independent Quebec, the Court suggested that in any negotiations towards a constitutional amendment to legalise secession, the borders of a future Quebec would be an agenda item in such negotiations. It is quite clear that the Court rejected the notion that Quebec's present provincial borders would be sacrosanct in the context of a negotiated secession of that province from Canada. On the other hand the Court observed that if a unilateral, but illegal, secession by Quebec took place, the secession, within existing provincial borders could become a reality if there was general recognition by the international community of Quebec's action.[23]

The Supreme Court decision in Canada has acted as a catalyst towards a clear polarisation of opinion on the logistics of secession, including the question of the borders of a future independent Quebec, between Canada's federal government and Quebec's provincial government. In April 2000 the federal parliament of Canada passed legislation, commonly referred to as the *Clarity Act*, in relation to the logistics of any future move by Quebec towards secession. In particular, the legislation stipulated that in any constitutional negotiations on secession the borders of Quebec would be a matter for negotiation (Article 3(2)). In response to the *Clarity Act*, in December 2000, the Quebec provincial parliament passed legislation, commonly referred to as *Bill 99*. A key provision in *Bill 99* is the assertion that Quebec's borders can only be altered with the consent of its parliament, and further that Quebec's government has a duty to preserve the territorial integrity of Quebec (Article 9). The Quebec government places great reliance upon the Badinter Borders Principle in support of the position it has taken in *Bill 99*.

In many respects the political battle lines drawn by these two acts reflect the political battle lines drawn in Yugoslavia in the late 1980s and early 1990s. Yugoslavia's secessionist republics all vigorously asserted that their internal republic borders would be future international borders in the event of secession. Serbia and Montenegro argued that if secession were to occur, border changes would have to be made. Indeed, in late 1990 and early 1991, these two republics were instrumental in proposing an amendment to Yugoslavia's constitution that would have

22 *Reference re: Secession of Quebec* (1998) 161 DLR (4th) 385.

23 P. Radan, 'The Supreme Court of Canada and the Borders of Quebec', *Australian International Law Journal*, 1998, pp. 172–5.

established procedures for determining such border changes in the event of secession by any of Yugoslavia's republics.[24] The enactment of these amendments was never a realistic possibility and subsequent events rendered them irrelevant as Yugoslavia quickly descended into violence following the unilateral secessions of Slovenia and Croatia in June 1991. The likelihood that Canada could experience violence in the event of Quebec moving to secession and insisting on maintaining its existing provincial borders cannot be lightly discarded. The First Nations of northern Quebec and a number of Quebec's Anglophone communities have strongly asserted their desire to remain in Canada in the event that Quebec seeks independence. In the case of the former, their spokespersons have openly admitted that any move towards independence by Quebec could result in violence.[25] Any endorsement of the Badinter Borders Principle by the international community, on the precedent of the former Yugoslavia, will only serve to increase the likelihood that these apprehensions of violence will become a reality if and when Quebec seeks its independence from Canada.

While any solution to the question of borders after secession may well have its own particular problems, there is little to recommend a solution based upon the Badinter Borders Principle. Rather, it is suggested that an approach based upon plebiscites and orderly and voluntary transfers of persons represents a far more palatable alternative, if only because fewer lives are likely to be lost and shattered. As Hannum observes:

> Self-determination should be concerned primarily with people, not territory. . . . If our concern is with peoples rather than territories, there is no reason to regard existing administrative or 'republic' boundaries within states as sacrosanct. In most cases, the best way of determining the wishes of those within a new state would be through a series of plebiscites to redraw what were formerly internal boundaries. . . . Accepting the possibility of altering borders might be a useful precondition for recognition of a new state whenever a significant proportion of the population appears not to support the new borders.[26]

24 M. Mitić, *Međunarodno pravo u Jugoslovenskoj krizi*, Belgrade, Službeni List SRJ, 1996, pp. 25–6.

25 P. Radan, 'The Borders of a Future Independent Quebec: Does the Principle of *Uti Possidetis Juris* Apply?', *Australian International Law Journal*, 1997, p. 214.

26 Hannum, note 5, pp. 15, 17–18.

Appendix

Table of cases

Aaland Islands Question: Report Submitted to the Council of the League of Nations by the Commission of Rapporteurs, The (1921) League Doc. B7.21/68/106.
Advisory Opinion of the International Court of Justice on the Western Sahara [1975] ICJ Rep. 12.
Arbitral Award About the Limits Between Venezuela and Colombia, 16 March 1891, in Moore, John Bassett, *History and Digest of the International Arbitrations to Which the United States Has Been a Party*, vol. V, Washington, DC, Government Printing Office, 1898, pp. 4856–61.
Argentine–Chile Frontier Case (1966) 16 RIAA 109.
Barcelona Traction, Light, & Power Co (Belgium -v- Spain) [1970] ICJ Rep. 3.
Beagle Channel Arbitration (1977) 52 ILR 93.
Boundary Case Between Bolivia and Peru (1902) 11 RIAA 133.
Boundary Case Between Honduras and Nicaragua (1906) 11 RIAA 101.
Case Concerning East Timor (Portugal -v- Australia) (1995) 105 ILR 227.
Case Concerning Kasikili/Sedudu Island (Botswana/Namibia) (2000) 39 ILM 310.
Case Concerning Sovereignty Over Certain Frontier Land (Belgium/Netherlands) [1959] ICJ Rep. 209.
Case Concerning the Arbitral Award Made by the King of Spain on 23 December 1906 (Honduras -v- Nicaragua) [1960] ICJ Rep. 192.
Case Concerning the Arbitral Award of 31 July 1989 (Guinea-Bissau -v- Senegal) (1989) 83 ILR 1.
Case Concerning the Frontier Dispute (Burkina Faso and Mali) [1986] ICJ Rep. 554.
Case Concerning the Land, Island and Maritime Frontier Dispute (El Salvador/Honduras) [1992] ICJ Rep. 383.
Case Concerning the Northern Cameroons Case (Cameroon -v- United Kingdom) [1963] ICJ Rep. 15.
Case Concerning the Temple of Preah Vihear (Cambodia -v- Thailand) (Merits) (1962) 33 ILR 48.
Case Concerning the Territorial Dispute (Libyan Arab Jamahiriya/Chad) [1994] ICJ Rep. 6.
Colombia–Venezuela Arbitral Award (1922) 1 RIAA 223.
Committee in Bernard Omivayak Chief of the Lubicon Lake Band -v- Canada, UN Doc A/45/40, vol. II (1990).
Cordillera of the Andes Boundary Case (Argentina/Chile) (1902) 9 RIAA 29.
Dubai–Sharjah Border Arbitration (1981) 91 ILR 543.
Eritrea/Yemen (*Territorial Sovereignty*) (1998) 114 ILR 1.
Guiana Boundary Case (1904) 11 RIAA 10.
Guinea/Guinea-Bissau Maritime Delimitation Case (1985) 77 ILR 635.
Honduras Borders (*Guatemala/Honduras*) (1933) 2 RIAA 1307.
Indo-Pakistan Western Boundary (Rann of Kutch) Case (India -v- Pakistan), The (1968) 50 ILR 2.
Ivancevic -v- Artukovic (1954) 211 F 2d 565.
Kitok -v- Sweden, UN Doc A/45/40, Vol II, App A (1990).

Legal Consequences for States of the Continued Presence of South Africa in Namibia (South West Africa) Notwithstanding Security Council Resolution 276 [1971] ICJ Rep. 16.

Loizidou -v- Turkey (Merits) (1996) 108 ILR 445.

Mišljenje USJ o suprotnosti odredaba Čl. 9A, 9B i 9C ustavnog zakona za provedbu ustava Republike Hrvatske sa ustavom SFRJ, 10 July 1991, in M. Buzadžić, *Secesija bivših jugoslovenskih republika u svetlosti odluka Ustavnog suda Jugoslavije, Zbirka dokumenata s uvodnom raspravom*, Belgrade, Službeni List SRJ, 1994, pp. 86–8.

Mišljenje USJ o suprotnosti ustavnog amandmana XCIX na ustav Republike Slovenije s ustavom SFRJ, 2 October 1991, in Buzadžić, *Secesija*, pp. 80–5.

Mišljenje USJ o suprotnosti ustavnog zakona za sprovođenje ustavnog amandmana XCVI na ustav Republike Slovenije i ustavnog zakona za sprovođenje ustavnih amandmana XCVI i XCVII na ustav Republike Slovenije u oblasti narodne odbrane ca ustavom SFRJ, 2 October 1991, in Buzadžić, *Secesija*, pp. 77–80.

Mišljenje Ustavnog suda Jugoslavije o suprotnosti amandmana IX–XC na ustav SR Slovenije s ustavom SFRJ, 18 January 1990, Službeni List SFRJ, 23 February 1990, vol. 46, no. 10, pp. 593–96.

Minquiers and Ecrehos Case (*France/United Kingdom*), *The* [1953] ICJ Rep. 4.

Odluka o oceni ustavnosti odredaba čl. 4. i 10. zakona o plebicitu o samostalnosti i nezavisnosti Republike Slovenije, 7 November 1991, Službeni List SFRJ, 28 February 1992, vol. 48, no. 14, pp. 189–90.

Odluka o ocenjivanju ustavnosti deklaracije o proglašenju suverene i samostalne Republike Hrvatske, 13 November 1991, in Buzadžić, *Secesija*, pp. 159–62.

Odluka o ocenjivanju ustavnosti deklaracije o suverenosti države Republike Slovenije, 10 January 1991, Službeni List SFRJ, 5 April 1991, vol. 47, no. 23, pp. 452–3.

Odluka o ocenjivanju ustavnosti deklaracije o suverenosti Socialističke Makedonije, 28 January 1991, Službeni List SRJ, 8 May 1992, vol. 1, no. 4, p. 61.

Odluka o ocenjivanju ustavnosti deklaracije povodom nezavisnosti, 9 October 1991, Službeni List SFRJ, 13 December 1991, vol. 47, no. 89, pp. 1427–8.

Odluka o ocenjivanju ustavnosti odluke o priznanju Republike Slovenije kao suverene i samostalne države, 29 January 1992, in Buzadžić, Secesija, pp. 165–6.

Odluka o ocenjivanju ustavnosti odluke Sabora Republike Hrvatske o raskidu državnopravne veze sa SFRJ, 25 December 1991, Službeni List SFRJ, 21 February 1992, vol. 47, no. 12, pp. 163–4.

Odluka o ocenjivanju ustavnosti osnovne ustavne povelje o samostalnosti i nezavisnosti Republike Slovenije, 16 October 1991, Službeni List SFRJ, 13 December 1991, vol. 47, no. 89, pp. 1422–3.

Odluka o ocenjivanju ustavnosti rezolucije o predlogu za sporazumno razdruživanje Socialističke Federativne Republike Jugoslavije, 2 October 1991, Službeni List SFRJ, 13 December 1991, vol. 47, no. 89, pp. 1426–7.

Odluka o ocenjivanju ustavnosti rezolucije o prihvaćanju postupka za razdruživanje SFRJ i o mogućim udruživanju u savez suverenih republika, 2 October 1991, Službeni List SFRJ, 29 November 1991, vol. 47, no. 86, pp. 1364–5.

Odluka o ocenjivanju ustavnosti ustavne deklaracije o Kosovu kao samostalnoj i ravnopravnoj jedinici u okviru federacije (konfederacije) Jugoslavije kao ravnopravnog subjekta sa ostalim jedinicama u federaciji (konfederaciji), 19 February 1991, Službeni List SFRJ, 20 May 1991, vol. 47, no. 37, pp. 618–19.

Odluka o ocenjivanju ustavnosti ustavne odluke o suverenosti i samostalnosti Republike Hrvatske, 16 October 1991, in Buzadžić, *Secesija*, pp. 156–9.

Odluka o ocenjivanju ustavnosti zakona za sprovođenje osnovne ustavne povelje o samostalnosti i nezavisnosti Republike Slovenije, 16 October 1991, Službeni List SFRJ, 13 December 1991, vol. 47, no. 89, pp. 1423–5.

Opinion No. 1 of the Arbitration Commission of the Peace Conference on Yugoslavia (1992) 31 ILM 1494.

Opinion No. 2 of the Arbitration Commission of the Peace Conference on Yugoslavia (1992) 31 ILM 1497.

Opinion No. 3 of the Arbitration Commission of the Peace Conference on Yugoslavia (1992) 31 ILM 1499.

Opinion No. 4 on International Recognition of the Socialist Republic of Bosnia and Herzegovina by the European Community and its Member States, 11 January 1992, (1992) 31 ILM 1501.

Opinion No. 5 on International Recognition of the Republic of Croatia by the European Community and its Member States, 11 January 1992, (1992) 31 ILM 1503.

Opinion No. 6 on the Recognition of the Socialist Republic of Macedonia by the European Community and its Member States, 11 January 1992, (1992) 31 ILM 1507.

Opinion No. 7 on International Recognition of the Republic of Slovenia by the European Community and its Member States, 11 January 1992, (1992) 31 ILM 1512.

Opinion No. 8 of the Arbitration Commission of the Peace Conference on Yugoslavia (1992) 31 ILM 1521.

Opinion No. 11 of the Arbitration Commission of the Peace Conference on Yugoslavia (1993) 32 ILM 1587.

Reference re: Secession of Quebec (1998) 161 DLR (4th) 385.

Report of the International Commission of Jurists (1920) LNOJ Spec. Supp. 3.

Rešenje o obustavi izvršenja pojedinačnih akata i radnji preduztih na osnovu čl. 4. i 10. zakona o plebicitu o samostalnosti i nezavisnosti Republike Slovenije kojima organi Republike Slovenije preuzimaju ustavom SFRJ utvrđena prava i dužnosti federacije ili kojima se jednostrano menja granica SFRJ, odnosno granica između republika, 8 January 1991, Službeni List SFRJ, 18 January 1991, vol. 47, no. 4, p. 64.

South West Africa Cases (Ethiopia -v- South Africa; Liberia -v- South Africa) Second Phase [1966] ICJ Rep. 4.

Tacna–Arica Question (1925) 2 RIAA 921.

Whispering Pines Indian Band -v- Canada, UN Doc A/46/40 (1991).

Select bibliography

Alvarez, A., 'Latin America and International Law', *American Journal of International Law*, 1909, vol. 3, pp. 269–353.

Antonopoulos, C., 'The Principle of *Uti Possidetis Iuris* in Contemporary International Law', *Revue Hellénique de Droit International*, 1996, vol. 49, pp. 29–88.

Bagwell, B., 'Yugoslavian Constitutional Questions: Self-Determination and Secession of Member Republics', *Georgia Journal of International and Comparative Law*, 1991, vol. 21, pp. 489–523.

Bartoš, Tomáš, '*Uti Possidetis, Quo Vadis?*', *Australian Year Book of International Law*, 1997, vol. 18, pp. 37–96.

Barutciski, M., 'Politics Overrides Legal Principles: Tragic Consequences of the Diplomatic Intervention in Bosnia-Hercegovina (1991–1992)', *American University Journal of International Law and Policy*, 1996, vol. 11, pp. 767–91.

Bello, E. G., 'The Effects of the Application of the Uti Possidetis Principle in Africa', *Proceedings of the Second Amsterdam International Law Conference on the Rights of Peoples and Minorities in International Law*, Amsterdam, 18–20 June 1992.

Bernárdez, S. T., 'The "Uti Possidetis Juris Principle" in Historical Perspective', in K. Ginther, G. Hafner, W. L. H. Neuhold, L. Sucharipa-Behrmann (eds), *Völkerrecht zwischen normativem Anspruch und politischer Realität, Festschrift für Karl Zemanek zum 65. Geburtstag*, Berlin, Duncker & Humbolt, 1994, pp. 417–437.

Bethlehem, D. and Weller, M. (eds), *The 'Yugoslav' Crisis in International Law: General Issues*, Part I, Cambridge, Cambridge University Press, 1997.

Bloomfield, L. M., *The British Honduras–Guatemala Dispute*, Toronto, The Carswell Company Ltd, 1953.

Bossuyt, M. J., *Guide to the 'Travaux Préparatoires' of the International Covenant on Civil and Political Rights*, Dordrecht, Martinus Nijhoff Publishers, 1987.

Braveboy-Wagner, J. A., *The Venezuela–Guyana Border Dispute: Britain's Colonial Legacy in Latin America*, Boulder, CO, Westview Press, 1984.

Brölmann, C., Lefeber, R. and Zieck, M., (eds), *Peoples and Minorities in International Law*, Dordrecht, Martinus Nijhoff Publishers, 1993.

Brubaker, R., *Citizenship and Nationhood in France and Germany*, Cambridge, MA, Harvard University Press, 1992.

Bučar, B., 'Mednarodni aspekti jugoslovenske reforme i osamostaljenja Slovenije', *Međunarodna Politika*, 1 June 1991, vol. 42, no. 988, pp. 3–5.

Bučar, B., 'The International Recognition of Slovenia', in D. Fink-Hafner and J. R. Robbins (eds), *Making a New Nation: The Formation of Slovenia*, Aldershot, Dartmouth, 1997, pp. 31–45.

Buchheit, L. C., *Secession: The Legitimacy of Self-Determination*, New Haven, CT, Yale University Press, 1978.

Burg, S. L. and Shoup, P. S., *The War in Bosnia-Herzegovina: Ethnic Conflict and International Intervention*, Armonk, M. E. Sharpe, 1999.

Buzadžić, M., *Secesija bivših jugoslovenskih republika u svetlosti odluka Ustavnog suda Jugoslavije, Zbirka dokumenata s uvodnom raspravom*, Belgrade, Službeni List SRJ, 1994.

Carrington, Lord, 'Turmoil in the Balkans: Developments and Prospects', *RUSI Journal*, 1992, vol. 137, no. 5, pp. 1–4.

Cassese, A., *Self-Determination of Peoples: A Legal Reappraisal*, Cambridge, Cambridge University Press, 1995.

Castellino, J., *International Law and Self-determination: The Interplay of the Politics of Territorial Possession with Formulations of Post-Colonial 'National' Identity*, The Hague, Martinus Nijhoff Publishers, 2000.

Cohen, L. J., *Broken Bonds: Yugoslavia's Disintegration and Balkan Politics in Transition*, 2nd edition, Boulder, CO, Westview Press, 1995.

Connor, W., *Ethnonationalism: The Quest for Understanding*, Princeton, NJ, Princeton University Press, 1994.

Craven, M. C. R., 'The European Community Arbitration Commission on Yugoslavia', *British Year Book of International Law*, 1995, vol. 66, pp. 333–413.

Craven, M. C. R., 'What's in a Name? The Former Yugoslav Republic of Macedonia and Issues of Statehood', *Australian Year Book of International Law*, 1995, vol. 16, pp. 199–239.

Crawford, J., *The Creation of States in International Law*, Oxford, Clarendon Press, 1979.

Cukwurah, A. O., *The Settlement of Boundary Disputes in International Law*, Manchester, Manchester University Press, 1967.

Dakić, M., *Srpska Krajina, Istorijski temelji i nastanak*, Knin, Iskra, 1994.

De Aréchaga, E. J., 'Boundary Disputes in Latin America: Uti Possidetis Doctrine', in R. Bernhardt (ed.), *Encyclopedia of Public International Law*, vol. 1, Amsterdam, North-Holland, 1992, pp. 449–53.

Dennis, W. J., *Tacna and Arica: An Account of the Chile-Peru Boundary Dispute and of the Arbitrations by the United States*, New Haven, CT, Yale University Press, 1931.

Duursma, J., *Fragmentation and the International Relations of Micro-States: Self-determination and Statehood*, Cambridge, Cambridge University Press, 1996.

Eastwood Jr, L. F., 'Secession: State Practice and International Law After the Dissolution of the Soviet Union and Yugoslavia', *Duke Journal of Comparative and International Law*, 1993, vol. 3, pp. 299–349.

Etinski, R., 'Has the SFR of Yugoslavia Ceased to Exist as a Subject of International Law?', in R. Petković (ed.), *International Law and the Changed Yugoslavia*, Belgrade, Institute of International Politics and Economics, 1995, pp. 19–68.

Fifer, J. V., *Bolivia: Land, Location and Politics Since 1825*, Cambridge, Cambridge University Press, 1972.

Fisher, F. C., 'The Arbitration of the Guatemalan-Honduran Boundary Dispute', *American Journal of International Law*, 1933, vol. 27, pp. 403–27.

Franck, T. M., *Fairness in International Law and Institutions*, Oxford, Clarendon Press, 1995.

Gow, J., *Triumph of the Lack of Will: International Diplomacy and the Yugoslav War*, New York, Columbia University Press, 1997.

Grafenauer, N. (ed.), *The Case of Slovenia*, Ljubljana, Nova Revija, 1991.

Hannum, H., 'Rethinking Self-Determination', *Virginia Journal of International Law*, 1993, vol. 34, pp. 1–69.

Hannum, H., 'Self-Determination, Yugoslavia, and Europe: Old Wine in New Bottles?', *Transnational Law and Contemporary Problems*, 1993, vol. 3, pp. 57–69.

Hannum, H., 'The Specter of Secession, Responding to Claims for Ethnic Self-Determination', *Foreign Affairs*, 1998, vol. 77, no. 2, pp. 13–18.

Hayden, R. M., *The Beginning of the End of Yugoslavia: The Slovenian Amendment Crisis of 1989*, Pittsburgh, The Carl Beck Papers in Russian and East European Studies, No. 1001, Center for Russian and East European Studies, University of Pittsburgh, 1992.

Hayden, R. M., 'The Constitution of the Federation of Bosnia and Herzegovina: An Imaginary Constitution for an Illusory "Federation"', *Balkan Forum*, 1994, vol. 2, no. 3, pp. 77–91.

Hayden, R. M., 'Bosnia's Internal War and the International Criminal Tribunal', *Fletcher Forum of World Affairs*, 1998, vol. 22, no. 1, pp. 45–61.

Hayden, R. M., *Blueprints for a House Divided: The Constitutional Logic of the Yugoslav Conflicts*, Ann Arbor, MI, University of Michigan Press, 1999.

Heraclides, A., *The Self-Determination of Minorities in International Politics*, London, Frank Cass & Co, 1991.

Holbrooke, R., *To End a War*, New York, Random House, 1998.

Hondius, F. W., *The Yugoslav Community of Nations*, The Hague, Mouton, 1968.

Howse, R. and Knop, K., 'Federalism, Secession, and the Limits of Ethnic Accommodation: A Canadian Perspective', *New Europe Law Review*, 1993, vol. 1, pp. 269–320.

Hyde, C. C., *International Law Chiefly as Interpreted and Applied by the United States*, 2nd revised edition, Boston, Little, Brown & Co, 1947.

Ireland, G., *Boundaries, Possessions, and Conflicts in Central and Northern America and the Caribbean*, New York, Octagon Books, 1971.

Ireland, G., *Boundaries, Possessions, and Conflicts in South America*, New York, Octagon Books, 1971.

Jennings, R. Y., *The Acquisition of Territory in International Law*, Manchester, Manchester University Press, 1963.

Jennings, R. Y., 'The Argentine-Chile Boundary Dispute, A Case Study', *International Disputes, The Legal Aspects*, London, Europa Publications, 1972, pp. 315–25.

Kingsbury, B., 'Claims by Non-State Groups in International Law', *Cornell International Law Journal*, 1992, vol. 25, pp. 481–513.

Korman, S., *The Right of Conquest: The Acquisition of Territory by Force in International Law and Practice*, Oxford, Clarendon Press, 1996.

Koskenniemi, M., 'National Self-Determination Today: Problems of Legal Theory and Practice', *International and Comparative Law Quarterly*, 1994, vol. 43, pp. 241–69.

Kreća, M., 'Succession and the Continuity of Yugoslavia', *Jugoslovenska revija za međunarodno pravo*, 1992, vol. 39, pp. 178–94.

Kreća, M., *The Badinter Arbitration Commission: A Critical Commentary*, Belgrade, Jugoslovenski pregled, 1993.

Kuzmanović, R., *Konstitutivni akti Republike Srpske*, Banja Luka, Glas srpski, 1994.

Lekić, B., 'Administrativne granice u Jugoslaviji posle Drugog Svetskog Rata', *Istorija 20. Veka*, 1992, vol. 10, no. 1–2, pp. 145–62.

Masot, O. V., *The Gulf of Venezuela: A Case Study of Historic Waters*, Carácas, Editorial Arte, 1991.

McCorquodale, R., 'Self-Determination Beyond the Colonial Context and Its Potential Impact on Africa', *African Journal of International and Comparative Law*, 1992, vol. 4, pp. 592–608.

McCorquodale, R., 'Self-Determination: A Human Rights Approach', *International and Comparative Law Quarterly*, 1994, vol. 43, pp. 857–85.

Milenković, T., 'Državne granice Kraljevine Srba, Hrvata i Slovenaca', *Istorija 20. Veka*, 1992, vol. 10, no. 1–2, pp. 9–25.

Milinković, B. (ed.), *Novi ustavi na tlu bivše Jugoslavije*, Belgrade, Međunarodna Politika, 1995.

Milojević, M. B., 'Mišljenja Arbitražne komisije o Jugoslaviji', *Anali Pravnog Fakulteta u Beogradu*, 1993, vol. 41, no. 5, pp. 559–83.

Mitić, M., *Međunarodno pravo u Jugoslovenskoj krizi*, Belgrade, Službeni List SRJ, 1996.

Moore, J. B., 'Memorandum on *Uti Possidetis*: Costa Rica–Panama Arbitration, 1911', in *The Collected Papers of John Bassett Moore in Seven Volumes*, Volume III, New Haven, CT, Yale University Press, 1944, pp. 328–56.

Musgrave, T. D., *Self-Determination and National Minorities*, Oxford, Clarendon Press, 1997.

Nelson, L. M. D., 'The Arbitration of Boundary Disputes in Latin America', *Netherlands International Law Review*, 1973, vol. 20, pp. 267–94.

Nikolić, P., *Od raspada do beznađa i nade, Svedočanstvo o jednom vremenu*, Belgrade, Filip Višnjić, 1997.

Pavković, A., *The Fragmentation of Yugoslavia: Nationalism and War in the Balkans*, 2nd edition, London, Macmillan, 2000.

Pavković, A., 'Recursive Secessions in Former Yugoslavia: Too Hard a Case for Theories of Secession?', *Political Studies*, 2000, vol. 48, pp. 485–502.

Pavlović, M. and Popović, N., *Secesija u režiji velikih sila, Od očuvanja do nametanja mira u građanskom ratu u prethodnoj SFR Jugoslvaiji*, Belgrade, Institut za političke studije, 1996.

Pellet, A., 'The Opinions of the Badinter Arbitration Committee: A Second Breath for the Self-Determination of Peoples', *European Journal of International Law*, 1992, vol. 3, pp. 178–81.

Pomerance, M., 'The Badinter Commission: The Use and Misuse of the International Court of Justice's Jurisprudence', *Michigan Journal of International Law*, 1998, vol. 20, pp. 31–58.

Radan, P., 'The Badinter Arbitration Commission and the Partition of Yugoslavia', *Nationalities Papers*, 1997, vol. 25, pp. 537–57.

Radan, P., 'The Borders of a Future Independent Quebec: Does the Principle of *Uti Possidetis Juris* Apply?', *Australian International Law Journal*, 1997, pp. 200–14.

Radan, P., 'Constitutional Law and the Multinational State: The Failure of Yugoslav Federalism', *University of New South Wales Law Journal*, 1998, vol. 21, pp. 185–203.

Radan, P., 'The Supreme Court of Canada and the Borders of Quebec', *Australian Journal of International Law*, 1998, pp. 171–6.

Radan, P., 'Yugoslavia's Internal Borders as International Borders: A Question of Appropriateness', *East European Quarterly*, 1999, vol. 33, pp. 137–55.

Radan, P., 'Post-Secession International Borders: A Critical Analysis of the Opinions of the Badinter Arbitration Commission', *Melbourne University Law Review*, 2000, vol. 24, pp. 50–76.

Radulović, S., *Sudbina Krajine*, Belgrade, Dan Graf, 1996.

Ratner, S. R., 'Drawing a Better Line: *Uti Possidetis* and the Borders of New States', *American Journal of International Law*, 1996, vol. 90, pp. 590–624.

Ratner, S. R., 'Ethnic Conflict and Territorial Claims: Where Do We Draw a Line?', in D. Wippman (ed.), *International Law and Ethnic Conflict*, Ithaca, NY, Cornell University Press, 1998, pp. 112–27.

Rich, R., 'Recognition of States: The Collapse of Yugoslavia and the Soviet Union', *European Journal of International Law*, 1993, vol. 4, pp. 36–65.

Sharma, S. P., *Territorial Acquisition, Disputes and International Law*, The Hague, Martinus Nijhoff Publishers, 1997.

Shaw, M. N. 'The Heritage of States: The Principle of *Uti Possidetis Juris* Today', *British Year Book of International Law*, 1996, vol. 67, pp. 75–154.
Shaw, M. N., 'Peoples, Territorialism and Boundaries', *European Journal of International Law*, 1997, vol. 8, pp. 478–507.
Smith, A. D., *Nationalism in the Twentieth Century*, Canberra, Australian University Press, 1979.
Stanković, Đ., 'Administrativna podela Kraljevine SHS', *Istorijski glasnik*, 1981, no. 1–2, pp. 33–46.
Talbott, R. D., *A History of the Chilean Boundaries*, Ames, Iowa State University Press, 1974.
Terrett, S., *The Dissolution of Yugoslavia and the Badinter Arbitration Commission: A Contextual Study of Peace-Making Efforts in the Post-Cold War World*, Aldershot, Ashgate, 2000.
Tomuschat, C. (ed.), *Modern Law of Self-Determination*, Dordrecht, Martinus Nijhoff Publishers, 1993.
Trifunovska, S. (ed.), *Yugoslavia Through Documents: From its Creation to its Dissolution*, Dordrecht, Martinus Nijhoff Publishers, 1994.
Trifunovska, S. (ed.), *Former Yugoslavia Through Documents: From its Dissolution to the Peace Settlement*, The Hague, Martinus Nijhoff Publishers, 1999.
Weller, M., 'The International Response to the Dissolution of the Socialist Federal Republic of Yugoslavia', *American Journal of International Law*, 1992, vol. 86, pp. 569–607.
Weller, M. (ed.), *The Crisis in Kosovo 1989–1999: From the Dissolution of Yugoslavia to Rambouillet and the Outbreak of Hostilities*, Cambridge, Documents and Analysis Publishing Ltd, 1999.
Wippman, D., 'Treaty-Based Intervention: Who Can Say No?', *University of Chicago Law Review*, 1995, vol. 62, pp. 607–87.
Wooldridge, F., '*Uti Possidetis* Doctrine' in R. Bernhardt (ed.), *Encyclopedia of Public International Law*, vol. 12, Amsterdam, North-Holland, 1990, pp. 519–21.
Zečević, M. and Lekić, B., *Frontiers and Internal Territorial Division in Yugoslavia*, Belgrade, Ministry of Information of the Republic of Serbia, 1991.

Unpublished dissertations

Hislope Jr, R. L., 'Nationalism, Ethnic Politics, and Democratic Consolidation: A Comparative Study of Croatia, Serbia and Bosnia-Hercegovina', unpublished doctoral dissertation, Ohio State University, 1995.
Lalonde, S. N., '*Uti Possidetis* and Internal Administrative Borders', unpublished doctoral dissertation, University of Cambridge, 1997.
Schoenberg, H. O., 'The Concept of "People" in the Principle of Self-Determination', unpublished doctoral dissertation, Columbia University 1972.
Wells, B. J., 'United Nations Decisions on Self-Determination', unpublished doctoral dissertation, New York University, 1963.

Index

For Product Safety Concerns and Information please contact our EU representative GPSR@taylorandfrancis.com
Taylor & Francis Verlag GmbH, Kaufingerstraße 24, 80331 München, Germany

www.ingramcontent.com/pod-product-compliance
Ingram Content Group UK Ltd.
Pitfield, Milton Keynes, MK11 3LW, UK
UKHW021513250926
475702UK00043B/456

* 9 7 8 0 4 1 5 2 5 3 5 2 9 *